Basic Education & Institutional Environments

Edited by
Jean-Paul Hautecoeur

Prepared by the UNESCO Institute for Education
with the collaboration of
The Ministry of Education, Government of Québec
The National Literacy Secretariat, Government of Canada
The Foundation for Self Reliance, Hungary
The Ministry of Education & Culture, Government of Hungary
The Office of National Minorities, Government of Hungary
The National Commission for UNESCO, Hungary
The National Commission for UNESCO, Canada

CULTURE CONCEPTS
Publishers
TORONTO, CANADA

UIE ISBN 92 829 1071 6
Culture Concepts ISBN 0-921472-30-7

Canadian Cataloguing in Publication Data

Main entry under title:

Alpha 97: basic education & institutional environments

Translation from the French by Peter Sutton.
Includes bibliographical references.
ISBN 0-921472-30-7

1. Fundamental education. I. Hautecoeur, Jean-Paul, 1943- . II. Sutton, Peter.
III. Unesco Institute for Education. IV. Quebec (Province). Ministère de l'education.
LC5161.A5613 1997 374'.012 C97-930974-3

Cover photograph:"Metropool", 1997 and Section Title Page Illustrations
By André Mathieu, sculptor
Translation from the French by Peter Sutton, Translator & Editor, UK.
Editor-in-Chief, Thelma Barer-Stein, Ph.D.
Typesetting by Accurate Typesetting Limited, Toronto.
This book is printed and bound in Canada.

UNESCO Institute for Education
B.P. 131023
20110 Hamburg, Germany

Culture Concepts, Publishers
5 Darlingbrook Crescent
Toronto, Ontario, M9A 3H4
Canada

CONTENTS

Section Four

North America

Section Five

From Alternative Visions to Politics

Previous titles in this collection:

ALPHA 90: Current Research in Literacy
ALPHA 92: Literacy Strategies in the Community Movement
ALPHA 94: LIteracy & Cultural Development Strategies in Rural Areas
ALPHA 96: Basic Education & Work

Orders may be sent to:
UNESCO Publishing, Commercial Services
7 Place de Fontenoy
75352 Paris, France

INTRODUCTION
Jean-Paul Hautecoeur
UNESCO Institute for Education

WIDENING THE FIELD

Alpha 97 looks back at three preceding publications in the series: *Alpha 92* on the voluntary sector movement in literacy, *Alpha 94* on cultural development in rural areas, and *Alpha 96* on basic education in working environments. While the approach adopted in these investigations was largely a collection of monographs focusing on the micro level and the experience of local actors, *Alpha 97* is different. Here there is an attempt to widen the field and examine the relationship between the micro and macro levels, between what happens and the structure that makes it happen, between the diversity of different practices and the major policy orientations that foster or limit this diversity. An ambitious task!

Alpha is a research program of the UNESCO Institute for Education specializing in alternative, experimental approaches to adult basic education. For once, it has been asked to take part in a larger forum, to share (perhaps to lose) its illusion of being unique, to change its scale and to risk exchanging ideas. We had no choice. After all, since we like to see ourselves as a "cooperative research" network, especially between Eastern and Western Europe; it would have been small-minded to refuse to widen the spectrum of cooperation. For a long time we have maintained that we are engaged in action-research; so it would have been illogical not to explore the means of making the action more effective for a larger number of people. As researchers, our intellectual strategy is that of opening up new pathways rather than closing them, of reporting on their fertility and of trying to spread their results.

Widening the field means looking at all the actors involved in basic education: participants, education and training agencies and their partners, sponsors, intermediaries, public authorities, policies, etc. It also means examining the range of activities and contexts where they take place; breaking down administrative, and professional and semantic divisions. It means going beyond policies and directives and looking at the values and social ethics underlying them, and at their purpose over a longer period than the short term of politics. It means taking an interest in the in-between, the hidden and the unsuspected, the unlawful, and what remains unsaid in ideological statements. It means taking inspiration from new ideas and new social practices outside the narrow field of training programs, and discovering *possible* forms, alternative education, and ways of offering political resistance to the order of things.

This in turn means having a better grasp and understanding of the complexity of reality, being in a better position to evaluate the results of local activities in overall terms and, most importantly, devising and proposing more useful, fairer and perhaps more effective plans of action.

The title of the present publication — *Basic Education and Institutional Environment* — also belongs to this movement of widening the field of adult education. It might have been simpler to give it the title "Literacy Policies in Industrialized Countries". However, we don't deal mainly with literacy in the ordinary sense, that is linguistic or educational. Neither do we deal with "politics" in the traditional sense, as if the political platform had to be high and distant from the practitioners and their practices. On the contrary, we conceive the "politics" of basic education as a negotiation between the people who initiate local projects and the institutions whose main function should be to facilitate the realization of these projects. The institutional environment means all the marks of a State on a social space, where people are once in a while customers of public services.

EDUCATION AND INSTITUTIONS

What do we[1] mean by basic education? In *Alpha 96*, we stated our position relative to *literacy* and *basic education*:

> Our critical approach obliged us to look for different words to observe, reveal and name experimental and marginal social practices that are, willingly or not, dissociated from dominant practice. Amid the often unbearable problems of everyday life for the groups and individuals who are discussed in this volume, there is rarely any thought of literacy. Literacy is a term used by professionals, politicians and pressure groups, and has not become part of the vocabulary of the citizens to whom it is applied. As for literacy provision, in reality this only covers an infinitesimal proportion of the population...
>
> We understood *basic education* in the anthropological sense, analogous to *basic personality*: a structure for assembling and transmitting knowledge, a generative grammar of total exchange. And as a skill particular to a group that was structuring its identity and transforming itself through chance events, encounters with other cultures, and a number of individual wills.[2]

We prefer to use the term *literacy* in the literal rather than the metaphorical sense, to restrict it to the linguistic register of learning and using the written word in communications. This is also the most common meaning. In our societies, adult literacy generally only concerns a small minority of the population. It is generally seen as an appendix to elementary school and as a first level of formal adult education.

Besides initiation into the written word, specific skills are expected in the various registers and contexts of written communication. They are coded, or normative to a greater or lesser degree. There are institutions that certify qualifications and people's order of attainment by means of examinations, tests, statistical surveys, interviews, etc. There is above all the force of ideology that imposes "normal" levels of qualification in present-day life, regardless of how useful or relevant they are. In the last ten years, the offensive to persuade the public of the need for functional literacy has been particularly sustained.[3]

Functional literacy is the term often used to mean the variable levels of skill that largely go beyond the linguistic register. In French, the equivalent term *littératie* has now been used for a while, obviously under the influence of English, but also to distinguish a contemporary phenomenon in the North from the former UNESCO slogan associated with literacy and development campaigns in the South.[4] We only refer to these terms from a critical stance, as they are so heavily loaded ideologically.

Our approach to *basic education* derives from the desire not to be shut in, either in the linguistic register of the written word, or in the institutional world of schools or labour force training. People, groups and communities have a heritage of knowledge (or cultural capital) that is the *basis* of their interpretation of the world. They express and transmit their knowledge in specific situations and in accordance with procedures that they recognize. Education and training of various types — there are so many different contexts — begin there, in people's lives, among their peers, with their own style of language, their customs, decisions and utopian ideals. Any educational enterprise must start by discovering and recognizing this vernacular education.

We work with people who are outcasts. That is another, fearsomely contemporary meaning of *basic education*. The goal of education in these circumstances is at least not to worsen their situation. At the best, it consists in recreating links that have been destroyed, rebuilding conditions for equal exchange, and establishing the means of existence — or survival — that suit partners' needs and aspirations. Restructuring work on this basis, which has little chance of external standardization, relying more on the ingenuity of the educators and their acolytes than on recognized skills. There is a shift from literacy using standardized codes to solidarity in communication; vocational training is *transformed* into appropriate self-help; on the fringes of the single market, new parallel networks for production and exchange of services are opened up — a giant jumble sale.[5]

Basic education goes in a different direction from the systemic education and training that follows the laws of the single market. It consists, in fact, in creating intermediate cultures, relationships, work and livelihoods for all those who have been expropriated by market forces and legal forces of a similar nature to the point where they lose their elementary rights of citizenship. The current practices of this popular education, which swims against the tide, are then in danger of running up against centralized training programs and sectoral policies dealing with unemployment, deviance and exclusion.[6] They are thereby exposed to boycotts and sanctions.

On the positive side, basic education initiatives provide new directions for the planning of social policies and local applications. They encourage unconventional institutional relationships that bring resources together rather than separating them, adding to the spirit of democracy. Community education is more easily adapted to the requirements and immediate needs of the milieu. It can make use of mutual assistance networks and donated services. It may be tied in with intermediary professional organizations that have broken away from the laws of the market. Such networks need to be linked institutional networks. More and more often, the two are mixed.

This leads to the inevitable question of the relationship between the *institutional environment* and basic education activities that are on the fringes of formal education policies and adult vocational training. *A* authorities work vertically in watertight compartments (in sectors with distinct jurisdiction), basic education proceeds by way of horizontal ramifications (cooperation and networking) and is pragmatic: open rules and global approaches within community limits that are formalized *a posteriori*. If basic education or popular education is included in adult education policy, there is a serious risk that it will be reduced to one dimension and will become marginalized and wither away. There is extensive evidence of this in the *Alpha* series.

By *institutional environment* we mean the structures of public organizations, their staffs, traditions and bureaucratic cultures, the statements governing their actions (legal, political and ideological), and also how they communicate with the outside and what are their power relationships in a locality or region. From our point of view, that of basic education rather than policy directives or public administration, the institutional environment is all that links these activities and structures to the state. These relationships still have to be specified, understood and evaluated, and means have to be found to improve them.

RESEARCH QUESTIONS

Alpha 97 is a synthesis that should be seen in its historical perspective. We must also acknowledge the main changes that have occurred over the last decade in the wider field of "literacy" and basic education. We should remember that it was at the 4th International Conference on Adult Education (Paris, 1985) that the preoccupation with *functional literacy* in the industrialized countries was brought to the attention of the international community and the General Conference of UNESCO. What are the main trends and priorities in basic education today?

The historical perspective is not uniform, especially if histories as different as those of the countries that have recently emerged from behind the Iron Curtain are included in one and the same piece of research. The comparative approach necessary between countries and regions, is made possible by collaboration between researchers with widely varied backgrounds and institutional links.. This helps particularly in sharpening criticism of the notions and practices that appear self-evident in our own mental landscapes.

We do not just record changes and differences from a distance. Since our research approach is linked to action, one of its objectives is to evaluate the results of basic education activities within their contexts and environments, according to the demands of those concerned. We therefore have to know the issues behind the initiatives, and what demands and real needs they are supposed to meet. We also need to know the terms of expression by the various interested groups. What distance separates institutional utterances from those that are given no recognition because they come from the outcasts and are therefore "illiterate"?

The questions raised in the course of our work can be summarized in the following way. In what cases does the institutional environment prove favourable to the success of local action? What are the possible areas of cooperation, antagonism and autonomy? Can these be generalized at local, regional, national and international level? What systems allow for plurality of initiatives without squeezing them? In what institutional areas have citizens' alternatives a chance of prospering? To what extent do central policies and directives meet demand? How far can one go to achieve the aims of grassroots action rather than those of professional organizations?

In the field of education, how can professional competence be reconciled with breadth and flexibility? How can disciplinary, corporate and institutional barriers be broken down if recognition and funding are still to be secured? How can competition from formal education schemes, which have little time for tolerance, be sustained? Where and how can a new team take over the education of trainers of adults, at a remove from basic education and vocational training?

Who defines the goals, objectives and methods of adult education at national level and at the level of local action? Who judges the quality of the results, and what are the criteria for this? How, locally at first, can power relationships be changed so as to achieve equitable and sustainable development of all resources, as an antidote to the "top-down" model?

THE REMIT

The issues set out above, were worked out collectively in two seminars; one with a team from Central Europe, and the other with a team from Western Europe and North America. All of the work that followed and is the subject of this publication is an attempt to respond to the issues.

The research program was initially couched in the following terms:

> There is frequent reference to the distance, and even the incompatibility, between adult literacy and basic education policies on the one hand, and the local reality of individuals' cultural practices within their communities, and the needs, rights and demands of local groupings on the other. Many factors are dangerously diminishing the possibilities of adapting the institutional environment to the needs and demands of local populations in relation to basic education. These include the globalization of markets, the devaluation of culture (where it is still relatively protected from the laws of the "single market") and the widespread attrition of government programs.

The main questions that have concerned us are:

- How can an institutional environment in different regional contexts be improved to ensure a sustainable development of community projects?
- How can educators and basic education programs cooperate to this end?"

The objectives of Alpha 97 can be summed up as follows:

- To evaluate what has been achieved, lost and changed in the field of basic education over the last decade
- To improve the effectiveness of basic education strategies in action

taken to combat poverty, exclusion in all its forms, and the systemic destruction of the resources of humanity and the planet

- To link the aims of basic education to citizenship rights (and not merely to technical competence), rights exercised through everyone's participation in the decisions that concern them and future generations
- To recommend to the organizations responsible measures that are necessary to create institutional environments more favourable to local initiatives

These were ambitious aims, but united all our collaborators and the organizations with which they were associated. This is how Mary Hamilton, of the United Kingdom, defined the current aims of the education networks in which she was involved:

> "Alternative visions of literacy are alive, but on the margins. What we have not learned to do effectively is to engage with the central processes of policy formation and decision-making, to use the powerful institutions of the media to put over these visions. Many of the resources available to us to do this have been removed during the last ten years by a government that is very adept at using these institutions for its own purposes. It is time for us, too, to focus on the big picture and how to redraw it."[7]

These are aims which pose inviting questions such as what approach alternative movements should adopt in their relations with the "great powers", how far one should compromise, and to what extent one should remain faithful to original values (P. Freynet, *infra*). The policy questions are at the heart of the exploration undertaken in this research.

PREMISES

The *Alpha* series is an area of a critical tradition within the applied humanities towards *literacy* and basic education, which have generally been free from controversy. The authors assembled here do at least share this deconstructive attitude towards statements of the obvious and the arm's-length utterances of professional and political lobbies. On the subject of policy and civil society's relationship with environmental institutions, we should spell out briefly the premises that we have in common and that are typical of our positions.

1. We do not have a specialized approach to the cultural, economic and psychological manifestations of social relegation: it seeks to remain *interdisciplinary*, globally anthropological, open to differences, sensitivities and imagination, and so on.
2. As adult educators and researchers in adult education, we keep our distance from corporate interests and institutional ways of thinking, seeing learning taking place in *all human activities*, particularly when these practices are devalued or simply suppressed (among the individuals and populations declared "illiterate").
3. Unlike the individual, behaviourist tradition of education, we give attention to the *cultural phenomena* that involve groups and communities in their original *environments* and their own historical experience. We see universality as a complex history of exchanges between

individuals and cultures, rather than as a statistical model.

4. Our intellectual commitment and professional interventions are not made under cover of some supposed scientific neutrality. Nor does the international nature of our organization mean that we have to be "diplomatic" in the face of social problems and national political interests. Basic education, in our sense means not only mobilizing technical skills but also, mobilizing *human and citizens' responsibilities*, which are therefore ethical and political.
5. All this means that our responsibilities are towards the "losers", the outcasts, the "disappeared" and the "extinct",[8] who are outlaws in the "new economic world order". It also means responsibilities towards situations in basic education that are most urgently needed to satisfy the needs and demands of local populations rather than the dominant paradigm of "retraining of human resources". We emphasize *cultural demand* rather than labour market entry provision.
6. To many of our collaborators, it is obvious that we are working on the fringes of the single market, and that there is little room in this market for all those who do not have the required "skills". There is little chance of access to it by the *alternative* route of education courses. We therefore have to find alternative ways of life that are more independent and equitable, collaborating with those who often have no choice but to be dependent on social services and unregulated, unskilled work.

COLLABORATION

This book is comprised of five sections. The first contains only one chapter, a retrospective of the international debate on literacy in industrialized countries. The second section presents six contributions from Central and Eastern Europe (unfortunately, a seventh chapter, from Hungary, was unable to be completed within the time frame). The third section presents five contributions from the European Union; the fourth one, five chapters from North America (including Mexico), and the final section is a synopsis of the main propositions presented in this book and in former publications of the *Alpha* series.

The team of collaborators for *Alpha 97* includes many who have worked on previous Alphas. At the outset, they represented 17 countries, and at the end they were from Albania, Belgium, Bulgaria, Canada, the Czech Republic, France, Mexico, Poland, Portugal, Romania, Slovenia, the United Kingdom and the United States.

The policy of the UNESCO Institute for Education's action-research program entitled *Literacy Strategies in Industrialized Countries*, is to allow researchers from ex-communist countries to take part equally. This biennial research program aims to expand intellectual cooperation in the fields of literacy and adult basic education, to support experimental education and to disseminate the results of its research internationally.

The implementation of *Alpha* projects would not be possible without the assistance of government partners and non-governmental organizations, or the voluntary collaboration of many researchers. *Alpha 97* has been supported by the Ministry of Education of the Quebec Government, the Literacy Secretariat of the Canadian Government, the Ministry of Education and Culture of the Hungarian Government, the National Office for Minorities of the Hungarian Government, the Hungarian UNESCO Commission, the Canadian UNESCO Commission and the Autonomy Foundation of Hungary.

In the organization of seminars and the preparation of the publication, we have been aided by the Directorate of Adult General Education and the Language Services Division of the Ministry of Education of Quebec, the Museum of Civilization of Quebec, and the Autonomy Foundation in Budapest.

We should like to thank the following people for their professional cooperation: Alain Mercier, Raymond-Marie Lefrançois, Anna Csongor, Brigitta Bicskei, Mihaly Rozsa, David Greig, Hélène Gravelle Korski, Peter Sutton and André Mathieu. We are also most grateful to all the authors and the institutions that made it possible for them to collaborate.

Notes

1. The use of "we" in the introduction and final section of this collective work does not imply a consensus of all the authors on all themes. It represents an attempt to produce a coherent meaning, which allows however, differences among the authors.
2. *Alpha 96 — Basic Education and Work*, Toronto, Culture Concepts and Hamburg, UNESCO Institute for Education, 1996, p. 2.
3. Jean-Paul Hautecoeur, "Is literacy "a good deal"? A critique of the literacy debate in Canada", *Alpha 96 — Basic Education and Work* op. cit., p. 57.
4. *Literacy, Economy and Society*, Ottawa, Statistics Canada and Paris, OECD, 1995.
5. Stanislav Hubik, "Television and literacy development in the Czech Republic", *Alpha 94 — Literacy and Cultural Development Strategies in Rural Areas*, Toronto, Culture Concepts and Hamburg, UNESCO Institute for Education, 1994, esp. pp. 197-199.
6. *Educations*, "Formation de base des adultes", issue edited by Veronique Leclerc, 8, March-May 1996.
7. Mary Hamilton, "Keeping alive alternative visions", above.
8. "The end of the job", *Fortune Magazine*, 19 September 1994, quoted in *Alpha 96*, p.7.

Section One

The International Discourse

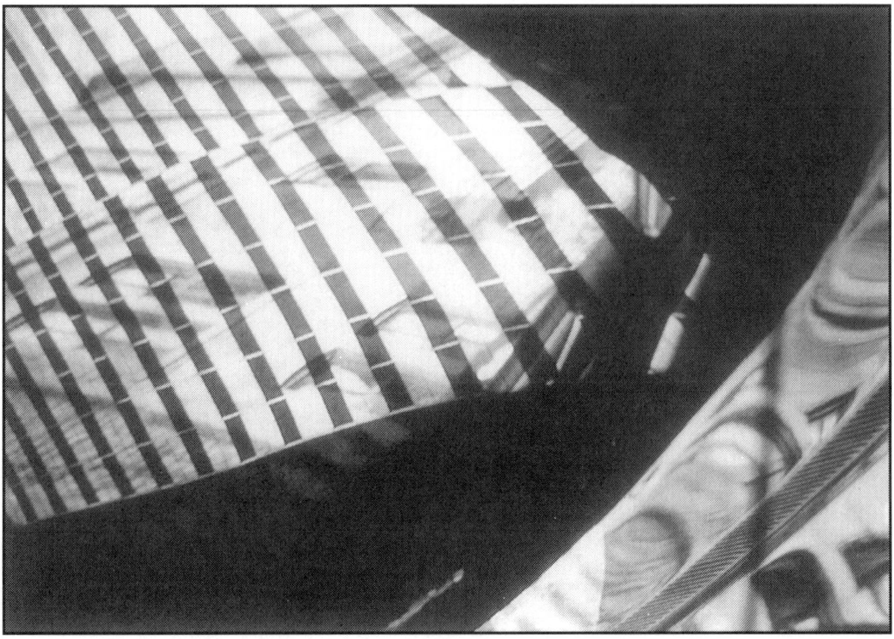

Chapter One
A POLITICAL REVIEW OF INTERNATIONAL LITERACY MEETINGS IN INDUSTRIALIZED COUNTRIES, 1981—1994

Jean-Paul Hautecoeur

A score of conferences, meetings and seminars have taken place since 1981 on the theme of "literacy in industrialized countries", a term that originated in UNESCO. The term was not created out of the air. In the geographical sense employed by international organizations, it referred to the world plan to eradicate illiteracy in Europe by the year 2000.

However, this is also the history of a social movement peculiar to Western Europe, North America and Australia, with little connection with Eastern Europe, the USSR, Japan and the newly industrialized countries. It is composed of two strands: literacy for migrant workers, strongly marked by the Third World movement, and popular education, with a Marxist and/or Christian allegiance, out of which the lifelong learning movement grew in Europe. In the 1980s, the literacy movement rapidly became more independent, created its own identity with national and international networks, and became a political factor in many countries.

Problems of terminology are inherent in the movement from the outset, and reflect its geopolitical ambiguity. From the world literacy movement it inherited the term "functional literacy", which was soon discredited. In France, the term "fight against illiteracy" was generally adopted; "basic education" quickly became current in the United Kingdom and the Netherlands, while "basic training" was applied to the world of work. But at the international level, under the aegis of UNESCO, the term "literacy" has persisted, despite the attempts of American multiculturalists to promote the plural form, "literacies".

Today, the dominant branch of the movement, largely English-speaking and North American, is playing an active part in the twin offensive of the privatization of education (the State being declared impotent), and the globalization of culture in partnership with business. It has taken the initiative and is striving for world leadership in a field long the preserve of others. The last three world literacy conferences have in fact been organized by non-governmental organizations, universities and U.S. private companies, together with UNESCO. As was said at a 1992 conference held at the UN Headquarters, "the new trend, is one towards serving whole human beings, not just literacy programs, but 360 degree programs that deal with people" (Somerfield, 1992:378), and "we really are just at the crest of beginning a job that stretches around the world. We will touch billions of people and confront circumstances that are very much the same. All over the world the stakes are the same" (Sawyer, 1992:8).

The purpose of the research into archives and contemporary events reported here is to provide access to meetings where documentation is scarce, to provide a global interpretation of trends, and to contribute to the debate surrounding the Fifth International Conference on Adult Education, to be held in Hamburg in 1997.

THE PROBLEM OF ILLITERACY

"It is obvious that there is a problem of illiteracy in the industrialized countries. This is not a temporary problem, it is growing."[1] This was the main message addressed to the international community by the Eastbourne Seminar (28 September - 2 October 1981), that brought together specialists from 16 countries in Europe and North America at the instigation of the International Council for Adult Education, the British National Institute of Adult Continuing Education and other British and international organizations, including UNESCO.

This first international meeting on literacy in industrialized countries was held in the United Kingdom, where a literacy campaign had been mounted some years earlier by voluntary organizations with the media support of the BBC. For some time to come, this television campaign was to remain the main source of inspiration and reference for the emerging literacy movement in Europe and North America. The idea of a national campaign, as promoted by UNESCO from the time of the Experimental World Program, was realized in the rich countries.

The problem is not the same in the industrialized and the Third World countries. In most industrialized countries, everyone goes to school, at least at primary level. Immigrants, dyslexics and the handicapped are no longer singled out, either. The problem concerns ordinary citizens who speak the national language, for whom the basic education they received does not give them the skills required in a world of complex communications. Although no one knows how many people are affected, it is known that the problem exists because many individuals ask for help when literacy servies are publicized.

Moreover, some countries already have a literacy movement, experienced staff, original knowledge and institutions specifically for adult basic education. The experience acquired deserves to be recognized, supported and disseminated.

The Eastbourne seminar recommended that:

- The problem of illiteracy should be *recognized* by governments;
- Large-scale information and *awareness* campaigns should be conducted at all levels of society, using effective means (the media);
- Governments should commit themselves to providing *long-term* financial support for literacy activities;
- The organization of literacy activities presupposed close *collaboration* between the public sector and voluntary organizations;
- Literacy required special *training* for teachers and a particular pedagogical approach. International co-operation should help to improve these and make them known.

In the same year, the Youth Forum of the European Communities held a meeting on "Illiteracy in the European Community" in Langen, Germany (16-17 November 1981).[2] This meeting was attended by adult educators, representatives of the Youth Forum, members of the European Parliament and officials of the European Community. The problem identified in Eastbourne was now described as a "scourge" to be combated. UNESCO's battle cry was now applied to Europe: to eradicate illiteracy by the year 2000.

It was estimated that the problem of functional illiteracy affected between four and six per cent of the adult population in Europe, and was growing. However, in a European survey, three countries stated that they had no illiteracy problem (France, Germany and Luxembourg), and the United Kingdom declared that 99 percent of its population was literate. Portugal proved the exception to this lack of awareness of the problem by admitting to an illiteracy rate of 23 per cent, and a semi-literacy rate of eight per cent (almost a third of the population in total).

Because of its social and economic implications, the struggle against illiteracy among young people was seen as a priority in Europe for the next ten years. Youth unemployment was considered directly linked to their poor qualifications for the labour market. Access to that market was governed by vocational training, that was closed to illiterate young people. *Basic skills* became the priority, and they were also needed to "prepare workers for periods of non-employment". Literacy was thus seen as a means of adapting to temporary unemployment, or rather, as a social treatment of economic exclusion.

Two other target populations were identified: rural women and the long-term unemployed. Basic education was prescribed in these cases as the solution to two sensitive social problems: the rural exodus and embedded marginalization.

The Youth Forum asked the Commission of the European Communities:

- to *assess* the scale of the problem of illiteracy in Member States;
- to make the struggle against illiteracy a *major priority* for the next ten years;
- to facilitate interregional and international *cooperation* (UNESCO) in order to improve literacy practices.

ANOTHER REALITY: SOCIAL EXCLUSION

In 1984 (6-8 September), European and UNESCO specialists took part in a national seminar in Brussels organized by *Lire et Ecrire*, "Illiteracy in Industrialized Countries". The meeting marked a further stage in the ideological definition of the "problem" of illiteracy and the development of policies to solve it.

In Brussels, it was reaffirmed that illiteracy affected wide sections of the population, and was not an individual but a mass problem. It would reach "such a degree of gravity that things cannot go as they were... Alarm bells have sounded." In consequence, preparations were made for a major awareness campaign aimed at public opinion and public authorities.

Illiteracy could not be reduced to a problem of education and culture; it was above all a social question. An illiterate was defined as "someone who cannot integrate into social life because he or she has difficulties, for example, in reading a timetable in a railway station." At a time of economic crisis, non-integration was in danger of degenerating into social exclusion. "Literacy is not limited to mastery of reading and writing. It is also a matter of mastering the techniques and the whole of economic, social and cultural activities."

The campaign prepared in Brussels had to start with what is known as prevention before teaching, in the schools and the community, and to continue afterwards into what was called, rather vaguely, "post-literacy". "This campaign must shed light on a different reality, social exclusion, the real lack of jobs and a whole range of brutal and retrograde steps." The struggle against illiteracy was henceforward identified with a political fight against social exclusion.

The proposals put forward at the conference can be summarized as follows:

- an awareness *campaign*
- the establishment of a literacy *network*
- professional *training* for teachers of adults, and recognition of a professional *status* comparable to that of schoolteachers
- a set of *preventative* measures in and out of school, in families and the community
- the selection of *priority education areas*, as in France, in accordance with the principle of "giving the most to those who have least".

A POLICY OF LIFELONG EDUCATION

The fourth International Conference on Adult Education (Paris, 1985) had recommended that UNESCO should become involved in functional literacy in industrialized countries. The "Technical Meeting of European Specialists on the Prevention of Functional Illiteracy and the Integration of Young People into the World of Work" (UNESCO Institute for Education, Hamburg, 1-5 December 1986) followed up this recommendation. This meeting, attended by participants from 23 countries in the extended European region, was the first occasion that UNESCO officially addressed the matter of functional illiteracy in industrialized countries, prepared the ground for inter-regional and international co-operation, and launched the project of an International Literacy Year.

Five years after the Eastbourne seminar, it was observed that the problem of illiteracy had been irrevocably admitted by governments, and that various measures to remedy it had been introduced, although the theme of young people and work did not feature greatly in the discussions in Hamburg. The definitions of illiteracy continued to vary between countries, and although there was no attempt to reach common criteria, each government was expected to set out its minimum requirements for basic education. The absence of statistics on illiteracy was regretted, but the figure was estimated at ten per cent, higher than in previous years.

Functional illiteracy was seen to be linked to poverty, to school failure and "cultural impoverishment" in the family, but literacy work could not be reduced to social work. It might also be the result of an intellectual handicap among some people, that called for types of intervention other than schooling and segregation in special classes.

Because of the strong link between illiteracy and unemployment among the young, there was a danger of relying on one-off job-creation schemes rather than a wider lifelong education approach combining personal education, with social and cultural development. The steps taken to integrate young people, with priority given to girls and women, consisted of preventing illiteracy at school and providing support for illiterates through training programs.

The British model of a media campaign needed to be complemented by other lifelong education activities, the prevention of school failure, social action among the disadvantaged and protection of the rights of the excluded. In addition to literacy activities addressed to target groups of persons brought up in the national language, great importance was attached to the encouragement of reading among young children, at school, in the family and in the social environment. (Immigrants and speakers of other languages, offenders, intellectually handicapped persons, the socially excluded, etc., were not mentioned.)

In the long list of recommendations, two priorities stand out: for governments, the creation of a *policy of lifelong education*, and for the international community, the strengthening of literacy cooperation with the declaration of an *International Literacy Year.*

The report of the meeting, attended by representatives of Eastern

Europe, never mentions these countries. At the subsequent seminar in Toronto, an official representative of the USSR declared that "the problem of illiteracy no longer exists in the Soviet Union." This attitude may explain the silence of the representatives of the Communist regimes.

A MOVEMENT FOR SOCIAL JUSTICE

An international seminar on "Literacy in Industrialized Countries — Focusing on Practice" was held in Toronto from 13 - 15 October 1987 at the instigation of the International Council for Adult Education. This meeting attracted over 300 people, from Europe to Hong Kong and from Canada to Australia. Specialists from developing countries were also invited in order to illustrate the world nature of literacy, as a mobilizing movement and a desire for cooperation between grassroots organizations "on a planetary scale".

The Toronto seminar proclaimed the world nature of illiteracy, linking it with poverty and social discrimination on grounds of race, class and gender. Illiteracy was in itself neither a scourge nor a handicap, but the evidence of unequal educational and cultural relationships between social groups. It was therefore illusory to pretend to be able to solve the problem of illiteracy by the year 2000 through campaigns that stigmatized individuals. In place of these, access to lifelong education, from basic to higher education, was proposed, along with access for all to information and other means of communication, free of discrimination, in every district.

The five points of the Toronto Declaration perceived literacy as a matter of universal rights, social justice, and changes to the living and working conditions of all people of the Earth. The Right to Learn applied particularly to groups that were structurally denied it: women, minorities, the voiceless, the excluded. It presupposed that access to education should be modified to suit the demands and needs of participants. That implied a range of programs, supplementary resources for the most disadvantaged, and a "major role for community organizations in policy making" (Gayfer, 1987).

Participatory democracy applied to literacy groups, between educators and learners, as much as to public authorities and non-governmental organizations at the national level. Grassroots organizations demanded greater freedom of action at the local level, and a share in decision making. In this respect, the seminar acknowledged Canada's innovative policy of literacy partnerships.

The fight against illiteracy could not be fought separately. It was at the same time a struggle against poverty and exclusion in order to improve local living conditions. It was an integral part of popular education, based on the dialectics dear to Paulo Freire: reading words in order to read the world better, to participate in it and transform it. It also presupposed some form of organization from the grassroots to the international level, in order to carry out mobilization within the literacy community and among the associations involved in activities demanding social justice, as well as in the whole of society. Literacy, claimed as a right to education for the whole of life, was defined as a political act: "helping the most disadvantaged to be aware of their rights and to organize in order to exercise them".

Carman St. John Hunter has given a definition of functional literacy that deserves to be quoted because it applies to the particular situations of individuals in their communities instead of trying to establish universal criteria of competence from on high or from outside:

> Functional literacy is the possession of skills perceived as necessary by particular persons and groups to fulfill their own self-determined objectives.... This definition ... suggests that *access* to information and skills may be as important as *possession* (St. John Hunter, 1987).

The Toronto seminar formulated four sets of recommendations:

- Universal free access to basic education for all individuals, the *right to learn* in one's mother tongue, and the recognition of the particular needs of women, oppressed minorities and the excluded.

- Literacy programs must respect the *autonomy* of grassroots groups, facilitate the *participation* of learners in all activities, and help to transform the living conditions of individuals and communities.

- Governments must fund and support a variety of programs, allocate *increased resources* to poor environments, and join with the literacy community in developing policies and respecting the independence of NGO partners.

- The literacy community must organize itself in coalitions, form alliances with organizations working for social justice, adopt democratic structures and involve all of society in the struggle against illiteracy.

GLOBAL INTEGRATED STRATEGIES

A seminar on "Functional Literacy in Industrialized Countries" was held in Ottenstein, Austria from 30 May - 3 June 1989 by the Austrian Commission for UNESCO and the International Institute of Children's Literature and Reading Research. It was attended by experts from 17 countries in the European region. This meeting was a follow-up to the Hamburg meeting (1986), and many themes in fact returned to the discussions and recommendations of that meeting.

Illiteracy "lays the foundations for a dual society". While the general level of literacy was rising, the gap between those who "know" and those who "don't know" was growing. Systemic illiteracy was a growing problem linked to poverty and marginalization, the symptom of a moral and intellectual crisis in a number of countries, and a consequence of technological and economic upheavals. It was therefore illusory to think that illiteracy could be eradicated within a short period.

The right to literacy was reiterated as the first point in the Right to Learn, and as a prerequisite for the exercise of the other Human Rights. However, unlike the agreement in Hamburg on the relativity of the thresholds of literacy, there was now a desire to apply an operational definition of literacy to all industrialized countries in order to set common goals and to obtain comparative data.

A European report on the fight against illiteracy had dwelt at length on schools as a factor in the persistence and growth in illiteracy. The report *Social Europe* proposed numerous preventative measures against illiteracy at all school levels, starting with nursery schools and stressing teacher training and opening up schools to the outside world, in association with parents and the community environment.

The Ottenstein seminar also considered the failure of schools rather than failure at school, as had been done in the past. "The school system is one of the major factors in illiteracy.... Schools are the cause of what they were supposed to cure." In place of literacy campaigns, global, integrated strategies were recommended: within the formal education system, in families and communities, with the aid of voluntary associations, whose role should receive greater recognition and support.

The participants recommended specifically that:

- the most disadvantaged groups should have priority in the application of "European *humanistic values*";

- basic education should be *revised* in line with the guidelines given by the 1988 Conference of European Ministers of Education;

- representatives of illiterate persons should be involved in decision-making agencies and in any strategy relating to literacy;

- all adult education programs should include literacy activities and require the presence of a *qualified person*.

THE END OF THE PIONEER ERA

In 1990, International Literacy Year, a number of international meetings and conferences took place. Two of them were interrelated, notably in terms of the profile of participants (researcher-practitioners) and of the dominant themes, and by the fact that they were addressed to the same European network: the Angers University Summer School, in France, "New approaches and challenges in literacy and adult basic education — A European perspective" (7-12 July), and the meeting "Literacy in the European Community" (Brussels, 14-15 May).

These two meetings held after the Jomtien world conference on "Education for All", stressed the imperative of making basic education accessible to all children, young people and adults, and the particular role of mothers in the education of their children. The priority given to young people in developing countries, especially to girls, had its counterpart in Europe where the theme of preventing illiteracy in schools, in families and in the community, was tending to take precedence over literacy work targeted at adults. Pierre Freynet and Alfonso Lizarzaburu provided the following report on Jomtien as an introduction to the Angers seminar:

> It is no longer possible to think only in terms of schools: schools are not the only place of education in a society; moreover, nothing can be achieved without the active support of parents, which explains the importance of adult education. It is no longer adequate, in developing or industrialized countries, to have literacy campaigns or isolated literacy initiatives: these are very likely to lead to failure if they are not immediately followed up by post-literacy measures.

In Angers, there was much discussion of pre-schools, after-hours schools and prevention of school failure in "at-risk" environments, of literacy for parents, partnership between children, their parents, the schools and the community. The authors of a Belgian survey entitled *Paths of illiteracy* concluded that the main task was to "build bridges between the school and the child's sociocultural environment ... which would make it possible to transform the relationship between the child, the school and the family". (Goffinet, 1986)

In Brussels, many participants had worked in "open" education or a "plural educational environment", in which dialogue and communication, participation and cooperation by many different parties replaced the former dualism between teaching and learning and between reading and writing in an enclosed world. Compensatory education was criticized in favour of a thorough change in the structure and culture of schools, in teacher training, educational social work and relations between schools and the local community.

Illiteracy was also brought into the open and linked systemically with poverty and unemployment in order to give an account of exclusion. The struggle against illiteracy was seen as one of the "preventative strategies" to combat exclusion". These consisted of an overall "reinforcement of economic and social cohesion ... to narrow the gap between highly literate and qualified young people and adults, and the disadvantaged and illiterate", or between the winners and losers. The talk was no longer of five, six or even ten per cent illiteracy in the adult population, but of one youngster in four failing at school and being in danger of joining the losing camp.

Large-scale long-term unemployment, coupled with changes in the organization of work, revealed illiteracy and under qualification as an "enormous wastage" of human resources. This theme, which had come to predominate in North America had been raised by the Director General of UNESCO at an earlier international meeting: "The problem is not trivial. Its human and social costs are enormous... We are talking in terms of billions of dollars." (Mayor, 1989)

On the one hand, the problem was one of loss of rights, refusal of citizenship and programed exclusion; on the other, of economic losses and the inadequacy of the social and educational systems. While little attention was given to Eastern Europe even though the communist regimes were collapsing, migrants and minority groups reappeared as legitimate concerns in the educational changes that were announced. Pluralist schools and society were to replace the homogeneous systems that in many countries were the justification for monolingual education in a unitary national culture based on traditional identity. Henceforward, there would be talk of a hybrid identity in Europe, and of new pluralistic identities to be created by means of intercultural education. This was typical of a school open to differences, to all citizens and all generations.

THE INDOCTRINATION AND SUBSERVIENCE OF LITERACY

Two other meetings were held in 1990, bringing together researchers and treated literacy in the context of wider issues. These were the European Conference of Directors of Educational Research Institutes, organized by the Council of Europe under the title of "Literacy and Basic Education on the Eve of the 21st Century" (Bled, Yugoslavia, 9-12 October 1990), and the seminar "Cultures and subcultures of orality, cultures and subcultures of the written word in French-speaking countries", organized by the Paris-Nord University of Paris-Nord together with UNESCO (Paris, 17-19 December 1990).

Discussion of literacy, but recently Manichean, became more complex and refined. But alarm bells were still being rung, ever more loudly. "Many people may consider themselves literate but in reality are not. In that sense, most people in industrialized countries are critically illiterate", Richard Hoggart (1992) said in his opening address in Bled. And the totalitarian systems in Eastern Europe were based on a model of programed communication and ideological control which Olga Kunst-Gnamus (1992), invoking Basil Bernstein, called "restricted literacy":

> A totalitarian system can be established only through restricted literacy, i.e. through the central and uniform planning and prescribing of pedagogical texts... [In] a school, metalinguistic knowledge is reduced to formal grammar rules, and the absence of semantic and pragmatic interpretation does not allow for critical reading...

What the totalitarian and the consumer societies supposedly had in common was the use of "functional" literacy for their own ends, as a tool of indoctrination into political or consumerist slogans. For Richard Hoggart, a restricted and uncritical level of literacy threatened to create a society of slaves, subject to commercial and political manipulation.

In another context, that of ethnolinguistic minorities subjected to monolingual institutions in dominant societies, literacy in the official language was described in Paris as a process of oppression and illiteracy, or imprisonment in the vernacular orality of a devalued language (French in Ontario or Creole in the French Overseas Departments), and as an act of resistance to assimilation. Functional literacy in French Canada was criticized by Serge Wagner, who argued for autonomous cultural and educational institutions that should be legally entitled to transmit the minority culture.

Criticism was also levelled at the obligatory passage from the oral to the written word, which was interpreted rather as a passage from silence to bureaucratic obedience. In Quebec, according to Vivian Labrie, the majority of literacy clients were recruited from among the recipients of social security, captives of "employability measures", which forced them to enrol by threatening to cut their benefits. Tutors were equally supposed to be subject to the control of social security officers. Labrie's conclusion was in tune with Hoggart's view: "Learn to read and write, and to query what is written. The third element is essential for survival." (Labrie, 1993)

Exclusion again: according to the French Deputy Thierry Mandon (1993), employment schemes based on linguistic skills were a failure, because there were no real jobs. Moreover, "when what identifies a group is a conflictual language in terms of the official language, it is reasonable to enquire into the status of the official language and whether it is rigid." For him, and for Bertrand Schwartz in France, the ability to read and write was not a precondition of entry into society, but a consequence. It was *employment*, and in a more general sense, *entry into society* that led to the acquisition of language and identity.

At the end of a history of education in France that spoke of the "invention of illiteracy" (rather than its belated discovery), Jean Hébrard de-dramatized the issue and shed a different light on it. On the one hand, reading was a difficult, abstract activity that could not be learnt in one year. On the other, longer years spent at school and mass enrolment in secondary education would have increased school failure as a matter of course. The professionalization of its treatment had amplified its importance. Also, the teaching of a trade in technical colleges rather than on the job had caused widespread illiteracy in schools.

The solution to illiteracy was less the provision of remedial schooling and investment in education, but rather to integrate minorities *culturally*, and to make it possible for the excluded to *participate* in collective life. The true task of literacy was to resolve

the contradiction between the inevitable acculturation and the expression of original cultures.

In the multidisciplinary arena of research, illiteracy ceased to be a minority group pathology, an educational anomie, a social injustice or an indicator of economic crisis.

Literacy was composed of a whole set of different analyses of the crises of contemporary societies that could not be synthesized into one single concept, be that school failure, poverty, discrimination, exclusion, ignorance, stupidity, domination or incompetence. This meant, in turn, that while there was agreement on the urgent need to collaborate in the face of serious risks of conflict, there was no magic formula for success.

MEASURING THE SCALE OF THE PROBLEM IN THE INDUSTRIALIZED COUNTRIES

In 1990, a seminar on "Functional literacy in Eastern and Western Europe" was held at the UNESCO Institute for Education in Hamburg (20-22 November 1990), attended by representatives of the OECD, the European Community, UNESCO and 17 countries in Western and Eastern Europe. The theme of this first East-West meeting was the analysis and application of instruments to measure illiteracy, from North America to the USSR, with the aim of making governments more aware and of documenting new adult education policies, particular in the countries "in transition".

North American and Western European experts led the discussion, but the criteria for measurement and the results of surveys differed widely: while it was estimated that functional illiteracy affected between one and five per cent of the adult population in the Netherlands, in France the figure was put at between nine and 22 per cent, in Greece at 20 per cent, and in Canada at 16 or 38 per cent, depending on the level of competence judged adequate. In conclusion, it was estimated that "between one fifth and one quarter of the adult population in the industrialized countries have serious difficulties in reading and writing", and that public measure to promote literacy were therefore called for.

Ongoing literacy work was justified particularly by unemployment and unemployed youth, groups "at risk" (of social deviation), prevention of school failure and dropout, ethnic minorities (a priority for the Council of Europe), the acquisition of reading habits at preschool age, and by rural underdevelopment. In the West, literacy was motivated largely by the adaptation of the labour force to the new labour market, the treatment of long-term unemployment, and the implementation of adult education policies. In the East, the overall historic changes and the emergence of unemployment called for basic education policies for groups "at risk". The restructuring of education systems was a propitious time to introduce the notion of functional literacy, which was alien to most of those countries.

Dissenting voices were nonetheless heard, denouncing "the simple transfer of illiteracy problems, including measurement techniques, from West to East, which is wrong and inappropriate". J.-P. Hautecoeur described illiteracy as a myth peculiar to Western societies, and suggested replacing standardized surveys of individual skills with written text by a contrasting analysis of the modes and means of communication used in different social contexts:

> The closer one comes to the presumed reality of illiteracy, the more problematic this reality appears, and the more alien to the people and environments affected. The more it appears also that literacy is evidently not a solution to problems that are either not a priority or quite frankly do not exist for the individuals supposed to be suffering from them... It has been proposed that the issue of literacy should be widened to include the material circumstances and social conditions of the use of means of communication, the different uses made by individuals according to their cultural heritage and place in society, and the literacy campaigns and the resistance of some groups to control or cultural domination.
>
> (adapted from ... J.-P. Hautecoeur 1992)

In a working document presented at the Tilburg Seminar (the Netherlands, 10-12 October 1991), Cesar Birzea described illiteracy as a structural element of the cultures of totalitarian regimes, rather than as a problem common to West and East. Illiteracy was not an individual deficiency or a mark of incompetence of certain groups "at risk", but a pathological mode of communication made necessary by totalitarian power and the whole of the society. The only way out was through global, social and political solutions, which presupposed revitalizing democratic participation, critical thought and a freeing of methods of communication.

In Bled, Olga Kunst-Gnamus (1991) had presented a similar opinion. Most of the participants from Eastern Europe, however, had remained quiet or had assimilated Western views. The report of the Hamburg meeting gives a brief summary of a new survey in five Central and Eastern European countries, based on what is done in the

West. This was the first stage in an *international survey* conducted later by Statistics Canada and the OECD, in which Poland took part. The results of the survey in that country appear problematic, to say the least.

THE IMPENETRABILITY OF CONTEMPORARY ADMINISTRATIONS

From 11 to 13 March 1991, the French Commission for UNESCO, in collaboration with the *Groups permanent de lutte contre l'illetrisme,* organized a European seminar on "Illiteracy and complexity of contemporary administrations". A number of European ombudsmen and senior staff of public authorities took part, together with the Director General of UNESCO. He stated that the topic of the seminar was indeed "the very condition of modern man": the growing difficulty of playing a role as citizen in a real democracy, in the face of the complexity and impenetrability of administrations (*Commission française pour l'UNESCO, 1993*).

The seminar set out to assess the action already taken in Europe to simplify administrative procedures and language, and associated training. It raised the issue of citizens' access to the administration, whether this meant the understanding of its codes or the use of its services. Numerous individuals, particularly the illiterate, encountered difficulties in their relationships with authorities. According to Véronique Espérandieu (1993), the major question was that of "the capacity of our society to be legible", rather than the ability of the public to make sense of administrative messages and procedures. Jean-Baptiste Foucault (1993) identified the problem as that of the "illegibility of administration, a particular form of illiteracy due less to people's inadequacies or handicaps than to administrative complexity". That complexity was perhaps reinforced by the large-scale introduction of new communications technologies.

Illiteracy was once more called into question. While there might be illiterates in Europe, they were the exception among those born in the country, and more numerous among those born abroad. Illiteracy affected people who had lost the use of the written word and found it difficult to communicate in writing (estimated as ten per cent of the adult population in France and 31 per cent among people born abroad). But they were not handicapped, marginalized or excluded, rather they were normal people who had not adapted to some forms of social life, were the victims of economic conditions, or of an abrupt change in their personal lives, and often "victims of administrative complexity". In France, for example, 16 million people every year were refused social security benefits because the form was incomplete. Ultimately, who was illiterate? Those who wrote texts in incomprehensible jargon or those who could not read them? Such relativism could not, however, disguise the fact that some people managed to deal with the complexity, while others fell victim.

The strategies proposed or implemented in certain countries to adapt official communications to the rights and needs of citizens were:

- A policy of *positive discrimination* towards the most disadvantaged, to be applied in all public sectors and including the simplification of procedures and the humanizing of communications;

- A policy of providing a *welcome* service, advice and personalized information;

- *Direct help* through ombudsmen at regional and local level and possibly involving voluntary organizations;

- *Administrative reforms*: decentralization, oral communication, giving local officers greater initiative, community information centres, etc.;

- *Training* for public service staff and civic education for the public in their community environments;

- *A national support service* to help people in difficulties, in collaboration with the voluntary sector; and

- An unconditional right to *work*, without regard to prior education. Training can take place during and after work, not necessarily before.

NO LONGER "HOW MANY?" BUT "HOW TO CHANGE?"

After the International Literacy Year, a seminar was held in Hamburg to evaluate the changes that had come about in industrialized countries since the first UNESCO Institute seminar of 1986, and to draw up guidelines for policy and research. Experts from 21 countries took part in this meeting on "The future of literacy and the literacy of the future" (4-7 December 1991).

Satisfactory developments were recorded. Awareness of the issue had spread; adult education legislation and initiatives had incorporated adults' right to literacy; services had expanded; enrolment had grown; the organization of the movement had become more efficient; partnership had helped to diversify activities; teachers were commonly more involved, even in research; educators were better trained; evaluation of outcomes, policies, benefits, learners' progress and educational effectiveness were commonly discussed; research was being conducted and better funded, etc.

There were also setbacks. Political commitment was tenuous; policies were short-term; the state was leaving the field to the private sector and NGOs, which sometimes had funding difficulties; workplace training stressed technical rather than humanistic skills; community organizations were marginalized; working conditions for professionals had not improved; quantitative approaches predominated, particularly in evaluation; and the adult literacy movement was isolated from schools, young people and other social movements.

There were positive changes in language and attitudes. Participants spoke of positive action, solidarity and human rights, participation and dialogue, not of a struggle or even of illiteracy. Learners' language and culture were valued, and differences were respected. The notion of "literacies" made its appearance, with an affirmation of the need for diversified education in several languages. These significant semantic changes were to be seen in the Declaration agreed by the seminar:

> We must not understand literacy as an indication of past failure, but as evidence that people are continuously constructing their own future... there are many literacies, reflecting adults' and communities' broad range of linguistic, cultural, ethnic, geographical and social backgrounds and situations... Present research has moved from the former assumption about learning difficulties towards the study of the cultural richness of adults. This means that literacy education is to be understood not as a remedial action, but rather as an advancement of the diversity which people have. (UNESCO Institute Seminar, 1986)

In this seminar, serious criticism was expressed, causing real "ruptures" rather than mere difficulties. First, the activism of the literacy movement disguised an uncomfortable fact: the low level of demand, despite mobilization and recruitment campaigns. As a result, demand was forced. Not to enrol could incur sanctions, a situation already denounced by Labrie (1993) at the Paris seminar.

Mass campaigns and public literacy programs had had the

pernicious effect of creating and stigmatizing a growing class of illiterates (30-40 per cent of the adult population), said to be "at risk". They were blamed for economic losses incurred by companies and public authorities. In Brian Street's (1992) words, "the reason for the failure of most of the literacy programs ... is the lack of this understanding that literacy involves ideological contests over meaning and power...".

Hanna Fingeret(1994) also criticized the neutrality of the literacy movement, observing that nothing had really changed in learners' lives because there was a refusal to confront the crucial issues of racism, sexism, social inequalities and poverty. Literacy was still perceived as an apolitical, individual academic activity separate from community development and movements working towards human rights and social justice.

Policy recommendations

In the policy recommendations, the seminar proposed that the promotion of basic education had to be part of national *cultural policies*, which needed to be multilingual and *multicultural*, with particular attention given to minorities. Literacy activities should be more closely linked to the prevention of illiteracy, lifelong education and vocational training, in a *lifelong learning* perspective.

The relationship between literacy at the workplace and the interest of productivity should be viewed more critically. The purpose of learning was to improve living conditions. Criteria for *évaluation* of the results of education should therefore include indices of change in the social environment and the economic situation of individuals and the community.

As for the controversial surveys, it was recommended in the Declaration that these should be conducted in countries as yet unfamiliar with the issue, but that literacy issues should not be reduced to individual deficiencies or a simple statistical analysis of needs: statistical measurement should be integrated with qualitative approaches in an attempt to grasp the reality of the people concerned.

Collaboration between learners and vocational organizations was recommended in the formulation of policies, as was the recognition of *partnership* between voluntary, commercial and public sector organizations. At the same time, grassroots initiative should be preserved.

HAPPENINGS IN THE UNITED STATES

The New York international conference entitled "Adult literacy: an urban perspective" (3-6 August 1992) was organized by UNESCO and the New York Literacy Assistance Center. It brought together 300 people from a score of countries to consider literacy strategy, policy and practice in major world cities. It was held at the headquarters of the United Nations, where the Book compiled by literacy learners worldwide had been presented to the world at the end of the International Literacy Year.

This conference was primarily American and Anglophone: half the speakers were American, the majority from the North, no one from Eastern Europe, and only a sixth from the South. It also attracted the "national literacy community", with the notable exception of the learners. And it was big: over sixty speakers at ten round tables over four days. The messages delivered were very varied, and the proceedings amounted to over 500 pages, but there were neither conclusion, recommendations nor declaration.

The predominant themes were:

- The *political* importance of literacy at national and world levels;
- The *professionalization* and standardization of services, quality criteria, measurement of returns and certification;
- *Partnership* and collaboration between numerous actors in the public, private, community and research sectors;
- The wide areas of intervention (*literacies* in the plural): the workplace, new technologies, family and intergenerational literacy, and the media; and
- The inevitable trouble spots: *women* and equity, *research* and criticism, *multiculturalism* and socio-demographic dangers.

Some traditional questions were not discussed. Concern with teaching materials was replaced by new technologies and evaluation methods inspired by zero-sum total quality: "It is an undeniable fact that literacy using new technologies is relevant to every individual of the human species" (Stone, 1994)

There was no further mention of steamroller campaigns: the

United States, Australia, the United Kingdom and the Netherlands had already adopted legislation on literacy or adult basic education, and significant results were expected from national programs. But in the Third World as elsewhere, post-modernism and the "single market" were in vogue, and references to the media were now to the private communications sector.

Positive discrimination in favour of the disadvantaged and links with employment gave way to quality, efficiency and visibility of results in a competitive environment. It was necessary to disinvest where education was making losses — Sweden was henceforward to follow the "Olympic model" (Abrahamson, 1994).

Alternative networks within the civil society and appeals to solidarity were out. Success lay in the *mainstream*, with recourse to companies, publicity and other marketing techniques to disseminate services and ensure results. The alliance between the National Center for Family Literacy and Toyota was presented as a new humanism, guaranteeing success, quality, participation and results.

There were dissenting voices recalling the tensions and conflicts in literacy, despite the predominance of affirmative reductionism, and sometimes evangelism. Among others, Harvey Graff challenged the myth of literacy as the solution to all the world's evils, the diagnosis of the decline of education, and the social apartheid built around illiteracy. Brian Street queried the normative nature of the debate, pointing to the variety of practice. Hanna Fingeret reiterated the need for solidarity among women in the interests of equity. Moacir Gadotti recalled the humanist aims of popular education and its different criteria of quality. John Garvey pointed to the non-participation of Blacks in the face of white power and racism.

But these were all from the "literacy intelligentsia". The legitimate political voices were in unison on the imperative of national and multinational cooperation in the offensive against illiteracy. There was curiously little reference to alarming statistics, but other dangers were alluded to: the fact that non-whites and non-English speakers would become the majority in U.S. cities; the rise in poverty and economic decline; the shortage of funds for education; the rise of violence, drugs, general urban lawlessness and the decrepitude of social security programs; and moral relativism in higher education, eroding traditional values.

The answer put forward given by the literacy community was a national education and basic training system to educate the groups that make up the society, starting with the family.

FAMILY LITERACY: A WORLD MOVEMENT?

A "World Conference on Literacy and the Family" (3-5 October 1994) was convened by UNESCO in Paris during the International Year of the Family. This was sponsored by an American company producing reading materials, and some 80 participants from 30 countries in the North and South took part. The aims were to call attention to literacy within the family on a world scale, to study its applicability to other contexts, and to promote educational action between parents and children in order to strengthen family ties.

The Director General of UNESCO described the theme of the conference as a matter of life and death for millions of children with no families, and as a moral challenge to humanity. The conference was a follow-up to the Jomtien Conference on Education for All, and sought links with non-formal and community education, particularly in developing countries; with the missions of UNESCO, UNICEF and the World Bank, to provide education as a basic human right in the service of peace and development; and with the major trend of contemporary history, the involvement of the private sector in education.

Many speakers spoke of the great potential of family literacy in resolving all manner of disputes. The American movement was described as a solution to undereducation, poverty, unemployment and criminality, restoring the educational role to the family, and there was an economic argument, according to Thomas Sticht (1995), that investment in family literacy brought a double return: the "double duty dollar".

Schools and traditional literacy programs had failed, particularly in "at-risk" environments. It was no longer possible to count on reform of the education system because of its "bureaucratic rigidity" and lack of resources. There was no longer an appeal to centralized institutions to plan and implement family education programs. Rather, the community was now seen as an extended family and as an irreplaceable resource for one-parent families. The state was expected to delegate resources and responsibility for education to local authorities, and standardized mass programs were to be replaced by small-scale, diversified provision integrated into everyday life. The movement made links with voluntary literacy organizations and the network of alternative associations engaged in popular education and community development. Even the World Bank was in favour of the approach: "We too recognize the role of the family in learning and favor programs that are rooted in community values and institutions."

The promoters of family literacy were seeking to disseminate its value worldwide. However, participants from the South were not all in agreement with this "Western model". Where there were insufficient resources to provide minimum schooling, the question was asked where these would come from to set up effective non-formal programs. Moreover, many literacy programs relied on traditional family structures, in an ideological context very different from the social and moral crisis of Western societies. And literacy was not universally an appropriate cultural intervention or an enduring precondition for development.

Finally, family literacy was defined as a broad framework for intergenerational learning. There was agreement on the need for experimentation, research, documentation and evaluation of results at an international level. The movement was seen as favourable to the emancipation of girls and women, and there was a wish for international *networking*, and a second conference.

But these action plans were feeble in comparison with the voluntarism and rhetorical power of the American movement. A new literacy *campaign* had been launched, as intended during the International Literacy Year. The movement found its charismatic leader in Barbara Bush, but other "personalities" were being sought in the world of sports and the media to give added impetus. The media were given a prominent place in spreading the value of literacy to *every home*, so that everyone could "take control of his or her affairs".

THE GEOPOLITICS OF THE INTERNATIONAL MOVEMENT

Two main observations have to be made about all these international conferences. First, there has been a trend towards Western independence from the world movement, followed by a world offensive, first under the leadership of the Europeans, and then the Americans. Second, 1990 was the key year, marked by the International Literacy Year, the Jomtien Conference, East-West reunification and the end of the Cold War.

In the 1980s, only one conference demonstrated the worldwide character of the literacy movement in the context of a wider militant sociopolitical movement, even though most of the participants were from the North: the Toronto Seminar organized by the International Council for Adult Education. The other meetings were dominated by the consolidation of a professional movement linking education, social work and the economy, and by the priority given to issues of unemployment in Europe.

The Jomtien Conference and the International Literacy Year restored a world perspective. Feminist movements and NGOs were given a hearing, but it was above all the World Bank and the imperatives of the new economic order that were the loudest voices. The three major conferences that followed were American initiatives and addressed skills, competition, quality, returns, participation, consensus and well-being. Less was expected of the state, more of local communities and companies, and American values were assumed to be valid worldwide.

In the 1990s, many states made Draconian cuts in adult education and gave priority to economic and labour questions, seeing basic education as providing vocational qualifications and employability training. Public authorities called on private enterprise to invest in workplace training, and responsibility for literacy was split between different partners. The encouragement of privatization was taken up by the family literacy movement. UNESCO came to realize that the literacy battle could not be won unless it involved everyone.

Some areas of the world were still absent: the north of the Far East, Eastern Europe and the former USSR. The "Japanese model" proclaimed zero failure among the labour force, lifelong training, loyalty of workers to employers and social consensus: there was no literacy problem. The Eastern Europeans, when they were invited, were imprisoned by the ideological insistence on capitalism as the source of the problem, but even after 1990, when this argument failed, they seldom participated.

CONCLUSION: TRENDS, TERMS AND APPROACHES TO LITERACY

There is a symbolic continuity to the literacy movement: the two key words are *campaign* and *struggle*. These presuppose a state of crisis, indicated by illiteracy, the complexity of modern life, unemployment and exclusion, the erosion of basic values, demographic dangers, economic decline and criminality. These signs point to crises in social relationships, between the generations, social classes, ethnic groups, the genders, etc. The answer has been to involve the whole of society, to rebuild skills and to trust in the value of literacy.

In the early stages, the trend was towards literacy work with adults *in isolation*. At the same time, those involved professionally were creating networks and demanding resources. This led to institutionalization, professionalization, intensified research and statistical planning, experimentation in teaching, specialized training for teachers, certification, evaluation, etc. In several countries, a *basic education system* was introduced to supplement formal education for young people.

At the same time, there were pleas for decentralization and the involvement of the other "actors", including learners. Budgets for non-productive areas such as positive discrimination measures were squeezed, and literacy found itself drawn increasingly to training for employment. In the face of rising unemployment and societal breakdown, there was talk of the failure of limited basic education programs and of systemic illiteracy.

Another trend came to the fore, that of *lifelong learning*, according to which education cannot be reduced to schools, or short-term campaigns. It was suggested that the field of action needed to be widened to all ages, in the family and the community, and involving voluntary sector organizations in partnership with public authorities. Illiteracy was linked to poverty and cultural indigence, so that *global approaches* were needed to combat exclusion. Literacy became one facet of cultural, social and economic integration, while the labour market and living conditions continued to deteriorate.

A minority on the fringe of the movement is critical of its Western identity, and invokes post-modern values of multiculturalism, multiple identities and deconstructed literacies, without attacking the notion of the literate society itself. A radical wing, in the tradition of *popular education*, and embracing feminist, anti-racist, community action and local development groups, was active throughout the history of the movement, constantly seeking links with other social action movements.

In the history of international conferences, this militant direction played a minor role, with the exception of Toronto. One of its major demands was to take positive action to recognize the rights of every individual, in this case, the right to literacy and all levels of education. Another was to delegate power and funds to grassroots organizations, which involved the learners themselves. There are clearly points of tension in the movement, which is centred on the English-speaking countries (elsewhere the term literacy is rarely used nowadays, training being preferred). However, all agree on the need to demonstrate its effectiveness. Given that the movement has succeeded in producing increasing figures for illiteracy, it is now expected to do something about it.

An Anglo-American approach that is of rising importance is that of *family literacy,* which draws on the original autonomous skills of reading and writing, on lifelong learning and the open school, on community solidarity, on new technologies and on the populism of the mass media. It goes back to the *symbolic tradition of the world literacy movement,* affirming the universal cultural value of literacy and seeks to shift responsibility for basic education from schools (seen as failing) to the private family and the surrounding community.

Another approach is to *simplify communications* between citizens and public agencies. Illiteracy is seen as being the fault of the writer of the institutional message rather than the recipient. The complex solution has been to simplify messages, open up channels of communication, train liaison staff, delegate functions to voluntary associations and stimulate civic responsibility.

At the periphery of the debate remains the demand for the *right to work,* which has scarcely been mentioned at conferences, despite growing unemployment. Basic education continues to be defined by employers, trade unions and employability programs funded by the state, in accordance with human resource theories and the globalization of the labour force. International conferences have made little reference to how some educators have adapted to community needs and cultures, and how other forms of basic education are transforming living conditions in environments reappropriated by those who live in them. This vast area is overlooked in literacy policy strategies. It takes the form of attempts to survive in parallel, even parasitical, economies, and falls outside the framework of literacy programs. But it is the only field in which genuine solutions are being sought — and sometimes found.

Notes

1. Archive copy of the report consulted in the library of the UNESCO Institute for Education, Hamburg.

2. Archive copy of the report consulted in the library of UNESCO Institute for Education, Hamburg.

References

Abrahamsson, K. 1994. Adult Literacy, Democracy and Economic Development. In *Adult Literacy: An International Urban Perspective*. New York: The City University of New York/The Literacy Assistance Center/UNESCO.

Austrian Commission for UNESCO. 1989. *Seminar on Functional Literacy in Industrialized Countries — Final Report and Recommendations*. Vienna: Austrian Commission for UNESCO/International Institute of Children's Literature and Reading Research.

Birzea, C. 1991. Literacy and Development in Eastern Euroepan Countries: the Case of Romania. Unpublished paper presented at the Tilburg Seminar, the Netherlands, 10-12 October 1991.

Commission francais pour l'UNESCO. 1993. *Illetrisme et complexité des administrations contemporaires. Dans la documentation française*.

Darling, S. 1994. Family Literacy: An Intergenerational Approach to Education. In *Adult Literacy: An International Urban Perspective*. New York: The City University of New York/The Literacy Assistance Center/UNESCO.

Delors, J. et al. 1996. *Learning: the Treasure Within. Report to UNESCO of the International Commission on Education for the 21st Century, Paris: UNESCO, 1996.*

Espérandieu, V. 1993. Allocution. In Commission française pour l'UNESCO, *Illettrisme et complexité des administrations contemporaines*. Paris: La documentation française.

Euroalfa. 1990. *Les nouveaux enjeux et les nouveaux défis de l'alphabétisation et de l'éducation de base des adultes — Une perspective européenne*. Angers: Centre universitaire de formation continue.

European Commission. 1988. *Social Europe — Report on the Fight against*

Illiteracy. Supplement 2/88. Luxembourg: Publications Office of the European Communities.

_____. 1991. *Meeting on Literacy in the European Community*. Luxembourg: Publications Office of the European Communities.

Fingeret, H. 1994. Women's Literacy, Equity and Reliance. In *Adult Literacy: An International Urban Perspective*. New York: The City University of New York/ The Literacy Assistance Center/UNESCO.

Foucault, J.B. de. 1993. Allocution. In Commission française pour l'UNESCO, *Illettrisme et complexité des administrations contemporaines*. Paris: La documentation française.

Freynet P., Lizarzaburu A. 1990. La conférence de Jomtien sur "L'éducation pour tous". In *Les nouveaux enjeux et les nouveaux défis de l'alphabétisation et de l'éducation de base des adultes — Une perspective européenne*. Angers: Centre universitaire de formation continue.

Gadotti, M. The State and Popular Education: Adult Literacy Initiatives in São Paulo, Brazil. 1994. In *Adult Literacy: An International Urban Perspective*. New York: The City University of New York/The Literacy Assistance Center/ UNESCO.

Garvey, J. 1994. Literacy and the Remaking of the Working Class. In *Adult Literacy: An International Urban Perspective*. New York: The City University of New York/The Literacy Assistance Center/UNESCO.

Gayfer, M. (ed.) 1987. *Literacy in the Industrialized Countries: Focus on Practice*. Toronto: International Council for Adult Education.

Goffinet, S. et al. 1986. *Les itinéraires d'analphabétisme*. Brussels/Luxembourg: Lire et Ecrire/Publications Office of the European Communities.

Graff, H. 1994. Literacy: Myths and Lessons. In *Adult Literacy: An International Urban Perspective*. New York: The City University of New York/The Literacy Assistance Center/UNESCO.

Hautecoeur, J.-P. 1992. Illiteracy: from the Myth to the Reconstruction of the Facts. In *Functional Literacy in Eastern and Western Europe* (79-103). UIE Reports 4. Hamburg: UNESCO Institute for Education.

_____. 1993. L'analphabétisme des pays industrialisés: du mythe à la reconstruction des faits. In *Teoría de la Educación* 5. Salamanca: Ediciones Universidad Salamanca.

Hoggart, R. 1992. Literacy and the Crisis in Europe Today (report by Leslie Limage). In *Literacy and Basic Education in Europe on the Eve of the 21st Century*. Strasbourg: Council of Europe/UNESCO and Amsterdam: Swets & Zeitlinger.

Huck, G. 1992. Functional Literacy in Europe on the Eve of the 21st Century. In *Literacy and Basic Education in Europe on the Eve of the 21st Century* (49-59). Strasbourg: Council of Europe/UNESCO and Amsterdam: Swets & Zeitlinger.

Kunst-Gnamus, O. 1992. Literacy at the Threshold of the 21st Century. In *Literacy and Basic Education in Europe on the Eve of the 21st Century*. Strasbourg: Council of Europe/UNESCO and Amsterdam: Swets & Zeitlinger.

Labrie, V. 1993. Brique, ciseaux, papier. Les dilemmes de la petite moitié de coq devant l'institution paperassière. In *Les actes du colloque Cultures et subcultures orales, cultures et subcultures écrites dans les pays de la francophonie*. Paris: UNESCO/Université Paris-Nord.

Lire et Ecrire. 1984. *L'alphabétisation dans les pays industrialisés — Actes du colloque*. Brussels: Lire et Ecrire.

Mayor, F. 1989. Address of the Director-General of UNESCO at the opening of the Media Colloquium. In *Report of the International Media Colloquium on Literacy* (Paris, May 16-17, 1989). Paris: UNESCO.

Mayor, F. 1995. Address by the Director General. In *World Symposium on Literacy and the Family. Final Report*. Paris: UNESCO.

Mandon, T. 1993. Allocution. In *Les actes du colloque Cultures et subcultures orales, cultures et subcultures écrites dans les pays de la francophonie*. Paris: UNESCO/Université Paris-Nord.

Statistics Canada/OECD. 1995. *Literacy, Economy and Society*. Paris: OECD.

Sawyer, T. 1992. Keynote Address. In *Adult Literacy: An International Urban Perspective*. New York: The City University of New York/The Literacy Assistance Center/UNESCO.

Somerfield, B. 1992. Intergenerational Literacy: Moderator's Remarks. In *Adult Literacy: An International Urban Perspective*. New York: The City University of New York/The Literacy Assistance Center/UNESCO.

Sticht, T. 1995. Family Literacy — A World Movement. In *World Symposium on Literacy and the Family. Final Report*. Paris: UNESCO.

St John Hunter, C. 1987. What Definitions Tell Us. In *Literacy in the Industrialized Countries: a Focus on Practice*. Toronto: International Council for Adult Education.

Stone, A. 1994. Tools for Adult Learners. In *Adult Literacy: An International Urban Perspective*. New York: The City University of New York/The Literacy Assistance Center/UNESCO.

Street, B. 1992. Sociocultural Dimensions of Literacy: Literacy in an International Context. In *The Future of Literacy and the Literacy of the Future*. UIE Reports 9. Hamburg: UNESCO Institute for Education.

_____. 1994. Research and Literacy. In *Adult Literacy: An International Urban Perspective*. New York: The City University of New York/The Literacy Assistance Center/UNESCO.

Torres del Castillo, R.M. 1994. The Recognition of Urban Literacy. In *Adult Literacy: An International Urban Perspective*. New York: The City University of New York/The Literacy Assistance Center/UNESCO.

UNESCO 1985. *Fourth International Conference on Adult Education. Final Report*. Paris: UNESCO.

_____. 1987. *Technical Meeting of European Specialists on the Prevention of Functional Illiteracy and the Integration of Young People into the World of Work — Final Report and Recommendations*. Paris: UNESCO.

UNESCO Institute for Education. 1992. *The Future of Literacy and the Literacy of the Future*. UIE Reports 9. Hamburg: UNESCO Institute for Education.

Université Paris-Nord. 1993. *Les actes du colloque Cultures et subcultures orales, cultures et subcultures écrites dans les pays de la francophonie*. Paris: UNESCO/Université Paris-Nord.

Vélis, J.P. 1990. Illiteracy/literacy in industrialized countries. In *Report of the International Media Colloquium on Literacy (Paris, May 16-17 1989)*. Paris: UNESCO.

_____. 1993. En avant, toutes? In *Les nouveaux enjeux et les nouveaux défis de l'alphabétisation et de l'éducation de base des adultes (Angers, France, 7-12 juillet 1990)*. Angers: Centre universitaire de formation continue.

Wagner, S. 1993. Minorité culture et alphabétisme. Les actes du collogue cultures et subcultures orales, cultures et subcultures ecrites dans le pays de la francophonie. Paris : UNESCO/Université Paris-Nord.

Section Two

Central
&
Eastern
Europe

Chapter Two
THE GYPSY MINORITY IN BULGARIA LITERACY POLICY AND COMMUNITY DEVELOPMENT (1985 - 1995)

Elena Marushiakova & Vesselin Popov
Minority Studies Society
Sofia, Bulgaria

The decade of 1985 — 1995 was a complex one for the development of Bulgaria. A long transition period followed the collapse of the Eastern European socialist system in 1989, when a modern economy, civic society and democratic political system were built in the midst of ongoing and difficult social, economic and political crises.

GYPSIES (ROMA) IN BULGARIA

The Gypsies (Roma) in Bulgaria, like Gypsies world wide, are not a homogeneous community. Typical of the Gypsy community is a complex ethno-social structure leading to important differences in the ethno-cultural traditions and socio-economic and educational features of its subdivisions. Gypsies have lived — and still live — in many countries with different historical circumstances and socio-cultural environments. Hence, the search for a universal approach to solve the "Gypsy problem" in all its dimensions and aspects is predestined to failure.

The Gypsies make up a considerable part of the Bulgarian population. The last population census of 1992 gave their number as being

313,000; but actually the people of Gypsy origin in Bulgaria are about 700,000-800,000, or approximately one tenth of the total population. Their ways of life and contemporary social and economic situations vary considerably. Large numbers of Gypsies live in a separate town or village *mahali*. Many of these *mahali*, especially in the towns, are "ghettos" where essential characteristics have been partially or completely lost and unskilled labour is the means of making a living. At present many Gypsies rely on welfare when it is available. Other, no less numerous, parts of the Gypsy population still adhere to group endogamous segregation and their traditional professional specialization that is often very much modified and successfully developed according to the new conditions.

On the whole the education level of Bulgarian Gypsies is much lower than that of the surrounding population. According to the 1992 census, in Bulgaria there are 464 Gypsies who are university graduates. Actually, the problems of Bulgarian Gypsies are not so much in the extent of their education as in the frequent lack of a wider social literacy. While this is a problem faced by Bulgarian society as a whole, it is especially pertinent for the Gypsies due to a number of additional factors including the negative attitudes of the macro-society towards them. In this respect the Gypsies' literacy problems cannot be made equivalent to the problems of school education.

Gypsy literacy exists within the traditional norms and values and is especially strong in the preserved groups and meta-group units. However, it is not sufficient in the modern era. Traditional literacy can function successfully and in reality it indeed does so within the specific community. A different type of literacy, corresponding to mainstream norms and criteria, is needed in Gypsy relations with the macro-society. It is much more appropriate to combine the two types of literacy (the traditional one of the Gypsy community and the modern one of the macro society) than to replace the first with the second. Gypsy groups who have preserved their traditional ethno-cultural characteristics adapt much more easily to the changing environment than those who have completely or partially lost these characteristics and are more vulnerable socially and economically. This often results in loss of ethnic identity, marginalization and anomie in parts of the community.

The attitude of the Gypsy community as a whole to the problems of literacy is rather complex and ambiguous. The majority of Gypsy intellectuals distance themselves from the problems of the community; many publicly refuse to be recognized as Gypsies. They see the solution to the problems in raising the level of education and culture of the Gypsy population according to the norms and criteria of the macro-society, would eventually mean a transformation of the Gypsies into Bulgarians. A Gypsy poet writes: "... so we can also become white people".

Most of the contemporary Gypsy leaders who were educated during the socialist era emphasize socio-economic problems such as unemployment, and they see their solution as the heal-all for all problems of the community. Relatively younger and fewer in number are those Gypsy leaders who view the problems of the Gypsy community from wider dimensions and raise the issues of equal rights within the community, equal status in Bulgarian society, equal education, and others. On the whole, however, the Gypsy community is relatively distanced from its leaders who usually are generals without an army; their efforts and activities are mostly unknown to the community.

POLICY OF THE STATE INSTITUTIONS AND LOCAL AUTHORITIES

The Gypsy policy of the State institutions and local authorities from 1985-1995 can be summed up generally as a denial of active politics, though the reasons for this approach differ over the years. Until 1989 Bulgaria followed a policy of "revival process" aimed at establishing the ethnic uniformity of the Bulgarian nation. For Bulgarian Turks the leading line was a "proof" of their Bulgarian origin and consequently their Bulgarian identity. Applying this approach to Gypsies was absurd even to the government, so officially Gypsies simply ceased to exist. Any mention of Gypsies in Bulgaria was avoided. The principle was "there are no Gypsies, so there are no problems"!

After the changes in 1989, the situation in Bulgaria was no longer the same. In 1991 a new constitution was adopted based on the presumption of individual civil rights and the denial of some collective minority rights. The most frequently cited Gypsy-related excerpt from this constitution is Article Six, paragraph two, that does not allow for "any limitations of the rights or privileges based on [...] ethnic belonging]...]". This text has taken on dimensions harmful for the Gypsies. Whenever there is a question of solving the problems of Gypsies, the typical reply is that according to the Constitution all Bulgarian citizens are equal and there can be no privileges. In November 1992 the Constitutional Court gave an interpretation to the above text that allows for "certain socially justified privileges" for "groups of citizens" who are in "an unfavourable social situation". However, this potential for providing some state policy in favour of Gypsies — even in a limited socio-economic field — has had no tangible effects.

The situation remained almost unchanged in the system of executive government despite the change of cabinets and political powers. For a few years there were discussions about having a special body of the Council of Ministers that would include representatives of various ministries and develop a coordinated State policy concerning Gypsies. Finally, in 1994 an Interdepartmental Council on Ethnic Problems was organized. In 1995, with the election of a new Bulgarian Socialist Party government, this council was transformed into the Inter-Administrative Council on Social and Democratic Issues. A complicated procedure determined the intended participation of representatives of the ethnic communities. So far this council has not actually functioned and it does not seem likely that this will change soon.

The main problem is the unwillingness of the authorities to acknowledge the "Gypsy problem". It is enough to mention the example of the Deputy Minister of Labour and Social Care, who represents Bulgaria in the Specialist Group on Roma/Gypsies and participates regularly in the meetings of this group in the Council of Europe in Strasbourg. Bulgaria is one of a few European countries that officially sends a high state officer to this specialist group, but this has never been officially announced in Bulgaria and the "specialist" himself has until now refused all invitations to participate in all kinds of Gypsy-connected initiatives.

The policy of local authorities towards Gypsies and their problems is no better. Local authorities are actually not obliged to have such a policy. Even if there is a will, it is hard to find a way to actualize it. Each county depends on government funding, and the opportunities to develop its own specialized policy — for example regarding Gypsies — are very limited. Despite limited opportunities there are some attempts in this direction, such as appointing local specialists on Gypsy issues (sometimes Gypsies themselves) although no results can be seen as yet.

Examples from existing practices

A future specialized policy should be developed through the active influx of experts and representatives of the Gypsy community. It is necessary to consider the ethno-cultural specifics of the Gypsy community as the basis of this policy in order to make it really effective and capable of solving the numerous problems of Bulgarian Gypsies. Here we will give some examples from existing practice that reflect the few actual attempts at such a specialized policy on the part of the State and local authorities. The teaching of the Gypsy language in Bulgarian schools deserves special mention. The study of the Gypsy language (Romanes), defined by the euphemistic terminology of the new constitution as a "mother tongue", is allowed for four hours a week as an optional subject (Decree #232 of December 10, 1991).

The actual implementation of this decision has encountered many problems, the first being the lack of sufficiently prepared teaching staff. The Gypsy language is not studied in any higher institution and its introduction in university curricula has been firmly rejected. The attempts to give certificates for "mother tongue" teachers to irregular teachers (Gypsies who are high school graduates and have attended special courses) are not welcomed by many school principals and teachers. The teaching of Romanes is not even allowed in many schools. The Gypsy community themselves do not have a unanimous attitude to the teaching of their language in schools. Moreover the mother tongue of some Bulgarian Gypsies is Turkish or Rumanian. As a result Romanes is taught in some parts of the country thanks only to the enthusiasm of Hristo Kyuchukov, a former expert in Romanes at the Ministry of Education, and a few Gypsy teachers. The outlook for the future is rather uncertain.

Another example of State attempts to solve a Gypsy issue by means of literacy comes from the Gypsy neighbourhood Stolipinovo in the town of Plovdiv. In 1993-1994 the Ministry of Labour and Social Affairs, in collaboration with the United States Department of Labour, began a program for literacy, professional qualification and employment in this neighbourhood. The Ministry had contradictory opinions about this long-term and expensive program. On the one hand it was defined as being a "pilot program" that should grow into a future national program. On the other hand, it was admitted unofficially that the program had not been able to accomplish its ultimate goals. The employment component providing temporary employment in public works, gardening and other occupations included only a few dozen participants and did not ensure long-term employment or qualification. Furthermore, participation in the employment program or the qualification training courses deprived families of unemployment benefits that were actually higher so there was no incentive for participation in the program.

The qualification program consisted of primary literacy courses and introduction into some professions, usually not taking the changes of finding employment into consideration, for example hairdressing courses for women. A few dozen people completed the qualification training courses and work placements were not provided for any of them. In other words, the most pressing need — for employment — was not met. Considering that the population of Stolipinovo is about 30,000 peole and actual unemployment is about 90-95 per cent, it is obvious that the program was far from accomplishing its primary goal.

This assessment of the ineffectiveness of the program was shared by outside experts, particularly in the US Ministry of Labour report. This report exphasizes that the program loses its meaning if it is not properly funded and especially if it does not accomplish its goal of providing employment; and there is no use repeating the program elsewhere in the same form. Nevertheless, this is exactly what is planned in 1996 — the beginning of a similar program for professional qualification and employment in Lom and most probably in Sliven as well. In the town of Lom where the Gypsy population is about 25,000-30,000, most of them unemployed, this program started with basic literacy for 40 Gypsies without providing funding for enlarging or following up the program and also without providing new work placements.

Such programs can be created *ad infinitum* and in practically every county. The county officers are no doubt very pleased with them because they increase the county's budget considerably, but their effect on Gypsies and their problems will be insignificant. The creation of a new large-scale program "To feed the poor" just after the completion of the program described above is evidence of such attitudes. This program, in Stolipinovo *mahala* in Plovdiv, is financed by the British Know How Fund and provides free distribution of food for Gypsies in need, an example of *charity* instead of *literacy*.

Another program of the same Ministry for the repatriation of emigrants (mostly Gypsies) had similar non-existent or negative effects. A 1992 agreement with Germany brought financial aid of 50 million German marks, intended for professional qualification of the contingent of re-emigrants and potential future emigrants. After long and bureaucratic negotiations it was decided to have three such centres, in Pazardjik, Stara Zagora and Pleven. Only the Pazardjik centre is functioning at this time. The centre, that was meant to provide basic education to Gypsies as a primary contingent at risk for illegal emigration, is now teaching computer design, and naturally there are no Gypsies among those attending it.

Unfortunately, State and local authorities have proved entirely unprepared to solve any of the problems of the Gypsy population, the literacy issue in particular. The measures undertaken so far have been incomplete, incompetent, ill considered and inefficient. They lead to a waste of funds, useless reporting of activities, even to corruption of officials and Gypsies involved in the programs. Given the present situation, Bulgarian Gypsies should be glad that other government or county programs are still only at the discussion stage.

THE NON-GOVERNMENTAL SECTOR AND THE GYPSIES

The non-governmental sector presents a similar situation, although much more dynamic and diverse. After 1989, the governmental sector in Bulgaria was created and supported by different programs and foreign foundations mainly from USA and Western Europe. The non-governmental sector had a powerful but rather specialized surge of development. This sector firmly believed that the problems of minorities, and specifically those of Gypsies, is a basic priority. Almost all of the newly emerged NGOs rushed to solve the problems of Gypsies, to help them and defend their rights, to address civic education, community development, conflict resolution and other areas. This simple terminology contains the magic words that can provide financial aid from abroad regardless of the actual activities of the organizations and whether they have the vaguest idea about Gypsies and Gypsy problems. A reference book published in 1995, *Non-governmental Organizations in Bulgaria* includes a total of 467 organizations (there are actually more) with more than one quarter of them listing minority rights as their priority.

However, these numbers should not mislead one. Neither Bulgarian society as a whole, nor the Gypsies themselves have a clear idea about the number of people and organizations "taking care" of them. Often a token Gypsy is included in an organization or project in order to facilitate funding. The argument is that minority representatives are active in the NGO. Another variation is keeping in touch with a Gypsy organization (often consisting of one or several people) and presenting a "joint" project of the two NGOs. Most of these organizations are semi-legal — they are registered officially and present their activities to sponsors from abroad while rigorously avoiding any mention of the activity in the Bulgarian media. For a survey on Gypsies and the NGO sector in 1994, we asked a dozen

NGOs who declared Gypsy-oriented activities for their Annual Reports or for information on their "Roma" Projects. The results were very striking and no commentary is needed — only two NGOs agreed to present us their materials.

THE RELEVANT PROBLEMS OF WORKING WITH GYPSIES

Projects for homeless children

In order to illustrate the relevant problems of working with Gypsies, we can analyze some especially poignant examples where the deficiencies of the third sector in Bulgaria are most obvious. For several years now there have been projects on homeless children in Bulgaria. This "fundable" problem has attracted some State institutions and a number of NGOs. The result was a multitude of projects with budgets enormous by Bulgarian standards, advertising campaigns in the press, heartbreaking reports, press conferences, charity balls and cocktail parties, gift-giving campaigns, associates hired to work with these children, and so on. The hypocrisy culminated in dressing a few of the children in costumes and taking them to the Sheraton Hotel so they could dance for the President of Bulgaria, diplomats and businessmen. Then they were changed into their old clothes again and sent back on the street.

These activities unfortunately distorted the nature of the whole issue. Various organizations would present the number of homeless children as so incredibly high that the problem acquired apocalyptic dimensions. The statistics of the Ministry of the Interior for the period 1991 — 1995 give the number of homeless children in Bulgaria as being about 3,000, although in reality the permanently homeless may number a few hundred, and a few dozen in Sofia in particular. Unfortunately this social issue was defined as an ethnic — i.e. Gypsy — problem, although not all homeless children were Gypsies. Thus, the negative stereotypes about Gypsies were confirmed in Bulgarian society. The mass media described Gypsies as people who did not take care of their children and who deliberately sent them out to beg, steal, become prostitutes and take drugs. Nobody, including the NGOs busily working on their projects, was willing to tell the truth: that there are a few dozen homeless Gypsy children in Sofia along with a few thousand "normal" Gypsy children, living with their parents, who have serious problems of a rather different nature.

The activities of the NGOs allowed the State to distance itself from the problem of homeless children and transfer the responsibility for them to the non-governmental sector. The official explanation was that the State is powerless since there is no law for child protection. That is actually far from the truth. According to current legislature parents who do not take care of their children may be deprived of parental rights and the children sent to special homes, but this has not been done in recent years. A shelter sponsored from abroad was finally built in Sofia and officially opened in the presence of State and diplomatic officials. Homeless children can come there to eat and spend the night, but they cannot stay there permanently. Here we are not talking about literacy, merely of minimal support for biological survival and an attempt to fulfil State responsibilities.

Universal opinion, including the opinion of those directly involved in this project that started off with high hopes and extensive advertising, is that it has been a failure. The situation of "street children" is still the same. The children spend all their time on the streets and have neither the wish nor the chance for a normal life. This is an illustration of how impossible it is for the non-governmental sector to assume all State tasks. At most it can undertake palliative measures. It is dangerous that the non-governmental sector not only does not urge the State to perform its functions, but also has allowed it to avoid the problem. At the last round table organized by the President of Bulgaria, the main idea was to enlarge the system of similar shelters for homeless children — funded by foreign sponsors of course — in the various counties. The contribution of the State was minimized to preparing a special decree of the Ministry of Labour and Social Affairs to regulate the procedures for opening and operating these shelters.

Projects of the Education of Gypsy Children

Another problem attracting the attention of NGOs concerns the education of Gypsy children. Segregated primary schools to the 8th grade have existed in Bulgaria since the 70's. They were built in the Gypsy neighbourhoods and are euphemistically called"schools for children with low living standards and culture". Gypsy children would leave these schools, if they managed to graduate at all, as illiterate or semiliterate unskilled workers whose later professional development was very difficult. In 1991 the special status of these schools was cancelled *de jure*, but *de facto* the situation the situation there has remained unchanged. The Ministry of Education has decreased its control, and because of the economic problems of Gypsy families, their lack of interest in such an "education" has become especially obvious. Theoretically, all children can enrol in the school of their choice, but in practice Gypsy children are denied access to regular schools under various excuses. More and more children from the Gypsy *mahali* fail to see any use in going to such segregated schools, and drop out of the educational process.

In their attempt to bring Gypsy children back to school and improve the conditions of schooling, a number of organizations including some Gypsy groups have created projects to repair existing schools and distribute free food to the children selected as most needy. This type of activity is harmless, but in the long run it is merely palliative and does not solve the educational problems of Gypsy children. Free food cannot be said to increase attendance or improve the quality of education in these schools. Parents who appreciate the importance of good education for their children try to enrol them in regular rather than "Gypsy schools" so they can receive an equal education. Also, inter-ethnic resentment is on the rise in Bulgarian society as a result of this activity; people perceive any aid given to "Gypsy schools" as a special preference for Gypsies.

Far more unsuccessful and negative are projects aiming to keep children in school by changing the curriculum or adding extra school hours. A typical example is the project "Let us bring the children back to school" financed by UNESCO through a Bulgarian foundation. In theory it sounds logical: it aims to attract Gypsy children to the schools by adding cultural activities such as lessons in music, dance, drawing, traditional Gypsy occupations and others. This "pilot project" (another magic word in the non-governmental sector) in five schools, has evidently increased the school attendance of Gypsy children.

However, there is another issue here. Should not the aim of Gypsy children's schooling be to increase their education level as a base for their future professional and social development? Gypsy children can and do dance, sing and acquire their own ethnic culture at home. It would be much better if the school could give them knowledge and skills for their life in the macro-society. Schools should attract children by improving the practical results of education. This is clearly not possible in segregated schools. The education of people graduating from "Gypsy schools" is second-rate no matter how regularly they have attended.

This project reinforces the existence of schools based on the segregation principle, instead of radically reforming or closing them down. A ridiculous situation has emerged: Bulgarian human rights activists launched a campaign against the segregation of Gypsy children while the high-ranking government officials responsible for the project claimed that "Gypsy schools" do not exist in Bulgaria at all. Even worse, this project has given the Ministry of Education the grounds to offer a return to the near past by introducing segregated professional education for Gypsy children from an earlier age. Since this would be at the expense of their general education, they will have less opportunity for future professional development. Despite the intentions of its organizers, the project "Let us bring the children back to school" has set the situation back instead of providing Gypsy children with new and equal opportunities. We can only hope that its underlying principles will not evolve into a national program for the educational development of Gypsy children.

Literacy projects for Gypsies

Most Gypsy literacy-related projects implemented in the non-governmental sector are rather harmless, but have almost no tangible results. There is no harm in having ten people receive office equipment and salaries for a year to prepare materials about the Gypsies and their history and culture for use in the school system. This project is financed by PHARE and coordinated by the Minority Rights Group of London. The fact remains that these materials could be prepared in two weeks by a few specialists, and the chances of their ever reaching the schools without preliminary coordination with the Ministry of Education are rather slim.

It is not clear what gives NGO sector "experts" the self-confidence to conceive programs for an ethnic community practically unknown to them. For example, a group of medical doctors from one NGO did "sociological research" among a few Gypsies in three Gypsy quarters, and on this basis proposed a national program for sexual education of Gypsy children.

The numerous and larger-scale projects on civic education, conflict resolution, "open education", sex education, family planning, protection of Gypsy women from violence and others follow a similar pattern. They usually take the form of endless courses and seminars with an insignificant effect on Gypsy literacy. Often the lecturers are highly qualified and well-meaning Western specialists who are totally unfamiliar with the specifics of the Gypsy community and the overall situation in Bulgaria. Many of the lecturers and "experts" do not know any Gypsies in their own countries, but this does not prevent them from giving generous advice on how to solve the "Gypsy problem" in Bulgaria. Usually the same people — most often teachers or social workers — and a small circle of Gypsies who have become professional "seminar attendants" take part in all projects.

The true level of interest of such projects and their participants in Gypsy literacy became obvious during an international meeting about the "Step by Step" program. This project of the Open Society Foundation network in Eastern Europe aims to provide an equal start for minority children through specialized kindergartens. The Bulgarian representatives at the meeting could not even answer the concrete question of whether there are separate Gypsy neighbourhoods in Bulgaria. There are no opportunities to apply what has been learned; this obviously does not appear to concern the organizers or their sponsors. At the end of a project, when the activities and expenses have been accounted for, what comes next? A similar project and its multiple copies!

Evaluating these projects

The evaluation of these many projects touches upon another problem: the unwillingness to inform society about NGO or finished projects. The above-mentioned "semi-legality" is evident here. Information about these projects can be found mainly in the reports of the sponsor foundations from abroad, but presentation in the Bulgarian media is usually avoided, and few of the Gypsy participants ever understand how many people and funds have been invested in their literacy.

Yet another problem is the common interest of most NGOs in receiving as much funding as possible without concern for its proper use. Increased funding usually results in hiring more staff, renting bigger offices and consequently seeking ever more expensive and inefficient projects to support the organization. There is an interesting phenomenon: the more expensive the project, the smaller the chance that the money will go to anything other than office rent and salaries. We often see curious situations, such as having a foundation sponsor with priority the projects of their own "experts". That is, the same people vote approval of their own projects, fulfil them and then report their success to themselves.

Their common self-interest stops project participants from criticizing other projects for fear of having the funding of the whole non-governmental sector stopped. A relatively small circle of people occupies key positions in the sector and to a large extent control and distributes the funds. However, despite the disadvantages described above and possibly others, the non-governmental sector still assists the positive changes in Bulgarian society.

GYPSY ORGANIZATIONS

The problems in State politics and the non-governmental sector inevitably reflect on Gypsy organizations. Since the changes of 1989, Bulgarian Gypsies have been given the opportunity of having their own organizations. Most often these groups are variations of similar organizations in the social and political life of the macro-society. Such organizations are Confederacy of Roma in Bulgaria, United Romani Union, Roma Social Democratic Union, Democratic Union Roma, Independent Union Roma and others. Initially, their primary goal was participation in Bulgarian political life and their ambition was to represent the whole Gypsy community. Their leaders were representatives of the "new Gypsy elite" formed in the "socialist era", with no real political experience and no significant influence in the larger Gypsy community.

Consequently, their activities were confined within a narrow circle of the community without receiving its total support. The strong politicization of these organizations was a result of the overall politicization of Bulgarian society. They did not grow into political parties, since the new Bulgarian constitution of 1991 forbade the existence of parties organized on an ethnic principle, but in reality their functions were largely political. However, the results achieved were insignificant and Gypsies were poorly represented in the government, mostly on a local level, without any real chance of influence on the development and implementation of State and local politics.

The emergence of Gypsy NGOs

Gradually however, under the influence of the developing non- governmental sector, Gypsy NGOs began to emerge that broke away from political ambitions and turned to specific projects. The specifics of Bulgarian law made them register as one-man foundations — such as Social Foundation "Roma", Foundation for Regional Development

"Roma", Foundation "New Life for Bulgarian Roma", Foundation "Social Roma Bureau", Foundation "Cebros" and others. The first steps of these organizations were marked with strong feelings of dependence on the non-Gypsy, the person in power, and the mediator in the non-governmental sector. For a long time Gypsies thought they were not able to prepare a project and work on it themselves. They thought they needed special blessings or joint activity with representatives of a higher institution or a wealthy foundation. (In Bulgaria these usually coincide; it is considered normal for a State official to be a member of the executive board of a foundation).

The appearance and activities of the Roma Soros Foundation in Bulgaria have brought about some important changes. The foundation's strategy is radically different from that of other foundations, including those within the network of Open Society Funds to which it used to belong. Its underlying principle is that Gypsies should work for themselves without the mediation of non-Gypsy leaders or organizations. Gypsy people and organizations have come to believe in their potential to determine their own destiny. They have started to write their own projects that they consider necessary — at first to Roma Soros Foundation and then to other foundations. They have learned from experience what they could not learn from the numerous courses and seminars on the development of non-governmental Gypsy organizations and project writing. The brief existence of a real Gypsy foundation had its effect, and the individual development of the Gypsy non-governmental sector could no longer be stopped however inconvenient it might be to many "mediator" NGOs whose existence and perspective no longer make sense.

The development of the non-governmental sector of Bulgarian Gypsies however, has not been all positive. Influenced by the example of the Bulgarian NGOs working with them, most Gypsy organizations soon began to copy their activities, thus repeating their major weaknesses. Meaningless projects are being offered that have real chances of being approved. The most cunning among the Gypsies has even registered several foundations (for example, one in a man's name and another in his wife's name) so they can have more opportunities. The work of the non-governmental sector is perceived as a special type of business conducted according to certain rules that should be followed. It should not be surprising that corruption on many levels and in many guises is another rule of this game for some of the NGOs in Bulgaria.

These disadvantages in the work of the non-governmental sector in Bulgaria should not by any means be perceived as a complete rejection of the purpose and importance of the sector. There are still some organizations that have useful activities related to Gypsies and their literacy. We would like to mention the "Human Rights Project". This is a Gypsy organization not limited to community frameworks; it also includes non-Gypsies and cooperates actively with other organizations in Bulgaria and abroad. The "Human Rights Project" was created as an organization for monitoring Gypsy civil rights in Bulgaria, and at present it has regional coordinators and a wider range of activities including an information base, contacts between Gypsies and international organizations and foundations, courses for Gypsy leaders, public awareness work, and others. It plays a successful role in Gypsy literacy. It is only normal that there are weaknesses in this multifaceted activity of the "Human Rights Project", but this is the direction that has the most potential. Other NGOs that are not specifically focused on Gypsies but include Gypsies or have active cooperation with representatives of the Gypsy community, have similar roles. These include the Bulgarian Helsinki Committee, the Minority Studies Society "Studii Romani", and others.

Another interesting issue is the way these processes of modern literacy enter and become part of the life of the Gypsy community. We can say with certainty that they concern only part of the Gypsy community, and only in some locations. Large subdivisions of the community remain virtually unaffected, including for example Romanian-speaking Rudari, many Turkish speaking Gypsies, many traditional Gypsy groups, and Gypsies in most regions of the country. Most Gypsy communities in Bulgaria stand apart from these processes. Many of them still rely on traditional literacy while others combine traditional with State offered education, insufficient as it is.

The formerly nomadic Gypsy community of Kardarashi is an example. These Gypsies have a closed way of life and strong cohesion within the community. Their ethnic and cultural traditions are rich and well-preserved, including internal self-government - the so called *Romano Kris* or Gypsy court. Their standard of living is high. In an attempt to partially legalize their business, they look for parallel forms of new social activities. They sent representatives to participate in the new system of Gypsy organizations, for example in the creation of the Foundation of United Roma Communities or Roma Soros Foundation and the Roma Program of the Open Society Fund. Recently there has been a noticeable transformation of the traditional forms of internal self-government, such as the creation of *Supreme Meshare* (Supreme Gypsy court) that acts as a fund, collecting money and investing it in the education of some community members. Thus, people are being educated to serve the whole community. So far only the first steps have been made towards realizing these intentions, but their potential should not be underestimated.

SUMMARY

The tendencies we can observe in the Gypsy community as a whole take two major directions. There is an underlying process of community self-closing, rejection of macro-society literacy, and the sole use of the Gypsies' own mechanisms. There is also the aspiration to win their own social and political presence and opportunities to participate in the decisions that concern the fate of their culture. Unfortunately, the surrounding population in the context of a difficult economic crisis and powerful political struggles relates this to increasing rejection of the Gypsy culture. The conditions are present for a crisis in inter-ethnic relations and their development into open conflicts. In fact this is already happening. In these circumstances the best course would be to combine these two tendencies and include them in the overall development of Bulgarian society if possible.

At present it is not easy to outline the potential for the development of Gypsy literacy. There are indications that the highest potential exists in the combination of traditional ethno-cultural forms with the capacities of the non-governmental sector. However, the complete implementation of this option will require too much time. Without participation of the State, at least in solving the most important problems of literacy (such as school education), and without provision of equal civil rights and opportunities, we cannot expect any essential changes. The palliative measures of the non-governmental sector with all their clearly negative aspects will still prevail. It is obvious that in the near future State and local authorities will have neither the will (considering the prevailing social attitudes to the Gypsies) nor the needed knowledge and skills for a special policy in this direction.

The non-governmental sector is working actively, but the actual results are unlikely to be seen soon. Attempts to create a civic society with a well-developed NGO sector in Bulgarian conditions, in a society with different types of social stratification and different cultural and historical tradition, has led to the formation of a small closed stratum of paid "NGO professionals" and "civic society fighters". These people are not really interested in the creation of a real civic society, because such a society would stultify their "missionary zeal" and negatively affect their financial situation. If this

Western approach continues unchanged, there is a serious danger of firmly establishing the pseudo-dissident "neo-nomenclature" in the non-governmental sector, that will work primarily for its own self-interest without contributing to Gypsy literacy. This will be the final compromise of the whole idea of a civic society in Bulgaria.

The paternal approach of the State and the NGO sector whenever literacy issues are addressed is especially negative for the development of the Gypsy community. A flagrant example is the attempt to present Gypsies as a destructuralized, marginalized community without their own ethno-cultural traditions. This has even been done in some quasi-scientific research works. The excuse that it has been done with the good intention of drawing public attention to Gypsies and their problems is rather suspicious considering the actual effect: funds coming from abroad for the "good" benefactors of the Gypsies, while the negative attitude of Bulgarian society towards Gypsies becomes entrenched.

This paternal approach of "the good white brothers" has a negative influence on Gypsies themselves. They are placed in a position of being forever taught and guarded. This destroys the adaptive mechanisms of the community and creates a layer of corrupt individuals who have benefited from the NGO sector and have no real contact with the community. A far more positive and effective alternative are the activities directed towards real learning about Gypsies and their ethno-cultural traditions, towards overcoming of the negative stereotypes in Bulgarian society, and towards the real equality of Gypsy civil rights.

RECOMMENDATIONS

We would like to conclude by pointing out some basic principles and recommendations for improving literacy-related work with Gypsies in Bulgaria:

- People who are very familiar with the specifics of the Gypsy community and their ethnic and cultural traditions should perform all projects and activities.

- Participation of Gypsies in solving their own problems should be mandatory, based on a truly equal cooperation.

- Approaches must not be copied directly from outside experience;

local specifics and the overall historical, ethnic and cultural context must be considered.

- There must be effective public control on the projects and their results. Their effect on the Gypsy community should always be considered.

- Independent specialists recognized in Bulgaria and abroad for their work with Gypsies should be involved in the evaluation and approval of the submitted projects and the analysis of the end results.

References

Aspekti na etnokulturna situatsia v Bulgaria. [Aspects of the ethno-cultural situation in Bulgaria]. Sofia: Centre za izsledvane na demokraciata, 1992.

Aspekti na etnokulturna situatsia v Bulgaria i na Balkanite. [Aspects of the ethno-cultural situation in Bulgaria and Balkans].Tom 2, Sofia: Centre za izsledvane na demokraciata, 1992.

Etnicheskata kartina v Bulgaria (prouchvania prez 1992). [The Ethnic Situation in Bulgaria. Research 1992]. Sofia: Club '90, 1993.

Kyuchukov, Hr. *Podgorovia za ogramotyavane v uslovia na bilingvisam.* [Preparation for Literacy in a Bilingual Situation]. Sofia: Sofia University, 1994.

Kyuchukov, Hr. *Romani Children and Their Preparation for Literacy. A Case-Study.* Tilburg: University of Tilburg, 1995.

Marushiakova, E. & Popov, V. *Tsiganite v Bulgaria.* [Gypsies in Bulgaria]. Sofia: Club '90, 1993.

Marushiakova, E. & Popov, V. "The Cultural Traditions of the Gypsies in Contemporary Bulgaria and the Attitude of the State and Local Authorities towards Them." - In *Gypsies in the Locality.* Strasbourg: Council of Europe Press, 1994, pp.111-116.

Marushiakova, E. & Popov, V. "Gypsy Schools' in Bulgaria."- Promoting *Human Rights and Civil Society in Central and Eastern Europe. Newsletter of International Helsinki Federation for Human Rights.* 4 (1994): 5.

Marushiakova, E. & Popov, V. (eds.) *Studii Romani.*, Vol. I, Sofia: Club '90, 1994.

Marushiakova, E. & Popov, V. (eds.) *Studii Romani.*, Vol. II, Sofia: Club '90, 1995.

Marushiakova, E. & Popov, V. *Tsiganite na Bulgaria. Problemi na multikulturalnata muzeyna expozitsia. / The Gypsies of Bulgaria. Problems of the Multicultural luseum Exibition.* Sofia: Club '90, 1995.

Nationwide Situation Analysis of Bulgaria's Children and Families. New York: UNICEF, 1992.

Sklar, M. *Doklad za poseshtenieto na rabotnata grupa na Departamenta na truda.* [Report on the Visit of the Work Group of the Department of Labour]. Sofia, 1994

Spravochnik. Nepravitelstveni organizatsii v Bulgaria. [Reference-book. Non Governmental Organizations in Bulgaria]. Sofia: Sajuz na balgarskite fondacii i Fondacia Otvoreno obshtestvo.

Tomova, I. *Tsiganite v prehodniya period.* [the Gypsies in the Transition Period]. *Sofia: International Centre for the Minority Studies and Intercultural Relations. 1995.*

Vrazli na savmestimost i nesâvmestimost vâv vsekidnevieto na hristiani i myusulmani v Bulgaria. [Relations of Compatibility and Incompatibility in the Everyday Life of Christians and Muslims in Bulgaria]. Sofia: International Centre for the Minority Studies and Intercultural Relations, 1995.

Zang, T. *Destroying Ethnic Identity. The Gypsies of Bulgaria.* A Helsinki Watch Report. 1991

Chapter Three
BASIC EDUCATION IN ROMANIA

Florentina Anghel
Institute of Educational Science
Bucharest, Romania

THE MEANING OF BASIC EDUCATION

This article presents experience of and critical reflections on basic education in the Romanian context, after five years' experience of literacy.

We should make clear what we mean by the concept of basic education, which has replaced that of literacy and that takes into account changes in grassroots practice in Romania, where the livelier and more meaningful *basic education process* "naturally" replaced the literacy process. Basic education has the sense made explicit in the *Alpha 96* projects:

> *Basic* does not have the usual meaning of the initial skills on which an educational curriculum can be based; nor does it mean minimal or prosaic skills, as though seen from a superior position and as though there were only one centre to the universe and one direction for history. We understood *basic education* in the anthropological sense, analogous to *basic personality*: a structure for assembling and transmitting knowledge, agenerative grammar of total exchange. And as a *skill* particular to a group that was structuring its identity and transforming itself through chance events, encounters with other cultures, and a number of individual wills.[1]

The concept of basic education has provided answers to questions that we asked in 1994:

> In Romania's case, literacy has to fulfill a training rather than an information function, because it is more than a sum of basic skills

(reading, writing, arithmetic). It is a way of raising consciousness of a social and cultural heritage that must be mobilized and revitalized. Enlightened (participative, involved) literacy training must become a basic framework for cultural development... as much an expression of the quality of new relationships between the individual and the community as the starting point for the individual autonomy that is necessary for Romania to consciously find a place in the outside world, to communicate with self or others, to participate more fully in social life. The overall purpose, in a word, is liberation, in its most generous sense.[2]

We are writing this at the end of the 20th century, in Europe, from a Romanian perspective, in a country with a range of problems that could hardly have been foreseen a decade ago. Romanian projects have benefited from the fall of political and ideological barriers in Central and Eastern Europe, from a change of paradigm on an international scale, from the trend towards the unification and integration of a Europe that has become considerably enlarged, and from North-South cooperation.

However other subtler barriers of an economic and cultural nature have appeared, maintaining the crisis situation and the inequalities between states (in the view of Andrei Plesu, the former Minister of Culture, the "silk veil" has replaced the "iron curtain"). Nor can we ignore the post-totalitarian "transition" process in the new democracies, which is longer and more difficult than had been foreseen.

In this context, adult education has been a very important factor in Romania. It has introduced a new strategy into education based on the generous principle of the right to education, calls into question the separation between formal and non-formal education, and gives a new impetus to literacy, not in itself but as a means of promoting individual and social development. After 40 years of "silence", a special place and role are accorded to voluntary associations, which are regarded as factors for change and alternative resources for the diversification of models of education.

Adults, with their real needs, are once again at the centre of education, embodying the ideal of a Copernican revolution that stresses the individual rather than the global, multiplies rather than simplifies, and makes individuals capable of participating in both their own transformation and the modification of the community. Participating in this transformation as conscious actors (subjects, not objects), and armed with their own recognized knowledge and capabilities to overcome individual crises during the wearying transition process, individuals are once more at the heart of things.

Nonetheless, critical attention should be given to the ways these broad ideals of adult education can be transformed into actual objectives at the *micro* level and into national or international strategies at the *macro* level, so that they acquire the necessary strength and do not open up too great a gap between individual and global needs.

This chapter poses a number of questions relating to the theme of *Alpha 97*, which seeks to match educational strategies with local resistance to marginalization and exclusion, and sets out to reduce the distance between literacy policies and local reality. The following questions are important:

- How can local solidarity be realized or "reconstructed" as adult basic education programs develop?
- Who are our true partners in basic education programs?
- What are the advantages and disadvantages of voluntary and unpaid work? Can this function at the local level?
- Is there a need for professionals specially prepared for these programs?
- What can be done so that activism and populism do not take the place of participation?
- Is it necessary to expunge concepts and activities that are "contaminated" by the ideological propaganda of the past? What can be done to "regenerate" them? How can new concepts be learnt and assimilated (adult education, basic education, literacy, partners, solidarity, voluntarism, awareness, non-formal education, intercultural education, civic education, etc.)?
- Who are the illiterates? What is illiteracy? Is it just an imported, fashionable notion?
- Can the problems be resolved only at the local level? Is there a need for decisions and strategies at the national level so that effective local programs can develop?
- Where is the funding to come from?

THE STAGES IN THE PROJECT

Any intellectual enterprise is an adventure. Today I am going to tell you about experience of the adventure called "action-research". I shall try to free myself from all prejudices about how to write in a newspaper, and from the notion that in our day we are no longer to write off the cuff, or to write about our personal memories. I don't know whether I shall succeed, but I can assure you that everything that I write will be true and first-hand. If you have any doubts, try to rewrite our experience. Don't try too hard to collect evidence. In any case, it won't replace first-hand experience. (Elena)[3]

From the outset, the "action-research" project proposed by the author more or less selected itself. It has been one of the most successful projects that, from the very beginning, refused to conform to the initial plans and behaved like a premature baby that adapts itself surprisingly well to its environment in order to survive, overcoming difficulties and taking advantage of any chance of survival. Our only merit is perhaps that of finding the environment and of acting as an intermediary in its development. Obviously, we acted advisedly to bring about certain attitudes and actions. At every moment we asked ourselves if we were doing what we did well. We asked questions to try to get answers from colleagues involved in the same types of "action-research" projects. We also made use of the advantages of what has been termed "cooperative research" in *Alpha* projects, an approach that aims to encourage cooperation in initiatives in the everyday context, and in discussions to try to find answers to real-life questions.

The stages in the program

The program evolved over a number of stages:

- ***The period 1990-1991***, the "period of enthusiasm", coincided with the shift of Romanian public opinion towards projects to update the education system in the direction of generally desired change. The international context was favourable both to Romania — as a country that had decided to give up a dictatorial communist system — and to matters connected with basic education. International Literacy Year made it easier for the states in Central and Eastern Europe to join in international exchange programs. Romania was able to take part in the UNESCO Institute project on "Literacy Strategies in Industrialized Countries", and received methodological assistance from Canada for the training of specialists and the design of statistical surveys of functional literacy.

It was possible to launch the first program aiming at raising public awareness of the seriousness of illiteracy and the right to basic education for all citizens in a country, including adults. After a period of "silence" and obfuscation that had lasted over 50 years, public opinion was alerted to the issue. We made the first timid, small-scale attempts at basic education programs. The first seminars and meetings at the Institute of Educational Science set out to identify the potential partners for an action-research program on basic education.

- *The period 1991-1993*, known as the "period of realism", was critical to the program. The country's "transition" to a different political and economic system proved longer and more arduous than anticipated. The crisis, conflicts and rival movements, and the global problems that made their appearance during these years in Romania changed the order of priorities for the solving of problems. Furthermore, the media persevered with a campaign about the situation of people with special needs in Romania. Sometimes poorly led, this may have had an adverse effect on adult basic education projects. In order to improve the "worsened" image of a Romania that had become a country of the handicapped, official propaganda launched a media counter-offensive focusing on gifted children and people with exceptional abilities (inventors, scientists, famous business leaders, etc.).

In consequence, it was impossible to appear "subversive" in a tense public atmosphere that even drove people to accuse anyone who stressed difficulties rather than achievements, of betraying the national interest. In the struggle to continue the process of public conscientization, people somehow or other forgot the real problem, the one they should all have been concentrating on.

From then on, we had to find another way of relaunching the whole question of basic education and illiteracy. Our awareness program restarted in another guise, in what at the time we called a "masked" form: while the term "conscientizing literacy" was retained in our research papers, it was eliminated from the activities that we organized with the representatives of the media, with teachers and public officials, and was replaced by that of "basic education". Even the surveys that we carried out with many different partners to assess literacy levels went under "clandestine" names. For example, the survey conducted in 1993 was called a "Survey of Everyday Reading, Writing and Arithmetical Skills".

We decided much later that the term "basic education" reflected much better the aims of our programs, which went beyond basic or functional literacy as such. We linked respect for the rights to education and development, with the recognition of community values and local culture, etc., to our basic education programs. In consequence, it was necessary to make an "invisible" population visible, by trying to mobilize the social actors involved in education and training programs (NGOs and government agencies) that were already running basic education and even conscientizing literacy without always recognizing that they were doing so.

We found that it was easier to associate our programs with European and international programs and networks, and that the barriers between us and other states were more easily overcome than our internal ideological barriers and differences, which were subtler and more resilient. Although we had wanted to launch the first educational stage of our program, we were obliged to delay it for another year.

- ***The period 1993-1994***, that of "truth" and "action", was also that of "reconstruction" and benefited from relative social and political calm. The data that we had collected following our surveys began to win recognition. The 30 or so radio broadcasts, four television broadcasts on public and private channels, and the score of articles published in newspapers and magazines started to produce visible results.

  In this short history of the *Alpha Botosani '94* program, mention should also be made of a few favourable circumstances that helped us. The laws governing "pilot centres" of educational reform were applied so that the Institute of Educational Science could set up action-research programs with institutional partners in the country. The relative autonomy in financial matters and action accorded to these "pilot centres", unlike the centralized national programs, enabled a number of alternative programs to gain accreditation.

  In consequence, our non-formal education program was able to grant its participants the status of "teachers" even though they were not qualified as such. Mention should also be made of the remarkable enthusiasm and professionalism of the Botosani Teachers' Centre in running the *Alpha Botosani '94* program and ensuring that the local media were drawn in.

THE ALPHA BOTOSANI '94 PROGRAM

> *I came to the Teachers' Centre with reservations about this project. I thought "I'll stay for the first day to see what it's about" (as I was curious all the same), but I could imagine myself falling asleep on my chair and waiting for the day to end, listening to lectures, advice and talk. But it wasn't like that: the whole time I felt obliged to think, and to involve myself in what the others were doing. I discovered that there were other people who had the same problems as me, that I could communicate with them because I was understood, that I was more intelligent than I thought, that I had some imagination, and that I could solve my own problems if I had some teaching.* (Anca)

The action-research program entitled "Basic Education and Literacy: Strategies for Participation, Awareness and Action" was launched in 1994 as a micro-community program as part of a project of the Institute of Educational Science called "Adult Basic Education and Functional Literacy in Romania".[4] With hindsight it can be said that the *Alpha Botosani '94* program focused on the concept of "basic education" — a skill to be built up in a group on the hypothesis that it would create genuine cultural capital, even though spread among various individuals — and that the literacy initiatives were only the *object* of our action-research. We assumed that the individuals taking part in the program had sufficient skills for cross-disciplinary research with the aim of transforming formal literacy programs and experimenting with a more effective approach.

The aims of the program were as follows:

- to revitalize traditional Romanian institutions (schools, cultural centres and churches) with the goals of literacy;
- to train animators and to motivate everyone involved in the program to take part in community life as "social actors and protagonists of local history";
- to discover specific methods of organizing locally on the theme of "local solidarity";

- to evaluate new partners (we intended to make use of a number of non-governmental agencies and organizations).

The program was run in Botosani, a picturesque region situated "way up in the north — where you put the pin in the map to hold it up", as the local inhabitants said jokingly, near the frontier with Ukraine and the Republic of Moldova. The region is largely agricultural, and fairly poor in comparison with other regions of the country from the economic point of view. But it is famous, like all of Moldavia, for its hospitality, spiritual wealth and tolerance (Romanians live side by side with Jews, Poles, Russians, Ukrainians, etc.).

The offer of accommodation for the program in the Teachers' Centre was easily accepted, on the basis that it was a good idea to start where we were warmly received. From the surveys we had carried out in 1990-1994, we estimated that some of the population would be illiterate, and that we could find partners willing to become involved in our program. Moreover, according to the data obtained the following year from a survey of education in deprived regions, Botosani could be declared an "educational priority area": there were 41 deprived schools located in isolated areas that were difficult to reach by road, with a shortage of qualified teachers and high rates of absenteeism, dropout, non-enrolment and illiteracy, and with low pupil numbers and an ageing population, out of a total of 1866 schools in a similar situation.

THE FIRST STAGE: THE ESTABLISHMENT OF THE GROUP

Tell me straight out: have we come here to forget or to learn? Why do you tell us that we're teaching you? I've come so you can teach us what to do and how to get money, if you from down there, from Bucharest, if you know how. That's what I wanted to ask, and I'm sorry to be asking it. (Ileana, recounting humorously the questions that were asked by participants on the first day.)

The first stage, that of "awareness", began in December 1993. Its aim was to establish a reflection and action group to launch programs "parallel" to the national curriculum with the objective of raising the awareness of young people and adults through literacy.

We did not fix too many restrictive criteria for the first meeting. The people invited to take part were those who felt responsible for education in their communities and were able to involve themselves in the non-formal basic education program, regardless of their education and backgrounds: representatives of the local school administrative authorities and schools, teachers, school heads, representatives of local NGOs and the media, and specialists from the Teachers' Centre.

The result was a large, polite but skeptical and cold audience. After a full day of talks, when we had set out the purpose and the way the next stage would run (the training stage that was planned almost like a traditional training program), after discussions and negotiations with the 50 or so participants, we adopted a new program that would better meet their needs for information and training. This new program defined in the main the approaches, know-how and behaviour required of potential partners in a conscientizing non-formal literacy program.

THE SECOND STAGE: THE TRAINING PROGRAM

The training program also fell into two stages, in spring 1994 and 1995. Over 30 people took part in the first program. School heads, inspectors, people not qualified as teachers, experts from the Botosani Teachers' Centre, public officials, teachers and journalists met and worked together. In one week, a timid group, held back by all manner of conventions, changed into a dynamic, productive group that was full of ideas, friendly, curious, "pupils and teachers" at one and the same time, creative, bold and even subversive. What came out of this was as follows:

- ***In terms of content***: From their personal and professional experience, participants identified and specified ways to manage an individual development project. We gave descriptions of types of non-formal education, modular learning, differentiated teaching, assisted independence and self-learning. We also explored the questions of evaluation and self-evaluation, and how to improve results. We tried practically to initiate the participants into the roles of animators, moderators, and mediators for adult basic education programs, especially with regard to techniques of mediation and individual consultation (in the case of adults who have their own individual or collective project) by giving them a minimum knowledge of guidance and negotiation.

  In terms of objectives: We found remarkable resources for what we have already called "subversion": the participants discovered the power of critical thought; they directly expressed their opinions, which were ideological rather than educational; and they examined ways to change the education, administrative and political systems locally. We thought at that moment that we had succeeded in quite quickly training true "change agents" for the community, and that we had found effective partners for our programs.

A year later, a score or so of very courageous and enthusiastic people took part in the second stage of the training program, containing a module to evaluate the results achieved by participants in their own programs. Right from the opening discussions, that set out to examine critically the results obtained by each participant in local programs, it was evident that there were both achievements and difficulties. Briefly stated, the problems were:

- **Resistance** on the part of colleagues and heads of the organizations to which the participants belonged, to the implementation of programs that did not conform to the classic algorithm and called for skills of self-organization. Such resistance made it difficult to repeat the initial program;

- **Inertia and formalities** during the accreditation and establishment of the programs, with central agencies refusing to give up their monopoly of the field;

- **Marginalization** of those who had tried to put the programs into practice and had finally been obliged to conform to the "central model". This was the only model recognized, even though in theory, according to the Education Act, "possible alternative forms of education" were lawful. Participants in programs were regarded as belonging to "minorities", especially in the schools where they worked. They admitted that the air of freedom and equality that they breathed during our courses made them feel more frustrated than ever, as they were not aware that such relationships could be established between basic education partners;

- **Accusations** that they were repeating slogans of the former regime that had achieved nothing (the ideas of "solidarity" and "group awareness", etc.);

- **Fragility and instability** of attempts at partnership with volunteers and unpaid workers;

- The **absence of a budget** of time especially for action-research (at first promised through a reduction in the school duties of the people involved); and

- The **lack of the minimum funds** required to develop the programs, and the lack of material help (promised by the Ministry of Education for participants in pilot projects), and the difficulty of finding sponsors, who would rather invest in more spectacular fields that would guarantee them publicity.

EVALUATION

> *Whenever you hear politicians speak, they're extremely liberal and full of pious words and good intentions when it's a matter of the disadvantaged, the illiterate and the unemployed. But they're less clear about a strategy to spell out effective action for such people or for the recognition and support of activities by organizations that want to practise a different type of education that's not the same as official teaching. That sort of liberalism may also mean fewer responsibilities.* (Maria)

One of the first conclusions drawn from the *Alpha Botosani '94* program was that local program of the type described, despite their considerable initial impact (they are effective and do without bureaucracy), *do not achieve the intended effects in the long term*. Moreover, because of their effects on participants' critical awareness, they may marginalize them in their communities. For that reason, we asked ourselves if we had done right to concern ourselves with a narrow section of the population, whose habits we had wanted to change and in whom we might have provoked a "crisis". An "objective, scientific and critical" outside observer, who might see things from the point of view of the formal education system, might have concluded that the programs suffered from empiricism and subjectivity, had modest ambitions, led to barely perceptible changes and offered little satisfaction in return for the effort put into running them.

Nonetheless, the local programs that grew out of our initial program, although still at the "micro" level, constantly multiplied and had a *dynamic effect, especially on existing programs in the official education system*. For example, they did affect the content, implementation and number of partners of education programs for some categories of adults and young people.

This was true of new basic education programs for recruits

organized by the Ministry of Defence, which involved various local partners, including the Church. These programs were organized by the Ministry of Justice for prisoners, and the content was improved and better addressed their learning needs; the experimental literacy programs organized by agencies responsible for caring for minors, which involved specialists who practised literacy through painting or music; the experimental programs of the Ministry of Education, for which the expertise and cooperation of the researchers at the Institute was called on to draw up the curriculum and specific adult education strategies, etc.

It can therefore be said that the existing programs for adults have been *influenced* by the new programs and that they have in consequence become more flexible and tolerant towards participants' needs and demands than compulsory education is towards those of children. Compulsory education programs are still subservient to external imperatives, are incompatible with non-formal programs, recruit teachers trained in the official, centralized system, and rely more heavily on *informing rather than educating*.

It is difficult to find out about non-formal basic education, as countries with a tradition in that field well know. In Romania, it seems even more difficult. Only after 1993 did adult literacy program receive official recognition. Some had operated "secretly" before, in prisons for example. They had existed more or less since 1974, when *Ceaucescu* declared in a speech that there were no more illiterates in Romania and some courageous person had "whispered in his ear" that there were still many illiterates in the prisons. A decree was then issued specifically on literacy for illiterate prisoners (and this might be called "secret literacy"). Since it is only now that formal program for adults have appeared, it is much more difficult to promote experimental non-formal literacy programs.

Another problem facing our program has been how to identify so-called "basic" skills and the criteria to describe someone is "functionally illiterate". What are the real needs of the people targeted by our programs? Is it necessary to teach them something more, or is it enough to make them aware of the wealth of skills that they have? We asked "tendentious" questions such as: Why do we have to remove the people that we want to educate from the environment to which they are perfectly suited? They live well; they communicate orally more quickly than they would by other media, which are still inadequate (especially in rural areas); they are happy, they fall in love, and have brought up their children for centuries without much knowledge of reading; they manage their affairs; and although they are officially unemployed, they get along far better than the staff paid by the state to teach them.

Among a number of possible answers, the best one was given during the last stage of the program by an (unqualified) primary-school teacher from the countryside. She asked a counter-question: Is a peasant woman whose daily work begins at four in the morning (at six in winter) and ends at eight or nine at night truly happy? She has to take care of her entire family, attend to her housework and work in the fields, and has no free time to worry about a better existence. Or the old potter in a mountain village who sees that out of the 150 families that practised that craft a mere 25 to 30 years ago, all that remain are three old men who have no one left to whom to pass on what they learnt orally from their predecessors, as has probably been done for more than 1500 years? To return to the initial question — who is illiterate? — can one say that the illiterate peasant woman is among the marginalized? And if so, "in relation to whom and to what?"[6]

All these thoughts led us to the realization that we had to rethink our criteria and to abandon our prejudices about who was educated and who was not. We had to do far more to help the people targeted by our program to discover and exploit the skills they already had and to play a part in passing them on to the generations to come.

Another problem came to light when we visited the schools that we thought were "deprived" and had studied with a view to special training for the teachers. These schools had serious equipment problems as they were, until 1989, among the former "closed units" that had been shut down under the so-called "urbanization policy" that destroyed many Romanian villages. These schools had been reorganized from 1990 in isolated regions (in the mountains or on the plane) to give an opportunity to children who had to travel between three and seven kilometres a day to get to school, and could now at least pursue basic courses closer to home.

By comparison with children in cities, if the criteria of evaluation were changed, these children were enjoying an education that was sufficient for local needs, were living much of the time in the open air, were spontaneous, went to church with their parents and grandparents, had a "natural and plentiful source" of teaching support, could walk several kilometres through the hills in winter to get to school, knew much about nature and life, and were attached to their teachers, who had often been their parents' teachers and would go on to teach their children. How could special training help those teachers, who were loved and respected, and were achieving results far higher (according to our criteria) than those of many teachers in large urban schools?

The question therefore arose again: who were the educated and who were the uneducated, *who was "trained" and who "needed training"*?

From the example given above, we came back to the issue of basic education. It was obvious that this has to be selective, even though knowledge is unlimited and cumulative. While for the (urban) formal education system, what is selected is artificial and tends towards the cumulative and excess of information that it is difficult to counter What is selected for children's and young people's education in rural areas is broadly "natural" and often sufficient for local needs.

Equally naturally, the focus shifts to methods and procedures, and an experimental attitude becomes part of the order of things: the *functionality* that has to be imposed artificially in urban environments appears of its own accord in rural areas. There, education has a collective function that is appreciated by the entire community, which makes an effort to educate its children. Our efforts to make education into social commitment in urban areas came a long way behind *the tradition of this kind of education in rural areas*. Often, after talking to people from town and country, we came to the conclusion that it was the town-dwellers who were disadvantaged.

POLICY IMPLICATIONS

Out of the Romanian experience, a few observations and propositions have taken shape:

Observations

- It seems clear that we should not overvalue or idealize the "micro" level. It will be inadequate until inequalities within and between regions (social, economic and cultural) are studied, analyzed and confronted by national and international initiatives. Failure to do so will allow a region, a population or a country to coordinate and manage its dependency, inequalities and poverty at the "micro" level. It may be better or worse off, but whatever happens, it will require considerable effort. It is equally risky to leave local initiatives with no connection to central norms. It is necessary to ***integrate one-off programs into national programs*** (that may be regional or inter-regional), and it may also prove very useful to link national projects in an international framework.

- *Change*, the declared aim of our basic education programs, does not always include development or, to put it another way, is not always associated with rapid development. Even if change is desirable, it often leads to an imbalance, in the course of which, unavoidable inequalities and unintended "boomerang" effects may appear. In a traditional democratic system. The negative effects are probably more easily countered, and in countries with a flourishing economy, they are not greatly felt by the entire population. In Romania, which faces a difficult situation in all respects, the implementation of such a program of "radical" change in one respect may well increase the marginalization of a region instead of providing it with support.

- ***The need for professionals and trainers of professionals*** is acutely felt in these programs, even if all are to supposed to participate on an equal footing. Roles remain different, and they have to be played well. Moderators, animators and teachers have to be prepared for the roles that they have to play in an action-research project. Usually, they have to acquire an awareness of the skills that they already have, and they must be supported in their efforts to develop them. Voluntary and unpaid staff participating in these programs are an instability factor. For those who have key roles in the programs, a period of training and stability is required. They have to learn to be change agents as this is, obviously, not a natural quality.

- A short-term view is generally typical of the program described. They are still more or less "experimental programs", benefitting research more than practice. ***There is a need for a long-term view***, a broader, coherent vision of basic education, and hence a vision of all the ways of linking micro elements with global social, economic and political elements, especially in countries "in transition". This would both make co-operation easier between programs of the same type and make it easier to form networks of local and regional actors. They could, in turn, be more easily identified and their cooperation better organized.

- The success of a future program also depends on the programs that have preceded it. ***Micro-level programs, which often take place in a closed environment, can easily dwindle if they are unsuccessful***. The failure of such programs can compromise any subsequent attempt of the same kind in the community concerned.

Propositions

The preceding observations allow us to formulate a number of propositions with the aim of making basic education programs in Romania more effective and transferable.

- Coordination at the local level is necessary to make existing international collaboration (through the UNESCO Institute in Hamburg) more effective. In Romania, basic education programs, which are fragmented, should be included in a *system of local, regional and national coordination*. The partnership desired by government institutions and non-governmental organizations cannot be achieved unless permanent relations are established between the actors participating in these programs.

- It takes energy, skills and responsibilities to increase the number of programs, however small. The generous autonomy granted by the state to partners that are not part of its system should not be confused with a rejection of responsibility. *Adult education in Romania must be declared a national priority*. The Education Act defines education as a whole as a national priority. This Act states, in article 136: "(1) For the education of adults and in order to support the education system in meeting its specific aims, institutions and open or distance educational networks may be established, with the agreement of the Ministry of Education, using modern communication and information-processing technologies"; and it continues, in paragraph (2): *"the expenditure required by these education systems shall be borne by their beneficiaries and the institutions concerned."*

- The actors involved in adult basic education key positions must be *professionals*. These persons must demonstrate competence in a range of activities (facilitating, providing information, mediating, evaluating, etc.). Voluntary and unpaid work, enthusiasm and charisma are no substitute for professionalism in key roles. Moreover, as we have not yet forgotten the infamous (communist) "permanent party staff", chosen as if on purpose for their incompetence, we cannot repeat that ridiculous experience. The training needed by professionals must be co-ordinated by specialists.

- A legal and budgetary framework must guarantee the right to basic education. Otherwise, the state merely guarantees an abstract right, a bit like the "Christian rights" of every mortal. Without the financial support of the state for priority programs of adult basic education, and without guaranteed conditions of participation by adults in such programs (that often involves family, occupational and social difficulties), there is practically no guarantee that the program will run, especially as it is not possible to rely on outside sponsors in this field.

that the program will run, especially as it is not possible to rely on outside sponsors in this field.

Notes & References

1. Hautecoeur, J.-P., 1996, «Introduction», in J.-P. Hautecoeur, (ed.), *Alpha 96: Basic Education and Work*, Toronto: Culture Concepts, Hamburg: UNESCO Institute for Education, p. 3.

2. Anghel, Florentina, 1994, «Functional Literacy in Romania — Between Myth and Reality», in J.-P. Hautecoeur (ed.) *Alpha 94: Literacy and Cultural Development Strategies in Rural Areas*, Toronto: Culture Concepts; Hamburg: UNESCO Institute for Education, p. 236.

3. The quotations that head sections of this chapter are extracts from the diary of the *Alpha Botosani '94* program, a collective work which reflects on and evaluates the outcomes and was compiled by participants in the program. This diary is a sort of spiritual last will and testament left to anyone intending to carry on similar program. If we had had sufficient money, we should have liked to publish it.

4. This project took place independently between 1990 and 1994. In 1995 it was incorporated into another Institute program, "Teaching in Deprived Regions". From 1990 to 1994, the project included, action-research, an assessment of the level of basic literacy of the population aged 12 years and over, and an assessment of the level of functional literacy of the population that had completed compulsory education. It also included a series of activities and surveys on the extent of non-formal education in functional literacy program and teachers' desire to take part in adult literacy, as well as numerous awareness programs about the right to basic education in Romania.

5. Jigua, Mihaela, (ed.) 1995. *Education in Deprived Regions* (part 2). Bucharest: Institute of Educational Science.

6. Dionne, Hugues, 1995 «*Les regions de la peripherie de quoi?*», *TRAMES* (October), Montreal: Institute of Urban Studies, University of Montreal.

7. One remarkably effective educational model "that takes place in its natural environement" is provided by the school in *Lop t reasa-Bisocu* a (headteacher Stana *Mih il*, teacher Costel Olteanu) in the mountainous region of the Department of *Buzau*. This might serve as an example to other schools of the meaning of community "solidarity" as well as the efforts the inhabitants (teachers, parents and grandparents) have made to educate the children of those who have not left the region where they were born.

8. Law no. 84 / 1995 — the *Education Act*. Part 1 (General provisions), article 2, notes: "In Romania, education shall be a national priority". In Part 3 (Content of education), section IV (Lifelong education), article 136, lifelong education only accounts for four articles out of the 185 in this vast Act.

Chapter Four
ADULT BASIC EDUCATION IN ALBANIA

Andon Dede
Institute for Pedagogical Studies
Tirana, Albania

In order to live and work, people need a set of basic abilities acquired from the family, school, mass media, and other life experience. With the passing of time, these skills become inadequate for current challenges and must be updated. Rapid development and change have made this dynamic a major problem in our times. Something valued as new and modern today may be seen as outdated when viewed from tomorrow's more practical and sophisticated perspectives. Yet in order to benefit from each new development, you must learn how to use it.

Today adult and continuing education has become a necessity for normal life and work. Unlike in the past, education is now a life-long process. It has broken out of "the walls of the school". This situation differs in form and degree from country to country. Literacy is not a uniform phenomenon. Even in a society that is supposed to have a high level of education, different social groups with different subcultures have different practices in their everyday life. If we do not keep this in mind throughout our investigations, we could make grave mistakes in our analysis of the situation and in the possible solutions we would recommend.

In Albania each of these factors has its own specifics, compared not only with developed countries but also with Central and Eastern European post communist countries. No other country's politics and ideology have resulted in such extreme oppression, isolation, and poverty. This is significant if we consider how much these influence people's development and education. During the dictatorship there was no mention of real and major themes like human rights, civics, sex education, etc. in our compulsory education. We were not aware of what we were entitled to, what were our rights to participate in decision-making or in the social-political life of the country — rights that are taken for granted by citizens of the developed countries.

THE NEW WORLD OF WORK

Structural changes in society and in working life are among the other factors that make adult basic education indispensable. These processes are present and permanent in every country of the world, but in Albania these developments have assumed extraordinary dimensions — both depth and breadth — in the past few years. As we change the social-political system itself (that is, from dictatorship to democracy, from a planned to a market economy, from a totalitarian to a legal state), we feel the need to become familiar with the system we have adopted, to learn about its components and how it functions. Every day we face terms, concepts and practices unknown and unheard of before. In other words we have had to deal with our "functional illiteracy". Our basic education is not sufficient. It must be enriched and re-dimensioned.

We soon became aware of this and in spite of other difficult problems during the transition, we began to work intensively on it. It would not be an exaggeration to say that we all, willingly or unwillingly, became "adult students". Besides organized forms like courses, seminars, conferences, and meetings, public and social places such as coffee bars and sitting rooms in homes were turned into classrooms. People of all ages and professions got acquainted with new terms and concepts, discussed and debated with one another about the various phenomena and processes we faced. Thus, everyone was a student and a teacher at the same time. This was our first adult education challenge after the victory of the democracy.

We are also aware that the new social political system which we have adopted with enthusiasm not only offers great opportunities from which everyone must know how to benefit, but also brings challenges and potential threats to be faced. For instance, it is common knowledge that technological progress is associated everywhere in the world with serious social problems; because among other things it cuts jobs, leading to unemployment. In Albania, this phenomenon is even more problematic for two reasons:

- The move to a market economy resulted in the closing of many enterprises and factories with old technology, leaving many workers unemployed. In order to find new jobs, these workers need to learn new professions.

- In order to meet the requirements of a more advanced technology, adult basic education must be constantly enriched. Training will always be an issue as workers must satisfy the needs of the new jobs. This is a key issue in our country. Extreme isolation and great poverty had left us with a technology backward beyond recognition: not decades, but centuries behind. This happens at a time when there is a very short period between scientific discoveries and their application in production.

Two phenomena, also observed in other Eastern European countries, seem at first glance to contradict each other. On one hand there is high unemployment because of the economic reforms and on the other hand there is a shortage of qualified workers with higher professional competence to satisfy the requirements of the new job market. This makes political and educational reform and a realignment of the work force indispensable.

During the years of transition, there was also a need for well-qualified workers and specialists with higher professional competencies for sectors such as finance, banking, management, marketing, etc., that were either unknown in the past or were of poor quality.

DEMOGRAPHIC CHANGES

Demographic movement is rapidly increasing in Albania. The old regime had prohibited by law the free movement of people inside the country and abroad. The peasants that comprise the majority of the population were obliged to live in isolated mountainous zones, having low incomes and living standards. After the overthrow of the dictatorship, there was a great flow of the population from the country to the towns, creating serious social, economic and educational problems.

These spontaneous and uncontrolled movements of the population hindered the normal functioning of formal education in the town schools. The schools were already overcrowded; now they had to respond to the newcomers as well. This affects the basic development of pupils, who will suffer the consequences later on in their lives. Filling the gaps created by this overload will be a goal of the system of adult basic education. It became even more alarming when these uncontrolled movements of the population also led to the increase in the school drop-out rate. Many students in compulsory education drop out for economic reasons, with or without their parent's permission, even though this is prohibited by law.

The movement of the population inside and outside the country has upset the balance of basic education even for adults, who now have to face new work and life contexts. The new conditions dictate new needs, and these new needs require new knowledge and abilities. This is faced by people of all ages, as well as those who have moved from the country to the town and those who have gone abroad as emigrants to do temporary work. Again they have to confront "functional illiteracy", but this time it is of a type perhaps unknown to developed countries which have been familiar with these factors and processes for some time.

MARGINALIZED PEOPLE

Another problem in Albania is that of abandoned or "marginalized" people. As in other countries, there are small groups like Gypsies and other ethnic minorities. But here I refer to children and youths that lack parental or even state care, such as orphans or abandoned children. The number of such marginalized people in Albania is relatively high. Special institutions have been established to help integrate them into society, but these are insufficient for the number of people needing their services.

ADULT BASIC EDUCATION AND THE INSTITUTIONAL ENVIRONMENT

After the Second World War

Before the second world war, a number of non-government organizations, usually of a patriotic and cultural nature, were directly or indirectly involved in adult basic education. I include in this the "sitting rooms", or men's gatherings as they used to be called, in some of our churches, mosques, etc. Throughout history these have made up for the lack of official educational institutions. (The first Albanian school was opened at the end of the last century.) In these environments fierce discussions took place, ranging from the most private problems to issues of world policy. We could call these settings institutions of adult education, because they really helped to address functional illiteracy. So, a kind of tradition existed.

After the second world war, that is during the communist dictatorship, various new institutions such as cultural palaces, cinemas and theatres, libraries and art galleries were created. As well, many social organizations for young people, students, women, veterans, etc., were established. This broad network of organizations carried out a rich and diversified cultural and artistic activity. There were courses for crafts, wood and metal work, sports,and so on. But in time these organizations became state institutions and were put completely under the control and at the service of the state-party of the dictatorship. They were politicized and ideologized and began to be used as a means to brainwash and manipulate the people. Their activities became monotonous, loathsome and without practical value. People participated unwillingly. Their material base was also poor. All these factors greatly diminished the efficiency of this institutional environment.

Transition from dictatorship to democracy

After the dictatorship was overthrown, many of these institutions were either damaged or closed just when at every step we were confronting our "functional illiteracy" in different forms and dimensions. But we were convinced that everything had to be changed from the foundation: the change of the social-political system required a new institutional structure. The old institutions began to be conceived of in a new way, in keeping with the new political, economic and social context. The rooms of the former institutions were turned into open classrooms, where local and foreign lecturers talked about themes such as freedom, democracy, market economy, rule of law, human rights, participation of people in decision making and other aspects of political and social life.

Another phenomenon just as important to us was and still is the reopening of the religious institutions of the different faiths and sects. The dictatorship had closed them three decades ago and prohibited by law the practice of religion. This reopening is an important event for our people, if we bear in mind the educational role of religion and its positive effect on spiritual life. In addition to the three main religions — Orthodox, Catholic and Moslem, other classic and modern sects have been introduced. This has greatly enlivened the spiritual life of the people.

The new democratic state established in 1992 paid special attention to adult basic education from the start. The main difficulty was lack of funds. At the time we could barely handle the emergency problems in the formal education system. Two ministries were directly concerned with this problem: the Ministry of Education and the Ministry of Labour and Social Assistance. But both of them were facing more pressing problems. So the issue was: who would take care of adult education; or more directly, who would pay for it? Education is generally seen as a non-productive sector. This unfair and inaccurate concept is very detrimental to the individual and society. Furthermore, where people do not enjoy economic and social rights, the principle of the right to education remains only a slogan.

We still have no special law about adult education, but this does not hinder adult learning alternatives. Article 50 of the Law about Pre-University Education stresses that "along with formal education, there also exist other supplementary structures that support and enrich the educational system".

NON-GOVERNMENTAL ORGANIZATIONS

Like other sectors, the educational sector was assisted by a number of international governmental and non-governmental organizations, associations, and foundations. Others were created inside Albania, and today we have a broad and complex institutional network of about 400 organizations across the country. Since 1993, a special Albanian Forum serves as an umbrella for 105 non-governmental organizations, helping and stimulating their activities and creating new NGOs. There are also many schools and courses which directly serve to enrich adult basic education and vocational training. A fair called "ALBINKUS '96" in Tirana, the capital city, aimed to present information on the "new world" of vocational education and training, with 30 institutions taking part.

It is clear that the institutional environment in Albania has been established and expanded. In fact, for a small country, Albania has more institutional environment than it needs. In some cases the establishment of new institutions has become an aim in itself. They do not justify themselves in terms of efficiency.

Problems of efficiency

At the beginning of the transition period, our people followed the seminars, lectures, conferences and other activities with great interest. This is understandable considering our hunger to learn about the new system we had adopted. But with time the interest began to diminish ; it was a kind of overload. People have become more and more pragmatic. They are interested in courses and seminars and speeches that are linked directly with their daily work and needs, such as foreign languages, computer skills, management and business courses. However, this does not negate learning about democracy, human rights, quality of life, ecology, the use of spare time, family planning, etc., which are ongoing issues in civilized society. We also have many gaps and deficits from the times when such themes were taboo and totally ignored. But in order to attract people to themes that have to do with their general cultural and democratic development, stimulating approaches must be sought, and material incentives offered whenever possible.

Although cooperation among these institutions is necessary in order to increase their efficiency, so far this has not been achieved. In particular, there has not been enough cooperation between the Ministry of Labour and Social Assistance and its regional offices with the Ministry of Education and the institutions that deliver the education. We have been hampered by our lack of understanding of the phenomena and processes of the system we have adopted. For instance some individuals and institutions did not have a proper understanding of decentralization. They thought that under democracy everyone can work at will and there is no reason to wait for plans, orientations and orders from higher levels. As a result, many solutions were spontaneous and not the most optimal, and examples of activities duplicated due to lack of coordination on the part of the organizers. Much better results could have been achieved with the same human and financial resources.

It is important to attend to the question of who is going to deal with adult education — the state? private business? non-governmental organizations? or the individuals themselves? What recommendations are provided by international experience or even our own experience during these years of democracy? For adult basic education to succeed, everyone must be interested in and contribute to it, because it serves everyone. From another perspective, people with insufficient basic development not only suffer, but are also a burden for others. Adult basic education also helps solve the unemployment problem.

The involvement of educators without proper training has lowered the effectiveness of education. These people were hired not because of their training and commitment but because of family and other connections. To some extent this is unavoidable in such a small country. We are "fixing the train on the way". We are behind schedule and have no time to stop, to study the situation, to search for and find the most qualified people and to make the most suitable recommendations. This will have to be done one step at a time.

The key problem: assessing the situation

The key to our immediate problem is to be able to assess adult basic education needs in relation to the current labour market context. The job market does not yet exist in Albania as it does in the countries of Western Europe. For now, we need to establish a system of information centres with social workers to identify job market needs.

The identification of priorities is also important: the ways, means, materials and human potential that lead to progress. We have discrepancies and gaps between the measures that must be taken on micro and macro levels of decision making and often the needs of the individual are different from those of the community but are not addressed in decisions or in programs. Responses at the micro level will help researchers and other stakeholders define the most important problems and themes, and aid in finding the most suitable solutions at the macro level: the institutional environment to be established, the policies to be followed, and so on.

Full and accurate assessment is also a precondition for drafting long-term strategies in the future. Many politicians and public servants are not aware of the deficiencies in people's basic education, so they do not intervene to make sure there is funding to help them. It takes courage to undertake special initiatives to address needs on local and national levels.

AN EXPERIENCE WITH SHORT COURSES

With the help of the SOROS Foundation, short courses were offered across most of the country during the summers of 1992 and 1996. These were at first one or two weeks long, and recently have been made longer. Teachers and specialists in different fields were very interested, and immediately began to submit projects. There were diverse themes, including teacher training, computers, foreign languages, the environment, and electronics. Participants included students, teachers, and other community members.

We followed their development closely, and the results were very encouraging. Beyond the practical benefits and credentials for the participants, these courses brought valuable experience to our developing system of adult basic education, showing great potential to consolidate and complete the knowledge and skills acquired at school. They also showed that participation is not a problem if subjects with practical benefits are offered. It is imperative that this type of education helps provide practical solutions to social problems. The courses also proved that for these activities to be effective, teachers must be committed and highly qualified.

Another positive factor in these courses was the cooperation with the communities. In many districts, the local authorities, heads of enterprises and schools made great contributions to the programs by putting at their disposal classrooms, laboratories, vehicles and equipment. This shows that they were convinced of the social and communal value of these activities. Of course we cannot count on having such support and appreciation from leaders in all districts. Only if you have a thorough knowledge of the regional context, the interests of the community and of individual participants, and then establish the proper institutional environment, can success be guaranteed.

CONCLUSIONS

Adult basic education in Albania has its own special characteristics. It is supported by a broad and complex institutional environment throughout the country. The main challenges we face in this field are:

- to make people aware that education now needs to be an ongoing process, and to teach people how to keep on learning;

- to increase the effectiveness of adult education by engaging the most qualified and dedicated people, and finding the most relevant and interesting contexts;

- to define the education requirements of the job market, as the basis for drafting plans, programs, policies, and structures related to this type of education;

- to find the financial resources to sponsor special projects with clearly defined objectives and schedules, and to use these funds efficiently; and
- to pass from "movements" and "initiatives" into a permanent system of adult education.

It would be very positive for Albania to establish a special institution for adult education like those of many other countries. For now there is no one institution to deal with this; it is in the hands of several ministries, departments and non-governmental organizations. Associations for adult education could be established, with teachers, specialists, parents, students, and within the Ministry of Education. In the Institute of Pedagogical Research, individuals or departments could be assigned to study the problems linked with this branch of education. International organizations, including UNESCO, could do much more than they have done so far.

By Albanian law, education has been sanctioned as a national priority. It deserves to be a priority because of all the benefits it provides to the development and prosperity of the individual and the society.

References

Jarvis, Peter. *Adult and Continuing Education*, (Second Edition), London, 1995.

Onushkin, V.G. and E.I. Ogariev. *Obrazovanie Vzroslih*, (Adult Education: Dictionary), St-Peterburg, 1995.

Skager, R. *Lifelong Education and Evoluting Practice*, Pergamon Press/UNESCO Institute for Education, Hamburg, 1979.

The Development of Education in Poland in 1990-1991, Ministry of National Education, Warsaw, 1992.

The International Encyclopedia of Education, (Second Edition), Pergamon, 1994, vol. 12.

The Law on Pre-University Education System in Republic of Albania, No. 7952, 21.06.1995.

The Swedish Way Towards a Learning Society, (A review), Ministry of Education and Science, Sweden, 1993.

Chapter Five
ANDRAGOGIC SUMMER SCHOOL: TOWARDS IMPROVING LITERACY AND LOCAL DEVELOPMENT

Dusana Findeisen
Ljubljana University
Ljubljana, Slovenia

ADULT BASIC EDUCATION IN SLOVENIA

Adult basic education in Slovenia in the new socio-economic and political situation is naturally concerned with skills like reading, writing, understanding written texts, and being able to perform some basic mathematical operations; though it is even more concerned with a far more complex ability to be self-reliant and self-sufficient. To make sound decisions in everyday life, however small they may be in the eyes of those who are generally considered socially mature and self-sufficient, one needs much more than writing and reading skills.

One should be able to identify one's needs and interests, to set up attainable short-term and long-term goals. Ideally one should also be able to perceive other people's needs. Perceiving the needs of others further means being responsible and committed. Thus one should learn the skills of participation and contribution to the communities to which one belongs. Such communities can be one's family, a working team in a factory or any local group. Talking about these skills in post-socialist countries may sound like saying slogans but we should bear in mind that these are also skills and essential values upon which to base adult basic education.

I would suggest adult basic education in the new socio-economic

and political situation in Slovenia should not be just about acquiring skills. It should also be about internalizing values related to the learning of social skills and skills that are traditionally those of adult basic education.

Consequently, there is a need to establish which key qualifications should be pursued in adult basic education to enable adults to function better in the changed conditions and to cope with situations they encounter. There is a fair number of Slovenians whose reading skills and numeracy may be quite developed but who have not acquired other skills that would make them self-reliant and self-sufficient. Accustomed to being sheltered by the Welfare State, they do not seem able to cope with the new situation. As a result they are often out of work or just waiting for their enterprise to go bankrupt, repeating to themselves and whoever wants to listen to them "They will have to do something about it. I don't know what, but something has to be done. "When asked who "they" are, they answer: "The State". And the State used to be "the others".

Further, adult basic education in this country has been related to full time employment. So, it was mostly taken care of by enterprises and the aim was to enable everybody to complete primary studies. Needless to say, most formal education focused on the program and much less on the individual. In addition, employment agencies also offered adult basic professional education. The situation is different now and an individual has to be prepared to cope with change. Thus, if we want our literacy programs to be effective, they should help an individual to develop "a new personality".

In conclusion, goals in adult basic education have changed and so should content, pedagogy, teaching and learning methods and techniques and evaluation itself. And if we want adults to become responsible and committed, learning should take place in natural environments in which responsibility and the spirit of enterprise would be real and oriented towards achieving practical and not just educational goals.

Furthermore, adult basic education has mostly been organized for workers, depending on their full time employment. When everybody had a job, it was relatively easy to spot functionally illiterate people. Nowadays they are getting out of reach. One of the few existing ways of reaching out to them is through employment agencies. But what about those who stay at home, idle, unemployed?

WHO IS MARGINALIZED AND HOW TO REACH OUT TO ILLITERATE PEOPLE?

When we introduced the Andragogic Summer School in Slovenia we started from the assumption that it is difficult to be certain which groups are marginalized in the new socio-economic and political conditions. Generally one could consider marginalized all those individuals and groups who are not able to be active citizens, negotiate with authorities, communicate in public and fight for their equal rights and opportunities: those who lack knowledge and skills to oppose or collaborate with those who hold the power. Marginalized are those who do not understand that in this newly established democracy they must have a say, that there are not yet mechanisms to protect them without their active participation. Active participation is a skill and it certainly presupposes knowledge.

Therefore adult basic education should also prepare people to play a more active role in society, since illiterate people are naturally even less able to be active citizens than those who are literate. Ten years ago we started the first Third Age University in the former Yugoslavia and we have been working and living with its members for the benefit of their "institution" or their educational movement as we call it. Now ten years later, they still seem to need to be taken care of. "We've just had an important exhibition in the town. We are good, we are getting better every day. Now the University should really take care of us!" When asked who is the University, they would say: "It's the leaders." "But the leaders are like you, people who are students or mentors, who are volunteers." "Yes, but there should be somebody." "No, there is nobody. The University is you." They regularly seem to have difficulty understanding this, and this concept is a part of the "new literacy".

People should be empowered. They should learn that they have knowledge and that they have the right to say what they know and to be listened to. They should be capable for example of opposing bureaucratic procedures and bureaucrats who sometimes lack the necessary legal knowledge, who can lack information and may commit mistakes without sanctions. Like all citizens, illiterate people should learn more about functions and missions of public institutions to be able to oppose, for example, a local government bureaucrat saying to them "I know that you are right, but you should engage a a procedure yourself. There is nothing I can do about it. It's too dangerous for me." They should know that State employees are there to listen to them and not to say "We don't let just any citizen enter the municipality building. If a citizen needs our services, he or she has to write an application." (An application of course, that not all citizens are able to write, that is rarely answered in time, and that blocks real communication.) Members of this society should know that public services are there for them and that they have the right to communicate with them. This is also a part of literacy.

The Andragogic Summer School focuses on identifying the needs and interests that local people share, with a view to starting local projects and groups. Moreover, it is devoted to reaching out to functionally illiterate people who are not easily accessible and who need to be animated for education. The School has further been designed to disseminate knowledge and offer field experience to adult educators, social workers and all other interested people who want to acquire the skills to animate local groups.

For functionally illiterate people, an animator should be able to understand not only their present needs and interests but also each individual's personal history and experience. An animator should recognize the skills, the psychological and social abilities as well as the work experience, to be able to animate each person for education.

REORGANIZATION OF THE LOCAL SELF-GOVERNMENT IN SLOVENIA

The principle of concentrating decision-making processes on the national and international levels has been opposed by the political principle of subsidiarity, according to which local communities should take over matters they prove competent enough to deal with. According to this political principle, State tasks have been decentralized to regions and further to local communities. The role of such a subsidiary State would be to offer help for local communities, and to back them in valuable local initiatives.

Recent Slovenian reorganization of local self-government, however, was not performed along these lines. That is, it has not been a techno-organizational modernization of local communities, but an establishment of a new State political system, i.e. the system of parliamentary democracy with a traditional type of local self-government. This system was meant to replace the old system of municipalities that acted as the first level of State administration but were more autonomous in their activities than the State itself.

The recent reorganization introduced a much greater number of municipalities (147 compared to 65). The establishment of new municipalities depended solely on the inhabitants' will and not on the capacity of the new local communities to perform certain tasks in their territory like improving economy, infrastructure, culture, education, health, etc... Moreover, the share of the communities in GDP has been ranging over the last years from 5.2 per cent in 1993 to 4.2 per cent in 1995. This demonstrates that Slovenia has allocated the smallest percentage of GDP to local communities. A relatively high percentage of the Slovenian public budget is channeled to the State and other centralized services and a relatively very low percentage to local self-government. Under these conditions municipalities mostly do not feel that they should take an active part in local adult education. The role of the Andragogic Summer School therefore is also to make local self-government aware that through adult education and truly local initiatives they could better establish their authentic local role.

Apart from the municipality, our efforts were directed to other institutions, especially the existing local groups, associations, the social centre, the local popular university, and the existing local projects. We also wanted to include local enterprises although we feel that in the present conditions they are struggling merely to consolidate their position in the new economic situation and most are not very interested in the people they employ. One of the findings of the Andragogic Summer School was that responsibility for development of local people should be therefore extended from them to the local community.

OBJECTIVES OF THE ANDRAGOGIC SUMMER SCHOOL

Some of the objectives of the Andragogic Summer School were set in advance and some only after the School started and following the initial findings:

- Once a year the School will gather adult educators, researchers, social workers and others who are interested in topics related to literacy and local development.
- Contrary to the existing tradition it will be set in a small town in order to make the participants get the feeling of a local community and how local issues are interlinked.

- Participants of the School will discover links that can be created among sectors, institutions, enterprises and individuals, as well as social groups that habitually do not go hand in hand.
- They will discover that in order to offer efficient help to marginalized groups through education, they have to work also with other social groups.
- This will enable the participants to relate to local people and share their knowledge with them.
- It will make it possible for the participants to understand that educational programs must be created around a need or an interest of local people or their community, this being even more important when they are meant for illiterate people.
- With the help of the School and the initial help of the participants some local projects will be started.
- Special interest will be paid to illiterate local people and to the animation of such people for education.

THE ANDRAGOGIC SUMMER SCHOOL — A WAY TO LITERACY AND LOCAL DEVELOPMENT

The Andragogic Summer School was set up in Ajdovscina in 1985. This locality had been chosen for various reasons, one of the most important being that it is small enough not to focus educational activities just on a town area but on the country town as a whole. Further, our thinking was that such a small, predominately industrialised town would offer participants of the School the opportunity to get in touch with low-educated inhabitants and start understanding their functional illiteracy.

For the next five years, the School would be dealing with the issue of action and socially oriented adult education and especially that of low educated people and local development. Thus, the first year it focused on the general introduction to community education for local development and its concepts.

However, the participants spent most of the time getting to know the town of Ajdovscina, its present and its past. Pursuing this aim, they were directed to the local library and the regional museum; they went through the local press and were introduced to the local radio and television; they were received by local industrial and trade enterprises, the presidents of the local groups and associations, and the representatives of the municipality. What is more, they learned how to get in touch with local people and had a number of meetings with some distinguished local inhabitants. They attended lectures on Ajdovscina, and became familiar with various approaches used mainly by community workers, for example street work. They also learned how to prepare a town appraisal in collaboration with local people. At the end of the School they presented their findings to the local people and the representatives of institutions.

Moreover, last year's School aimed at the recognition of sectors, institutions, enterprises, associations, local groups and local governmental bodies and individuals whose knowledge, culture and experiences might be applied to one goal, i.e. local development. A list of them was established with the joint help of the School participants and local inhabitants.

From the very beginning, we gave our attention to the problem of literacy, this issue having been previously recognized by some adult educators and researchers and the National Andragogic Centre as one of the most important ones in any of the Slovenian local communities. It has been estimated that the majority of long-term unemployed Slovenes are illiterate. They had been trained for a specific work station, for handling a specific machine or device — their whole life had been organized around a full time job. The new economic and social situation squeezed them out of the job and most of the time they are left to themselves, spending their time waiting for a change to come. Illiteracy had been recognized as a major problem in most Slovenian communities by adult educators and researchers but not by the central and local governments. Thus we discovered once again that if we want to promote social change and act towards local development by means of adult education we have to act along different lines. We have to:

- recognize the life and not only the educational needs and interests of inhabitants, especially the poorly-educated ones;
- get to know the community, its past and present and the existing plans for the future;
- make an audit of common needs and interests and of the community capacity;
- enable and sometimes empower the local government to set up structures and mechanisms responding to the local people and their needs;

- launch a vast and long-term campaign raising awareness of the existing community problems and of the existing literacy and self-reliance problem;
- help the local community to animate its low-educated members to pursue education;
- assist the local community in setting up the first educational projects;
- back up local communities in setting up local campaigns; and
- start a national campaign with a view to recognizing the literacy problem.

INITIAL RESEARCH INTO LOCAL NEEDS AND COMMUNITY CAPACITY

Since the topic of the First Andragogic School was Education for Local Development, we organized it around the aim of the participants' getting familiar with the town and its surroundings.

Prior to the First School, some students of andragogy from Ljubljana University learned about the past of Ajdovscina and the surrounding villages through interviews with local inhabitants. Many local associations of cultural and economic nature existed there till 1942 when most of them were abolished by the Italian government. After the war authentic local groups led by the inhabitants and based on their needs were not restored; on the contrary, they were replaced by kwango organizations like the Youth Association, and community centres were built up in most settlements all over the State. The socio-cultural activities of the Catholic church were abolished too. The findings of this research were important since they disclosed a forgotten community capacity to take care of its own needs and to pursue its interests.

During the School the participants, many of them coming from small towns and settlements and from Ajdovscina itself, were introduced to various aspects of street work, i.e. of getting to know people. We did not focus our attention on specific age groups or social groups since our topic was local development. All the participants were taught some basic interviewing skills. A questionnaire for a focused interview was established based on initial contacts with local inhabitants, some lectures and presentations and some individual studies the participants carried out beforehand about Ajdovscina. They agreed that if there is a lack of communication, there is no community. Therefore they decided to find out what communication means existed in the town and how good the communication was.

Most of the interviewed inhabitants were in favour of setting up a small information centre where it would be possible to get all kinds of information as well as advice concerning important aspects of their life and community. The respondents stated that they would like it to provide information and advice concerning their health, education, social welfare rights, and so on. They would also like the person employed there to help them with writing things like applications and complaints. The participants of the School were introduced beforehand to various case studies enabling them to suggest to local people a number of solutions to their needs.

Another interest was in how local people were able to take care of their health. It was amazing to learn how many aspects of life were not controlled, or not controlled enough by individuals but were controlled by institutions, professionals or disciplines. Thus people did not learn to take care of their health on their own. Health promotion had not been developed and most health staff had not been trained to share their knowledge with patients. Further, the patients had not been empowered to ask questions or to participate in their therapy. The situation has not changed much. Thus the majority of our respondents when asked "If you get ill, where do you get advice about the treatment?" answered "I go to the doctor." "Right, but do you always go to the doctor? The doctor is not always available." "In that case I ask my wife or my mother or my step mother or, even better, I go to the Maksl's (a local inn).

We found out that empowerment of the inhabitants concerning various aspects of their lives would be one of the major tasks of educational and local development workers. The level of literacy in the field of health is generally very low and raising awareness of people would require the systematic use of the most powerful media.

The respondents agreed that written information about their town should be available all over the town, wherever people meet: in banks, shops, the health centre, the church, local inns, the post office, the local library, and so on. Written information was practically non-existent and the majority of the above-mentioned places were not ready to disseminate information leaflets other than those concerning their own activity. We also discovered that written communication with local inhabitants had not been well-developed in the past, and that most of the information existed in peoples' minds.

The participants of the School went around the town establishing photo documentation about good and bad examples of visual communication. They discovered for example, that most respondents could not locate the local Popular University. The photo documentation showed that in fact it was impossible to locate it because there were no signs and the entrance was not visible. Nor was information available in the town. Most of the respondents did not know what programs were offered there. If we wanted to use the popular university as a place for illiterate people to gather and learn together, the way to its building should be clearly marked and information about its activities should be available all over the town.

It was further discovered that the local school, although it does not function as a community school, was a place where children could get a lot of information important to them and their family. Most of the young respondents get information from their teachers. Information about literacy programs should therefore be available at school and other institutions.

Most of the respondents did not know what the role of the municipality was. They were convinced that there "your papers can be sealed". Last year the municipality building did not offer much written information about its work and functions to the inhabitants. We discovered that work would have to be done in order to make people and institutions understand what they can do in the field of communication and that written communication is important — it saves time and effort and disseminates knowledge and ideas. The participants of the School discovered that local people would need education in the field of visual literacy, organization of written informative texts, and so on.

This year the participants of the School themselves learned how to communicate with the town, how to inform the town about the School using various means: personal contact, information leaflets, posters, local media, industrial enterprises' newsletters, local newspapers, the radio, and others. They learned how make their information visible, and where and how to make contact with local people.

An important part of the School was relating to the representatives of the municipality and of the local enterprises and associations. It was important for us to discover that there was no real developmental strategy in the town. When we asked the Mayor what the strategic targets of the municipality development were, he answered that its major plan was "not to worsen the situation". As a result of this, we decided that education for local development should go along two lines:

1. education of local people including those who are low-educated and are difficult to reach, and

2. education of the most influential representatives of the municipality.

In other words we found out that it is not only the local people who should be empowered. The same goes for the local government which is far too dependent on the central government, longing for past autonomy and having little room left for its own local initiatives.

Another of our major findings was that for an integrated local development, institutions and enterprises need to be educated along with local people and local groups. The inhabitants should start thinking about the future of their own town. It used to be a military and a heavily industrialized country town and it had some leading industries whose output was not sufficient to meet the needs on the ex-Yugoslav market. The situation altered when Slovenia separated from Yugoslavia. Some of the smaller enterprises had to close down, but nevertheless the number of unemployed people is not very high. More changes are expected when Slovenia joins Europe. But then the town has good tourist perspectives.

Therefore the inhabitants and the employees of the local hotel, shops, restaurants etc., should be educated accordingly. The participants of the School also found out that the hotel staff was unable to give relevant information about the town. Information leaflets at the reception desk, for example, invited guests to travel to distant foreign countries but they would not do the same for local sights.

ANIMATING ILLITERATE PEOPLE FOR EDUCATION

The Andragogic Summer School of 1996 was mainly devoted to animating local low-educated people for education. We assumed that they would be extremely difficult to reach under local conditions, so we first tried to reach some of them with the help of some of our local participants.

When asked to receive our participants and to "have a talk with them" they said "No, I really can't." " Why not?" "I'm so busy, I really have no time." Unable to reach them in this way we decided then to get in touch with them by surprise. We went to some old buildings which used to belong to local industries and rang the bell. Most of the time the lodgers did not answer it. We entered the room. In most of the apartments the TV set was on, and even the young people were lying on beds. Some of them did not seem to have noticed us. They appeared totally passive. When we introduced ourselves they were at first not ready to talk to us and tried instead to involve somebody else in the conversation.

Our initial idea was to apply a modified Eurodelphi questionnaire, but finally we agreed that anything prepared in advance would block the conversation, deciding instead to ask people about their hopes, plans, anxieties, expectations, work experiences, hobbies, family, and so on. This lack of structure helped us to remain free to listen to people. We made a number of discoveries:

- Illiterate people were not easy to reach and would be ready to receive us only if we approached them by surprise.

- They were not accessible at public places like members of other marginalized groups.

- They were not mobile, and tended to stay at the same place, so we should come to them.

- Often they belonged to minority groups (for example, Muslims) and establishing an educational program for them would require taking their culture into account.

- Those who were young lived in flocks, while those who were elder were very isolated.

- They all complained that life was not fair to them and that people were mean. Also they seemed to be very emotional about what had happened to them (losing their job, for example). Somebody said to us "How could the Slovenian Railways fire me? Me who had discovered five bombs hidden on trains!"

- In the course of the conversation they all seemed to become interested in our plans for them.

- **The best way to animate these people for education might be direct personal contact at first and perhaps also at the beginning an individual program built around their immediate needs. Any institutional "entremise" would make the project much more difficult to**

start. Illiterate people in this country are afraid of institutions.

In addition, during this second School the participants learned about other possible ways of animating illiterate young people — through photo novels, comic strips, personal stories on the front pages of local newspapers, graffiti, and so on.

HOW CAN EXISTING INSTITUTIONS OFFER SUPPORT?

We invited the participants of local institutions to take part in the School. These included the popular university in the first place, the local library, the planning and urban department of the municipality, the social centre, and the local secondary school. Also present were colleagues from the National Andragogic Centre and some people from the Ministry of Education. We believe that in addition to other national institutions the existing networks like those of popular universities and social centres and perhaps also the Chamber of Commerce, could contribute to setting up a literacy policy and should also play an active role in preventing and combating illiteracy. We are convinced, however, that at first they should help to educate individuals who would like to take part in such activities.

Some of it has already been done by the Andragogic Centre of Slovenia and as a result some centres for younger illiterate adults have been created. But we feel that in addition, combating illiteracy should go into the hands of enlightened and properly educated individuals who are ready to help illiterate people on a one-to-one basis not only to acquire skills but to grow as persons. At this first stage, combating illiteracy should be on a very personal level. People in this country would need to be animated for literacy work by exerting an impact on their values people. For example, voluntary work should be promoted as a value.

WHAT POLICY CHANGES ARE NEEDED?

First, we should launch a vast campaign to help the general public understand that illiteracy is a problem in Slovenia and that no minister has the right to answer the journalist's question "What will happen to the dismissed workers?" in the following way: "Well, what *will* happen to them? Doesn't everybody know it? Nothing nice will happen to them." This simply cannot be the answer of the Central Government. The Government must have a policy concerning illiterate people and our task is to make them aware of solutions. The solutions are not in hoping for new big industrial systems, but in working with people, finding out what they can do and what they could do, and how they could integrate in society so as not to become exploited service proletariat. Therefore functional illiteracy should be recognized as a national problem and mechanisms should be provided for backing up local initiatives in addressing it. Further, all public institutions should become responsible for "developing people". A regular part of their activity should be sociocultural animation. An appropriate State policy should make it possible for them to carry this out.

EVALUATION OF THE PROJECT

The Andragogic Summer School was conceived as a five-year project designed first to raise awareness of the existence of functional illiteracy and of local capacity among professionals, the general public and the local government; and second to help local initiatives get started.

There are several ways of raising awareness. We deliberately chose the way which was meant to have a multiplying effect over Slovenia. Thus our primary intention was not to set up local pilot projects but to start working on a wider scale to raise awareness in those who might be concerned by literacy and local development and to offer them some basic knowledge and skills in the field. The results and findings have been as follows.

- Where institutions fail, adult educators and other professionals or interested and properly informed individuals can succeed. It is easier to reach out to functionally illiterate people and to break into their social isolation by establishing personal contact in their natural environment.

- The School has shown that in local conditions, prevention and remediation of functional illiteracy should be first entrusted to people in the community and then to institutions.

- A program for illiterate people or local communities starts by an in-depth analysis and understanding of personal and community issues and needs.

- This can be done by talking to people about themselves, their life history, their hopes, their anxieties, their plans, their wishes, life in their community, and so on.

- The Andragogic Summer School has been an important experience for many adult educators making them aware that adult education of the marginalized means understanding these people not as learners but as people.

- The School established an awareness of the need for communication in local communities and what that communication means. The participants learned about the importance in a community of written communication focused on people's needs and understanding. In doing so they discovered functional literacy in relation to themselves and not only in relation to those who are to be included in adult basic education.

- The participants themselves grew into a community through living, learning and working with local people and experiencing how a community can grow if its needs and interests are taken into account and if its members share a relevant "developmental topic" and have learned the skills of participation.

- During the School we encouraged local people to have a say on the local radio and to experience appearing in public and the importance of being empowered. For many participants this was a first experience of working with media. It turned out to be an important part of the experiential learning we have stimulated in the School.

- A club for unemployed young people was set up with help of the local Social Aid Centre, and is run by an animator and the young people themselves. One of the first workshops will be devoted to understanding and writing graffiti. The participants of the School managed to raise awareness in local people and institutions that unemployed young people can be approached and animated to take part in a local project.

- Through the accompanying cultural program, we stirred local people's interest in their cultural identity and highlighted their existing cultural efforts and achievements. The Centre for Urban Planning at the Municipality regularly issued a leaflet on cultural events in the valley that is now available at public places in the area and some other Slovenian towns.

- The local government is planning to set up a type of citizen advice bureau run by local people themselves. The town appraisal conducted by the participants of the School helped the representatives of the local government to grasp this idea.

It turned out that it was difficult to combine an Andragogic School with its timetable and learning imperatives together with meeting and fulfilling local needs. Many personal and common needs were identified and at least some of them will have to be met in local projects. It is true that the School raised many hopes in local people and the participants themselves. The latter spontaneously offered to share their knowledge with local people during the next Summer School.

The percentage of the local participants in the school has been relatively small (6 per cent), not enough to enable a greater number of local initiatives to come into existence. We had planned to help them set up a number of projects, especially those for low-educated functionally illiterate young people but we did not plan to live with them. One of the findings has been that a school like ours should be conducted to ensure continuing professional follow-up help to local educators and animators; and that at least one of the school organizers should remain in the town sharing life with local people, working with them and helping them to get started. Since we can not do this, we suggested that we help the local library to set up a Third Age University in this coming September. A group of educated elderly adults will then start a program for functionally illiterate people based on the identified needs.

CONCLUSION

The Andragogic Summer School is an important step toward preventing and combating functional illiteracy but it is only one step. Based on our long term (12 years) practical experience with conceiving, maintaining and developing the Third Age University in Slovenia, we did not choose to start this time by setting up a pilot project for remediating functional illiteracy.

We wanted to give local people and adult educators an opportunity to start projects themselves by offering them experiential learning; enabling them to get the basic knowledge and skills before undertaking a project in practice. This may seem a slow approach to improving literacy for those who would like to achieve quicker and more tangible results on the local level, but it does enable us to engage in both practice and reflection on a wider scale. Moreover, it has the potential of making professionals, governmental bodies and local people more aware of the existence of functional illiteracy and of local capacity; and of ways to prevent or combat the first and to use the latter for local development.

References

Andragogic Perspectives, the first Slovenian Journal of Adult Education, to appear in October 1996.

Doherty, Caroline & Peter Firkin. 1993. *Developing Skills to work with Professionals*, NCVO, London.

Henderson, Paul & David, Thomas. 1994. *Skills in Neigbourhood Work*, Routledge London.

Krajnc, Ana & Dusana Findeisen. 1990. *How we were conceiving The Third Age University*, The Third Age University of Slovenia, *Ljubljana*.

Mijoc, Nena, Ana Krajnc & Dusana Findeisen. 1992. *Study Circles*, Andragoski Center Slovenije.

Chapter Six
BASIC EDUCATION AND COMMUNITY DEVELOPMENT IN POLAND

Ewa Solarczyk-Ambrokik
Adam Mickiewicz University
Poznan, Poland

THE BROADER CONTEXT

The process of leaving behind the previous political and economic system in Poland has been accompanied by the restoration of democratic procedures in public life and the creation of new platforms for political and economic activity pursued by individuals and social groups. The removal of barriers to free associations and unrestrained expression of group interests has led to the emergence of new institutions, characteristic of democratic societies.

Under the old political system, institutions were created by the decisions of centralized political bodies. The institutions were then organized into hierarchical structures and placed under strict control of the ruling party's political machine. Once new opportunities emerged, opening doors to the rise of a democratic society and individual entrepreneurship, a number of grass-roots democratic institutions were established, such as political parties, associations of manufacturers and consumers, co-operatives, private schools, and local unions (Grabowska, 1994). The main characteristics of the new social order include a gradual limiting of state dominance and stimulation of individual and group initiative. The new order has also brought freedom of speech and the right to true information, but also entails greater responsibility for one's own decisions and individual life.

Under the previous political and economic system the state exercised control over nearly all spheres of social life, and provided individuals with complete job security regardless of their performance. Such a high degree of state control combined with a sense of security produced a prevalent syndrome of "acquired helplessness" (Ziolkowski, 1993:47). This passive attitude resulted from the fact that many individuals in Poland had limited opportunities of exerting influence on various spheres of life, and especially on the functioning of the public industrial sector. The consequence was a subjective sense of being powerless, which in turn provided an excuse for lack of involvement and responsibility (Koralewicz, Ziolkowski, 1990:30).

Although the current political and economic transformations facilitate the development of a democratic society, they also bring about new tensions connected with the loss of a sense of security, and increase social inequalities. Sociologists point out that people accustomed to state leadership and its mechanisms of control, but now forced by the operation of free market mechanisms to make individual decisions and take initiative, tend to long for the lost sense of security and the comfort of no risk and little responsibility for their lives. They feel uneasy deprived of the protection of the state. Similar trends can be observed at the level of institutions. Once centrally controlled and managed, institutions are now experiencing a legal void, a lack of guidelines and regulations (Ziolkowski, 1993:47-48).

We can thus conclude that the period of transformation has its own logic and dynamics, which generates a wide range of tendencies contradictory to the rules of free market and democracy (Kolarska-Bobinska, 1991). The result is a certain ambivalence of social attitudes, especially towards the state. While the state is expected to perform its protective functions — an attitude rooted in the old political and economic system which suppressed individual entrepreneurship and ingenuity, still, people demand that state dominance be reduced in all spheres of life. A similar contradiction can be observed in attitudes towards the new economic order. The majority of Poles support free competition, which is one of the fundamental principles of a free market, while at the same time advocating full employment, which characterizes state-run centrally managed economies devoid of free market mechanisms (Koralewicz, Ziolkowski, 1990:44).

Interestingly, although the society views market economy and free competition as a means to achieving freedom, it also perceives them as potential threats to individuals, especially the old and the unemployed, incapable of adjusting to the new situation. The majority of Poles have no experience in coping with the realities of a market economy. The growing freedom to engage in economic activities, pursue one's interests, and express one's opinions, has generated social inequalities, rendered individual choices more risky, and increased the scope of individual responsibility (Wnuk-Lipinski, 1990).

The above contradictions are further aggravated by the lack of a mass pro-market promotional campaign or even modest educational initiatives aimed at boosting social awareness of the new principles of public life and of new rules for self-advancement.

BASIC EDUCATION

The goal of the above analysis of socio-economic phenomena occurring in Poland in the period of system transformation is to demonstrate the need for creating strategies and undertaking actions oriented to developing skills helpful in adjusting to changes and participating in the decisions affecting one's life.

In a broader context, these problems require the creation of a system of basic adult education in the pragmatic sense of developing competence of both individuals and communities. Thus, besides such tasks of adult education as stimulation of social life, and changing the professional make-up of the society, new equally important tasks appear in the field of individual development which are ultimately aimed at activating local communities.

Unfortunately, the only way of measuring the extent of functional illiteracy available to us at this time is to rely on the existing statistics regarding elementary education. Such statistics are not an adequate basis for evaluating the extent of the problem, since completion of elementary education does not guarantee adjustment to society, especially in the radically changed socio-economic conditions in Poland. The goal of the literacy drive during a period of socio-economic transformation is to equip individuals with skills to enable them to adjust effectively to new economic, political, and social conditions; and allow them to secure and hold jobs and to actively participate in a democratic society through involvement in the local community.

The process of decentralization of the state resulted in the creation of local self-governments which by now have become relatively effective. Nevertheless, a number of difficulties still remain, particularly in the area of laying foundations for a grass-roots reform. Local communities are still incompetent with regard to voicing opinions and defending their interests. The new social space has to be filled up by the citizens themselves. As mentioned earlier, this new space is both confusing and challenging (Blok, 1995). Sociologists describing the problems of helplessness and dependency in public life argue that action must be taken to eliminate them. Such action could include the creation of new structures and the development of new practices, ideas and behavior patterns. They point out that the "advocates of change" are more likely to focus on common values than on common interests of social groups (Kolarska-Bobinska, 1990).

The goal of all basic adult education programs designed to stimulate and support various forms of self-help, self-organization, interest groups and citizen activities should therefore be to:

- ensure that individual needs and the needs of social groups functioning in local communities are easily identifiable and can easily be voiced ; and

- establish groups whose objective is to pursue common interests.

Accomplishment of these goals will in effect enhance problem-solving and coping skills of people classified as illiterate.

THE LAZARZ COMMUNITY DEVELOPMENT PROJECT

Having presented the broader context of socio-economic processes taking place in Poland, I would like to focus on the specific example of a community development project implemented between 1994 and 1995 in the Lazarz area of Poznan. The project was designed to solve the community's social problems. It was developed by the research staff of Adam Mickiewicz University in Poznan within the framework of the European TEMPUS Program, whose aim in Poland was to introduce the system of social work.

The goal of the project was to improve the social skills of persons and groups who are unable to articulate and pursue their own interests, remain passive in contacts with various institutions, cannot express their own needs and make demands of the political system (this involves the social policy of the state) and have no influence on the political decisions made at the regional level. The project was initially launched on the assumption that individuals, social groups, organizations and institutions which comprise local communities will eventually get involved in its implementation.

The authors of the project also expected involvement of various non-governmental organizations as well as of non-profit and for-profit organizations having their seats in given communities, regardless of their reach. Most of all, they counted on the participation of organizations and institutions involved primarily in social work such as institutions of education, cultural centres, institutions of social welfare and social control. The objective was to create a local (and therefore a natural) horizontal platform for coordinating the efforts of these institutions with the goal of identifying and solving the problems faced by local communities (Ambrozik, Wlodarek).

The project was implemented in three stages. Stage one involved the selection of a local community for the implementation of the project, and the identification of social problems faced by this community.

Stage two, referred to as mobilizing the community's social forces toward specific goals, involved an extensive promotional campaign designed to bring information about the project to the residents of a selected area of the city and to all local organizations with a view to finding potential partners to support the project.

Stage three involved the formulation of task teams. At this stage concrete action was taken to resolve problems detected in the assessment phase. In forming these teams, the organizers considered the competence of the persons and organizations involved as well as their personal preferences (Ambrozik, Wlodarek).

PROJECT IMPLEMENTATION AND RESULTS

The project was implemented in the Lazarz area of Poznan with a population of 18,000. A factor which contributed to the selection of this particular area was the "higher than average indicator of social neglect, and a good tradition of educational and cultural work". Lazarz is a hotbed for such problems as unemployment and the resulting widespread impoverishment, lack of housing, alcoholism, and crime. Another distinctive feature of the area is an above average percentage of residents in their retirement age. A related statistic is an unusually high percentage of single persons (over 39 per cent), especially elderly women. As many as 8.8 per cent of the area's residents take advantage of social assistance provided by the local Welfare Centre. These residents qualify for welfare support by virtue of their low income, lack of professional qualifications, an extended illness, permanent disability, unemployment, raising a child as a single mother, raising a disabled child, etc. (Ambrozik, Wlodarek).

Three sets of problems arose during the first stage of project implementation, which became the focal point of efforts aimed at preparing the institutional environment for the development of local initiatives. They included:

- the problems of elderly people,
- the problems of families and children at risk of social deprivation,
- the problems of children with physical and mental disabilities and the problems faced by their families.

As indicated in the report by W. Ambrozik and J. Wlodarek, the first promotional conferences under the program were held in early 1994. The events attracted an impressive turnout by representatives of over 30 Lazarz and Grunwald organizations. Simultaneously with the conferences, an informational campaign was launched in local press and radio. In addition, training seminars were organized for the staffs of social institutions with lectures given by German and Dutch speakers.

A number of Lazarz area institutions centred around the problems of children in danger of becoming hardened juvenile delinquents and the problems faced by dysfunctional families. These institutions included: the Board of Education's Youth House, two elementary schools, a District Welfare Centre and the Lazarz-Poznan Police Department. The institutions used the project as a common ground for coordinating their efforts. A special contribution was made by the students of the Pedagogy and Sociology Departments of Adam Mickiewicz University. The students worked toward establishing contact with the families of the above-mentioned children and toward involving the children in a wide range of activities.

Unfortunately, as has been indicated by the authors of the report, all attempts to procure the parents' commitment to working with educational institutions toward realizing what in fact were their own interests, failed. Equally unsuccessful were the attempts to stimulate some local organizations such as scout groups, the local Cultural Centre and sports clubs.

The following Lazarz area institutions, organizations and individuals proved willing to focus on assisting families raising children with disabilities: the Association for the Assistance to the Mentally

Handicapped, a Disabled Children's School, a Catholic Mission for Disabled Children, the "Children's Friends" Association, and social workers. The efforts of these institutions and individuals focused on getting the parents involved in work for the benefit of their children and, with the help of the parents, on enabling the children to participate in the activities of the various local institutions. The attempts to stimulate parents were met with "wait-and-see" attitudes or expectations of financial assistance. These phenomena are difficult to interpret, especially in an environment teeming with efficient non-governmental organizations involved with parents of children with a variety of disabilities. The majority of these associations, however, are national and regional rather than local in character. (Ambrozik, Wlodarek).

The third problem, the living conditions of the elderly, attracted organizations which had already been involved in helping old people in their predicaments. These organizations included the "Bamberka" Senior Citizen Club at the "Krag" Cultural Centre, a day program for elderly people, a Retiree Centre at the Polish Teachers' Association, and social workers. The chief problem of elderly people in the area turned out to be loneliness. Therefore efforts to solve old people's problems within the framework of the program focused on creating self-help circles. Thus the "Golden Autumn" Senior Citizen's Club was established at St. Ann's Parish. Special steps have already been taken toward that end.

The activities of other cultural and educational institutions in local communities were stimulated by the role of the "Krag" Cultural Centre in community involvement of elderly people. "Krag", and especially the affiliated "Bamberka" Senior Citizen Club, have been acclaimed by the Lazarz community as a model organization for its role in integrating elderly people. In addition to its undeniable accomplishments in the area of Social care for senior citizens, the Club has won public acceptance in the district as well as city-wide for its achievements in promoting educational and cultural life. Credit for the success of such activities is due to members and voluntary activists performing their labor of love and contributing to the Club's success. The same people also constitute a part of the audience at which such programs are targeted.

Among the cultural events held at the "Bamberka" Senior Citizen Club are the weekly concerts given by professional musicians. Performing artists from the Poznan Philharmonic Orchestra offer courses in musical education, providing an opportunity for the elderly to broaden their knowledge of music and perfect their singing skills. These activities have resulted in the formation of a highly successful band named the "Lazarz Circle". One of its accomplishments is its distinction at the Polish Festival of Amateur Bands. The senior citizens of "Krag" give concerts for residents of homes for the elderly, members of cultural centres in other areas of Poznan and at various cultural centres. Proceeds from the events go to support the "Satis Verborum" Association for the Disabled.

Besides the above activities, the members of the Senior Citizen Club are involved in theatre and comedy performances. They also write poetry, song lyrics and comedy scripts and perform in theatres, social care homes, homeless shelters and often on the local radio. In the several years since the establishment of the stand-up comedy circle, a number of amateur comedians joined it and acquired experience and stage skills. Some of them went on to work in other clubs, others left to establish their own. The air of enthusiasm projected by the older members of the "Bamberka" Club spread to the younger ones, helping them to develop their talents and gain self-confidence.

Some of the most interesting areas of activity promoted in the "Krag" Cultural Centre include lectures and exhibitions. They are aimed at enhancing local communities and creating a platform for the educational and cultural needs of Lazarz residents. The Club also houses a permanent exhibition of amateur artists, members of the Poznan Creative Arts Association and has also initiated a diary contest: "My Lazarz", and a photography contest: "Impressions of Lazarz", with photographs displayed on Club premises.

The Cultural Centre is also the organizer of educational events such as talks, lectures, language courses, and sight-seeing tours. It provides a meeting place for the "Gran" Mountaineers' Club, the Polish Society of Astronomy Lovers, the Wielkopolska Societies of Esperanto Speakers, Stamp Collectors, Embroiderers and Dowsers. Especially popular among the elderly are seminars conducted by medical doctors on topics ranging from health to dieting and from nutrition to disease prevention. The activities of "Krag" Cultural Centre have generated a wide range of initiatives by elderly persons and have resulted in an increased popularity of events.

A noteworthy event, well-established in the Poznan cultural scene, is the annual Lazarz Festival organized over the last several years by the "Krag" Centre. The Festival features a music marathon, a festival of amateur musical bands, presentations by the students and graduates of music schools, art exhibits, operetta and theatre performances, singing contests, exhibitions, art sales, etc. The Festival is preceded by a promotional campaign in the press, radio and television. It is held in primary schools, parks, school and community playing fields and in "Krag" facilities.

The relatively efficient coordination of actions within cultural and educational associations and institutions, and the impressive achievements in the area of stimulating community involvement in cultural affairs by elderly residents of Lazarz, underline the importance of the institutional environment for the efficient functioning of basic adult education. An additional factor contributing to the success of the third objective of the TEMPUS Program which embodied the stimulation of local community involvement are the long-standing traditions of cultural and educational work in the Lazarz area.

Although the program presented here was aimed at community development and specifically at resolving social issues, it is obvious that adult education has become one of its spin-off results. What has been produced here as a side-effect of general program efforts is an education in citizen cooperation. The big challenge is to educate people who spent their lives in and grew accustomed to the realities of a non-democratic social order.

In searching for a justification for such educational programs, one should take into account the political, economic and cultural context of the educational efforts on the one hand, and the expectations of individuals with respect to the final shape of such programs on the other. As can be seen from the results of the program, the educational needs are a function of the scope and type of life experience acquired by the adults and by the social and cultural environment they live in. The values promoted in such educational programs based on involvement in the life of a democratic society are self-reliance, ability to self-organize, as well as improvement of the quality of both the collective and individual life.

ASSESSMENT OF THE POTENTIAL TO STIMULATE LOCAL COMMUNITIES

Progress analysis of the Lazarz community development project aimed at developing individual and community competence, shows only limited success of efforts to stimulate non-institutional social forces. As described earlier, stimulation of elderly people's community involvement, both in the area of social work and cultural and educational activities, is an exception in this regard. The reason for this lies in the lack of a sense of common interest in the targeted community and the general withdrawal from social life observed in big cities. Another factor is the long-standing tradition of central organization of social life coupled with the novelty of the concept of self-government (Ambrozik, Wlodarek). According to Ambrozik and Wlodarek, the remnants of the old centralized management system are still present in many institutions. Its characteristics have also been found lingering in the Lazarz community. Local Lazarz institutions are still reluctant to surrender to a horizontal organization. They are also hesitant to engage in cooperation with other institutions toward realizing common goals.

In light of the above analysis of local communities, one can see distinctly the vital role basic adult education plays in satisfying new social needs arising out of socio-political transformations. One of the major challenges to adult education is functional illiteracy. Here, illiteracy is defined in its broadest sense of not only having no or limited education or inadequate reading skills, but also as inability to use the written word in all practical aspects of daily life, being underqualified in a given work situation and with cultural aspects of poverty, a symbol of more or less generalized exclusion (Hautecoeur, 1992:10-14)

Studies of functional illiteracy frequently point to the lack of informal education to compensate for the inadequacies of the existing school system. The extent of the problem is further evidenced by international studies which suggest the need to expand the existing continuous education programs (*Literacy, Economy and Society*, 1996). The important thing is not so much the possession of a degree but rather the quality of one's education and the ability to apply the acquired knowledge toward improving the quality of one's life.

The changes taking place in Polish adult education are very much in line with the overall transformations occurring in other countries of Europe. One of the strongest new trends in adult education in Poland is to conform to the demands imposed by the market. Thus, some of the key new goals of adult education are to offer competitive skills and knowledge and to help graduates obtain and hold jobs. Adult education is therefore associated with vocational education whose sole objective is to respond to market demands. We can thus speak of commercialization in education. The trend is a typical market reaction to educational voids brought about by socio-economic change (Solarczyk-Ambrozik, 1996). The transformation of the political system opened up opportunities for unrestricted establishment of socio-economic and political institutions. This newly-gained freedom also included the educational system where a number of institutions have been created at all levels of education.

It must be emphasized, however, that liberal commercialization of educational services will not eliminate all of the existing educational inadequacies troubling Polish society. The essential problem is that the lower the education level of potential participants, the less likely they are to actually enroll in adult education programs. The paradox is that persons whose education falls below a certain minimum necessary for coping in this increasingly complex world and who are in the most desperate need of the benefits of education, are also the least likely to choose to take advantage of the educational system. Thus the number of unmet educational problems remains basically unchanged.

Among the most pressing of such problems is functional illiteracy. There is a need to create institutions of adult education and to design curricula with a strong focus on social needs, not only the needs related to the market economy and the job market. Therefore, a key responsibility of adult education is to set education strategies designed to promote the development of competence in adults.

Today's adult education differs greatly from the traditional system. It no longer gives top priority to the ideological objectives emphasized so much under the previous political system. Education today is oriented to a number of goals never before pursued to such a large extent. The goals are selected in response to the new social and economic environment of the transition Poland is currently undergoing, as well as in view of the new challenges dictated by advancing global civilization which includes such factors as transformation of the work system, education in flexibility and innovation, and a new relationship between education and work. Adult education no longer plays the role of social stabilizer. Rather, it has become a key factor contributing to increasing the dynamism of social life.

The primary tenet of adult education is the emphasis on the individual, a consequence of the existential and social role it has been given. The emphasis on the individual, necessary as individuals acquire more educational competence, incorporates reaching such target goals as self-improvement, self-realization, the realization of one's needs and aspirations, a life oriented to work, social involvement and recreation. One should therefore say that besides such objectives of adult education as stimulation of social life and social restructuring in terms of vocations, a number of new ones have emerged in connection with self-development and acquisition of the skills and knowledge needed to actively participate in the changing reality (Solarczyk-Ambrozik, 1995).

The victory of democratic forces created bright prospects not only for business ventures but also, as has been demonstrated earlier, for a broad range of educational activities, including those promoting basic adult education. So far the results achieved in this area have been mixed. On the one hand, the system is plagued by the persistent shortcomings of the educational reform. On the other, there is a strong drive toward sweeping structural and program transformations. As has been shown earlier in this paper and as is clearly evident from the presented case of stimulation initiatives in the Lazarz community, advances in basic adult education are doomed to failure without consistent support from local communities.

References

Ambrozik, W. (not published). Z doswladczen w aktywizawaniu spolecznosci lokalnej wokof zadan socjulnych.

Ambrozik, W., Wlodarek, J. (not published). Funkcje specznosci lokalnej w rozwia-zywaniu problemow spolecznych

Blok, W. 1995. Social Work in an Open Democratic Society, (A lecture for Adam Mickiewicz University), Poznan.

Hautecoeur, J.-P. 1992. "Illiteracy. Direction? Action? Results?", in J.-P. Hautecoeur (Ed), *Alpha 92: Current Research in Literacy* (9-2 7), UNESCO Institute for Education and Ministry of Education, Quebec.

Kolarska-Bobinska, L. 1990. "Civil Society and Social Anomy in Poland", in *Acta Sociologica* (33), 4: 277-288.

Kolarska-Bobinska, L. 1991. "Role panstwa w procesie transformacji", in Studia Svejologiczne 3-4.

Koralewicz, J., Ziolkowski, M. 1990. Mentalnosc Polakow, Sposoby myslenia of polityce, Warszawa: PWN.

Literacy, Economy and Society. *Results of the First International Adult Literacy Survey*, 1995, Organisation for Economic Cooperation and Development, Canada.

Polacy wobec ladu postmonocentryczuego. Spoleczenstwo polskie i jego instytucje w 1992r, M Zio kowski (Ed), 1993. Warszawa: PAN.

Solarczyk-Ambrozik, E. 1995. "Zmiany spoleczno-gospodarcze w Polsce a system oswiaty doroslych", in L, Przyszczypkowski, e. Solarczyk-ambrozik, *Zmiana spoleczna a kompetencje edukacyjne doroslych, Koszalin.*

Solarczyk-Ambrozik, E. 1996. "Spoleczne i ekonomiczne wyznaczniki zmian w praktyce o—wiaty dorostych", in *Możliwości i zagrośenia reform edukacyjnych*, Kazimierz Dolny.

Wnuk-Lipinski, E. 1990. Rozpadpolowiczny, Warszawa: Instytut Studiow Politycznych PAN.

Chapter Seven
ADULT BASIC EDUCATION ENVIRONMENTS FROM DISCURSIVE INTERPLAY AMONG LEGISLATURE, ECONOMICS AND INSTITUTIONS

Stanislav Hubik
Czech Republic

FROM THE HISTORY OF THE ADULT EDUCATION INSTITUTIONAL ENVIRONMENTS IN THE CZECH REPUBLIC

To understand present institutional environments of adult basic education, i.e. community-based adult education in the Czech Republic means to grasp an historical background. This is needed because after the 1989-90 sociopolitical changes in the Czech Republic, new phenomena emerged in the area of adult education. The question is , "From which sources did these phenomena emerge?". The answer is: most of so called "new things" are only revitalized and renewed structures produced by society during the 1860-1948 period.

The significant landmark in constituting an institutional basis for adult education in Bohemia was in the 1860s, and with the approval of the so-called *Association Bill*, the possibility of establishing nationality, educational and other societies and associations emerged. This process culminated for the first time in the 1890s when educational institutions for adults were founded: the Worker's Academy (*Delnická akademie*) in 1896, or the Central Workers' 'School (*Ústrední škola delnická*) as a centre of national workers' clubs and unions in 1898.

Initiated by the National Czech Council (*Národní rada Ceská*), and approved by political parties of that time, the League of Popular Cultural Activities (*Svaz osvetový*) was established in 1906 as a "non-political organization in which members of all parties striving for progress and the people's well-being, could work side by side for the benefit of the Czech people". Beginning in 1908, this league struggled to legalize popular libraries in the Czech Lands that, however, did not happen until the Republic of Czechoslovakia was declared. That same year the Czech Popular Cultural Activities (*Ceská osveta*) magazine was founded.

So the activities of the nationality and workers' associations were bearers of adult education development in Bohemia before World War I and during the period of struggle for a new independent Czechoslovakian state.[1]

After the birth of Czechoslovakia, in October 1918, three popular education bills forming the basis for legislative amendments of adult education were passed over the next two years: the *Act of Organizing Popular Courses of Civic Education* of February 7, 1919 (No. 67 of the *Code — O organizaci lidových kurzuobcanské výchovy*), the *Act of Public Libraries* of July 22, 1919 (No. 430 of the *Code - O verejných knihovnách*) and the *Act of Community Books of Memoirs* of January 30, 1920 (No. 80 of the *Code - O pametních knihách obecních*). Resting on these three legislative pillars, popular education had been the most widespread way of realizing adult education, up until the Nazi invasion in March 1939.

Popular education was even introduced in the army (as early as 1918) and by 1926 there were about 270 military seclusions in the army. The popular education activities were coordinated by the District Corps of popular Cultural Activities (*Okresní osvetové sbory*). In 1919 there were in total 230 of them in the Czech Lands, in 1926 there were 569 of them on the whole territory of the Czechoslovakian Republic, and 9000 local committees (*komise*).

The legislative basis of popular education was liberal with a considerable role given to the state. The preamble to the 76/1919 bill reads: "The state itself is obliged — as one of its foremost and noblest tasks — to assume superintendence over the political education of all citizens. [...] The state will accomplish this education both at schools and especially through popular education." In this respect, the 530/1919 bill was of principal significance. It imposed upon "every municipality to establish and maintain a public library".

In 1925, the League of Popular Cultural Activities was changed into the Masaryk Institute of Popular Education (*Masarykuv osvetový ústav*), and mass popular education acquired a high-quality centre.

The legislative process was continued. The *Ministry of Education and National Popular Cultural Activities Decree* of November 10, 1923 (*Výnos ministerstva skolství a národní osvety*) supplemented with a decree of 1932 amended possibilities for free educational courses, and popular education congresses (held in 1928 and 1938). This contributed to a better interpretation of basic legislative texts, as well as to better implementation. The whole process of building and developing the system of popular education as an important part of lifelong learning was interrupted by the occupation of Czechoslovakia and World War II.

After 1945, the strategy of popular education and other adult education patterns proceeded from the *Kosice Governmental Programme*. On October 26, 1945 *Edict No. 130 of State Care of Popular Cultural Activities* (No. 130/1945 of the *Code - Dekret c. 130 o státní osvetové péci*) was adopted. This document determined the position of boards of popular cultural activities (*osvetové rady*) in the educational system and created a basis for establishing the State Boards of *Popular Education (Státní lidovýchovná rada*) within the Ministry of Education and Popular Cultural Activities.

Based on the *Edict*, important *Provisional Instructions and Information for Popular Cultural Activities Inspectors and Library Inspectors (Prozatímní pokyny a informace pro osvetové inspektory a knihovnické inspektory*) were issued (the Ministry of Education and popular *Cultural Activities Decree No. B-161659-IV, November 28, 1945). The Czech Popular Cultural Activities* magazine (*Ceská osveta*) resumed publication in 1946, while other work in this area of education was specified by the *Circulars of the Country's Popular Cultural Education Board (Obezníky zemské rady osvetové*) — controlling, for example, the relationship between the people's schools of popular cultural activities and trade union schools of work.

In February 1948, political power in the Country was taken over by the Communist Party, and in May 1948 a new *Constitution* was adopted that meant a basis for additional modification of legislation.

In August 1948, the third popular education congress took place, defining the main objectives and methods of a new communist strategy in the field of popular education and adult education. To a great extent, the whole sphere was linked to the leading ideology, and gradually the old contents of the popular education actions were removed. The ruling party placed a great emphasis on this area of education. The *Ministry of Information Decree* No. 136564/48-VII modified in a considerable way the operation of people's schools of popular cultural activities. The *Organizational and Curriculum Regulations for Public Schools of Popular Cultural Activities (Predpisy o organizaci a ucebních osnovách verejných osvetových skol)* were issued and their organizational structure was altered. These schools were divided into three levels: school of popular cultural activities (*SPCA*), higher *SPCA* and people's academy of popular cultural activities. In the first half of 1950s, due to a decision by the Ministry of Education and Popular Cultural Activities there were 2,200 *SPCA* established.

In June 1952, the Czechoslovak Society for the Dissemination of Political and Scientific Knowledge (*Ceskoslovenská spolecnost pro sír ení politických a vedeckých znalostí*) was founded as a new methodological and organizational centre of adult education outside schools and outside the framework of trade-union and party training. The need to provide education for new politically desired personnel in different leading positions (nomenclature) resulted in the founding of *SPCA for workers (Osve—tové skoly pro pracující)* — see the *Ministry of Culture Decree* No. 172/54, June 1, 1954. Thus, a very dense network of continuing adult education was completed, supplementing the similarly dense network of trade-union training as well as training within the Communist Party. Through this, not only continuing education was assured, but also a permanent ideological influence on adult citizens was exercised. In practice, each citizen was incorporated in some of the forms (of popular cultural activities, trade-union, party) of continuing education that was gradually understood more and more as a lifelong learning.[2]

Major impulses for the present changes in Czech society generally, and education in particular, stem from the political changes in 1989 and from the consequent profound rearrangements in all areas of Czech social life. Special note should be given to the break-up of Czechoslovakia that generated two independent states, the Czech Republic and the Slovak Republic. This accelerated and intensified the economic and political transformation already in progress. First of all the old constitution (*The Czechoslovak Socialist Republic Constitution*) had been amended. After the country split up, a number of new bills and legislative decrees have been approved following the adoption of the new Czech Republic Constitution. This process continues.

PRESENT STATE OF INSTITUTIONAL ENVIRONMENTS AS A PRODUCT OF DISCOURSE BETWEEN LEGISLATURE, INSTITUTIONS AND ECONOMICS

The unitary (highly centralized) legislative regulation of the whole system has been abolished and only the school education is consistently legally regulated. Development of private primary and secondary schools was made possible.

Legislature

That is why the responsibility (also in legal sense) for all forms of out-of-schools adult education is in the hands of participants, employees, trade unions and various other NGOs. The first "participant" of the treble environmental discourse (legislature-institutions-economics) emerges from the legislature.

Legal base for the responsibility consists of the school acts and the general codes: *The Work Statute Book (Zákoník práce)* and *The Business Book (Obchodní zákoník)* and *The Act on Citizens Associating (Zákon o sdruzování obcanu)*. Institutions were constituted according to these three types of acts: government and non-government. The non-government institutions are assigned (and typologized) by *The Business Statute Book* (limited companies, etc.) and from 1995 also by *The Act on General Welfare Companies* (so called "non-profit organizations Act").

The whole area of adult education is closely connected with this triangle of the acts: *the school acts, The Work Statute* Book and *The Business Statute Book*. But the area of adult basic education is formed by following this square of the acts:

The Act on Citizens Associating

The Business Statute Book **The Work Statute Book**

The Act on General Welfare Companies

Here we can formulate our definition of the institutional environments for adult basic education and understand another highly important concept, that of the base of adult basic education.

Institutional environment for adult basic education is a possibility produced as a result of discourse with the existing institutions, legislation and economics. The expression "limited by real responsibilities" changes that possibility into the actual state of affairs. This "by real" provides the real base for adult basic education in the Czech Republic and it is not possible to understand the question **"What is "the base" of adult basic education and its institutional environments?"** without knowing the history and its silent role in the process of revitalizing basic education environments during the last three, four years.

Economics

The second "participant" of the treble environmental discourse (legislature-institutions-economics) emerges from the economics. The following description affirms an analytical remark on political economy of education of P. Belangér: "In this new political economy of education, the role of the state will no longer be the one that has been institutionalized in prior phases of the history of education, a time when education was equated with initial education."[3]

In accordance with institutional structure of adult education in the Czech Republic, funding depends on various sources: the state (ministries and grant agencies, European included), the private economy (company-based education/training), the sponsoring bodies and the private individuals.

During the last five years the quite new system of funding emerged in the sphere covered by the state. As an example we can take new *Act on non-profit organizations* (of September 1995) and system of grant agencies (Grant Agency of Government of the Czech Republic, Grant Agency of the Academy of Sciencies, grant agencies of Ministry of Education and Ministry of Culture and other agencies).

An important way of funding adult education on the local and regional level is a grant system of the Ministry of Culture. As an example, in 1995 this *Ministry* advertised a contest directed towards four educational thematic groups: development of educational activities for children, youth and adults, development of methods and forms of education, problematics of lifelong learning, education and non-artistic activities and activities for unemployed and for risk-groups of population.[4]

Another way of supporting is by NGOs. As an example we can take *Grant Program for Adults (Project for realizing of social and culture activities)* of the *Open Society Fund*. This grant program is specified for "all projects for any actvity of cultural, educational [...] character"[5], first of all on the local and regional level.

Institutions

The third "participant" of the treble environmental discourse (legislature-institutions-economics) emerges from the institutions. From the *ALPHA 97* viewpoint, it is the most important and essential "participant". It represents the visible form of the institutional environments for basic adult education.

By 1990 the important organizational and methodological basis for further adult education in Czechoslovakia was represented by a network of cultural centres and clubs of popular cultural activities. Their structures were related to the administrative division of the country: before 1993 Czechoslovakia was divided into 10 regions, 112 districts, and had over 9,000 municipal units. Each region had its own cultural centre that directed particular district cultural centres. Others operated on the territories of the capital cities of both republics of the federative state, in Prague and in Bratislava. However, in every larger municipal unit, the club of popular cultural activities functioned through voluntary members.

The activities of the cultural centres were closely related to The CSSR Socialist Academy (at present *Jan Amos Komensky Aacademy - JAKA*), and to other cultural institutions, theaters, trade union clubs and libraries (before 1990 Czechoslovakia had the most developed network of theaters in the world, and owing to the *Masaryk Act of Libraries (Act of Public Municipal Libraries* of July 22, 1919). This was the most developed network of libraries in the world (the act ordered the establishment of a public library in every municipal unit). This very dense network of cultural institutions, subsidized by the state, municipalities, trade unions and cooperative farms, represented an extraordinarily effective body of institutions dealing with adult education, as well a influencing the adult population both ideologically and politically. After 1990, this network was partially transferred into the form of private cultural and educational agencies and has partially lost its former state support, and partially ceased to exist.

Generally speaking, this network of the culture centres is transformed into the new or renewed forms of activities and into the new institutional structures that are the axis of the new institutional environments.

In total, the network of cultural centres,the clubs of popular cultural activities, and the *CSSR Socialist Academy* (excluding analogical institutions, e.g., several thousands of cultural centres in trade unions and cooperative farms) comprised approximately 250 institutions operating on a professional level, and several thousands of institutions functioning on a voluntary level. All the professional institutions were systematically engaged in adult education and basic education.

Although this area has changed to a significant degree we can observe its revival and stabilization based on the quite new economic, legislative and social platform, as the tradition in the Czech Republic is very strong in this respect.

Basic structural and organizational units of this community-based cultural/educational practice consists of the local culture centre (*Kulturní stredisko or Kulturní a informacní stredisko* or *Osvetová beseda*), local NGOs (eg. *Sokol* or *JAKA* etc.) and any local (regional) culture institution (gallery, museum etc.). There are three specialized research institutions in the Czech Republic (covered by the Ministry of Culture) that are monitoring this mass base for various educatioonal activities: *CIK (Centrum informací o kulture - Centre for culture information), REGIS (útvar pro místní a regionální kulturu - division for local and regional culture) and ARTAMA (útvar pro neprofesinální umení a estetickou výchovu - division for non-professional arts and aesthetic education*). Results of their researches and monitoring are presented in the periodical *Místní kultura* (*Local Culture*) that is the best source of information concerning adult básic education. To obtain a good picture of educational activities, institutions and networks in the field of adult basic education, means to observe what happens with local/regional cultural practices. This is an extremely important area for adult basic education dating from the national enlightenment period (19th century) as a real, vital and living example of mass adult basic education.

Most importantly, the activities in this sphere of community-based cultural/educational practices are mostly voluntary. Now we can answer the question "What is really "the base" of adult basic education and its institutional environments?" quite plastically: the result of discursive practices among the existing institutions, legislation and economics, is only limited by the real responsibilities for adult basic education in these different sectors is created by a triangle :

local culture centre **local NGOs**

local/regional
culture institutions
(gallery, museum etc.)

Local *NGOs, like Pionýr* (transformed organization of children and youth), *Junák* (an organization of children and youth), *Sokol* (an organization for sports and physical education) includes more than 500 civic associations. Among these, an important role is played by the various social movements that have a stable institutional base. These include ecological movements with their own educational institutions and network such as *Brontosaurus Movement, Deti zeme (Children of the Earth), Poslední generace (The Last Generation)* or *Duha (Rainbow)*, and some include an educational dimension : *EkoCentrum (Centre of Environmental Information), Environmental Education Houses, Houses of Environmental Conservation* etc.

The voluntary and democratic character of the practices produced in the above triangle framework are very similar to the other process of adult basic education moderated by multimedia. The research project realized with help of the UNESCO Institute for Education (UIE) *in the framework of ALPHA 96 — Literacy and Work in the Czech Republic* was meant to prove highly effective at connecting alternative ways of production and reproduction of literacy and literacy strategies based on bricolage with mass-media respecting and methodically using bricolage. The subject of this research was the mass-media complex of the *Receptár* (*The Book of Prescriptions*) institutions, which enables the exchange of those alternative approaches towards solving various problems like adult learning. The practical results of the effect of the TV program *Receptár* on the adult learning process is extraordinary, and worthy of attention from people dealing with adult basic education problems.[6]

The *Receptar* educational project is from an institution that has two types of mass media, television and periodicals. The organizational structure of this institution is shaped by a weekly TV program, a monthly magazine, a club and a club foundation (with its own periodical). In addition, there is a telephone line that can be installed in every major municipal unit in the Czech Republic. The publishing institution that focuses only on publications for the audience of the *Receptar* is another, loosely associated but very important, organizational component. In total, the bricolage institution referred to as the *Receptar* involves every week about 1-1.5 Million individuals or small groups.

The principle determining the shape of the whole educational project is quite simple: the team of the *Receptar* personnel gathers information (knowledge, ideas, minor educational projects, know-how) continually. At the centre it is selected and distributed back to the audience, either in the overall scope (TV) or as far as special interest is concerned (to magazine readers), and purposefully (to club members).

The result of this is bricolage as a process of disclosing hidden cultural codes that, by providing adequate intervention from outside, may change into an alternative educational project/process and may initiate the desirable impulses of social and cultural mobilization of individuals, communities and regions.

In this sense the *bricolage* is one of the most important activities in adult basic education. In the form of "mass bricolage" mediated by TV and other medias there is a "small" parallel of it in the form of various activities produced by the triangle local cultural centres — local NGOs — local/regional culture institutions.

During the last eight years (1990-97) the new institutional environments emerged, but its structural elements (as the products of treble discourse between legislature, economics and institutions) are not quite new: rather, they are renewed older structures produced mostly in the 1918-1948 period andpartly during the 1948-1989 period. Nevertheless, the result is quite new system up to this time *in statu nascendi. The real and concrete state of the institutional environments depends on the third discursive "participant" (not represented by the picture) — on the economics.*

We can demonstrate the institutional environments of adult basic education in the Czech Republic by following picture:

The Act on Citizens Associating

The Business Statute Books

culture centres

NGOs

local or régional

culture institutions

The Work Statute Book

The Act on General Welfare Companies

THE NEAR FUTURE OF THE INSTITUTIONAL ENVIRONMENTS FOR ADULT BASIC EDUCATION

The nearest aim of the adult basic education policies is to balance the roles, interests and goals of these three most important discursive "participants": legislature, economics and institutions themselves. The axes of this balancing would have to be principles of democracy, solidarity and community based interests. That is why the role of the state will be limiting not only through the "new political economy of education" but also through the regional and local politics.

Space created for educational environments during the last eight years provides a sufficient number of formal opportunities for adult basic education. This fact is limited by the economics that is in this way limiting real opportunities of adult basic education. There is also a paradoxical situation caused by the fact that the field of adult basic education is principally covered by the Ministry of Culture *(see e.g. ARTAMA* or *REGIS* activities) rather than the Ministry of Education. This factor complicates the creation of the educational environments in general and rational funding.

This is just the time for the creation of the framework of international cooperation that can influence further modifications of the educational environments in the Czech Republic and model it in accordance with the EU and UNESCO standards. In connection with this, a clear justification of the role of adult education is needed. What is missing is such legal norm like the Further Education Act comparible with the similar norm of EU.

To justify the role of adult (basic) education means **to identify basic needs of regional and local communities**. This can be a matter of the special cultural/educational researches initiated and covered by governmental institutions and agencies like the. grant agencies. As in other countries, **here there is a gap between real needs and official declarations**. There is a serious legislative debt of the government — to create the higher regional and administrative units in the Czech Republic and in such way decentralize three main "participants" that are the discursive producing environments.

References

1. Trnka, T. 1970, Lidová výchova, její teorie, slozky, metody a organizace (*Popular Education, Its Theory, Parts, Methods and Organizing*), Ostrava 1970, pp. 202-5.

2. Skoda, K. 1968, Kapitoly z dejin ceské osvety (Chapters from Czech *Education History*), Praha (OU) 1968.

3. Bélanger, P., Lifelong Learning: the Dialectics of "Lifelong Education". *International Review of Education*, Vol. 40, 1994, p. 374.

4. Ministerstvo kultury — vyhlásaení konkursu (*Ministry of Culture — Advertising a Contest) 1995. Místní kultura* (Informacní servis) IV, p. 6. The *Ministry* also advertised other contests directed to the non-professional arts with directions as follows:

   1. the traditional Czech musicality,
   2. literary branch, dramatic creativity, workshops and seminars including,
   3. non-professional creating of the arts, photopgraphy, audio-, *amateur* movies and video,
   4. all sorts of dancing [...],
   5. child aesthetic activities with a stress on the preparation and education of the leaders of child/youth collectives.

5. Grantový program pro dospelé. Projekt na realizaci spolecenských a kulturních aktivit. Open Society Fund (*Grant* Program for Adults. Project for Realizing of Social and Cultural Activities). **Místní kultura**, IV, 1995, nº 6, p. 28-9.

6 Hubik, S., An Alternative Literacy and Work: *Bricolage* and Mass Media. In: Hautecoeur, J.-P. (ed.) 1996, *Basic Education and Work. ALPHA 96*, Toronto and Hamburg (UIE and Culture Concepts), pp. 301-321.

Section Three

Western Europe

Chapter Eight
KEEPING ALIVE ALTERNATIVE VISIONS

Mary Hamilton
Lancaster University, United Kingdom

INTRODUCTION

The last decade has been a time of radical change in the political, social and educational landscape of the UK and a crucial time for adult basic education (ABE). We have moved from the literacy campaign of the mid-seventies to a permanent and increasingly formalized system of learning opportunities for adults, but with this has come a redefinition of what counts as literacy, the goals of literacy learning and the means for achieving them. In some ways this has been progress, but in others, especially for those of us committed to ideals of community-based literacy practice, it has been a dispiriting journey in which our particular visions of literacy have moved further into the distance.

The main focus of the ALPHA 97 project is on the relationship between policies, institutions and local actions concerning literacy, and the extent to which these reflect the literacy practices and expressed needs of local communities. I take this to be, at base, a practical focus, about the points at which ideals meet reality and what is possible to achieve in this translation. As suggested in the overall project outline, I will explore the issues under three main headings:

1. How has the relationship between policy, institutional settings and local literacies changed in the UK over the last 10 years?

2. What are the constraints or antagonisms which may interfere with communication between these three levels?

3. How can we make policy and institutions more responsive to local needs and marginalized communities so as to develop sustainable literacy projects?

I have been connected with literacy work since the adult literacy campaign of the early 1970's. I am currently based in a university where I am involved in a range of research projects, including documenting some vernacular literacy practices outside of educational settings. I am a founder member and current chair of the Research and Practice in Adult Literacy network (RaPAL) which promotes participatory research, and makes links with community-based projects and learner centred practices wherever they occur.

For this article I have drawn on a number of documentary sources, including government policy documents and research reports. I have also consulted a range of projects in the UK that are working responsively with local needs and agendas.[1] I have seen this process of consultation as a kind of action research which could help us begin to articulate the current concerns of local communities and formulate some new directions for policy. Sanguinetti (1995) suggests that action research of this kind can provide the opportunity for participants to develop alternative discourses which can be used to visualize and argue for change. This is especially important in the current UK context where one of the profound ways communities and literacy projects are disempowered is by the lack of alternatives to a strongly dominant centralist discourse which legitimates only one version of the work that is going on (Hamilton, 1995).

The process of consulting has already been an education for me. It has revealed many creative and determinedly resistant responses to current constraints, important regional differences in the policy context (especially in Scotland and Northern Ireland) and the research has generated conversations in which people challenged the prevailing language and definitions of "market led" literacy as well as some of the assumptions underlying my own thinking.

THE LAST 10 YEARS

The policy and institutional context of literacy work in the UK is multi-layered. To understand how it has been shaped we need to consider the European, national, regional and local levels all of which determine the actual learning opportunities available to particular adults. We also need to know something about the broader context of political and cultural change during this period which has both local and international dimensions to it.

Developments in adult literacy programs have been taking place within the bleak context of increasing poverty and social exclusion for a significant minority of the population. For example, the Child Poverty Action Group and others have documented the increasing differentials in wealth that have led to nearly a quarter of households with children living under the poverty line in the 1990's (Oppenheim and Harker, 1996). Particularly worrying from the point of view of literacy are Department for Education and Employment figures showing that more children than ever are now being permanently excluded from school because they are judged to be disrupting classroom life. The figures have increased from 11,000 in 1993 to 15,000 in 1996 (National Guardian newspaper report 23/4/96). In her analysis of a series of riots that took place across the country in the summer of 1991, Bea Campbell describes the ways in which whole communities have been abandoned by employers, by their official political representatives and by the police, living in a state of emergency, without resources, and treated as beyond the pale, criminalized but not protected (Campbell, 1993).

National political changes have included the erosion of local democracy and corresponding mechanisms for planning and allocating resources at the same time as tightening control from the centre. Many elected and accountable bodies have been replaced by unelected "quango's"[2] disbursing money from central sources. All public services — transport, health, education, social services, prisons — have been scrutinized. Government funding has been reduced through privatization and the introduction of a contract culture and an "internal market", whereby different parts of a public service buy goods and services from one another or elsewhere in a system of competitive tendering. The notion of public service has been replaced by the metaphor of the market place. This has been accompanied by a conscious change in the vocabulary of social relationships. So for example, users of public services are now referred to as "customers" or "consumers".

One of the most significant developments has been the dismantling into smaller units of the larger, metropolitan district authorities such as the Greater London Council and, most recently, Lothian Regional Council in Scotland. These authorities coordinated the provision of many resources for local communities and have tended to be generous and frequently creative in their support for community education and development activities.

Recent changes in the funding arrangements for social welfare and community development programs have also had knock-on effects to learning opportunities, for example, for members of linguistic minority groups, refugees and asylum seekers. The introduction of integrated social funding through a "single regeneration budget" has been important for urban areas that qualify for such funding but many smaller towns and communities do not have access to it. Such funding can have divisive effects and as Rutledge (1996) points out "encourages a peculiar form of local politics. The structure is headed by an unselected quango, with a number of subsidiary groups seeking to gain resources (often sorely needed) for their own constituents, and in direct competition with each other". As another writer puts it, groups are compelled to compete with one another "on the basis of their level of misery or the respective skills of bidders" Reeves et al (1993:98). The short-term nature of much project funding also leads to a huge burden of paperwork, insecure staff contracts and the impossibility of forward planning.

Funding through European Community is now an important source for many projects, and comes with its own set of criteria, target group definitions and paperwork headaches. In general it has been useful in allowing developments that could not have happened with national resources and political priorities over the last 10 years. Women, and communities with high unemployment have particularly benefited from this funding. Special funding has been available to Northern Ireland through the "peace and reconciliation" program. Exchanges and visits are often part of funded programs, as a powerful way of creating a new European identity.

Changes in culture and community life have been brought about by the emphasis on individual competitiveness, rather than cooperative strategies, in all areas of public and private life. This has led to fewer collective resources and more fragmentation in community initiatives. The government now advocates individual solutions to social problems within the market place, rather than the welfare policies that framed the original literacy campaign in the early 1970's and which are now denigrated as both inefficient and patronizing (Hamilton, 1996; Withnall, 1994). The national lottery has become an major new focus for the financial hopes of both individuals and the community groups who bid for grants from its profits.

New media developments are changing the role of literacy in people's day-to-day lives for example in the widespread use of video libraries and home computers. These changes have been strongly encouraged by a government that places a high value on new technologies and the consumer goods that accompany them — home videos and computers, mobile phones and so on — such that these have become symbols of status and prosperity as well as offering new possibilities for communication.

Changes in the organization of the workplace and the structure of paid employment have led to the weakening of traditions of collective action through Trade Unions and a corresponding erosion of working conditions. "Flexible working" has led to a huge increase in temporary and part-time jobs which do not offer access to training (see Frank and Hamilton, 1993). There is significant unemployment, including many people who are out of paid work permanently or on a long-term basis (Unemployment Unit, 1996). These changes are the product of global economic trends combined with regressive government policy on employment and industrial relations. We are encouraged to blame unemployed people and those who are low-skilled for the country's economic problems. International comparisons are not argued through in terms of the global market and the power of international business. Neither do they explore what "flexible" working means in terms of peoples daily lives, health and the security of their families.

Broader reforms have taken place in the education and training system within which adult basic education and literacy are minor players. Changes in ABE programs are motivated by top-down policy decisions enforced by financial incentives or penalties. In many instances, ABE workers are having to deal with the unintended consequences of legislation designed for other constituencies or purposes, rather than a coherent policy aimed at developing and supporting literacy and adult learning (Fullan, 1991; Derrick, 1996).

Most notable among these changes has been the Further and Higher Education Act of 1992 which separated vocational, qualification-bearing courses from non-vocational courses for adults. In England and Wales ABE was placed within the vocational sector so that the institutional setting of literacy programs has changed, away from community settings towards the greater formality of Further Education Colleges.

The separation of "vocational" from "non-vocational" is particularly unhelpful to ABE. Neither category is adequate to define the range of functions that literacy programs should be able to fulfil and the division contradicts a long tradition of viewing liberal or community education as having many functions — from cultural, community development and citizenship roles, to making early steps back into the employment market (Tuckett,1991 and also the Scottish Community Education model which currently preserves this integrated view). The Act has made this questionable distinction into a solid legal entity and further redefined "non-vocational" as "leisure". Thus any activity that cannot be linked to direct employment outcomes is classed as a luxury commodity and therefore expendable (Derrick,1996). This particularly discriminates against older adults who have retired from paid employment and poses problems in resourcing courses for adults with serious disabilities or learning difficulties. It results in a two tier system, one highly resourced and closely monitored and the other fragmented and marginalized.

Adult literacy educators have now forged better links across different levels of the education system (for example links with Higher Education through concerns for students who find academic writing difficult and links with schools via family literacy programs). There are stronger links with employers and vocational training. But these educators have also lost many of the local and regional networks that used to be an important part of staff development opportunities. The many locally responsive projects keep in touch by informal means, but often feel isolated or invisible.

There is rhetorical support for the notion of lifetime learning, both at national and European level but considerable reluctance to invest public money to improve opportunities for adult learning (National Institute for Adult and Continuing Education, 1996). England and Wales have a government-funded central agency, the Basic Skills Agency (BSA) which formulates policy and resulting in a higher profile for adult literacy issues than in Scotland or Northern Ireland where there is no similar agency. Through the BSA, and by controlling funding, the government exerts strong central pressures on programs and projects for accountability, quality control and accreditation. Outcomes are measured by nationally defined standards and a body of skills rather than in terms of individual profiles or the impact of projects on communities. Expansions in recruitment are motivated by money, maximizing the number of student enrolments, rather than *rights* to education.

The internal market in education has taken the form of local management of schools and colleges (see Tuckett, 1991) whereby each institution is funded directly from central government and operates as an independent business. Democratic control of programs has been eroded at many levels, including the representation of student and staff voices and control over curriculum and assessment (Smith, 1994). Collective action and representation has been replaced by the idea of "consumer power" at the individual level.

The research base of adult literacy has grown but has had a limited impact on practice. The national Basic Skills Agency (BSA) limits itself to "research into the scale and characteristics of basic skills need and the effectiveness of basic skills programmes" (BSA, 1995) and has tended to fund quantitative, policy driven research that assumes, rather than explores the needs and interests of local communities. Academic research in higher education on the "new literacy studies" has been developing alternative notions of literacy as social practice (Mace, 1993, 1995; Barton, 1994; Street, 1995). These ideas have underpinned much community-responsive literacy work, especially within non-government funded organizations in the UK and internationally. This cultural approach to literacy emphasizes the significance of local contexts and purposes for literacy but it has not found a sympathetic climate in government policy circles. Gaining a positive platform for these ideas has been hindered by the entrenched views of the media reporting on literacy and by the traditionally distant and mistrustful relationship between Higher Education and ABE practice in the UK.

EXAMPLES OF PROJECTS WORKING IN A RESPONSIVE WAY TO LOCAL AND MARGINALIZED COMMUNITIES

This section offers some examples of responsive projects that have been developed over the last ten years. These projects show how responsive literacy work can still be carried on despite the difficult climate outlined above, and the principles on which it is based. I have included examples of different kinds of institutional partnerships that span the possible range in the UK and illustrate different strategies and priorities.

Community Projects Funded by Non-Governmental Sources

Pecket Well residential college for adults opened in 1992 in a rural location near Halifax in the North of England. Courses are run for students and by students and the college welcomes adults with disabilities or learning difficulties. It has been developed by a small group of committed people and is based on principles of democratic learning which show themselves at all levels in the running of the college: learning methods, course design, relationships between workshop leaders and participants (who at different points in time, may be the same people), management of the college, researching local community needs through employing outreach workers and through students' activities on courses.

Pecket Well raises money for its activities from a range of sources including trusts and the European Community. So far, the college has been able to operate in an independent way but even a small, independent project like this cannot escape the effects of bigger changes in policy. Increasingly it is under pressure from founders to target, label and measure the people who come onto courses:

> It is very difficult the constraints the founders put on us. They try to turn us more formal, make us less democratic. Certain funding restricts many people, for example age, time to complete courses, background, culture, areas of residence etc. Accreditation is also "forced" upon us. (interview notes, July 1996)

Pecket Well has made use of the media to publicize itself as a unique project and to explain the importance of residential courses — frequently a life-changing experience for the adults who take part. It uses these opportunities to challenge mainstream language and assumptions about literacy and put over students' views.

One of its strengths is the emphasis it places on developing a public voice for students at the college through collectively documenting and publishing the writing that is done in courses (Pecket Well, 1994; 1995). In this, the college is supported by a national network, the Federation of Worker Writers and Community Publishers (FWWCP) which offers national events and exchanges with other projects that promote student writing, contacts and ideas.

Local government funded community education services

In local areas where there are a large proportion of bilingual speakers, a number of innovative initiatives have developed within the statutory sector, despite the fact that only English and Welsh are recognized for support within literacy programs. There are no state funded heritage or community language programs, either for children or adults and this is a deliberate policy decision. This means that the language needs and literacy practices of bilingual ethnic minority groups are not generally acknowledged within literacy programs.

A notable exception to this is the Sheffield Black Literacy Campaign that started with the Yemeni community in 1989 and has continued to the present, adding new community strands to its activities (Gurnah, 1992). The campaign is organized by the Sheffield Unified Multicultural Education Service(SUMES) within the Local Education Authority, in partnership with the black communities and a local university which trains literacy assistants as part of a year long access course. The literacy assistants are young, unemployed members of the black communities who recruit and teach learners as part of their outreach and development work in the community. At the same time they themselves get a training which offers access to further study and employment.

There are other examples of responsive developments in local government-organized community education services that have circumvented the prevailing models (Lucero & Thompson, 1994). Key factors in the successful development of these programs seem to be a political will and committed and informed decision-makers within local councils to respond to community needs; involvement of younger members of local communities; partnership funding from a range of sources and creative use of existing funding criteria.

Further Education Colleges with a Strong Community Focused Service

There are also examples of further education colleges developing a wide range of community learning opportunities. For example, Bilston College in the West Midlands of England operates with a strong held view of itself as a community college engaging with "popular education" (Reeves et al, 1993). Based in an area of former steel works with high levels of unemployment and poverty, resources in the local community are scarce and those offered by the college are valuable. It sees its brief as "not merely to visit community groups to tell them about the college, but to participate on an equal basis in community organizations and where relevant, to identify with their objectives".

It has gone to great lengths to develop courses in community venues that respond to local needs, including courses for women and older adults, and separate centres for Afro-Caribbean and Asian Education and Training that teach in community languages. A Basic Skills Partnership links the college with local community organizations and a well-resourced "Key into Learning" centre is a main focus of the college effort where adults from the local communities can obtain help with reading and writing as well as computer skills. The college organization reflects its underlying commitments. It has a number of directorates including a "community" directorate and a "quality and equal opportunities" directorate which enable these goals to be properly planned and linked in with all areas of the college's work.

Bilston College is unusual in having such explicit, well-thought through and high level management support for community access. Having set out its values and vision, it is then able to re-interpret and take control of the demands that founders make on it, enthusiastically develop new technologies in ways that do not isolate and disempower students, and argue for definitions of "quality" that take into account local conditions and resources. Bilston College is still limited by its role as a government funded tertiary college but it offers impressive evidence of how a strong and explicit community mission can be used to challenge the barriers resulting from funding constraints and open up the institution to local community involvement.

Partnerships with University based Continuing Education

In a climate where local education authorities and voluntary groups have struggled to support community education initiatives, sometimes partnerships with higher education have produced innovative responses. Coare and Jones (1995) report on a writing project that was set up between the Continuing Education Department at the University of Sussex in Brighton, England and a local organization for homeless adults. This project built on writing activities associated with the BIG ISSUE — a national magazine written by and for homeless people and sold on the streets to finance shelters and as a means of livelihood for the sellers. The magazine distribution offices also function as advocacy and advice centres for homeless people (Guardian newspaper report 2/10/96). The BIG ISSUE has become a familiar part of street life in all major cities in the UK. and was originally started with help from a business. In itself the magazine is an example of a creative literacy response to a social need that has grown to affect the lives of thousands of people.

The Brighton project used a local day-centre for homeless people and was able to be very flexible in what counted as "attendance" on the course and outcomes from it. This was important because of the chaotic and unpredictable nature of participants' lives, and their changing needs. Such flexibility is not easy to obtain through more mainstream funding but is an essential part of responsive literacy work with extremely marginalized groups such as people living on the streets.

Networks supporting Community-Based Literacy

There are many other initiatives of the sort mentioned above, which seem to form a strong but largely invisible thread running alongside the mainstream, official version of what is happening in literacy work. It is a problem that such projects do not have a louder public voice because their contribution is not properly acknowledged and they are unable to contribute directly to shaping the future through policy debates and decisions. In such a context, national networks that can help draw together the contributions of local projects and work that is not recognised by the mainstream ABE providers are potentially very important.

Few networks have survived the changes of the past decade. One of these has already been mentioned, the Federation of Worker Writers and Community Publishers (FWWCP) which was founded in 1976. It is almost entirely invisible in the mainstream of ABE which does not highly value the activities of student writing and publishing, despite the fact that it still exists in some form in many programs (O'Rourke & Mace, 1992; Mace, 1995).

Another network is the Research and Practice in Adult Literacy Group (RaPAL) which started in 1985. RaPAL links practitioners and researchers together, publishes a regular newsletter and supports participatory research activities which include students. A self-funded network for workplace trainers has also recently been started, reflecting new developments in workplace basic skills programs.

The National Literacy Trust is an umbrella organization, launched in 1993 and supported by a major publishing company. It sees its role as encouraging access for all citizens to a literate culture, and to this end it works across all sectors of the education system, children and adults. It encourages partnerships with other cultural organizations, such as libraries, publishers, newspapers, the British Film Institute, arts councils, and with charities and businesses to find ways in which all of these can put their resources to work for local communities. It works with the media and offers its services as a consultant and broker to policy-makers, schools and colleges, parents and pressure groups. It is currently publishing a position paper on the future of literacy, drawing on the perspectives of all these groups. One of its main strengths is that it can work across the boundaries imposed on many literacy-oriented groups and one of its key notions is that of literacy for *pleasure*.

In a climate where all programs to develop literacy have to justify their activities in terms of the functional and vocational, insisting on the importance of pleasure to literacy learning is a gesture of challenge! However, the NLT is not a political organization and is reluctant to engage with partisan views. It will be interesting to see how much influence it can have in the longer term working on this basis.

Constraints on Developing Community Responsive Literacy

Over the last ten years, adult literacy and basic skills has become a permanent and accepted area of provision in the UK. However, the more these programs have been accepted into the mainstream of post-school education and training, the more pressures there are on them to become standardized and therefore less responsive to the needs and priorities of local and marginalized communities. There is consensus about how this has been achieved. The mechanisms have been clear, open and brutally applied: the introduction of outcome funding and quality criteria, standardized accreditation, devaluing of outreach and development work, a vocational slant on courses which marginalizes those who are not looking for direct employment outcomes.

Those of us committed to community responsive literacy do not believe that this is an inevitable effect of the process of "mainstreaming". More creative and responsive ways could be found of developing a system of securely funded and high quality learning opportunities if the political will existed. The projects described above show some of the many ways this can be done. The very different way in which Scotland has developed its ABE service within a strong community education framework offers another model.

The factors that contribute to the current "gap" between the perspectives of national policy-makers and local communities are summarized below.

First, there is a lack of real knowledge about the priorities and practices within local communities by those making decisions and setting up programs to develop literacy. Restrictive funding mechanisms limit the possibilities for the necessary research and consultation to be carried out and for project workers to develop their knowledge and feed it back to policy makers. Time and again this is mentioned by project workers as a frustration and an essential component of more measurable work they do. It is also a key issue in literacy in other countries, where it often goes unrecognized by policy makers.

Second, centralized control of policy decisions, and the corresponding erosion of local democracy and fragmentation of collective organizations contributes to the "gap". A description in the Adult Literacy and Basic Skills Unit (ALBSU, now the BSA) Annual Report of how the recent family literacy initiative was developed illustrates the policy process that currently takes place. There were discussions between ALBSU and various government ministers; ALBSU staff carried out research into family literacy elsewhere in Europe and visits to programs in the USA which were considered as models for developments in the UK. Finally, ALBSU visited "programmes and projects that work with children and parents and talked with several experts" (Adult Literacy and Basic Skills Unit, 1993:10). This looks like a very top-down process. Importing social and educational policy ideas from the USA has been a common strategy in recent years (Finegold et al, 1993). Within this strategy there is little room for consultation with local communities or participants in existing ABE programs and there are certainly no *rights* for such groups to be involved in the decision-making process.

Third, hierarchical, undemocratic learning institutions (mainly further education colleges) work in isolation and in competition with one another within a "market driven" economy, vying for students and unable to share information and referral systems that would put the interests of students first, rather than the interests of the institution itself. As we have seen, under these conditions, change and expansion is determined by financial incentives rather than developed in partnership with project workers and participants. But, as Reeves points out "against a background of thinly-spread educational resources, widespread social deprivation and educational underachievement, the idea of encouraging competition between educational institutions makes little sense" (Reeves et al 1993:10.)

Similarly irrational, even in terms of the government's own priorities, is the decreasing support given to the voluntary sector in terms of the partnership funding which in the past has helped many projects keep afloat. This wastes cost-effective resources that already exist in local communities to support literacy.

Finally, we suffer from narrow and elitist assumptions about what is of cultural value in terms of literacy and other popular media; simplistic, utilitarian views of literacy and of what counts as "the community interest" (i.e. the business community first and foremost). As I have discussed above, the separation of "vocational" from "leisure" is particularly restrictive and the legal redefinition of ABE is one way in which the **discourse** of literacy has changed since the early days of the campaign.

A powerful feature of the policy process is that it labels and categorizes groups of people, institutions and activities and then gives weight to this classification system through selective allocation of funding. Politicians and the media legitimize these categories and devalue alternatives views through what Ball (1990) has called "a discourse of derision". This process constructs a strong notion of "the other" to exclude some people and target others for support, and is extremely oppressive if not accompanied by consultation with those affected by it (Stuart & Thomson, 1995). Narrow and rigid views of how literacy is important to adults' lives that mean consultation with local groups is not seen as important, the answers are known in advance, provision is offered rather than negotiated.

Even more fundamentally, experience from international adult education work suggests that as long as ABE remains solely within the domain and discourse of education and training it will deny community aspirations, focusing on individuals rather than on group concerns and cooperative activities (Rogers, 1992).

There is at present a lack of opportunities to develop and make public *alternatives* to this dominant, legitimated, government discourse. Alternative discourses are needed that can voice the concerns and priorities of local and marginalized communities in order to regain control of the literacy agenda (Wickert, 1996).

WHAT SHOULD WE DO?

Recommendations for action at three different levels suggest themselves from the discussion above. They correspond roughly to the levels of local communities, institutions and central policy and they are based on some general understandings. First, that we need to view literacy holistically, in the context of peoples' full lives and community context. Second, that strong democratic consultation and decision-making mechanisms are essential to developing truly responsive community literacy. Third, that it is also essential to have the desire for and practical possibility of cooperation and partnership between all interested groups and organizations. Fourth, we must create opportunities for open debate about the local uses and meanings of literacy and develop alternative public discourses of literacy through publishing and other mass media.

1. **Networks: In our current context we lack the networks that need to be in place to ensure a flow of information and debate between actors at different levels and to ensure the visibility of community concerns.**

There is a role for a coordinating body to link non-government funded organizations, as exist in some developing countries. This could act as an alternative focus for policy discourse and a critical voice, as well as being a resource and information exchange.

Such a body could encourage the active support and involvement of students and their communities in lobbying the media and policy-makers. Equally, they could support strong professional networks of teachers and community workers across the whole range of literacy related programs.

Research and development skills and strategies need to be developed with resources devolved to local communities for this purpose. A possible model for this can be found in Australia's research networks which fund practitioner-based research projects through links with local Higher Education Institutions. The Higher Education institutions are vehicles for these activities but do not own the resources.

Finally, international links and exchanges develop understandings of the global influences on local decisions and the range of solutions discovered in other countries. These can all inform a national policy.

2. **Institutional Systems are the bridge between community networks and policy, and as such they can open the way for mutual learning and dialogue, or deter this process.**

We need institutional systems which can support a range of learning opportunities on the spectrum from informal to formal learning as stepping stones for those who need them. As part of this, we need to work out a productive and complementary relationship between statutory and voluntary organizations. Institutions should also aim to support the general development of a culture of literacy and enabling access for all. This is not just an educational issue but many cultural institutions should be involved in partnerships for cultural action — for example libraries, arts projects, community publishing and other media.

To achieve these things we must have democratic management in the institutions themselves so that community concerns can shape the curriculum and ensure dialogue between informal and formal systems.

Finally, institutions should critique sterile notions of competency based education and training and insist on alternative forms of assessment and measures of quality including input, process as well as output. A great deal of this knowledge already exists, for example in the widespread experience of Open Colleges around the country that have found flexible ways of accrediting courses, tailored to local needs.

Policy Changes

3. **Policy is about planning and allocating resources and designing effective mechanisms for doing this. Top level policy can dampen or stimulate energy at the level of institutions and communities to develop literacy. Policy can also have unintended consequences for groups who are not the main focus of the initiative and we need action to protect their interests.**

We need to make it possible for representatives of local and marginalized groups to have the right to input into policy decisions, at all levels, not just to be occasionally consulted.

It is essential that literacy initiatives be coordinated with other social policy initiatives so that they are not happening in isolation. Literacy is not just an educational issue but must be linked with the broader culture and socio-economic conditions of peoples' lives which may be working against life-long learning and community development — such as unemployment and insecure jobs, poverty and homelessness, fragmentation.

We need staff development to be taken seriously as a policy issue, with programs that aim to produce reflective professionals and a real sense of professional community and voice, to input seriously into policy. There are a number of higher education institutions ready to contribute to this, and the Research and Practice in Adult Literacy group also has a potential role to play.

Positive action programs should be put in place that resist the imposition of monocultural, monolingual approaches to literacy education and recognise the resources that are available in bi-lingual communities.

Finally, we need to review the role of a central agency for literacy taking into account the contrasting experiences in England and Wales, Scotland and Northern Ireland, and examining the solutions adopted in other countries. We should consider other mechanisms that could be put into place which might better meet the current demands of the field.

Gaber-Katz and Watson (1991) in their discussion of community based literacy, talk about *building* community not just responding to what is already there. They point out that poverty and stress limit peoples' aspirations as they struggle with the day-to-day tasks of survival, and part of the role of community literacy is to enlarge people's own vision for their lives and strengthen the resources available to them. This seems very relevant to the depleted communities of turn-of-the millennium Britain and is recognized by many working at the local level.

The consultation I report in this article reveals that many of us in the UK are well-practised in the art of working in the cracks, finding the spaces to do what we know to be important. Alternative visions of literacy are alive but out on the margins. Finding ways of moving them into the centre is the challenge we face. What we have not learned to do effectively is to engage with the central processes of policy formation and decision-making, to use the powerful institutions of the media to put over these visions. Many of the resources available to us to do this have been removed during the last 10 years by a government that is very adept at using these institutions for its own purposes. It is time for us too, to focus on the big picture and how to redraw it.

Notes

1. I am very grateful to the following people and organizations that have taken time to contribute their ideas, views and comments on the issues covered in this paper. I have been unable to do justice to all of the information and ideas they offered me within the scope of this article, but I hope to be able to develop this project in the near future. The analysis offered is mine and does not necessarily represent all the views expressed to me. I take full responsibility for all errors and ommisions: *Pecket Well College, Calderdale; Jan Thompson, Westminster Adult Education Service; Tricia Hartley, Access Unit, Nelson and Colne College; Kate Pahl and Neil McLelland, National Literacy Trust; janet Ash, former chair of the Adult Basic Education Section of National Association of Teachers in Further and Higher Education; Alan Rogers, Education for Development; Catherine Macrae, Margaret Teale, Mhairi Gilfillan, Maureen McQeenie, City of Edinburgh Community Education ABE Team; Rob Mark, Institute of Continuing Education, Queens University of Belfast; participants at NIACE Annual Conference, Warwick University, March 1996; participants at the Lifelong Literacies conference, Manchester 31st May-1st June 1'996; members of the RaPal working group.*

2. Quasi-autonomous non-government organizations.

3. Recent changes in the BSA however threaten to reduce the attention given to adults: from 1995 the words "adult literacy" have been dropped from its title and it now has a remit that extends into compulsory schooling with the pre-sixteen year old age group.

References

Adult Literacy and Basic Skills Unit. 1993, *Annual Report 1992-3.*

Barton, D. 1994. *Literacy: The Ecology of Written Language*, Blackwells.

Ball, S. 1990. *Politics and Policy Making in Education*, Routledge.

Basic Skills Agency, 1995. *Annual Report 1994/5 Spreading the Word* BSA London.

Campbell, B. 1993. *Goliath: Britain's Dangerous Places Methuen.*

Coare, P. & Jones, L. January 1996. "Inside-Outside: A Homeless People's Writing Project" in *Adults Learning*, Vol. 7/5 pp. 105-106.

Derrick, J. 1996. *Adult Learners in Colleges and the FEFC*, paper presented at the NIAE Annual Conference, Warwick University, March 1996.

DfEE, 1996. *Lifetime Learning: A Consultation Paper*, HMSO Publications.

Dept of Education for Northern Ireland, 1996. *Lifetime Learning: A Consultation Paper*, Training and Employment Agency.

Finegold, D., L. McFarland & W. Richardson (eds). 1993. *Something Borrowed, Something Blue? A Study of the Thatcher Government's Appropriation of American Education and Training Policy*, Triangle Books, Oxfordshire.

Frank, F. & M. Hamilton 1993. *Not Just a Number: The Role of Adult Basic Education in the Changing Workplace*, Report to Leverhulme Trust, June 1993.

Fullan, M. 1991. *The New meaning of Educational Change*, London, Cassell.

Gaber-Katz, E. & G.M. Watson, 1991. *The land that we dream of: a participatory study of community-based literacy*, OISE Press, Toronto, Ontario.

Guardian Newspaper "New School option for boy in strike row" Guardian front page report, April 23, 1996 quoting DfEE statistics.

Gurnah, A. (ed). 1992. "Literacy for a Change: A Special Issue on the Black Literacy Campaign in Sheffield", *Adults Learning*, Vol. 3, N°8, Leicester.

Hamilton, M. 1992. *The Development of Adult Literacy Policy in the UK: A Cautionary Tale*, in the *International Yearbook of Adult Education*, Bohlau Verlag, FRG.

Hamilton, M. 1995. "Networks and Communities in Adult Basic Education", in F. Savitsky ed, *Living Literacies: Papers from a conference on Multiple Literacies and Lifelong* Learning, London, London Language and Literacy Unit.

Hamilton, M. 1996. Adult Literacy and Basic Education, in R. Fieldhouse ed, *A Modern History of Adult Education*, NIACE.

Lucero, M. & J. Thompson, 1994. *Teaching English Literacy Using Bilingual Approaches*, RaPAL Bulletin No25, Special Theme Issue on Bilingual Literacy.

Mace, J. 1993. *Talking About Literacy*, Routledge.

Mace, J. led). 1995 *Literacy, Language and Community Publishing: Essays in Adult Education*, Multilingual Matters, Clevedon, England.

National Institute for Adult Continuing Education, 1996. *LifeTime Learning: Response to the Government Consultation Document*, NIACE, Leicester, UK.

Pecket Well College, 1994. "Forging a Common Language, Sharing the Power", in Hamilton, M. Barton and D. Ivanic eds, *Worlds of Literacy*, Multilingual Matters/OISE Press: Clevedon, Philadelphia, Adelaide, Toronto.

Pecket Well College, 1995. *Changing Lives. Annual Report 1994-5*, Halifax, England.

Oppenheim, C. & L. Harker, 1996. *Poverty: The facts* 3rd edition, Child Poverty Action Group, London.

O'Rourke, R. & J. Mace, 1992. *Versions and Variety: A Report on Student Writing and Publishing in Adult Literacy Education*, Avanti books, Stevenage.

Reeves, F. & colleagues, 1993. *Community Need and Further Education: The practice of community-centred education at Bilston Community College*, Education Now Books in partnership with Bilston Community College.

Rogers, A. 1992. *Adults Learning for Development*, Cassell.

Rutledge, H. 1996. "Empowerment, Education and Citizenship: A Local Study", in *Adults learning*, March 1996, Vol. 7/7, pp. 172-4.

Sanguinetti, J. June 1995. *Evaluation as Discursive Resistance*. Paper Presented at LERN Conference, Australia.

Smith, M. 1994. *Local education: community, conversation, praxis*, OUP.

Street, B. 1995. *Social Literacies: Critical Approaches to Literacy in Development, Ethnography and Education*, Longman London and New York.

Stuart, M. & A. Thomson (eds). 1995. *Engaging with Difference: The "Other" in Adult Education*, NIACE.

Tuckett. A. 1991. "Counting the Cost: Managerialism, the market and the education of adults in the 1980s and beyond", in Westwood, S and J.E. Thomas eds, *Radical Agendas? The Politics of Adult Education*, NIACE.

Unemployment Unit, *Working Brief*, Issue 76, July 1996, UU: London.

Withnall, A. 1994, "Literacy on the Agenda: The Origins of the Adult Literacy Campaign in the United Kingdom", *Studies in the Education of Adults*, Vol. 26, No[1]. pp. 67-85.

Wickert, R. 1991. "Maintaining Power Over the Literacy Agenda", in *Open Letter*, Vol. 2, No[1].

Chapter Nine
THE INSTITUTIONAL ENVIRONMENT OF THE STRUGGLE AGAINST ILLITERACY IN FRANCE

Pierre Freynet
Continuing Education Centre
Angers, France

QUESTIONS OF TERMINOLOGY

'Basic education' is not the most commonly used term in France, the country which coined a new expression, *illettrisme*. This term, which was created originally by the organization ATD-Quart Monde to replace *analphabétisme,* which was thought too pejorative, spread following the publication in 1984 of the official report *Des Illettrés en France* ("On the Unlettered in France"). Since then, it has acquired a meaning closer to what most countries call "functional illiteracy". [No distinction is made in English between the French *analphabétisme,* which implies total ignorance of the system of writing, and *illettrisme,* which suggests being unlettered, unfamiliar with the literate world — both are usually translated as "illiteracy", but in this chapter the French term *illettrisme* is used where necessary to avoid confusion. [Translation]

It can therefore be said that two terms coexist in France: *analphabétisme,* which roughly corresponds to the definition given by UNESCO ("a person shall be considered illiterate if he is unable to read and write, with understanding, a short simple statement of facts relating to his everyday life"), and *illettrisme,* of which the definition recently given by the *Groupe permanent de lutte contre l'illettrisme* (Standing Group to Combat *Illettrisme,* GPLI) seems to be generally acceptable:

> The GPLI regards those persons as in situations of *illettrisme* who are over sixteen years of age, have attended school and do not have sufficient mastery of the written word to meet the minimum demands placed upon them in their working, social, cultural and personal lives. These persons, who have been taught literacy at school, have left the school system having acquired little or no knowledge and/or have never acquired a taste for applying it. This refers to men and women for whom the use of the written word is neither immediate, spontaneous, nor easy, and who avoid and/or are afraid of this means of expression and communication.[1]

The term "adult basic education" is not used at all in France. As for the term "literacy" (*alphabétisation*), this is generally used only in respect of people with a foreign mother tongue, especially migrants. Businesses refer rather to *training for low-level skills* or *training for adults with low levels of skill*. Some authors also speak of "basic skills".[2]

The term "basic education" is not yet commonly accepted, but it is used increasingly among writers, educators and persons responsible for education and training, who prefer it to "the struggle against *illettrisme*", which they think inadequate and too demeaning of learners. The Upper Normandy Region has, for example, developed a network of "basic education workshops". Its use may well grow as it more closely relates to what is actually done on the ground.

THE CONTEXT OF BASIC EDUCATION IN FRANCE

For a better understanding of what is meant by the "struggle against *illettrisme*" in France, it is necessary to remind ourselves of some of the characteristics of French society.

A changing economy

As Alain Lebaube has said, "In the way in which it organizes work, France has, more than other countries, sunk into Taylorism, and doubtless to a lesser extent into Fordism, both of which are now outdated. By comparison with the United States, and even more so with the other industrialized countries, she has been the scion of the creed of modern production, from the beginning of the 20th century up until the recent past."[3] This type of organization worked well for some time. The French economy, like that of other developed countries, has experienced extraordinary quantitative growth since the last war, and it is common to speak of the "thirty glorious years" to refer to the period ending in the early 1970s.

This type of Taylorian system then proved far less suitable. The period that followed showed much less spectacular quantitative growth, but had considerable qualitative effects, especially in terms of productivity, thanks to new ways of organizing work, made possible partly by the widespread introduction of automation and information technology. These new ways of organizing work, and the use of new technologies, were in turn translated into a growing need for people with higher and higher qualifications who could handle modern communication tools. Despite these changes, in March 1984, according to the National Institute of Statistics (INSEE), 19 percent of the working population were still in unskilled jobs.

A population with few formal qualifications

In fact, despite a considerable growth in the number of pupils in schools and the duration of their schooling, this rapid shift in the policy of business created a significant mismatch between the needs of the economy and the public's level of education and training. The 1990 national census revealed an average level of education that was appreciably higher than in the previous census (1982), but it was still very low: 48.2 per cent of the population of metropolitan France aged 15 years and above had at most a certificate of primary education, or no qualifications at all (60.2 per cent in 1982). These averages of course hide wide differences: from 75.3 per cent among those aged 65-74, the rate fell to 26.1 per cent among those aged 25-34. In any discussion of illiteracy and school failure, the progress made should not be forgotten.

Concern with unemployment

The economic crisis, associated with gains in productivity and restructuring, led to growing unemployment. The figures published on 31 July 1996 by the Ministry of Labour showed three Million unemployed. According to the norms of the International Labour Office, one French person in eight is unemployed (12.5 per cent). There are two aspects to this unemployment in France: young people find it increasingly difficult to get a foothold in the labour market, particularly those from "disadvantaged backgrounds", and a significant number of the unemployed find it difficult to get back into work.

These are the "long-term unemployed". In March 1995, 39.5 per cent of the unemployed had been without a job for one year or longer.

Among those with no qualifications, the figures of the National Institute of Statistics showed unemployment of over 20 per cent.

Growth in poverty and exclusion

This quantitative approach to unemployment is not enough. The border between being employed and unemployed, which used to be relatively clear, has become increasingly fluid and imprecise, with the spread of what are sometimes called "atypical jobs": paid training, part-time work, short-term contracts, employment-solidarity contracts, intermediary voluntary associations, early retirement, etc. It is therefore necessary to add the number of workers with unstable jobs, some two Million persons, to that of those who are unemployed in the true sense.

This is one of the features of the evolution of the economy which has contributed to instability, instability of employment bringing social instability in its train. Moreover, as a recent survey has shown[4], a job is not an absolute guarantee against poverty. Another survey published in February 1994 went so far as to estimate that almost half the active French population was, to a varying degree, suffering from "economic and social fragility", that is, at risk of economic and social exclusion[5]. At the present time, according to some estimates[6], four Million people in France are living on 3,000 F per month, one French person aged 18 or over in ten! (Note that in July 1996, the guaranteed minimum wage was about 5,000 F net per month.)

Voluntary social action

In order to handle this growth in difficult situations, a certain number of new measures were taken in addition to traditional social security. The best known were the creation of "works of public utility" (TUC), which then became "employment-solidarity contracts" (CES), and encouraged people into or back into work through part-time paid jobs, and the establishment in 1988 of a "minimum job entry allowance" (RMI) for people whose circumstances gave them no claim to any income. From 300,000 in 1994, the number of recipients of RMI rose to 940,000 in 1996. Many measures were also adopted to encourage employers to take on staff.

Over these 20 years, the social professions developed considerably, both quantitatively — between 1974 and 1994, the numbers of social workers grew from 22,500 to 37,000, and of special education staff from 9,000 to over 42,000 — and qualitatively: the changing economic situation and decentralization gave rise to new occupations and new jobs concerned with entry into the labour market, urban policy, etc. In the early 1980s, social workers played (and they still play) a major role in many places in awareness-raising and implementation of measures in the struggle against *illettrisme*.

A very lively voluntary sector

Social workers made use, in their various initiatives, of a highly developed voluntary sector, much of which was unpaid. The power of unpaid work and voluntary associations was to be found in different fields: culture, social work, support for schooling, etc. The struggle against *illettrisme*, particularly in the early stages, was helped substantially by the voluntary sector, and still receives such help.

However, the voluntary sector covers a wide spectrum, from small groups of unpaid workers to enormous associations which are in effect performing a public service. The Association for the Vocational Training of Adults (AFPA), for example, a semi-public agency subordinated to the Ministry of Labour and employing several thousand paid staff, is still subject to the 1901 law governing clubs and societies.

A French model of individual integration

In its political traditions, France has always favoured a model of integration based on the individual. This notion is found both in the French education system and policy towards immigrant populations. It is also to be found operating in continuing vocational education in the concept of "second chance". While other countries speak of the "community", France prefers to talk about the "territory", which is something quite different. **This reluctance to take communities into account, and the stress on the individual, doubtless have consequences for the field of basic education, as they have had in schools**. In this respect, the "collective" education that has been carried out particularly in the north and east of France at the instigation of Bertrand Schwartz is something of an exception.

A highly centralized, unequal education system

One feature of the French education system is the important role played by the state. Decentralization nonetheless transferred significant power to local groupings, and was accompanied by the splitting-up of some decision-making powers at the level of the regional *rectorats*, and by increased independence for those bodies. But this decentralization and splitting-up remained very limited, since the state retained its monopoly over:

- the recruitment and remuneration of teachers;
- the design of national curricula; and
- the awarding of university qualifications (the first level of which is the *baccalauréat*).

Another feature is that education grew very rapidly. As Paul Sylvestre remarks, "between 1950 and 1985, the school population rose from five to 14 Million pupils, almost triple the number".[7] At the present time, the total number of pupils, students, teachers and other staff working in the education system amounts to 28 percent of the population of the country.[8] Such a sudden growth was not without its problems. In particular, it brought a new population into secondary education which, by supplementing the traditional population of the *lycées*, raised problems of differing levels that the education system has still not resolved. School failure has thus been a recurrent topic of educational debate ever since the school system was (at least formally) unified.

Despite the democratization of education, school failure remains statistically closely linked to the level of education and social and occupational backgrounds of parents: 72 percent of the children of administrative staff achieve the *baccalauréat*, compared with 19 percent of the children of manual workers.[9] The education system is thus a poor observer of its principle of equality of opportunity, equal education leading to inequality in career paths.[10] This situation has been further aggravated at the present time by the fact that "given a similar level of qualification and social background, young people are less successful than their parents at entering the labour market."[11] Many young people face alternating periods of unemployment, training and temporary jobs, and they are bitterly disillusioned.

The difficulty of finding a first job

In 1981, the report by Bertrand Schwartz on young people's entry into society and the labour market revealed that 200,000 young people finished compulsory education with no qualifications or vocational training.[12] Since then, the figure has fallen markedly, to 88,000 pupils in 1991, according to an OECD report. Despite this progress, young people's entry into the labour market remains a troubling problem in France. In March 1994, 45.7 percent of 16-25 year-olds were in education or training. Some 850,000 were unemployed, 10.2 percent of the whole age group (compared with 9.4 percent in the previous year), and an unemployment rate of 23.2 percent (i.e., the percentage of young people in the labour market who were unemployed).

Moreover, 2.8 Million jobs occupied by young people, more than one in five, were under apprenticeship contracts or various job creation schemes. Of the 800,000 young people completing their studies each year, fewer than 60 percent were actually in the labour market nine months later (the others being in training, apprenticed, doing their national service, etc.). **Of the 60 percent, almost 45 percent were unemployed! The ease with which they could find a job was proportional to their level of education, young people with no qualifications suffering the worst.**[13]

From adult education to continuing vocational education

The law of 16 July 1971 on "Continuing Vocational Education within Lifelong Education" required businesses employing at least ten paid staff to contribute 0.8 percent of the total salaries and wages bill to the continuing education and training of their staff. This law was limited in some respects. Businesses kept absolute control over how their money was spent on education and training: the national education system no longer had a monopoly, nor did the state in a wider sense. **Above all, the training was of particular benefit to those who were already the best educated. It did not therefore perform its intended function of compensating for inequalities in initial education.**

The traditional sources of funding for public adult education thereby absolved themselves of the obligation. In a sense, it is no exaggeration to say that the 1971 law, which was peculiar to France, sounded the knell for public education, which withdrew, for good or ill, into socio-cultural programs and job entry training for "young" age groups.

On the other hand, this law — and the many that followed it (especially the law on individual educational leave), did create:

- a real education and training "market";
- a new occupational sector, with its own practices, rules and norms; and above all
- a new institutional framework (legislation on continuing vocational education was henceforward part of the labour code), which would not only serve not only for business but also for the state and regional groupings. In particular, the funds provided by the state for the struggle against *illettrisme* would increasingly be managed within that framework.

In 1994, the total spent on education and training rose to 131 Billion francs, funded largely by the state (46%) and business (39%), far ahead of the regions (5.9%) and UNEDIC, an agency with equal representation by employers and employees (5.8%). More than one person in three in the active population — 8.2 Million people — took 913 Million hours of continuing education and training. These figures put France in first place among European countries.

A tradition of literacy work

Having developed conveyor-belt production and drawn a good part of the former rural population into its factories, the French economy looked to the former colonies in the 1960s and '70s for the unskilled, cheap labour which it needed. Hence, a mass of unskilled workers and usually illiterate workers entered the French market, many of whom did not speak French (illiteracy sometimes being a condition of recruitment!).

The education offered to these populations, and in particular the literacy work, was generally carried out by the voluntary sector. Often, it was "militant" education, perceived above all as an instrument of emancipation and struggle against exploitation and oppression.

Immigration was abruptly slowed by the advent of the economic crisis in the mid-1970s. The official report of 1984 on *illettrisme* in France, by stressing those who were *illettrés* in French as a mother tongue, paid rather little attention to literacy among migrants, although they were particularly affected by unemployment.

However, over the years, this provision did serve a wide population, and gave rise to considerable educational research and production. Among the problems addressed and the ideas discussed, most did not generally concern the "immigrant" population and looked at the entire "disadvantaged" population: problems of social integration and labour market entry, the link between education and employment, and even problems of a cultural nature. As Gilles Verbunt puts it, "The presence of immigrants in France, and the discovery of their cultural differences, paradoxically led many educators to notice cultural differences also within the French population itself."[14]

If one compares the problems encountered in the struggle against *illettrisme* with those met with in literacy work with migrants, one quickly finds that the similarities are far greater than the differences.

Major problems of *illettrisme*

Since there are no exact common definitions and criteria, the various surveys conducted into *illettrisme* in France do not give us a precise figure for the population affected. The surveys of INSEE, for example, include people who do not speak French. The surveys carried out among young recruits to military service measure the reading performance of male persons in a very restricted age group. It is therefore only be means of extrapolations that it is possible to conclude, as certain media have not been slow to do, that "one French person in five is *illettré*." In fact, figures can vary from one study to another by a factor of two. The OECD survey conducted in a number of industrialized countries does not mention France.[15]

In any event, even if the statistics have to be viewed with caution, they suggest orders of magnitude which are worrying and are closely relevant to the conclusions of the 1984 official report "On the *Illettrés* in France": "The number of complete illiterates is certainly small; however, it can be stated that the number of people without mastery of reading and writing or facing serious difficulties in applying these must be counted in Millions rather than in hundreds of thousands."[16]

THE INSTITUTIONAL FRAMEWORK OF THE STRUGGLE AGAINST *ILLETTRISME*

French policy

This is the background to the actions taken by the GPLI. Unlike most other European countries, France did not make use of the national education system to implement its policy of "struggle against *illettrisme*", or of its tradition of public adult education, or even of continuing vocational education. Nor did it draw on its experience of literacy work with people with a foreign mother tongue, and still less on literacy in developing countries. Instead, at least in the early stages, it turned to existing social work in order to create a new area of activity.

The approach was primarily concerned with *poverty* and exclusion. In the context of a program combating poverty, the Council of Ministers stated its position on 26 January 1983 as follows:

> Illiteracy is a major obstacle to any coherent policy of socialization and entry into the world of work. An interministerial group has just been set up to draw up a diagnostic report and to make proposals. Moreover, the initiatives already taken in this field, notably by voluntary associations and social workers, will be encouraged.

The group in question met between January and July 1983, and the official report "On the *Illettrés* in France" was published in 1984 on the basis of its work. This policy, which was intended to be a policy of general mobilization, made full use of *unpaid work* and hence of the *voluntary sector*. In the early 1980s, as will be seen, many examples of initiatives taken in the struggle against *illettrisme* by social workers relied on unpaid help, which led to the establishment of voluntary associations to carry on the struggle.

Given this general mobilization approach, another concept was also widely promoted, that of *partnership*. At the national level, the GPLI was an interministerial group, and at the local level, collaboration between institutions was encouraged.

In the twelve years of its existence, the French approach to the struggle against *illettrisme* has changed considerably. At the outset, the role of the GPLI was seen as that of awareness-raising, stimulation and co-ordination. The GPLI had a modest permanent staff and its own budget. Over the years, it acquired a national network of regional and *département* agents, which enabled it to expand its presence. It also had increasing funds allocated to the struggle against *illettrisme* (55 Million francs in 1995). These funds were for vocational education and training, managed in a decentralized manner by regional representatives for labour, employment and vocational education.

This feature, in combination with a concern increasingly focusing on "employment" and "employability", helped to make the purpose of the struggle against *illettrisme* into that of *continuing vocational education*. More and more of those involved chose to speak of "basic education", a less demeaning term. The tools available, and the training of the educators, were also based on this reasoning, which led in turn to a professionalization of the sector.

The legislative framework

Unlike the situation in some European countries, the French approach of a struggle against *illettrisme* did not rest on one particular law. At most, the internal circulars of various ministries were concerned with the issue of *illettrisme*: the Ministries of National Education, Labour, Justice, Defence, etc. The most significant official action was without doubt the creation of the Standing Group to Combat *Illettrisme* (GPLI), followed by the decision to set up regional and *département* agents throughout the country.

The legislative framework to which reference was made became, without anyone's noticing it, that of continuing vocational education. This was also the framework within which the major part of the funds for the struggle against *illettrisme* was managed.

The GPLI has been at the heart of the approach since, on the one hand, it is responsible for handling general policy and, on the other, it gives coherence to the work of the various national partners and to national and local planning. Numerous institutions are represented on the Governing Board of the GPLI: ministries, secretariats of state, government departments, public and semi-public agencies, voluntary associations, etc. The chairman of the GPLI is an elected politician appointed by the Prime Minister. It has a permanent staff headed by a Secretary General, whose role is to implement the guidelines laid down by the Governing Board by stimulating and coordinating the action taken by the various partners of the GPLI.

At first, the GPLI was attached to the Ministry of Social Affairs and National Solidarity, and was then moved to the Ministry of Labour and Vocational Training, which has since become the Ministry of

Labour and Social Affairs.

The regional and *département* agents of the GPLI play the same role of stimulating and coordinating action at the local level as the GPLI itself at national level. However, these agents carry out their duties in connection with the struggle against *illettrisme* in addition to their usual activities.

Each ministry and major government department is involved in accordance with its field of operation: National Education in preventing school failure and in teacher training; Culture in providing access to libraries, Labour in training those seeking work and employees with "low skill levels", Social Affairs in combating exclusion, Justice in preventing delinquency and providing education for prisoners, and Defence in providing education for conscripts.

There is thus a twofold aim: to enable the GPLI to benefit from the knowledge of the different ministries and departments, and to encourage these to incorporate the struggle against *illettrisme* into their several policies. By involving the different ministries and departments, the struggle against *illettrisme* covers a very wide range of activities.

Decentralization and derogation

The publication of the official report "On the *Illettrés* in France" and the establishment of the GPLI came shortly after the adoption of laws on decentralization (1982-1983), which passed the responsibility for social work to *départements* and that for continuing vocational education and apprenticeship to the regions. These transfers of responsibilities did not of themselves do away with the role of the state: far from it, since regional expenditure on continuing education was, until the five-year law of 1993, only 20 percent of the total public funding.

Decentralization not only created a new level of regional power through the new responsibilities given to the regions and *départements*, but it was accompanied by a policy of *splitting up* some state decision making at regional and *département* level.

- Thus, the regional councils, as part of their responsibilities for vocational education and apprenticeship, were able to fund initiatives for people who were *illettrés*, but the Regional Labour, Employment and Vocational Education Directorate also played an important part in managing derogated state funds, particularly those for the struggle against *illettrisme*. Regional policies could henceforward be combined with those of the state in "State-

Regional Planning Contracts" laying down joint policies over a number of years.

- The *départements* could do more within the context of their responsibilities for social work. Their projects therefore fell largely into the area of combating exclusion. Through "urban policy", the prefectures of the *départements* played a major part in responding to those seeking work.

- The municipalities could act under several headings: social work, urban policy, prevention of delinquency, etc.

From the early 1990s, "*illettrisme* resource centres" were opened at regional and *département* level. These resource centres, usually co-funded by different partners, played a role which went well beyond that of mere documentation centres: they organized awareness-raising and information days, trained educators and even carried out action-research.

Partnership

The voluntary sector has been widely involved in the struggle against *illettrisme*: not only local but also regional and even national associations, some of which are represented on the GPLI Board. This also has representatives from charitable associations such as ATD-Quart Monde, popular education movements such as the Léo Lagrange Association, associations for the education of migrants such as CLAP, which are increasingly dealing with people of French mother tongue, and more "educational" movements such as the French Reading Association, which has wide membership among teachers and is widely known for its teaching materials, etc. At the local level, the voluntary associations carry out the bulk of the activities of receiving enquiries, giving information, teaching, and socialization.

Business devotes considerable sums to the continuing training of its staff. But in most companies, the least educated population is not the priority for training. As Elisabeth Charlon has observed, "for every hundred trainees in a company, six are unskilled, while these make up 16 percent of the total number of employees."[17] Moreover, depending on the sector of activity and the size of the company, the chances of an unskilled worker's being offered training can vary from 1 to 40. Some businesses have nonetheless become aware of the problems posed by the underqualification of their staff. Unfortunately, it has often been at times of "social plans" (mass redundancies) that education and training have been provided for people with "low levels of skills". When they do not provide their own training, companies usually turn to private training agencies rather than to the voluntary sector.

By virtue of the staff involved, and the interest in educational experimentation which is to be found in it, business is a major partner in the French basic education approach.

The teachers

The teachers are of course a key element in the approach. The variation in their status and profiles reflects that of the agencies which employ them. A significant number are unpaid. Often, those who are paid have no job security, being on temporary, part-time or sessional contracts, etc. They also vary widely in qualifications, experience and motivation. Their training tends, if not uniform, at least towards being structured and standardized. The coexistence of paid and unpaid staff sometimes poses problems.

The place of the *illettrés* in the picture

So far, little attention has been given to the *illettrés,* although in principle the entire setup is for their benefit. It has to be said that because of the multiplicity of approaches and ways of speaking about them, it is difficult to gain an exact impression of them, especially as they are themselves seldom the ones who talk about *illettrisme*. In the absence of a sufficiently reliable definition and criteria, the various national quantitative studies have to be handled with care.

The qualitative studies of the field reveal a kaleidoscope of widely varying situations, reporting on populations thought to be at greatest "risk" of *illettrisme,* and ranging from "fourth world" people in situations of extreme exclusion to people whose culture has not yet fully incorporated the written word, such as boat-people (on inland waterways) and gypsies, and including young people who "resist" the culture of the school, people with low levels of skills who are in search of work, etc. Aside from their common negative characteristics of failure to master skills associated with the written word, it is questionable how much they have in common besides being the targets of different aspects of the struggle against *illettrisme*.

HOW THE APPROACH WORKS

Decision-making and funding

The general policy guidelines are laid down by the GPLI and its Governing Board. However, over and above these general guidelines, a ministry can decide to devote particular effort to one aspect or another of the struggle against *illettrisme*. For example, the Ministry of National Education may decide on special measures to improve the learning and development of reading at school, or the Ministry of Labour and Vocational Education may decide to reserve some vocational training places for people who are *illettrés*. Once these decisions are taken at the national level, the relevant funds are apportioned at regional and *département* level.

The regional and local authorities (regions, *départements* and municipalities) are, for their part, entirely autonomous in deciding whether to allocate funds to combating *illettrisme* and in choosing the agencies which they will use. Similarly, companies have complete autonomy in how they design their training policies.

Out of the GPLI's budget of 55 Million francs in 1995, around 44 Million were devoted to regional programs: 2.3 Million to those run with the Ministry of Defence, 4.5 Million to those run with the Ministry of Justice, and 4.4 Million to other national programs. These funds involved a large number of partners and projects.[18]

To these funds should be added those allocated by the various ministries to preventing and combating *illettrisme*: the funds of the Social Action Fund, with which extensive collaboration has developed; the funds of the regional and local authorities ; the funds allotted by the European Social Fund ; the budgets devoted by companies to the continuing education of their staffs, the help received from foundations, etc.

The significant sums represented by these funds have created a "market" for training agencies, teacher training agencies, publishers of educational materials, research centres, counselling agencies, etc. They have also helped to establish a new occupational sector.

Relations between partners

Since activities are generally arranged on a contractual basis, in a market framework, it is possible to distinguish between the funding and commissioning agencies on the one hand (the GPLI, the ministries, government departments, regional and local authorities, and business), and the bodies which provide services locally or nationally, on the other (voluntary associations, and public and private continuing education agencies). The negotiations between the various ministries and administrations concerned can take place in the Governing Board of the GPLI or, for more important decisions, through the usual channels (the Council of Ministers). Similarly, at the regional and local level, or between different levels, they follow the normal procedures.

The relationships between decision-makers and service providers are always set out contractually, sometimes through a tendering process. In an education and training market, educational agencies are in competition. Some regional services which manage decentralized funds for continuing vocational education have nonetheless tried to establish more lasting, deeper relationships with selected agencies that agree to submit to criteria of educational quality laid down in a charter. An example is provided by the Upper Normandy Region and the "basic education workshops" network which it set up, or by the Brittany Region and its "Permanent Workshops to Combat *Illettrisme*".

Cooperation has also been established at *département* level between agencies working in various geographical areas, often at the instigation of the *département* agents of the GPLI.

From unpaid work to the market

Among the agencies of widely varying type and status are to be found public institutions, voluntary associations, private training agencies, etc. However, the vast majority are voluntary associations. These may consist entirely of unpaid workers, but may also employ paid staff. The peculiar situation then arises that a governing board made up of unpaid volunteers manages what may be substantial funds and employs the paid staff of the association. Many of the unpaid volunteers have no preparation for this role, which explains the difficulties encountered by numerous associations.

Many associations involved in combating *illettrisme* were set up in the early 1980s on an unpaid basis, often with the help or at the initiative of social workers. Their aim was largely to serve those left out of account by the system, whose very low level of education did not enable them to take part in the continuing education schemes established by the state.

Gradually, in order to obtain funding, these associations adopted the reasoning of the funding agencies, which was increasingly that of continuing vocational education and training. The associations thus became more and more like other agencies of continuing education, or were at least subject to the same constraints. If the associations recruited paid staff, especially teachers, they were often forced to implement certain measures in order to maintain the jobs created.

Over the years, there has thus been a definite slide, from the dyad of social workers and voluntary associations combating *illettrisme,* to that of basic education agencies and public authorities, based on a continuing education and training market and on one-off contracts for which education providers compete. The problem is that this major change has taken place within the self-same associations, with the self-same people. The change has often brought about some distortion within associations, which have been faced with a choice between hanging on to the values which led to the creation of the association, and the need to adapt to the new context, if only to ensure that the association survives.

Partnership seen from below

The GPLI had largely based its activities on "partnership" with the aim of mobilizing the maximum number of partners. At the grassroots level, it must be said that this partnership was not viewed in the same way. At the risk of simplification, it is tempting to say that they saw it only in a "negative" sense.

- What was called the "linkage between the national and local levels" was seen very differently by those running associations, who were constantly being referred from one level to another: the region, in the belief that it was not a matter of continuing vocational education but of social work, referred them to the *département,* which in turn thought that it was a school issue and passed them on to the Ministry of National Education, and so on.

- "Partnership between institutions" did not exist spontaneously. It often proved very difficult to make the different public authorities work together. Associations had either to seek out the various institutional partners and convince them to help mount a project, or to reply to invitations to tender issued by the various partners.

That means that each association was obliged to work with a significant number of partners in widely varying projects and programs (basic education workshops, training for job-seekers, socialization training, prison education, urban policy, CES and RMI training, etc.), each project naturally having its own tendering, implementation and evaluation procedures. For those running associations, that meant considerable time spent in "ringing front-door bells" and filling out forms.

- This situation obliged the associations, if they wanted to survive, to go on adapting to the one-off schemes launched by the various ministries and government departments. Not only did that constraint cause some associations entirely to lose sight of their original aims, but in some cases also their identity. Moreover, it precluded any long-term policy, which was prejudicial not only to the associations but also to those who were primarily interested, the adults undergoing education and training.

From personal development to basic skills

The changing context of the struggle against *illettrisme* had an influence on the very nature of the education and training provided. The associations which had attacked *illettrisme* at the outset did so in the name of certain values: the restoration of human dignity, in the case of charitable associations, political and social emancipation in the popular education movement, etc. These values implied an educational approach focusing on personal development.

The change in the demands made by the various decision-makers meant that this overall aim had to move closer to that of continuing vocational education. The various funding bodies, particularly in the present economic situation, have become increasingly preoccupied with the *employment* and *employability* of the trainees. Employability ranges from education leading to qualifications to the acquisition of vocational skills. The term *basic education* became associated with that of *basic skills*. Education thus became ever more technical training, focusing on the acquisition of basic skills. The notion of "benchmarks" for basic skills and "basic knowledge" began to spread.

CONCLUSION

Ten years ago, the GPLI was intended to be a simple structure set up to stimulate others. It now has a large secretariat, a national network of regional and *département* agents, and a considerable budget. At grassroots level, 21,000 people took part in 1995 in activities funded specifically under the heading *illettrisme*, and some 300 agencies were involved nationally. To these figures should be added all those persons and agencies that took part in activities to combat *illettrisme* through schemes set up under other legislation.

This scheme has essentially been run under the rubric of continuing vocational education: the specific funding has been for vocational education and training and social advancement, which are handled by the decentralized services of the state. Everything has been done as though a specific section had been set up within the national policy of continuing vocational education to combat *illettrisme*.

What will be the long-term effect of this professionalization on the existing voluntary associations? For the moment, it rests on a contradiction:

- an ever stronger demand for quality and professionalism on the part of the agencies involved, especially the voluntary associations; and

- a renewed reliance on unpaid work and the voluntary sector.

Will France follow the example of the Netherlands and the Flemish Community of Belgium, which have set up a real public adult basic education scheme (that leaves out unpaid volunteers)? Or will it continue to make use of the voluntary sector? It has to be recognized that, the way things have turned out, the voluntary sector has been caught in something of a trap. It carries out national and regional policies which it has had no part in deciding.

It is true that the funds devoted to combating *illettrisme* have grown considerably in France and that the grassroots associations have far more money than they used to. At the same time, the market, contracts and competition have made them far weaker since they are heavily dependent on funding bodies for their survival, having taken on paid staff. They are in danger of becoming interchangeable elements of the basic education market. While they played an extremely active part in the early 1980s in raising awareness and launching innovations, they have become mere providers of services.

It should be remembered that in France, the voluntary associations account for the bulk of the work on the ground. Local projects do not happen "spontaneously", at the behest of the people concerned; if they are to happen, they require the creation of an association, usually with the help of unpaid volunteers, and often with the support of professionals, especially social workers, who become temporary "promoters of local development".

In the light of the new situation of the struggle against *illettrisme*, what strategy might the voluntary associations adopt? In our view, it should have two aspects:

- to take advantage of the positive developments in terms of professionalism: a better integration of the professional dimension in training, a more rigorous approach to teaching and evaluation, and improved training for teachers; and

- to maintain their individuality and to go on defending the values, principles and aims which lay behind their creation, especially the attention given to the most disadvantaged populations within a global perspective of education that is not restricted to vocational skills. They should also, in our view, retain their "political" dimension, which is their *raison d'être*, and their role of influencing opinion and public authorities.

In order to respond to this double challenge, voluntary associations have to undertake two difficult tasks:

- not to reject unpaid volunteers, but to review the conditions under which they take part in the life of the association, and to find their proper place within it; and

- to redefine their own place in the general environment of basic education, which means establishing new partnerships and alliances with public authorities, businesses and local groupings. From this point of view, it is they that can compensate for the lack of real partnership between institutions.

All of this presupposes changes within the associations themselves, which can no longer operate as they did when they were composed of unpaid volunteers with the guidance of social workers. It is no longer possible to count the number of basic education associations that have had to call in auditors to get them out of impossible situations.

But it also assumes changes in the relationships between associations: the context of continuing vocational education has placed them in competition with each other, which contributes to their weakness. They will only be able to make their collective voice heard if they form a strong enough block. It is up to the voluntary sector to recover the initiative.

Notes

1. GPLI. 1996. *Répertoire de la recherche: Illettrisme, accès et rapport á l'écrit.* Paris: Ministry of Labour and Social Affairs.

2. 'Dartois, Colette. 1996. Savoirs de base: de quoi s'agit-it? *Educations* 8, March-May.

3. Lebaube Alain. 1995. Employ et travail. Grandes tendances. *L'état de la France 95-96.* Paris: La Découverte.

4. Gilles, Marie-Odile & Legor, Michel. 1995. Our certains, le travail d'empêche plus pauvreté. *Consommation et Modes de vie* 100, September-October.

5. Paugam, Serge; Zoyem, Jean-Paul & Charbonnel, Jean-Miche. 1994. Précariteé et risque d'exclusion en France. *Documents du CERC* 109. Paris: la Documentation française.

6. *Alternatives économiques*, supplement 26. 1995, 4th quarter.

7. Sylvestre, Paul. L'école aujourd'hui. Fonctions et dysfonctionnnements. *Sciences humaines* 10, October.

8. Emin, Jean-Calue & Fallouard, Pierre. 1996. Létat du système éducatif français. *INSEE: Données sociales.*

9. Estrade, Marc-Antoine. 1995.Les inégalités devant l'école. Influence du milieu social et familial. *INSEE Première* 400, September.

10. Ibid.

11. Ibid.

12. Schwartz, Bertrand. 1981. *L'insertion professionnelle et sociale des jeuns: Rapport au Prier Ministre.* Paris: La Documentation française.

13. Balan, Danièle & Minni, Claude. 1995. De l'école à l'emploi. Les jeunes en mars 1994. *INSEE Première* 365, March.

14. Verbunt, Gilles. 1994. Le formateur confronté aux différeces culturelles. *Hommes et migrations* 1177, June, p. 7.

15. OECD. 1995. *Literacy, Economy and Society. Results of the first international survey of adult education.* Paris: OECD.

16. Espérandieu, Véronique & Lion, Antoine (with Benichou, Jean-Pierre). 1984. *Des illettrés en France. Rapport au Premier Ministre*. Paris: La Documentation française.

17. Charlon, Elisabeth. 1996. Du côté de l'entreprise. *Educations* March-May.

18. GPLI. 1996. *Lutte contre l'illettrisme. Bilan des actions et programmes de travail 1995-96*. Paris: GPLI.

Chapter Ten
30 YEARS OF LITERACY WORK IN BELGIUM: WHERE HAS IT GOT US?

Catherine Stercq
Literacy Collective
Brussels, Belgium

In spring 1996, at the time of starting this article, secondary education (12-18 years) has been on strike for six weeks. The issue at stake is the abolition of 3,000 teaching posts as from September 1997, the "last straw" of five years of successive budget cuts. These cuts have also affected adult education, personal services, culture, and so on: cuts across the board, combined with huge national and regional public deficits in the interest of creating a European economy. The cuts have led to attempts at institutional destabilization (separatism and transfers of responsibilities in all directions) and a breakdown of policy, against a background of social, cultural and economic underdevelopment.

I can only hope therefore that this report on the relations between adult basic education policies and recent local initiatives will help to *preserve what has been achieved*.

Today, our task is not to create an institutional environment that will encourage community initiatives and link basic education with citizenship rights. This environment already largely exists. Four elements are basic to an understanding of it:

- a strong and dynamic voluntary tradition which plays a part in policy-making and has developed the sector of education for adults with little previous schooling;

- an absence of literacy and adult basic education policy and practice within the Ministry of Education;
- a recognition of literacy and basic education in cultural policies and policies linking these practices with citizenship rights; and
- a place for literacy and basic education in regional social integration and labour market entry policies, co-funded by the European Communities.

Our task today is:

- to defend what has been achieved and is under serious threat;
- to admit that there is often a wide gap between practice and discussion of it, and that there are many dysfunctions, unintended negative effects and contradictions;
- to investigate the causes; and
- to explore possible new perspectives.

I propose to develop these points, using the history of the Literacy Collective (*Collectif d'alphabétisation*), in which I have been involved for 25 years, as the starting point. For 30 years, the Literacy Collective has been organizing literacy courses for adults in Brussels, in working-class areas with a high proportion of immigrants.

30 years ago: a dozen unpaid staff; today, 30 full-time paid staff

30 years ago: refusal of any form of funding; today, a constant quest for funds

30 years ago: a public composed of organized workers; today, the majority are unemployed, isolated and increasingly marginalized

30 years ago: an association set up to meet the needs of a community; today, what are we playing at?

In order to answer this question, I have tried to uncover the history of the association, to find out who has been involved and what their interests were, where there have been breaks, and where there has been continuity.

1967 — A POLITICAL PROJECT: THE DEVELOPMENT OF A COMMUNITY

At the outset, in 1967, militants from an immigrant community who were involved in trade union activity turned to Belgian teachers to give literacy courses to workers from the community in the premises of a trade union branch office. There were three bodies involved: the immigrant community, Belgian teachers, and a trade union, with three purposes that informed the discussion and the disagreements for the first ten years of the association's existence: immigration, trade union and political commitment, and the teaching of literacy. There was then no mention of exclusion, citizenship or labour market entry and socialization. And although the term literacy was used, no one talked about illiterates.

This was the "golden sixties". At that time of full employment, Belgian employers recruited workers from the countries of the South. Decolonization was recent, and the development of the South was in vogue. It was the eve of the cultural revolution of May '68. Liberation theology and pedagogy were the order of the day. Numerous Marxist groups were created, of varying tendencies.

The project

In this context, the immigrant militants designed a literacy project on the basis of their assessment of the situation of immigrant workers, both in their countries of origin and in Belgium. *Their aim was economic and democratic development in their countries of origin*. Literacy and vocational training were to be tools of development when these workers returned to their countries.

Our association was therefore born in the context of the development of a community, but a particular context, as the development was that of the country of origin. Literacy and vocational training were *"to change their situation back there"*.[1]

The trade union

For the group of immigrant militants, the trade union was the workers' organization. Everyone had the right to a corner where they could organize themselves and take on responsibilities, within a united working class. Further, the trade union represented a safe haven which offered protection and confidence in the face of the political policies of the time.

Three areas of distinct responsibility were marked out: teaching methodology, which was the role of the group of teachers (who were to teach French), the organization of courses and workers, in the hands of the immigrant group (who were to teach courses in arithmetic and the mother tongue), and the premises, the responsibility of the trade union. It goes without saying that this situation led to many disagreements with the trade union that was unaccustomed to autonomous groups within it making their own arrangements.

The teachers

To begin with, most of the teachers were university lecturers, conscious of the underdevelopment of immigration and with close ties to the trade union or various Marxist groups. Their commitment centred on what is now coyly called "North-South links", and was then called "economic imperialism". Over the years, this group renewed itself and expanded, notably by the addition of manual and clerical workers who were involved in various ways in trade union activities.

The teachers defined themselves as *"a group of democrats carrying out anti-imperialist work"*, and saw their activities in a political context: "It is a matter of addressing the mass of immigrant workers here for whom reading and writing are a necessity ... Literacy becomes a means of fighting against the underdevelopment caused by imperialism." They were engaged in a project serving immigrant workers, and "motivated by opposition to all exploitation and all repression in a spirit of militant democracy."

In 1974, the teachers drew up a manifesto that defined

> the political aims of the literacy courses from a global perspective: to give workers the means to understand the world outside and their own situation in relation to it; to enable them to master the economic and political mechanisms which govern these relations so that they can free themselves from the exploitation, domination and repression to which they are subjected by imperialism in all its forms ... to organize and develop forms of struggle to transform social, economic and political relationships so as to establish the bases of a new society.

Their pedagogical guidelines were:

- to present an alternative to the dominator/dominated relationship which was typical of the traditional mode of transmitting knowledge;
- to arouse collective responsibility among the workers; and
- to raise the workers' level of conceptualization.

Lastly, they organized themselves in an autonomous "literacy group" and set out to develop literacy by:

- creating new experiences;
- expanding links with other groups working on the same basis; and
- providing information to other groups about literacy and immigration issues.

This did not all go smoothly. There was a significant turnover in the teaching force, and arguments were needed to make them arrive regularly and on time, and to take their responsibilities seriously. It was not easy working in partnership, and the many conflicts between different tendencies within the immigrant community, and the allocation of the tasks defined at the outset, quickly focused on the teachers' contribution of teaching methodology. Here too, the gap between what was said and what was done was sometimes a wide one.

Many discussions were held in these early years. They concerned the target population — "There is no question of giving priority to workers who are already coping passably well; we have to address the great mass of illiterates from the mountains and the countryside" — the aims, organization and functioning of the group, political commitment and educational aspects — notably the refusal to use textbooks — and funding.

1967-1976 — REFUSAL

For the first ten years of its operation, the group of teachers, who came together voluntarily, refused all forms of funding, whether from the trade union or public authorities. The teachers thought that they would lose their independence if they accepted it, and that money was "an ideal way of controlling the courses, and hence a large proportion of the immigrant class."

Later, the group split into those who thought that they should accept the funding that was offered, and those who preached rejection. All agreed on the need to "guarantee the independence of the group from all official institutions". There was also general agreement that acceptance of the money would not in fact bring about a loss of independence. Rejection was based on other arguments: "Carrying out political activity with means that go beyond our real needs is dangerous. Politics must be in command. It is the political imagination and the militant spirit that must ensure the continuity of our experiment."

Eventually, in December 1976, when the group had laid down ethical rules for funding and had restated that money "is never given freely and that every time it is necessary to examine carefully both sides of the exchange", it accepted a funding proposal from the "Immigrant Action" fund of the Ministry of Culture.

After this first application for a subsidy, a new phase was quickly opened up: the remuneration of full-time teachers in programs run by the Ministry of Labour to reduce unemployment.

1976 — From the Third World to Belgium

More than seven years after the group was founded, for the first time references appeared, in connection with funding, to the public authorities as actors in the literacy project. Until then, the topics, problems, statements of principle and partnership had all been related to the trade union. If the state had been present, it was as the abstract target of anti-imperialist utterances. The reality had been the workers, employers, trade unions, and the context of the exploitation of the South for the benefit of the North. Our links with the state were not related to literacy but to immigration and the investigation of its cause: imperialism. We demonstrated for the legalization of illegal immigrants and supported national liberation movements and striking workers.

Up till then, our political purpose had not been literacy but the fight against underdevelopment. The first application for a grant occurred at a moment when the project was teetering between *a political project to combat Third World underdevelopment and a political project to develop literacy in Belgium*.

This break was against a background of:

- an economic crisis and growing unemployment;
- the emergence of the issue of illiteracy in industrialized countries;
- the development by the public authorities of policies of lifelong education and reducing unemployment; and
- the development of adult education within the voluntary sector.

The economic crisis and growing unemployment, and the failure of liberation movements, brought about the end to hopes of a return to the home country and disorganized the immigrant militants who had started the literacy project. The extreme left-wing movements disappeared, leaving no real political alternative. In this context, the group of teachers fell back on the area for which it had been made responsible: teaching methodology and literacy.

With the economic crisis there emerged the awareness of the persistence of illiteracy in Belgian society. ATD Quart-Monde, and then the European Communities, called on governments to recognize the continued existence of illiteracy. The campaigns of ATD and the campaign conducted in the United Kingdom, and the timid appearance of Belgians in our groups of immigrant workers, provided the justification for our project of "literacy development".

Among the public authorities, two policies were to be of major importance for the development of the voluntary sector in general, and for adult education in particular: the decree on lifelong education issued by the Ministry of Culture, and the programs of the Ministry of Labour to reduce unemployment.

In April 1976, the French Community adopted a decree on lifelong education, which had been obtained by workers' movements in order to fund political action in adult education. This decree recognized and gave funding to:

- voluntary lifelong education organizations which are led and managed by private persons and aim to bring about and to develop, principally among adults:
- awareness and critical recognition of the realities of the society;
- the ability to analyze and choose, to act and to evaluate;
- attitudes of responsibility and active participation in social, economic, cultural and political life.

> In order to carry out such education, each organization shall use the methods and techniques which are best suited to the aims intended and to the needs defined by the populations concerned.[2]

As can be seen, the aims set out by our association in 1974 fitted perfectly into this framework. Given our position on funding, we nonetheless did not ask for recognition until 1982.

The Ministry of Labour set up programs to reduce unemployment. Voluntary sector projects might help to create jobs. "Special temporary posts" of limited duration in fact became an open-ended "third track of employment". They were widely derided as being "sub-status". Some people consistently refused to have anything to do with them, but most made wide use of them. These programs became of major importance for our association.

At first sight, there was no connection between these two policies other than the simultaneous offer of "capital" to the same "clients", and the nature of those "clients': workers' movements and voluntary movements, which had always been the pillars of Belgian social organization. It was, however, the conjunction of the two that made it possible — with the support of European funding — to set up associations of a new type, termed "development, employment, training and socialization associations".

The first of these associations, FUNOC, was established in Charleroi in June 1977. It stated its purpose as follows:

> To offer to the working public and anyone with a low level of education the opportunity of education in which they can acquire the tools of analysis necessary to master their environment, and the intellectual means necessary to resolve their problems. In this perspective, it will develop a growing number of activities that will take account of the objective educational needs of adults with little previous schooling: the need for education associated with vocational and social skills; and the need for basic education that is a prerequisite for all other skills.

Other, similar associations were set up in the major cities in the country. In 1982, their common declaration stated their approach to be as follows:

> These associations have thus developed integrated action within their regions. Firstly, these associations coordinate and involve educational, cultural and social institutions by seeking to make maximum use of their resources.... Secondly, these associations attempt to build up

educational provision which will give basic education to people who have need of it, as an indispensable precondition for access to vocational training and participation in social, political and cultural life.

In fact, in the context of economic crisis, they were to design, create and run — *in the place of the public authorities* — a network of education for adults with little previous schooling.

The words "disadvantaged", "excluded" and "illiterate" made their appearance. In these short extracts, the emphasis on both the aspect of *employment* (vocational skills) and on that of *lifelong education* (social, cultural and political skills) is also noticeable. This peculiarity was linked with the definition of the projects in terms of the needs of adults with low levels of education that were encountered by the associations, with the militant profile of the associations, and with the policies outlined above: employment, and especially the decree on lifelong education that legitimized political and cultural action.

There was also, for the first time, a reference to the Ministry of Education: on the one hand, to denounce widespread school failure, the persistence of illiteracy despite the existence of compulsory school education since 1919, the mismatch between initial education and the changing society, and the almost total lack of basic education for adults; on the other, to seek recognition as a partner (open university projects) or recognition of training and to obtain certification. There was — and still is — huge resistance and refusal to collaborate, not only with the voluntary movement but also with other ministries. There was — and still is — no public "second chance education" service.

Hence in 1983, on the basis of the experience of the Literacy Collective and ATD Quart-Monde, the development, employment and socialization organizations set up *Lire et Ecrire*, a pluralist association which set itself the aim of launching a widespread literacy campaign throughout the French Community. This campaign would lead to the creation of a literacy network based on unpaid voluntary work. The French Community thereby acquired a basic education system at low cost (60% of the literacy teachers were unpaid).

In spite of its links with the grassroots and its good intentions, the literacy campaign had numerous undesirable effects:

- the designation of a proportion of the population as illiterate, this designation rather than their illiteracy itself causing their exclusion;

- rapid mass recruitment of many new teachers who had been brought up with the emotional sensitivity of the "cultured classes";
- the development of an academic type of literacy, despite the aims of lifelong education, due to the lack of guidance, training and reflection among the teachers; and
- the development of a "service provision" approach with little attention to community development.

1977-84 — A POLITICAL PURPOSE: THE DEVELOPMENT OF LITERACY

For our organization, this period was one of transformation, expansion and rapid changes, and of coming to terms with change:

- the first paid staff;
- the creation of a documentation centre for teachers;
- the expansion of courses in other neighbourhoods;
- the renegotiation of the partnership between the trade union and the immigrant militants;
- new partnerships;
- participation in the literacy campaign and the creation of *Lire et Ecrire;*
- participation in vocational retraining projects;
- expansion of the target population to women, Belgians, and a growing number of nationalities;
- the change from 30 to 300 people being educated each year. etc.

This period was marked by a move away from reflection and pedagogical practice and policy. Attention was concentrated on organization: the solving of accommodation problems, administration and training for new teachers.

In 1982, the questions raised in evaluation related to the status of teachers, internal organization, and the direction taken by our courses. In 1983, the problems raised were funds, the employment of teachers, the expansion of our services in order to respond better to needs, links with the Ministry of Education, and the real prospects of jobs and socialization. Such questions are still current!

The year 1984 was one of stabilization. Projects developed that were driven by people now called "participants" rather than "workers": newspapers, drama, and a highway code workshop. Reception procedures were rethought, and courses also became workshops. Stabilization — the structures and teachers were in place — enabled attention to be given once more to teaching methodology and the direction to be taken by the association. A new manifesto was written, stressing "policy aims", now focusing on literacy and the Belgian context "because we think that in our society, illiteracy is an obstacle to democracy", and mentioning the problems of exclusion that are still current: "illiterate people, who do not have the necessary tools, are indeed excluded from real participation in social, occupational, cultural and political life."

Given the involvement of professional teachers, the issue of unpaid voluntary work was raised for the first time. Paid staff had opened day-time courses, and volunteers were continuing evening courses. The militants who had been behind the project had gradually become engaged by the association or had started other associations. There were then a large number of unpaid volunteers. We were worried by the difficulties of coordinating and training these tutors, and of involving them in the association. In the light of these difficulties, we decided some years later no longer to use unpaid staff.

The activity report stressed teacher training and team working, which made it possible to "deschool" our work as intended in 1984. But, despite redefining our aims and making pedagogical changes, the issue of the direction of our activities remained:

> The issue of post-literacy, socialization and labour market entry is becoming increasingly evident among our unemployed public, for whom the prospects of a job are almost nil. Some will, of course, find work or realize their professional "aims", and others will enrol in vocational training. But for many, for whom work would have meant socialization, the notion of "going to school in order to learn to read and write" has been turned on its head and has become "learning to read and write in order to go to school". Attendance at a literacy centre is a social experience and becomes an aim in itself.

In the light of this situation, which contradicts our aims and the role we

> defined for ourselves, we have to ask ourselves some questions. Literacy by itself does not guarantee a job or socialization. It has to be part of a wider project, which is neither that of going to school nor that of learning to read, but that of learning to read *in order to* [do other things].

The question of purpose was that much more pressing because 65 percent of our public were over 45 years of age at that time. The purpose of our work was perhaps (certainly?) to provide a sort of transition for "first generation" immigrant workers between active life and sudden, compulsory early retirement, a bridge between hopes of returning to the home country and definitive settlement in Belgium.

In 1985, the partnership with the trade union and the immigrant militants that had launched our association came to an end although, in principle, we continued to stress the importance of the link with the union "which can support our claims for such things as the right to education for all", and "the importance of offering participants the chance of acquiring literacy in their mother tongue."

Instead, we emphasized other partners:

> The presence of different associations (medical organizations, homework clubs, immigrant associations, youth support groups... enables us to respond better to the issues that arise in urban areas and hence to plan integrated action. We believe that the presence of these different associations encourages encounters between Belgians and immigrants and mutual respect for each language and culture.

1985 — A POLITICAL PURPOSE: PERSONAL AND CULTURAL DEVELOPMENT

During the preceding period, we had succeeded in developing literacy, but we had lost the sense of the activity. In order to find an answer to this question of purpose, we focused on pedagogy, which had the effect of making us swing from community development to personal development, from the definition of a concept of literacy work to the development of the "illiterate" personality.

We should like to quote two pedagogical texts, one from 1975 and the other from 1985, both of them "political", and to examine the differences.

1975

Last year, the group organized solidarity with the strike in Court-Saint-Etienne ...

Our courses this year will concentrate specifically on:

- the general study of the mechanisms of emigration. In the style of an illustrated story (the *Persian Letters* of Montesquieu) we shall write a novel telling the story of a landless peasant from a poor country who goes to look for work in the city and ends up emigrating in order to feed his family ...

- the socio-economic study of Belgium and Morocco in parallel (the importance of industry, agriculture, etc.), with reference to the economic and political systems and the level of development.

The aim is to make a link between a mechanism and a specific situation which gives rise to that mechanism. We shall endeavour nonetheless not to overlook:

- their factory work and daily battles (wages, jobs, conditions of work), the economic crisis and its repercussions on the working class;

- the struggle in our context, i.e., the struggle for trade union democracy;

- the problems associated with their situation as immigrants in Belgium: discrimination, wages, work, accommodation and democratic rights.

All of the above will be set in a democratic, anti-imperialist perspective whenever possible so that our teaching will encourage them to join workers' organizations.

1985

The topics addressed were:

- the general election,

- the armaments race and pacifist movements,

- South Africa and apartheid,
- the issue of naturalization,
- the economic crisis,
- the Palestinian question

We believe that we are still very unambitious when we talk about what should be the purpose of basic education. We still see it in terms of the functional dimension: the goal of learning in order to manage everyday life better, to catch a train, fill in forms, read street names, and so on. All of that is doubtless indispensable, but it is not sufficient for our purpose .... But there is also the use of language as a means of creating and communicating more complex thoughts, which are in the hands of a minority who thereby exercise considerable social power.

Thus, from two angles, it seems to me to be indispensable to ensure that participants somehow acquire French as a tool with which to develop complex thought, as they will otherwise be limited to a few bits of French that may be useful functionally (from an educational angle) and will always be deprived of the basic means to query their position in social relationships (the political angle).

We therefore have to devote time to creating a good library... Some of them may thus become readers ...

In both texts, the problem is posed in terms of class power: "the working class and imperialism" in 1975, and "the thoughts of a minority who thereby exercise considerable power" in 1985. Between 1975 and 1985, there was a shift from the collective to the individual, from workers' organization to the individual acquisition of a tool of thought.

This shift was both a step both forwards and backwards. Backwards if the redevelopment of the pedagogical aspect was marked by the cessation of collective action, and if the new focus on learning was at the expense of the power of the individual over his or her education.

1975	1985
The political angle *Thematic approach, linked to current events* *One objective: to make it possible to analyze economic and social mechanisms*	
Analysis in terms of economic and political power	*Analysis in terms of intellectual and political power*
Collective aim, external to literacy and learning: awareness-raising and developing solidarity between workers	*Individual aim, both internal and external to literacy and learning: acquiring a tool of thought and becoming readers*
So that they can join a collective organization	*So that they can query their position in social relationships* *And join a library?*

'Forwards' to the extent that the pedagogy was redefined to match the politics. The methodologies used had themselves to be liberating and participatory. It was a matter of finding approaches which enabled real access to the written word. 'Forwards' if the progressive field of education (the Freinet movement, *Education nouvelle*) coincided with the sociocultural field and enabled the latter to enrich the input of Freire's approach to learning in general and reading in particular. 'Forwards' if it gave the "excluded" the tools to speak and if it responded to people's demand to be regarded as individuals and not as an abstract unit, a social grouping.

This new focus on individual pedagogy led to the development of ongoing educational research conducted by the teachers, who designed original cultural approaches that promised a way of solving the problems of society that we face every day. New projects came about, in which literacy was no longer a goal in itself but a tool to do something. Hence, one of our local centres developed a network for the exchange of knowledge and the creation of a local base, in successful partnership with other associations. Very many writing workshops were organized, among them a collective writing group, led by writers and involving illiterates, teachers, and indeed anyone.

There was thus an attempt to escape from "course cocoons" and "illiterate ghettoes", and in our actions then and in subsequent years we doubtless moved closer to the aims laid down in our 1974 manifesto. On the other hand, the questioning of the power of the teachers, relationships of dominance, collective action and social and political participation, disappeared. Paradoxically, at the time when tools for "gaining one's voice" were being given, the focus was on the society outside. The voice of the participants inside, within the association, was often quite feeble. Generally, it was neither the people attending our courses, nor the particular communities that had been behind the projects that had a controlling voice, but the teachers and institutions.

1992 — FROM PERSONAL DEVELOPMENT TO THE DEVELOPMENT OF CITIZENSHIP

While there had always been references to culture and work ever since the first manifesto had been drawn up, the term "citizenship" appeared for the first time in 1992. It was certainly a positive move to replace "illiterates" by "citizens". There was a need to re-emphasize collective action. But what was the meaning of the loud cries heard in regional politics for working towards citizenship?

Having laid the foundations for the present-day scheme of adult education, members of associations were now charged officially, by means of injunctions and key funding, to encourage their publics to take part in the process of political decision-making. What was the sense of that in a context in which the majority of the population in our areas had no right to vote, there was no longer work for all, finding accommodation was difficult, and the Ministry of Education was laying people off?

In the early 1990s, the public authorities, especially the Brussels Region, in the light of:

- the growing deterioration in the socio-economic situation;
- the severe tensions crystallizing around cultural differences (the rise of the extreme right and young people rioting in immigrant quarters); and
- the inability of traditional forces to deal with and resolve the crisis situation,

concluded that:

- exclusion was caused by a series of factors and that it was therefore necessary to implement inter-related policies to attack these various factors; and
- neither the public authorities nor the voluntary sector could hope to attack them successfully on their own.

They therefore decided to link the public and voluntary sectors:

- by giving local political authorities responsibility for taking initiatives to deal with the rise of exclusion in their areas; and
- by creating a public/private interface: "local missions" to manage and develop dynamic new policies.

Four regional policies were instituted:

1. an education, socialization and labour market entry policy for people with few skills, a policy which recognized the network that had been developed since 1977 by the voluntary movement and tried to link it to the public vocational education network;
2. a policy of "harmonious cohabitation and integration between the communities" in the problem communes, largely focusing on young people and partnership between local authorities and voluntary associations;
3. a policy of urban renewal and restoration of the social fabric in problem communes: "local contracts"; and
4. a new policy driven by the federal authorities rather than by the regions: the "security policy" and security contracts.

What were the effects of these "solutions" implemented by the public authorities?

- An avalanche of responsibilities passed from federal to local authorities. In the face of problems that were becoming international, action was taken at a micro level of society. Although there was real work to be done at this "micro" level, it could not disguise the need for real policies at a macro-social and macro-economic level.

- A plethora of policies: instead of questioning (analyzing, modifying or strengthening) existing policies (such as lifelong education), new layers of policy were created, with new funding and new rules.
- These layers of policy led to a diminution of the number of agencies involved, which sometimes acted in concert but often did not know of each other's existence, and at worst fought against or cancelled each other out.

These new regional policies, only the first two of which concerned basic education, did have some positive aspects: the renewed involvement of local political authorities in their areas, recognition of the work of voluntary associations, and the requirement for the latter to examine the quality of what they were doing. But they were not able to change rapidly a poor situation, and their effects were not immediately in proportion to the funds invested. It required less superficial work that was less "visible to the electorate" and was hence frequently revised and rearranged so that it was "visible".

There were also wide differences in the results depending on the way in which the policies were carried out. While in some districts, they brought the inhabitants together and made it possible to strengthen local development work initiated some time previously by voluntary associations, in others, the new activities were launched by associations directly dependent on the communal authorities, at the expense of existing activities.

Depending on the way in which local decision-makers and associations interpreted these policies, they thus allowed local community development to be maintained in some cases, and in others served to reinforce social control.

WHAT POINT HAVE WE REACHED TODAY?

Without the hindsight needed to see exactly the point when the change came, we are today at a new turning point: in society, in education policies, and in our activities.

From economic crisis to social crisis

The crisis is not only socio-economic. It is a deep crisis, which calls into question our traditional values: a cultural and political crisis, accompanied by instability for a growing proportion of the population, including our public, in the real context of an "under-developing country". It is a country in which the rich are getting richer and the poor poorer, where there is no longer any creativity or political drive. The government goals of reducing unemployment will be met only by statistical manipulation. The employers hold the cards, and the problems remain in terms of "social class", with the hesitant emergence of some new collective actions led by certain categories of the excluded and those in receipt of social security assistance.

From recognition to subcontracting

Many changes in the funding of the voluntary movement have today taken effect or are in preparation, principally in socialization and labour market entry programs. In 1995, the Brussels Region recognized the network set up by the voluntary movement as its system for the socialization and labour market entry of people with low levels of skill. Our association, like others, was approved under this scheme.

It is pleasant to see the aims and quality of our work recognized. But now that we are part of a regional development policy, it is that policy which may in future define what sort of education should be developed and funded, and what should be discontinued and no longer funded, by means of top-down "invitations to tender". The associations which organize this vocational education and training will thus become training enterprises, no longer responding to demand from a particular public, a local community, but adapting to the market of public provision.

In addition, by organizing legitimate complementarity between the different sectors, such policies see the voluntary sector as subcontractors to the public vocational training agencies. The latter offload the people with the greatest difficulties and entrust the associations with education for "pre-entry preparation" while trying to impose their norms (of teacher training, pay scales and programs).

We are thus witnessing a real privatization of the public sector by associations which are in danger of becoming completely controlled by others, of seeing their particular roles and the conditions which enable them to provide education of quality disappear. (They are abandoning the principle of analyzing the needs of the people whom they meet every day and designing activities as a consequence, which have often anticipated awareness of those needs on the part of the public authorities.) It is vital to resist these undesirable effects of recognition today.

From the development of literacy to the defence of the illiterate

Having defended the right to literacy, we now have to "defend" the rights of our illiterate public in the face of social policies which increasingly resort to compulsion and are addressed to individuals. We are of course still defending the right to literacy, and we still fight for its recognition and development in all the sectors concerned.

But today we have to defend also the rights of illiterate people: rights which include the right to literacy teaching of quality, given by experienced, trained teachers, which is far from being the case with us. But the rights of illiterate people also include the right to refuse literacy, which is nowadays offered systematically to anyone designated illiterate, whatever their aims in life. The rights of illiterate people also embrace their rights to culture, work and vocational education. And these rights are far from guaranteed today.

1997 — FUTURE DEVELOPMENT

Three observations stand out from our history: two distinct changes, and a large measure of continuity in the quest for a sense of direction.

Two distinct changes

In 1976, the association shifted from an aim of development in the countries of the South to that of the development of literacy in Belgium, and from the refusal of public funding to applications for literacy funding from public authorities. We question this today.

Can we be completely subsidized by the public authorities without being entirely controlled by them? Are we able to maintain our own orientation and hence, should the case arise, to decline funding if we cannot accept its aims and constraints, given the consequences for jobs? Or has the employment of our teachers become our first priority?

The year 1976 was also when public policies based on the current "landscape" of basic education were implemented in the French Community. Today, this landscape is under great tension, the contradictions in this form of development becoming increasingly great.

Two articles that appeared in an issue of the *Journal de l'Alpha* devoted to citizenship bring out these contradictions clearly.

The first reveals the political choices made in the decree on lifelong education, the decree on cultural centres, the decree on youth organizations, the support given to many initiatives emanating from communities of foreign origin, and policies aiding "citizens' associations" that aim to help their members "to become active, responsible and critical citizens within the society."[3]

The second reveals the misconceptions in these policies:

> We thus witnessed the birth of new associations alongside the working class movement and public service organizations which are led by a small number of citizens and permanent staff. They encountered new social needs and were progressively subsidized by the state. These associations rapidly took on a democratic legitimacy in the face of major institutions which were 'well equipped'. While the sudden growth of these associations had a positive side, it rested nonetheless on a misconception. The state thereby discovered new social needs. It was keen to leave the initiative in the hands of a few committed citizens... . The whole ideology of cultural development and of some corners of socialization and labour market entry policy derives from this misconception.
>
> The state manages its cultural, social and preventative policy through citizens, by giving low-cost subsidies to workers. I do not deny the good intention of leaving the management of these state policies to citizens. But one does wonder why this is only conceivable on the fringes of social and cultural activities.[4]

One might add, and in the education of the "excluded"!

A large measure of continuity

Aside from these questions, and despite the changes in its political purpose and socio-economic context, the Literacy Collective has until now been able to keep to the general direction set out in its original manifesto. This contained:

- **An object, a "job": literacy**. Thirty years later, this is still the only aim of the association, and it is still a real job for 30 teachers.
- **Reference to the Ministry of Labour**: literacy in order to have access to vocational education, which was necessary for the

dedevelopment of the country of origin, and reference to change and *to culture*; literacy as *"in-depth cultural preparation"*. In fact, labour and cultural policy were to be the two pillars of our development.

- **Partnership** between different actors. Although partnership is today a political constraint in the funding of our activities, the Collective has always worked in partnership, always with many difficulties, but always to its benefit.

- **A clear division of tasks between the partners**. This division — in simple terms, policy to the workers' organizations, and teaching to teachers — created problems that are still unresolved as workers become unemployed and workers' organizations prove incapable of organizing the working class outside the framework of work.

- **Educational aims** that we still have to defend: *"a job of basic education: reading, writing, speaking and calculating. Through this basic education we have to give workers the capacity to take charge of their circumstances.... We must go forward keeping in mind all the elements, all the difficulties.... We must not therefore tie ourselves to a rigid program.*

  "It is the continuity in our work that creates the climate of confidence in which people can grow. And it is ongoing discussion between the teachers that enables us to correct certain errors, to establish a program that is sufficiently flexible and to clarify the goals to be achieved."

Through wind and storm, the teachers stick to their task.

- **And organizational guidelines**: continuity — autonomy — and continual discussion between teachers, which requires an organized group that functions democratically. For 30 years, this tradition of group discussion and teacher training has withstood every change in the status of either the association or the teachers.

More than any government policy, it is these traditions, forged through grassroots work, that have been our strength and have enabled us to keep our own personality, to remain at the service of the same public, to develop activities that largely anticipate "invitations to tender", and to respond to the criteria of being an association: free choice in joining, definition of a common purpose, a democratic way of operating, attention to the most basic expectations and needs, questioning of the social and political system, and establishment of a real partnership with public authorities.

Then, as the 1983 report emphasizes, "the implementation of all these activities has been made possible thanks to an enthusiastic team of animators, both 'voluntary' and 'professional', who have been able to develop the Literacy Collective while remaining at the service of the illiterates."

Given the funding constraints laid down by the Ministry of Labour, the creation of jobs in the association led to the recruitment of teachers from widely differing backgrounds: unqualified long-term unemployed people who found a professional commitment in literacy that matched their democratic ideals, but also made it possible for them to develop as people and to realize their worth.

Thereafter, teachers were principally recruited from among qualified school teachers, who stood out from the school system by their educational and social commitment. But whatever they were, whatever their status and "creed", the teachers have remained militant, i.e., "members of an organization who take an active part in the life of that association" (*Petit Robert* dictionary). First, because they can participate in the organs of decision making (the Governing Board and General Assembly), and second because they have the opportunity within the association to develop new projects and *"fight for their ideas"*.

Finally, the policies introduced in 1976 by the Ministry of Culture and the Ministry of Labour gave us the *long-term funds for a global project,* which are the preconditions for the development of high-quality work: the global nature of the funding enabled us to develop our activities in response to the needs discovered; and their long-term nature enabled the teaching force to be stabilized, and the quality of their work to be enhanced in consequence.

The quest for a sense of direction

From 1983, the problem of the sense of direction of our activities was constantly raised, despite the educational quality of our literacy project. In our 1983 report, we wrote: *"At this time of long-term unemployment, the problem of the aims of our courses is raised. What viewpoints do we offer?"*

Almost 15 years later we can say that the trends of the preceding year have — unfortunately — been confirmed: the increasing spread of short-termism, uncertainty and impoverishment among our public. This raises the issue of the purpose of our work:

- In relation to ourselves: how to survive these situations and to become involved without destroying ourselves.

- In relation to the dynamics of the groups, which is more difficult to manage with a public suffering from uncertainty that exacerbates problems between individuals.

- In relation to the object of our work: in these circumstances, why teach literacy?

- In relation to social services: we are not a social service and have no intention of becoming one. But, can we ignore the question if a participant is in urgent need of accommodation?

- In relation to culture: when they have attended a writing workshop, they go home and empty the rubbish bins in restaurants.

- In relation to labour, the immediate, burning concern: at the "micro" level, some people find a job; at a "macro" level, there is no hope.

- In relation to the obligation to provide training: do we have to?"

We are convinced that people are illiterate, become illiterate and remain illiterate despite attending literacy courses because they are not part of the social, political and economic circle of participation, communication and expression, and hence have no reason to read.

We have developed a social, political and economic circle of participation, communication and expression which makes little sense today if we do not continually ask ourselves questions about the society and its politics.

Until now we have always thought that these questions should be addressed in other structures and that our role was not to organize the participants who take part in education within our association, but to support their participation and organization in the "natural" places: trade unions, neighbourhood committees and various movements. Can we maintain that role today?

Can we go on working at the level of the individual? Reinforcing their exclusion and developing a new type of corporatism (defending illiterates, junkies and young school dropouts)? Being an interface between them and the society, while defending our own interests?

Or shall we be able, together with our public, to confront what is today not only an economic crisis but also a cultural crisis? Shall we be able to allow everyone to reflect on their identity, history and way ahead, while supporting new projects to give them a voice and collective action arising from our courses?

Shall we be able to set our activities once again in a global perspective of combating the underdevelopment of our society?

Notes

1. Unless otherwise stated, all the texts in italics are extracts from meeting reports or activity reports of the Literacy Collective.

2. Ministry of Culture of the French Community of Belgium. Decree of 8 April 1976.

3. Zwick, J. 1996. Une option de la Communauté française: promouvoir la citoyenneté. *Journal de l'Alpha* 93, March-April.

4. Mangot, T. 1996. Citoyenneté et action socio-culturelle: quels liens? *Journal de l'Alpha* 93, March-April.

5. As defined by the Voluntary Associations Charter compiled by CIRAT (Interregional Coordination of Associations and their Workers).

Chapter Eleven
SKILLS, SCHOOLS AND SOCIAL PRACTICES
Limits to the Basic Skills Approach in Adult Basic Education in Flanders

Nathalie Druine and Danny Wildemeersch
Catholic University of Leuven
Leuven, Belgium

INTRODUCTION

> The task of Adult Basic Education (ABE) is to equip lowly skilled adults with the essential basic qualifications needed for effective functioning in the community (Decree on Adult Basic Education).

This statement by the coordinator of the Flemish Adult Basic Education Foundation (VOCB) is an illustration of the particular way in which today, people in charge of Adult Basic Education (ABE) in Flanders legitimize the societal function of their organization (Verdurmen, 1993:4). In the eyes of political elites and policy-makers, ABE is seen today as an important instrument in the fight against educational subordination and unemployment. They increasingly judge the societal contributions of the sector in terms of its problem-solving capacity and hence, ask for measurable results. Mainstream ABE tends to endorse this socio-economic policy orientation and justifies its actions predominantly in terms of the dominant discourse of "utility". In this discourse the concept of "basic skills" is of central importance. ABE is said to guarantee the acquisition of the basic skills necessary to function in the community and on the labour market. Especially with reference to the unemployment issue, this labour-market orientation is considered to be of central importance.

At first sight, it is hard to object to these orientations. People indeed have the right to be qualified for the labour market, or to acquire basic skills that help them to survive. A professionally well-organized ABE-provision meets these basic social rights. On second thought however, some critical comments concerning these orientations are justified. There is the major observation, that ABE is shifting rapidly towards a schoolish institution, leaving behind many of the broader socio-cultural options that inspired its activities in the past. Such comments are formulated today at various levels and by different spokespersonS, both in practice and in the academic world. Yet, mainstream ABE does not seem to bother. How can this be explained?

We first will show in a historical outline, when and how literacy work in Flanders originated, expanded and developed towards its actual form. We will illustrate the central decisions that were made over time concerning institutional environment, pedagogical orientations and professionalization, and examine to what extent other perspectives also make sense. We thematize some of the critical questions raised by the literacy field (concerning the societal goals of ABE) and by theoreticians of literacy education and of adult education, and we conclude with some suggestions for further discussion and research.

From a literacy movement to adult basic education

We will limit ourselves to a brief description of the evolution of adult literacy work towards the present day situation. More details are given elsewhere (Goffinet & Van Damme, 1990). Before the end of the seventies, there was little adult literacy work in Flanders. Some isolated literacy courses for migrant people were organized, together with a four-month literacy course for recruits of the Belgian army who had problems with reading and writing. Illiteracy was not considered a problem, neither among the Belgian population, nor among the policy-makers.

When a radio program in 1978 highlighted illiteracy problems of native Belgian adults, including the absence of a well-organized literacy provision (apart from the army), the literacy movement took a start. The reactions of people who wanted to work as a literacy volunteer were numerous. Some months later, the first literacy group could start its work. This group took the shape of a foundation and had an exemplary function. After one year, some twenty volunteers, one conscientious objector and two persons on a temporary contract, experienced that there was a real need for literacy activities.

Most of those activities were supported (and funded) by existing non governmental organizations for adults (welfare organizations or organizations for general adult education) until they were strong enough to function autonomously. The result of this evolution was a wide diversity of local projects each developing their own accents and particular frameworks. Soon, the need for more cooperation and coordination generated the establishment of the Foundation *Alfabetisering Vlaanderen* (Flanders Literacy) in 1981. The organization was responsible for the support and the defence of interests of the local projects and for preparatory policy activities (Gehre, 1992). One of its first aims was to attract money from the government while funding criteria were to be defined by the literacy field itself. In 1981, the Flemish literacy movement received temporary funding from the Ministry of Culture. The role of the government was limited to the provision of funds. It had no other responsibility concerning the literacy work. The (political) responsibility was in the hands of the local (non governmental) organizations and social movements. The volunteers of the literacy movement were convinced that they were best placed to interpret the needs of the participants.

Another important issue for the literacy movement in those days was the necessity find agreement on the main principles regarding content and method. Literacy was seen as a way to give people better opportunities to participate in society and to eliminate arrears. People were considered to have the right to learn to read and write. An emancipatory approach was advocated, with the main focus on empowerment of the participants and on experiential learning (the learners have a voice in the definition of learning; learning should reflect their own life-world, experiences, concerns and ways of expression). Traditional schooling was often repudiated because of its status quo orientation. Furthermore, the role of volunteers was strongly emphasized, with reference to the presupposed equivalence of participants and educators.

institutions for adult literacy, wanted more say in literacy matters and wanted to free literacy work from the influence of the "mother organizations". They further argued that the particular problem of adult illiteracy calls for a specific approach.

Opponents of this position however, feared the risk of fragmentation (specialization in literacy and numeracy) at the expense of a more global approach. They considered illiteracy as only one factor in a whole range of disadvantages. An integrated approach was thought to be necessary. Separate institutions for illiterates were considered to have a stigmatizing effect. Nevertheless, just like in Great Britain (Hamilton, 1992) and in The Netherlands (Hammink, 1990), the history of the Flemish literacy work is marked by increasing professionalization and a growing autonomy and functional differentiation.

While the number of local projects was increasing in the years that followed and although more funds were obtained, the needs were growing and the sector was unhappy about the poor financial support. Moreover, the eighties were characterized by conservative policy tendencies. Social expenditures were cut back and an ideological warfare against the welfare state took a start. In these days, the idea took shape to limit the social interventions of the state to particular key issues. Against this backdrop, the discussions about the future institutional forms of adult literacy education took place.

Due to the growth of numerous projects for lowly educated adults, more coordination in the fragmentated landscape and an integrated and coherent provision were thought to be necessary. The Flemish government reserved special funds to set up five "experiments of basic education", in cooperation with existing initiatives for literacy education, socio-cultural organizations and local authorities. The aim was to generate knowledge to prepare a new policy on basic education. The main orientations of the model under construction (and that still is the model for the Centres for Basic Education today) were the following (Document, 1986, p. 66 e.v.):

- develop an integrated and coherent provision, whereby traditional borders between education, vocational training and general adult education are crossed;
- develop a coherent policy for ABE, with specific responsibilities for the different (local, federal) authorities;
- improve the quality of the provision by means of the professionalization of the sector;

- develop new counselling and guidance strategies;
- promote a broad social embedment of the centres (cooperation with other organizations).

Although the existing literacy movement had supported the new developments in adult basic education, it also felt some ambivalence towards recent evolutions. Basic education would probably make an end to the fragmentation of initiatives for lowly skilled adults and guarantee more professionalization. At the same time, some fears were expressed that "the real literacy work", with its emphasis on small groups, de-schooling, emancipatory objectives, attention to the structural embedment of literacy problems [...] would disappear in favour of a one-sided schoolish approach.

At the end of the experimental period and after the adoption of the "Decree on Basic Education" in 1990, which was the result of a controversial debate, the adult literacy work, now adult basic education, was removed from the Ministry of Culture to the authority of the Ministry of Education. There, the basic education approach was being privileged. Other existing initiatives of adult literacy had to cope with a minimum of financial resources. Many of them could not survive. Today, only a few projects of that kind still organize adult literacy, in a context which differs very much from the official organizations. The most extensive projects with respect to participant hours, local institutions, finances etc., are of course organized by the Centres for Basic Education, which in their turn are methodologically supported by the VOCB (Flemish Adult Basic Education Foundation).

Adult basic education today

After the Decree on Basic Education was passed by Flemish parliament in 1990, 29 centres for basic education took a start in Flanders (Verdurmen, 1993). The centres were the continuation of different initiatives, over the last fifteen years. The basic education centres offer schemes (literacy and numeracy, social skills, social formation and preparation to work or further studies) for lowly skilled adults. Different groups of adults are addressed: "functional illiterates", migrants, housewives, unemployed people, people living on an existential minimum. All activities take place in one integrated organizational framework. This is meant to put an end to fragmentation. Basic education in Flanders now is part of a general arrangement on the education of adults and ensures a provision along two lines:

- a basic provision of training and education, aimed at the acquisition and improvement of basic skills that are essential to function in personal, social and professional situations;
- a channelling provision aimed at directing people to other training and education schemes.

The 1990 decree strongly emphasizes the cooperation of different educational sectors such as vocational training, socio-cultural work and school education. Cooperation between local authorities and private initiatives is obligatory. A broad social embedment is pursued. Other points of attention in the decree are the professionalization of the literacy teachers and an organizational scaling up to guarantee the viability and the possibility to create varied programs for different target groups. Although basic education is part of the larger system of education for adults, its own specific place and particular pedagogical concept are emphasized.

This short description of the basic education centres makes clear that the literacy field in Flanders has dramatically changed. Adult literacy no longer is a marginal activity, run by volunteers with improvised learning materials. The conception of literacy has changed in both political and in theoretical respect during the last decades. Similar evolutions have also taken place in other Western European countries. According to van der Kamp, Scheeren and Veendrick, "there seems to be a shift from the concept of "analphabetism" (sic), i.e. the classic rather dichotomous view of (il)literacy, via "functional literacy", i.e. literacy seen as contextbound language and numeracy skills, towards a concept of "basic skills", i.e. broader skills specifically needed on the workplace." (1995:159)

From literacy to basic skills

These three main conceptions of literacy are presented by van der Kamp, Scheeren and Veendrick in an illuminatory overview in which they link the conceptions of literacy to differences in value orientations, political responsibility, content etc. The diagram is of course an ideal-typical interpretation of the developments in the literacy field. Differences are stressed to contrast the conceptions. In the field of practice, the evolutions are more gradual and different conceptions overlap.

It is enlightening to use the same framework to interpret the history of the Flemish literacy work. Adult basic education in The Netherlands has even further evolved in the direction of the basic skills-approach, but considering previous developments in both countries, we may expect the same evolution to be carried through in Flanders. In the initial stage, the literacy work was not considered a governmental task. The responsibility was completely in the hands of non governmental organizations and social movements. The rationale behind their actions was to fight against poverty and social exclusion by stressing the emancipation of the migrants, the poor and the unskilled people. Today, the target groups of ABE have moved from unskilled people over drop outs or people with almost no schooling to lowly schooled people or (unemployed) workers.

The rationale of current literacy work now is participation to society, c.q. to work. The first provisions for "illiterates" were the literacy campaigns, while from 1975 onwards, initial education, basic education and later vocational education became more important. The advocated approach is gradually shifting from community development and group work methods, via remedial teaching and special programs to vocational training and on the job training. Related to this, the content of literacy education has changed from a focus on reading and writing via literacy, numeracy and social skills to instrumental and vocational skills. Professional educators have replaced almost all volunteers. The authors conclude that the current dominant literacy concept of basic skills has a broad content, but a rather narrow economic focus.

It is clear that ABE in Flanders, supported by the government, has narrowed its orientation from a societal function towards an economic utility. The developments in the Flemish ABE correspond to the international tendency which reveals a stress on the economic priorities of literacy programs aimed at a better participation of adults in economic life (van der Kamp et al, 1995). Literacy and ABE are increasingly seen as an instrument creating opportunities for individuals to enter the labour market. The same authors formulate some critical remarks with respect to this conception of ABE. One of the questions they raise is whether such basic skills are really "basic" and significant in the daily life of many citizens (i.e. older adults). Many older adults maintain that they do not experience insurmountable problems in daily life in situations in which literacy skills are needed (van der Kamp & Veendrick, 1996:9). Often they are very clever in avoiding such situations. The size of their social network is important (cf. infra). Moreover, it is difficult to grasp the labour-related literacy requirements (Hull, 1993). "One can argue whether the perceived changes in production-concepts, technology and flexibility within labour organizations really demand such high levels of literacy and basic skills of workers [...] in the lower jobs" (van der Kamp and Veendrick, 1996:11). The authors argue that a strong emphasis on the global economic function of ABE goes at the expense of social and cultural functions.

Questioning societal goals

Also in the field of practice of adult basic education, similar criticisms on the narrow basic skills approach and on the increasingly influential economic rationality in ABE are heard. At the occasion of the fifth anniversary of the decree on ABE, the Flemish Adult Basic Education Foundation (VOCB) established a reflection platform to discover and develop relevant themes for the years to come. These themes would give rise to "renewal projects" for the two following years. Adult educators and board members of the local centres, representatives from institutes, organizations, governmental services and other interest groups were invited to participate. Participants of the platform could form project groups and develop a project proposal. Only a small number would be selected because the VOCB financed the execution of the projects.

Different projects were formulated, among which quite a few originated from the Flemish Foundation e.g. educational methods in adult literacy; position and relation to other aspects of formal adult education; course offer, etc. Yet, the two themes that obtained the support of most representatives of the local organizations — contrary to the preferences of the "Flemish Foundation" — were: the role of basic education with respect to the underprivileged in Flemish society, and the issue of the societal goals of adult basic education. We had the opportunity to take part in the last project group and to discuss the problems with people from the field.

Their concern was to keep alive the question of the societal goals of adult basic education and to stimulate critical reflection about its institutional context.

The members of the project-group claimed that adult literacy work today in Flanders is directed too much by unquestioned concepts which strongly refer to an economic discourse framing people's problems and the solutions to their problems in individualistic terms. ABE was said to consider the participants predominantly as individuals who lack skills, thus decontextualizing the whole issue of illiteracy and unemployment and emphasizing the helplessness of the learners. Furthermore, it was argued that the orientation of the work had shifted dramatically towards the technical improvement of the curriculum and towards the positioning of ABE within broader qualification frameworks. The members of the project group suggested an open dialogue about the underlying concepts of the work and about the institutional context of current basic education practice. They invited professionals at all levels to reflect intensively on current societal evolutions and to think about the consequences for their own practice.

From the very start, the participants of this project group expected some opposition against their project proposal on behalf of the Flemish Foundation. They expected the foundation to argue that a debate on the societal goals of ABE would not contribute to the affectivity of the work in the local centres and that the renewal projects were expected to produce concrete results. These expectations recently came true, as the project proposal was rejected by the board of governors of the Flemish Foundation, thereby denying the concerns of a vast majority of the workers in the local centres of adult basic education in Flanders.

Two approaches to professionalism

The request for a dialogue about the underlying principles of ABE refers to an enlarged conception of professionalism. Professionalism in literacy work firstly means that literacy education becomes an activity exclusively executed by professionals. These professionals are considered to be the technical experts who guarantee the quality of the work. The above mentioned decree enabled this type of professionalism. Local centres are today supported by an overarching national centre which gives professional advice, produces courseware and teaching materials, conducts research and gives information. ABE workers have to participate in retraining schemes. Their efforts are rewarded by the allocation of average teacher's wages by the state. One can not deny that this form of professionalism is a necessary prerequisite condition for good adult basic education. Underprivileged learners have the right to competent teachers. This right was often overlooked in the pioneering days of ABE, when professionalism was not widespread.

Yet, professionalism also has a second meaning. The above mentioned project group insisted that professionalization means more than developing technical expertise. Next to technical reflection, critical reflection is also necessary. This means that literacy professionals can reflect on the evolution of the sector and on society at large and on the consequences for the learners.

According to Jansen (1996), "acting as a professional educator means not just to perform circumscribed tasks and functions, but also to inhabit a specific image of the world, a specific way of being-in-the-world. And this construction of reality not only favours certain perspectives on the role of educators in processes of social transformation, but also excludes other ones". In other words, we have to be aware of the bias produced by economic rationality in ABE which makes that "skills are listed as abstract competencies and represented as context-free and universal" (Hull, 1993 :34). The economic discourse is fallacious because it promises (better) jobs and social participation, once the workers or unemployed have acquired the necessary basic skills. Yet, this "partial picture of reality" ignores the crisis in the labourmarket, the structural lack of a job for everyone, the growth in poverty (Hautecoeur, 1996:79).

The strong or almost exclusive emphasis on the first meaning of professionalism went hand in hand with other processes of institutional and organizational change which we have witnessed in various north-western European countries. A particular emphasis on affectivity almost necessarily provokes farreaching processes of centralization and standardization. Centralization is the process whereby all local literacy programs — in order to obtain state funding — have to fit in a "national" framework.

Of course the central production of teaching materials for adults is of good help to teachers, but we must not neglect the experience that (voluntary) literacy workers have built up over the years. Do course materials, developed in close collaboration with the learners not better meet their needs? In a centralized model of ABE, can the cooperation between different local providers of adult education and other (socio-cultural, welfare) organizations really be assured? Moreover, the standardization of ABE (i.e. the unity in form, content, method [...]) is important for a clear ABE policy. Formal institutions for people who had no chance to learn to read and write are indeed necessary. Reading and writing are important tools to participate in and change society. Yet the question remains whether in such a standardized and regulated approach the diversity in participants' needs is met.

Neglecting the multidimensional perspective

One could argue that the dominant processes of standardization and centralization in present-day ABE in Flanders also entails a unidimensional approach. In this approach, basic (literacy) skills are considered to play a catalyst role in a process of social integration. It is taken for granted that there are clear links between illiteracy, poor job performance and the declining economy, so adult (basic) education is promoted in order to improve employability (Hull, 1993; Barton, 1994).

We argue that this conception is inspired by a traditional notion of literacy, which isolates learning from people's social context and biography. Due to the exclusive attention paid in current ABE logic to the integration of basic skills in one's personal skills repertoire, other dimensions such as biographical integration and social integration are neglected. This doesn't mean however, that they do not play a role any more in the daily practices of ABE.

Many workers know that in their daily activities, there is more at stake than the skills-acquisition business (Janssen, van der Kamp, Suhre & Harskamp, 1993). They know that people try to keep the narrative of their own life course going, while trying to find answers to the disturbances they cope with (biographical integration), and that they want to meet other people and if possible, establish new relationships and friendships in the context of work, family life and leisure time (social integration). Moreover, illiterate adults often have other and more important difficulties such as poor housing, health problems, lack of self confidence, etc. Those are not directly addressed by a basic skills approach. Yet, the necessary multidimensional character of everyday ABE practice is not reflected in the official vocabulary of current ABE rationale. The dimension of skills-integration obtains all formal attention, whereas the dimensions of biographical and social integration are neglected.

The justification of this one-sidedness is grounded in a linear problem solving conception which puts skills acquisition in the first place and assumes that social integration (e.g. via the labour-market) and new autobiographical balances will automatically follow. Although experienced educators know that this is a fallacy, the current ABE rationale leaves little room to conceive of ABE as an integrated practice which equally and simultaneously emphasizes the dimensions of skills acquisition, of biographical integration and of social integration. Together with the above-mentioned project-group on societal goals, we wonder whether the "education works" — rhetoric responds to a social reality, and if this rhetoric does not hide ongoing mechanisms of social exclusion. Is ABE in terms of learning basic skills really a "global solution for the active population" (Hautecoeur, 1996, p. 80)? Are one's chances to succeed without those skills really limited? Advocates of the "new literacy studies" (NLS) warn us for the delusions of the literacy myth which at regular occasions takes new shapes.

The literacy myth

In the "new literacy studies"[1], the traditional notion of literacy is under pressure (Gee, 1988, 1990). Giving an overview of all the contributions to this field of study, would defeat our object. At the risk of being too simplistic, we will limit ourselves to a very short overview of some conclusions we think to be relevant for ABE.

Critical analysis of the role of literacy within the larger complex of social development was first undertaken in the study of modern history of the western world. The motive for the new approach was an increasing skepticism about the one-sided appreciation, claiming only positive effects of literacy for both society and for woman. With his book "The Literacy Myth" (1979) together with more recent work (1987a, 1987b), Harvey Graff created a furore. Extended diffusion of literacy was almost universally assumed to have powerful effects. "Primary schooling and literacy are necessary, it is so often repeated, for economic and social development, establishment and maintenance of democratic institutions, individual advancement, and so on". All this, regardless of its veracity, has come to constitute a "literacy myth". (Graff, 1979 : xvi)

Graff shows that literacy has no effects (no meaning) apart from particular cultural contexts in which it is used, and it has different effects in different contexts. He illustrates that already in the 19th century, education and reading and writing skills were seen as a prerequisite for occupational and economic success. However, systematic patterns of inequality and stratification — by origin, class, sex, race, and age — were deep and pervasive, and relatively unaltered by the influence of literacy. An analysis of literacy's role in a specific work situation showed that literacy was related to occupation, but not completely, and very little to remuneration (Ibidem, p. 222). The capacity to read and write offered good perspectives for certain individuals, but not for deprived classes or ethnic groups as a whole.

Concerning employment, Graff found that ethnicity played a much more important role than literacy. His work and that of other historians showed that literacy, socio-economic and cultural development (modernization) could not simply be connected to each other. There are different uses of literacy, with different effects. While workers (in the 19th century) were led to believe that acquiring literacy was to their benefit, literacy training served to regularize and discipline behaviour: "promoting discipline, morality, and the "training in being trained" mattered most in the creation and preparation of a modern industrial and urban work force". These were the purposes of the school — and one use of literacy (Ibid.:233). Graff's work again shows that there is no neutral perspective to literacy. Literacy is always linked to a political vision and ideology.

One could interpret the recent evolutions in Flemish ABE as an illustration of the powerful belief in the literacy myth. Together with Van Damme (1987, 1992) we are convinced that, since the 1980s onwards, illiteracy has no longer been considered as a complex social phenomenon that should find a solution on broad policy-making level but has been reframed as a narrow, educational problem. While in the original literacy campaign, the explicit link between literacy and broader social problems was recognized, "illiteracy" — in its new significance — has become a task for education. This explains the shift of ABE from the cultural department to the educational departments, and the ongoing effort to further integrate ABE into the larger structure of formal education for adults.

Some of the main arguments here claim that via ABE people have access to the media, to sources of information, to further training or schooling, to a place on the jobmarket, to a better participation to social life (Verdurmen, 1993:2). According to Van Damme (1992:52) it is commonly assumed that adult basic education can compensate for social marginalization and educational deprivation and that, both on the individual and on the social level, emancipation will be the result. "Besides the fact that in this educational ideology, illiteracy risks to be confined to a technical problem and that neutral concepts of "functional literacy" become dominant, this educational ideology tends to simplify a complex social phenomenon into a problem that can easily be cured by educational correctives" (Ibidem).

Literacy as a social practice

With reference to this debate, Scribner and Cole (1981) introduce the notion of "literacy as a social practice". The pioneering work of both crosscultural cognitive psychologists with the Vai in Liberia challenged the claim that literacy leads inevitably to higher forms of thought. In addition to English literacy, acquired in formal school settings, the Vai have an indigenous script transmitted outside an institutional setting as well as a form of literacy in Arabic, used in religious contexts. So, the different literacies are acquired in different contexts (environments) and serve different purposes. Scribner and Cole assessed their subjects with different categorization and cognitive ability tests.

They concluded that the environment in which learners acquire skills, has a major impact on the way in which these skills operate in daily life. Hence, they choose for a practice account of literacy, arguing that literacy can only be understood in the context of the social practices in which it is acquired.

> "This notion of practice guides the way we seek to understand literacy. Instead of focusing exclusively on the technology of a writing system and its reputed consequences [...] we approach literacy as a set of socially organized practices which make use of a symbol system and a technology for producing and disseminating it. Literacy is not simply knowing how to read and write a particular script but applying this knowledge for specific purposes in specific contexts of use. The nature of those practices, including, of course, their technological aspect, will determine the kinds of skills (consequences) associated with literacy" (Scribner & Cole, 1981, p. 236).

Referring to the above-mentioned discussion on the basic skills-approach, we argue that the acquisition of skills only makes sense when the process of skills acquisition really matches the life context of people, their environment and their biography.

A small study by A. Fingeret (1983), exploring the social structures illiterate adults create, and their relationship to notions of dependence and independence, shows that basic skills are not always essential for many adults. According to this author, adult basic educators continue to define their student populations in terms of incompetence even though this "deficit' perspective is under attack in a variety of social science studies. Yet, most of the illiterate adults she studied, did not necessarily see themselves as dependent simply because they lack reading and writing skills. Rather, they were part of social networks that are characterized by reciprocal exchange. "Networks offer access to most of the resources individuals require, so that it is unnecessary to develop every skill personally" (Ibidem:134). Adults who preserve their independence tend to have strong inner social networks typified by mutual exchange relations. Only a very small number in the study is considered dependent. They "have inner networks that are asymmetrical; there is not a reciprocal exchange" (Ibid.:140). She emphasized that it was not literacy itself which made them dependent, although it was a part of the dependence. Literacy contributed but was not the cause (Barton, 1994:201).

This research contradicts the assumption that illiterate adults cannot function competently in a society dominated by literate culture and traditions. The data from this study underline the importance of social networks and show that adults enrol in literacy programs when their social networks are in flux, due to factors such as new children, new jobs, new geographic locations or the changing status of network members. Fingeret concludes that "educators must become involved in the social networks of illiterate adults and must recognize that the development of literacy skills, even for one individual, entails a broader process of social change" (1983 :145).

From deficient objects to responsible actors

We have repeatedly argued that adult basic education in Flanders and elsewhere today is increasingly conceived as a technical intervention aimed at stimulating the acquisition of basic skills. We want to finish this contribution by again emphasizing some of the negative effects of this tendency, and by drawing attention to the necessity of a more integrated, multidimensional approach. Some of these ideas we have already been developed elsewhere, in collaboration with other partners (Jansen & Wildemeersch, 1996). Various authors have convincingly argued in the past that processes of adult and continuing education do not come about in a social vacuum. Today, we again feel obliged to remind ABE of this argument because it seems to have forgotten that the discussions and decisions on basic skills reflect the existing power relations among social groups in society. In other words, the skills catalogues that are currently under construction in adult basic education tend to emphasize the shortcomings of people and neglect their competencies. The effect is that participants' social identity cannot be formulated in positive terms, unless they have acquired the appropriate qualifications through education and training.

So, in order to increase their social autonomy ABE participants are expected to first internalize a negative image, reflecting a "deficient identity" attributed to them by others, and moreover, identify themselves with "roads to normality" again defined by others. Anyone who is unable or unwilling to meet these requirements will, according to this rationality, remain a second-rate citizen. In this way, a social integration policy based on "objectively necessary" formal basic skills tends to reproduce and legitimize social inequality.

Finally, it should be emphasized that this inequality is individualized by linking social integration to self-help. The individual becomes personally responsible to "catch up" and acquire the appropriate skills via adult basic education. Hence, individuals are to blame if they fail to seize the opportunities offered. As a result, the individual's responsibility for personal well-being not only becomes *the* vehicle for social integration (Van Onna, 1990), but at the same time it pushes questions about the significance of social responsibilities into the background. The discourse on individual social rights, however important it may be, may partially blind the dimension of social responsibility related to adult basic education. This development is part of a broader process of "de-contextualization of self-responsibility", in which the impact of social (power) relations and structures on the differences in social opportunities disappears, and the emphasis shifts to people's will and efforts to qualify for a higher social status.

It is important therefore, to relate practices of skills-acquisition to broader issues of identity development, social integration and social responsibility in different contexts of life. These contexts of life include: work, leisure, family life, social, cultural, religious and political movements. The adult is thus considered a member of the community who takes responsibility for that community, rather than just an individual to whom maximum opportunities for personal development should be offered. In such contexts, adults are not primarily approached as deficient citizens, but as responsible actors in social, cultural and political projects. Let us finish here with the message that such an orientation not necessarily invalidates the achievements of a well-organized and professionalized institution of ABE. On the contrary, we are convinced that these achievements match with continuous attempts to question the often unintended assumptions and effects of institutionalized action.

Note

1. Literacy has been a focus of research for a long time, but in the last decade, a new set of assumptions and methodologies in the study of literacy education has emerged. In the so called "New Literacy Studies", approaches from a variety of disciplines are integrated: psycho linguistics, anthropology, sociology, history, politics, economics and education.

References

Barton, D. 1994. *Literacy. An Introduction to the ecology of written language*, Oxford: Blackwell.

Documenten. 1986. *Vorming Vlaanderen*, 1 3/4, pp. 65-92.

Fingeret, A. 1983. "Social network: a new perspective on independence and illiterate adults", *Adult Education Quarterly, 333*, pp. 133-146.

Gee, J. P. 1988. "The legacies of literacy: from Plato to Freire through Harvey Graff", *Harvard Educational Review, 58*, pp. 195-212.

Gee, J. P. 1990. *Social linguistics and literacies: ideology in discourses*, New York: The Falmer Press.

Gehre, G. 1992. "Basic Education in Flanders: Strengths and Weaknesses". In J.-P. Hautecoeur Ed., *Alpha 92. Current Research in Literacy*, pp. 427-444. Hamburg: UNESCO Institute for Education.

Goffinet, S. A., & Van Damme, D. 1990. *Functioneel analfabetisme in België*, Brussel/Hamburg: Koning Boudewijnstichting/UNESCO Institute for Education.

Graff, H. J. 1987a. *The labyrinths of literacy. Reflections on literacy, past and present*, London: The Falmer Press.

Graff, H. J. 1987b. *The legacies of literacy*, Bloomington: Indiana University Press.

Graff, H. J. 1979. *The literacy myth: literacy and social structure in the nineteenth-century city*, New York: Academic Press.

Hammink, 1990. *Analphabétisme fonctionnel et éducation de base pour les adultes aux Pays-Bas*, Hamburg: UNESCO Institute for Education.

Hamilton, M. 1992. "The development of adult literacy policy in the U.K.: a cautionary tale". In J. H. Knoll, *Internationales Jahrbuch der Erwachsenenbildung, Alphabetisierung und Grundbildung Erwachsener in europaischen Industriestaaten*, Band 19/20, pp. 45-57, Köln: Bohlau Verlag.

Hautecoeur, J.-P. 1996. "Is Literacy, "A Good Deal"? A Critique of the Literacy

Debate in Canada". In J.-P. Hautecoeur Ed., *Alpha 96, Basic Education and Work*, Hamburg, UNESCO Institute for Education, and Culture Concepts, Toronto, Canada.

Hull, G. 1993. "Hearing other voices: a critical assessment of popular views on literacy and work", *Harvard educational Review*, 631, p. 20-49.

Jansen, T. 1996. *Social transformation and the culture of professionalism*, Key note abstract at the International Expert Conference "The professional in formal and non-formal adult and continuing education. Profile, position, legitimation", Leuven, pp. 18-20 September.

Jansen, T., & Wildemeersch, D. 1996. "Adult education and critical identity development". From a deficiency orientation towards a competence orientation, *International Journal of Lifelong Education*, 5, in press.

Janssen, T., van der Kamp, M., Suhre, C., & Harskamp, E. 1993. *Basisvaardigheden in de basiseducatie. Meningen over basisvaardigheden op het gebied van taal, rekenen en sociale vaardigheid*, Amsterdam: Swets & Zeitlinger.

Scribner, S., & Cole, M. 1981. *The psychology of literacy*, Cambridge: Harvard University Press.

Van Damme, D. 1987. "Contradicties van alfabetisering. Historische en vormingspolitieke bedenkingen bij een actueel 'probleem'", *Comenius*, 25, pp. 3-26.

Van Damme, D. 1992. "Social change and educational optimism". Notes on the limits of a modernist idea. In D. Wildemeersch, & T. Jansen Eds., *Adult education, experiential learning and social change. The postmodern challenge*, pp. 51-62. Gravenhage: VUGA.

van der Kamp, M., Scheeren, J., & Veendrick, L. 1995. "Van geletterdheid naar basisvaardigheden". *Comenius*, 15, pp. 159-178.

van der Kamp, M., & Veendrick, L. 1996. *Different views on literacy*. Paper presented at the conference "Reconciling the irreconcilable'. Leuven, 9-11 May.
Van Onna, B. 1990. "Individualisering en sociale interventie". TvA, 192. pp. 88-101.

Verdurmen, H. 1993. "Basiseducatie in Vlaanderen". *Gids sociaal-cultureel en educatief werk*, Afl. 4, pp. 1-18.

Verdurmen, H. 1995. "Decreet basiseducatie geactualiseerd". *Gids sociaal-cultureel en educatief werk*, AO 5, pp. 11-18.

Verdurmen, H. 1994. "Reikwijdte, eindniveau en minimaal redzaamheidsniveau in de basiseducatie". *Gids sociaal-cultureel en educatief werk*, AO 4, pp. 9-12

Chapter Twelve
THE ROLE OF THE STATE IN BASIC ADULT EDUCATION THE PORTUGUESE EXAMPLE

Maria José Bruno Esteves
Ministry of Education
Portugal

To grasp the current context of adult education in Portugal, it is not enough to focus merely on the last ten years. The revolution of 1974, put an end to the long 40 years of dictatorship of Portuguese society. Any analysis requires the consideration of the periods before and after 1974. In a country where democracy has existed for only two decades, nothing is definite. The whole Portuguese society is still learning what democracy really means.

Some of the fundamental aspects of Portuguese culture are deeply rooted in traditional values. Nevertheless, the strong will to attain development and to be free of the recent past contributes to making the country one of the more advanced democracies.

The confluence of traditional and innovative democratic values gives rise to situations which the old democratic nations have some difficulty understanding. In many aspects, the laws and rules are quite advanced, whereas the practice of institutions and individuals is still constrained by traditional values.

This confluence of values is quite evident in education, and especially in adult education.

Basic Adult Education in Portugal: Evolution of Practice and Concepts

The development of adult education in Portugal was very slow compared with other European countries. While illiteracy rates decreased elsewhere, in Portugal they remained unchanged, despite the continual efforts of "eradicating illiteracy" expressed in official texts and legislation.

Adult education provision was mainly based on the literacy training of populations who could not read or write. For many years this resulted in adult education policies based exclusively on traditional and more elementary concepts of literacy training. This is evident when one considers the adult literacy examinations, which were aimed to award a school leaving certificate equivalent to the fourth year of compulsory schooling.

Although the conceptual terminology adopted by international organizations was often integrated in the official discourse — concepts of adult education, popular education and in the 1970's, permanent education — the prevailing approach was the school-based model. The cleavage between conceptual terminology which was sometimes innovative, and the traditional, school-based practice is evident throughout this analysis.

After the 1974 Revolution, adult education expanded to the point of being considered by some authors as "popular education[1]". Two types of strategy were used, which had fairly opposing dynamics:

- **local initiatives** organized by neighbourhood or workers' committees, populist education associations, recreational associations, and other cultural groups which were emerging all over the country; and

- **establishment initiatives** with strong centralizing tendencies, organized by the authorities or by social and political forces during the period of provisional governments (before the first general elections).

Other authors argue that the cultural and educational advancement of the revolutionary period was developed from the centre to the periphery, from the cities to the country. Even when the popular education movement was most dynamic, the "cultural dynamization", as it was called, was led by the urban populations. The spirit of the "campaign", which aimed at "eradicating" illiteracy, overlaid the regional and local cultures.

After the revolutionary period, the new State departments directly responsible for adult education provision, although preserving a global democratic model, centralized the education system and confined popular education to a marginal, mistrusting ghetto[2].

Local *animateurs* and trainers, often members of the communities, are teachers on the staff of the ministry of Education, and their assignment is to act as mediators between national policies and local needs and concerns.

In the 1980's, however, institutional actions tended to respond to the needs of local development. Integrated development projects, with adult education as either the promoter or an important partner, emerged all over the country. The support of local associations by the State took a significant role among the activities of central and local offices in charge of adult education.

BASIC ADULT EDUCATION SCHOOLING

In view of the large number of people who have not attended or completed their compulsory schooling, the State offices of adult education concentrate on providing courses to respond to the needs for basic schooling completion. Until the mid-1980s the demand was centred around literacy and first cycle courses, which correspond to four years' schooling. Afterwards, the second cycle courses, corresponding to six years' schooling, were in greater demand especially by young adults.

Social and educational inequalities are evident in the access to education, the schooling pathways and results. Due to academic failure and dropping out, large numbers of young people are left underschooled. When no compensatory education or priority programs exist, adult education is the only possible alternative for adolescents to engage in a second chance schooling.

As a response to the increasing educational demand from a younger population, adult education offices are compelled to organize more and more adult schooling courses. The escalating of adult schooling excludes community action and divides educational activities into training and community education.

The Comprehensive Law on the Education System, dated October 1986, echoes this division by separating recurrent education from "out-of-school" education. Recurrent education is school-based and conforms to the rules of the education system. Out-of-school education is left to the initiative of local agents (adult education officers) who, having no financial resources, manage to promote some activities by using local facilities and voluntary teachers and *animateurs*. Out-of-school education earned its place in the legal framework but became powerless.

Local development is also omitted by the law. The experience of the 1980's, which created a network of community projects was completely forgotten by the new legislation. As a result of local strategies during this period, some activities stood their ground: the job-related and socio-educative courses, and the State's support to community libraries and local associations are enshrined in the law.

Although the adult education legal framework established the structure for out-of-school education, the measures to foster and develop this modality of adult education were never defined. Its continuity depended more on the will and the initiative of the communities than on the support and strategies' outlining by the State. As a matter of fact, out-of-school education has become less and less important at central administration level.

A note must be made on the role of the local adult education officers, who, being institutional representatives, fulfil the role of local development agents. Local dynamics are often the result of their voluntary work. With a modest budget from the ministry of Education for the support of socio-cultural and out-of-school activities, they promote a number of activities with the financial aid of other agencies, namely the local authorities. This is one of the characteristics of adult education agents in Portugal. Being civil servants — teachers or officers — they are the pivotal organizers of adult education. They move between national policies and the needs of the communities; they are simultaneously the representatives of those policies and the defenders of the rights of the populations they work with. They often are members of local associations, where they can expand the scope of educational action. In some rural areas where employment opportunities are few, they are also local development agents, fostering occupational activities that can give rise to self-employment enterprises. The creation of cooperatives of women artisans is a case in point.

Illiteracy in Portugal: Is it becoming Extinct, or is it Expanding?

Although basic adult education provision has been centred on recurrent education, the results do not indicate an increase in educational demand nor the fulfilment of the provision's goals. The number of persons who seek the education system has little import when compared to the number of persons without the four-year or six-year schooling.

From the comparison between the data issued by the population censuses of 1981 and 1991[4] it is evident that, in view of the educational investment, the decrease of the underschooled (less than six years of compulsory schooling) is insignificant: 76 percent in 1981 to 62 percent in 1991.

Levels of education of the resident population 15 years of age and over

Levels of education	1981		1991	
Cannot read or write	1,506,205	20.6%	951,021	12.1%
Reading and writing skills; no schooling certificate	1,194,192	16.3%	1,097,563	13.9%
Basic education - 1st cycle (4 years' schooling)	2,847,739	38.9%	2,871,014	36.4%
Basic education - 2nd cycle (6 years)	775,139	10.6%	1,182,355	15.0%
Basic education - 3rd cycle (9 years)	473,022	6.5%	804,792	10.5%
Secondary education (12 years)	256,563	3.5%	602,050	7.6%
Post secondary education	166,196	1.6%	98,218	1.2%
Higher education (bachelor and post-graduate)	155,284	2.1%	183,862	3.6%
Total	7,324,230	100%	7,890,875	100%

National Institute of Statistics — Population Census XII and XIII, 1981 and 1991

Portugal is a semi-industrialized country, having some characteristics of a traditional, non industrialized society (rural zones of the interior) and of a modern, industrialized society (urban zones near the coastline). Consequently, illiteracy takes different aspects according to the type of region where it exists.

Those living in urban, industrial areas who can read and write but do not have a compulsory schooling certificate, can hardly participate in the economic and community life. In rural areas illiteracy is not a determinant to the full participation of the individuals in community life. Therefore, the higher illiteracy or semi-illiteracy rates come from rural areas.

As we have said before, the economic and political situation in Portugal until 1974 did not encourage the generalized schooling of the population. This was particularly evident in rural zones, where the family income also depended upon the work of the younger ones, and where the schools were too far away for regular attendance. Moreover, the migration to the cities, and specially to industrialized urban areas, contributed, in absolute terms, to the large concentration of illiterates in urban zones. A significant part of these populations "has been confined [...] to new forms of need and exclusion, and are a very important part of the urban poor who tend to crowd together in slums, degraded inner cities and old welfare housing"[5].

However, modern economy has produced a kind of illiteracy which cannot be defined as the inability to read and write; now illiteracy has a wider sense and applies to a population having some literacy skills and school attendance but who did not complete compulsory schooling.

The "new illiterates" are unqualified or underqualified in terms of economic and social standards. According to Jean-Pierre Vélis, they are those whose "rudimentary knowledge is not on a level with the demands of today's society. And even less on a level with tomorrow's society"[6]. Therefore, the high percentage of unschooled Portuguese citizens in 1991 indicates high illiteracy and functional illiteracy rates, particularly among the working and the younger segments of the population.

For the majority of the population, compulsory schooling does not last for six years; only 20 percent of the resident population who were over 14 years of age in 1991 are legally bound to a compulsory attendance of six years. The six-year schooling certificate is now essential for obtaining access to the labour market, and also for keeping a position and obtaining access to professional improvement. Some researchers have pointed out however, that schooling of at least 12 years of compulsory attendance is needed to prevent the acquired knowledge from being completely forgotten[7].

The large percentage of the population who do not have a six-year basic education indicates the scope of the precariousness of the population's knowledge, and the resulting precariousness of employment and the possibility of access to vocational training[8].

Population 15 years of age and over
who do not have a six-year schooling certificate

Age Group	Total	Men	Women
15-19	21,4282	23.1	19.8
20.24	38.1	29.4	26.9
25-29	47.8	38.4	37.8
30-34	63.0	46.9	48.6
35-39	68.7	61.1	64.9
40-44	75.6	65.7	71.5
45-49	82.0	71.2	79.6
50-54	85.7	77.8	85.8
55-59	88.1	82.5	88.5
60-64	91.0	85.2	90.6
65+		88.2	93.1
Total	**62.3%**	**59.4%**	**65.0%**

National Institute of Statistics
Population Census XII and XIII, 1981 and 1991

The table above shows that 62 percent of the Portuguese population over 14 years of age — that is, five million people — has schooling levels of less than six years. For the needs and concerns of the older population, the very high percentages are admissible, as compulsory schooling only began in 1967. However, in the case of the younger population, especially the 15 to 24 age group, the situation is alarming. It means that one fourth of those young people should have completed their compulsory education and did not.

Although the statistics point to the existence of large segments of population with a still very rudimentary knowledge, the tendency is to ignore the new contours in illiteracy, encompassing semi-illiteracy through to functional illiteracy. Whenever the results of a new census are published, the media's and the politicians' only concerns are to see that the illiteracy rates have decreased and to congratulate themselves for it. The high percentage of young and working population who have no four-year or six-year compulsory schooling — a percentage that should be considered a semi-illiteracy or functional illiteracy rate — is simply ignored.

Basic Adult Education Policies in the Last Ten Years

Portugal is a very centralized country where private initiative is rare. The associative movement that took form during the revolutionary period has begun to fade, or tends to pursue less collective-oriented goals.

Welfare policies have always been undertaken by the State. There is no organizational tradition at community level. The few welfare non-governmental organizations that exist are relief associations with a structure and a dimension that keeps them as removed from the populations in general as the State is. Among these associations, the *Misericórdias* have for the last five centuries been devoted to health and welfare relief; now they are providing training for young people in depressed circumstances.

At community level, associations are usually oriented to sports and recreational activities; during the revolutionary period, from 1974 to 1976, the populations have organized (or have been organized) to fight illiteracy and improve their cultural level. After that period, educational initiatives have been gradually assumed only by the ministry of Education and their adult education offices, although many community associations have continued their cultural activities, and namely theatre, music education and folk dancing.

When Portugal joined the EEC, adult education reached a new dimension due to the funding of vocational training by the European Social Fund (ESF). The ministry of Employment developed vocational training and qualification projects for the working population. The majority of the projects, however, were targeted to the schooled public.

The ministries of Employment and Education were partners in the creation of an intermittent education system targeted to a younger population. The system however, proved to be inadequate to the needs and interests of disadvantaged young people, as it favoured them less than economic objectives and interests. Both the location of the courses away from the area of the trainees' residence and a heavy schedule, restrained the access of young people from rural areas and of those who had experienced a difficult school integration and dropped out.

The lack of a system that could respond to the needs of under-schooled, disadvantaged segments of the population who could not obtain access to vocational system, prompted the adult education offices of the ministry of Education to suggest the organization of a new system to the ESF. For the first time it was possible to associate technical training to basic adult education already provided by the ministry of Education (which the younger and more disadvantaged population were beginning to find inadequate).

This innovative experience provided a kind of training that seemed to give a better response to the young public's needs, and to be more motivating for those who had found some difficulties in integrating the recurrent education modality.

The organization and implementation were the responsibility of adult education offices and, although the courses took place in basic or secondary schools, they were not subject to regular school rules. The timetables were devised to accommodate the trainees' schedules. The courses were nearer to the area of the trainees' residence or work. The trainers were selected in terms of their pedagogical profile and their experience in adult education work. Being a vocational training program, this system differed from other educational supplies as it was not isolated from basic adult education.

The results of this experience led to the negotiation of a specific subprogram for adult education within the Educational Development Plan for Portugal (PRODEP).The courses were suggested by local adult education officers for approval, which took into consideration the dimension of the project and its accordance with the national priorities and goals.

The approval of a project considered, among other aspects:

- the conditions of functioning;
- the guarantee that educational standards were maintained;
- the expected output in terms of opportunities for bettering the trainees' working situation;
- the articulation with other local development projects; and

- the articulation with other institutions, namely enterprises, schools, local authorities and associations.

The program began in 1990 and until 1993, during the four years of administration, reached 42,632 young adults throughout the country, from the inner cities to the remotest villages, and had special significance in the interior, where no such educational opportunity had existed before. It aimed at raising the educational level of adult population and advance better vocational qualifications while providing literacy education and compulsory schooling and qualified pre-vocational training. The demand was evidently high, and often exceeded the organizational possibilities. Year after year many projects and courses were suggested but could not be selected, because the budget was insufficient to implement them.

Another important aspect, indicating the positive output of these courses, was the considerable decrease of drop-out rates in comparison with other courses that did not offer vocational training.

According to pedagogical methods, the program was considered to be innovative. The integrated management of the two curricular components — General Education and Technical Training — increased the possibilities to provide a model for intermittent education in small communities that could reach unmotivated or isolated publics. According to the external evaluation of the program, "the success of this innovation is attached to the levels of operation of the program and the effective contents of the pedagogical process offered by the DGEE [the adult education central office within the ministry of Education] for local application"[9].

The Subprogram for Adult Education, although restricted to the economic trends of the 1990's, was an opportunity to guarantee a dynamic adult education that could develop permanent education concepts, namely the articulation between school and out-of-school education, and bring together people and institutions around local education projects.

Nowadays the model is still active, but the project's dimension and resources are considerably attenuated. Most actions take place in regular schools. At community level some out-of-school activities are maintained but they are now marginal projects. The ministry of Education is now evaluating adult education provision, and defining new strategie. With a view to improving the opportunity of EEC funding, community development associations were created. Some of them engage in adult education activities, but these are often undertaken in connection with local adult education offices and the tendency is to follow external models of dynamic adult education, especially in rural areas.

Adult education activities are also offered by associations of African immigrants from the PALOP (African countries that use Portuguese as their official language), and these are still confined to the metropolitan area of Lisbon.

Teachers and Trainers

One of the current problems is trainers and teachers' training. The trainers working in the adult education system are the same who work in the normal education system. The priorities of adult education trainers are defined by each Regional Directorate of Education. These are :

- recruited teachers working full-time in adult education courses;
- teachers in the normal school's staff who opted for evening courses;
- recruited teachers working part-time in adult education courses cumulatively with their normal school teaching;
- teachers and other professionals working as vocational trainers; and
- voluntary teachers, trainers, and *animateurs* who are granted a subvention for their participation in out-of-school education and community education.

Most of these teachers and professionals have not been trained to work with young drop-outs who show a negative behaviour towards the education establishment, or to understand the paces and needs of adults. The fact is that teacher education institutions show no particular concern for this type of education. However teachers can at any moment apply for, or be recruited to basic adult education evening courses.

Teachers have a hard time adapting their styles and methods to courses where adolescents, young adults and adults mix. How could these teachers, whose training was based on the expectation of an untroubled school progression, find it easy to work with publics who have rejected school?

Although the recruitment of normal system's teachers has hindered adult pedagogical adequacy, it is a fact that it would have been impossible to carry out adult education programs without them. Considering the crisis in voluntary teachers' and adult education organizations' supply, the existence of an official provision that resorts to its agents (the teachers) has permitted the survival of the system. However, the operation of the non-formal education system is hindered by its association with the normal (formal) education system. The rules of the normal system are too rigid to ensure the success of an education that aims to be flexible and adaptable to the needs of the target publics. Moreover, the schools have some difficulty to manage and adequately provide adult education methods and ambiance. This situation engenders an incoherence between theory and practice, and often the more innovative and flexible postulates are put into practice according to traditional patterns by teachers who had not been trained to act otherwise.

The Construction of Supply and Demand in a Local Context

The adjustment of the types of supply to the needs of the demand is an issue bearing close relation to the choices that are constantly being made by the political power. In spite of that, the supply is structured at the local level, and local dynamics offer the opportunity for such an adjustment.The local construction of supply and demand generates dynamics that in some ways may determine the variables in the supply/demand model. Although the pressure of demand may condition the general supply policies, such as training priorities and strategies, on a local level demand does not always determine supply. The dynamic relationship between supply and demand is conditioned by the mediators, who construct local supply.

The research on the construction of supply and demand in a local context[10] proved that the demand of education is not always dependent on the will of the population, it often depends on the supply's structural factors. One of these is the dynamics created by the ministry of Education's regional and local officers. The coordination of local efforts and resources are fundamental to the creation of supply and local authorities (city mayors, city councils, parish representatives, etc.) can contribute to the organization of supply as a response to the needs of the demand. Local governments are the oldest and more traditional partners of the ministry of Education in promoting these courses. But this is not always the case: some local authorities engage in this collaboration, while others are unresponsive.

The organization of the courses in the target-public's area of residence is fundamental to the construction of demand, specially in what concerns the underschooled population. This fact is not a determinant because when transportation allowances are available, the people are not reluctant to participate in courses. Based on this, we can safely say that the mobilization of the population is related to the supply's structural factors.

Research also proved that the types of supply are directly linked with the educational priorities defined by each municipal office, especially the definition of priority target publics. The choices made by local adult education officers depend on the value they bestow upon the criteria used to appraise the supply. However, the choices that are made are not always the most adequate to the needs of the population, and may have considered only some segments of the population.

Therefore, it seems that at local level demand is conditioned by the supply dynamics. People choose to engage in education and training activities according to the supply's accessibility and response to their needs. Nevertheless, the construction of demand does not derive merely from the supply's structural conditions. The demand has its own dynamics, which arise from the population's individual and social characteristics. There are profiles that show more readiness than others.

THE CONSTRUCTION OF DEMAND: THE PUBLICS

Based on the clientele analysis, we have defined several profiles. Although the education supply follows the same model, the participants are of different ages and have different life and education stories. Together with working adults, who have very definite professional objectives, there are young people in their teens (14-18 age group) who had abandoned normal schooling due to retardation or failure, and engage in adult education courses to complete their compulsory education.

The adult participants, men and women, have abandoned school in their childhood to help the family income. Those from rural origins, they are typical of a generation who seldom progressed within the education system beyond the four years of primary schooling. With very different occupations (housewives, domestic helpers, cleaning ladies, industrial or construction workers), they now seek adult education courses to improve their employment situations. Although showing some learning difficulties due to their age and disused knowledge, their motivation is high.

The younger participants have attended the normal education system until the expected age limit (14 years of age) without obtaining the compulsory schooling certificate. Most of these young people leave normal schooling to enter evening courses, increasing the number of participants in adult education courses. They usually come from broken homes, and they have a clashing relation with the education establishment. If their notions about the education system are not altered by their relationship with the new teachers, the conflicting relation will tend to persist and a second failure will be the outcome.

Recurrent adult education, as well as the normal education system, has adopted a cross-cultural quality, as the number of participants from the so-called minority cultures and linguistic references has increased and demand special attention to their learning processes. In the Lisbon metropolitan area the majority of these participants come originally from African countries, and namely from Cabo Verde. Among these, the number of women participants exceed the number of men participants, but there are also groups of Portuguese-African young people who, like their suburban peers, enrol in adult education courses after having failed the normal schooling progression.

In sum, the adult education publics are heterogeneous and when they are brought together in the same courses, pedagogical situations may be difficult to deal with.

Obstacles to Participation

There are many reasons for the absence of demand, which can be identified as causes of the estrangement of the major part of the unschooled and underschooled population. Some of these causes may be related to structural factors of the supply dynamics; others may derive from the population's characteristics.

Shame, self-indulgence, family opposition and misinformation are the most commonly mentioned reasons for the lack of demand in what concerns underschooled young people and men. Participation in adult education courses has too many associations with illiteracy and the negative (sometimes traumatic) memories of past school days. In other ways, the needs of those segments of the population are not transparent. The working population does not always consider that acquiring a higher educational level is relevant to their professional advancement, especially if they already have the four-year schooling certificate.

Designed for an adult public, the courses are attended by adolescents, who "did not succeed their first schooling and were challenged by the explicit or implicit social demands of having a certificate[11]. In the courses, the adolescents mingle with younger and older adults, and the trainers try to motivate a number of people who do not have the same interests and motivations at the outset.

Going back to school as a participant in adult education courses "tends to reduce the former penalization. Having a second chance at education is, for a large part of these young people, having a second chance at failure"[12]. The abandonment rates are high among the participants, and particularly among the younger ones, which corroborates this second failure.

The new training models must be realistic and more attractive to the younger publics. Intermittent vocational training is in many countries a measure designed to attract this kind of public who is in danger of becoming marginal people. However, it is necessary that the contents and methods be adequate, and that the education project encompasses the counselling that these young people need during the transition from school to working life.

Heterogeneity of demand does exist in a metropolitan area, but it is not met by diversity of supply targeted to different cultural and age groups. The training model is but one. However, there is some local autonomy that allows for the adaptation of supply to various demands. As a consequence, local supply differ from national policies.

When the model allows some flexibility and a better adaptation to demand (as it is the case of PRODEP courses with vocational training areas), we have found that the local dynamics created by organizers and trainers have potentiated or conditioned that flexibility. This leads to the conclusion that the genesis of the supply is done in a local context. At national level, laws may be passed and innovations may be suggested, but only at local level can the supply be constructed — as it is constructed by local factors that determine both the extent of the demand and its success.

RECOMMENDATIONS

We feel that we can move on to offering some suggestions towards the construction of success.

The school-oriented instruction model does not motivate the larger part of the unschooled or underschooled population, simply because this type of training is not engaging to rural and urban populations of illiterate culture and specially to the most disadvantaged segments of the population. Where extreme poverty or even delinquency exists, education is not a priority. Only specific provisons that could combine literacy training and social work can induce disadvantaged populations to participate in adult education activities.

The programs for rural areas ought to be different from programs designed for urban areas. The literacy courses targeted to a certification according to academic parameters may be an adequate response to the expectations of the urban illiterates, but not to those of the rural illiterates; the literate culture seldom meets their needs. It seems that in certain situations literacy instruction could be an adequate response in rural areas, provided that such an instruction is integrated in larger, popular education or community education processes. Certification does not always appeal to adults who developed an illiterate culture and knowledge of their own.

In what concerns young and long-term unemployed, and even the ethnic minorities in conflict, there are problems of difficult solution all over Europe. Education could be the answer — but what measures can alter this situation? The traditional education system is unable to respond to the populations' needs, unless new models can be constructed that would consider these needs and foster a qualitative change in the target publics.

On verifying that instruction and employment policies are irrelevant if isolated from other measures, new challenges must be met by education. According to the Council of Europe, the answer could be found in a new concept of education, which develops new skills through a symbiosis between general education and technical instruction and helps the publics to face the current changes. The new education is not achieved through vocational training, but through a general, comprehensive, flexible education in a local context. It is an education for life.

In moments of economical crisis such as the one we live in now, adult education loses its developmentalist logic. Social problems are so large, and they reach so deeply, that adult education cannot offer a solution by itself. Unemployment, poverty, health problems, the pace of life-style changes, are some of the problems traditionally met by adult education, but their dimension has increased so dramatically that only a radical change of policy could solve them.

We believe that the new paths of adult education lead to the existence of local programs, in which local agencies — both governmental and non governmental — should participate, within the framework of, and supported by, national policies. The experience of the PRODEP courses has proved that it is possible to engage local economic forces in adult education programs, provided that local organizers are able to articulate the economic and social actions of the different partners.

Another aspect that needs some attention is training for the trainers. No training system exists yet. The only training is provided by the ministry of Education but on a rather slim dimension; the mobility of the teachers and the lack of a specialized pre-service training makes it almost impossible to secure their effective training in adult education methods. The answer seems to be the creation of a local staff of adult educators, including teachers and other professionals — such as sociologists, social workers, community development agents, psychologists — so that the trainers' reality context would not be so remote from that of the adult trainees.

For the adolescents who failed their compulsory education, steps should be taken to ensure their integration in the normal education system instead of rejecting them on the grounds that they could not complete their compulsory education within the time determined by the law.

The system must be prepared for the diversity of students, it must ensure equal education opportunities, and prevent early school leaving by offering new alternatives to help those who have learning and integration problems. It cannot continue to cast out thousands of adolescents each year.

Notes

1. Alberto de Melo, Ana Benavente, *Educacao Popular em Portugal (1974-1976)*, Lisboa, Livros Horizonte, 1978.

2. Stephen Stoer, *Educaca, Estado e Desenvolvimento em Portugal*, Lisboa, Livros Horizonte, Biblioteca do Educador Profissional, 1982, p. 83.

3. The Passing of the Comprehensive Law on the Education System marks the beginning of a new period in educational policies, namely in what concerns

adult education. According to the new structure, the educational system is divided into three sub-systems: pre-school education, school education and out-of-school (or further) education. **School education** includes several modalities, described as «special types of schoolings», such as vocational training, recurrent adult education and distance education. Any of these three modalities can be organized for adults and young people, but **recurrent adult education** is stated to be especially organized for «people who are no longer of thenormal age for attending basic and secondary education» and it is «also designed for people who did not have the chance to benefite from the education system at the normal age, and is particularly geared to eliminating illiteracy».

4. Maria José Esteves, *Os Novos Contornos de Analfabetismo. Analfabetismo ou iletrismo: O que é? Quem são? Onde Estão?* Ministerio da Educação, Departamento da Educação Basica, 1996.

5. Joao Ferreira de Almeida et al., *Exclusão Social — Factores e Tipos de Pobreza em Portugal*, Oeiras, Celta Editora, 1994, pp. 7, 48. The research on poverty in Portugal has shown that some of the population who are underhoused and/or live in the slums are characterized by limited or non existent schooling and vocational training, and can hardly obtain access to better wages, resorting to precarious labour conditions and odd jobs.

6. Jean-Pierre Velis. *La France illettrée*, L'Épreuve des faits, Paris, Édition du Seuil, 1988.

7. Ana Benavente and Alexandre Rosa interviewed by *Noticias da Educaçao*, 18, February 1995, Lisboa, Ministerio da Educaçao, pp. 12-13.

8. The compulsory schooling certificate is an access requirement for attending vocational courses promoted by Vocational Training institutions.

9. CIDEC/CIES. *Avaliaçcādo do PRODEP/Subprograma de Educação de Adultos. Relatório Final*, Ministério da Educação, Departamento da Educação Básica, Lisboa, 1995, p. XV.

10. This research was conducted in two municipalities of the Lisbon metropolitan area, where the diversity of publics and supplies permits to establish the relations between national policies and local practices.

11. Augusto Santos Silva, *Tempos Cruzados. Um Estudo Interpretativo da Cultura Popular*, Porto, Edicoes Afrontamento, Biblioteca das Ciencias do Homem, 1994, p. 357.

12. Ibidem.

Section Four

North America

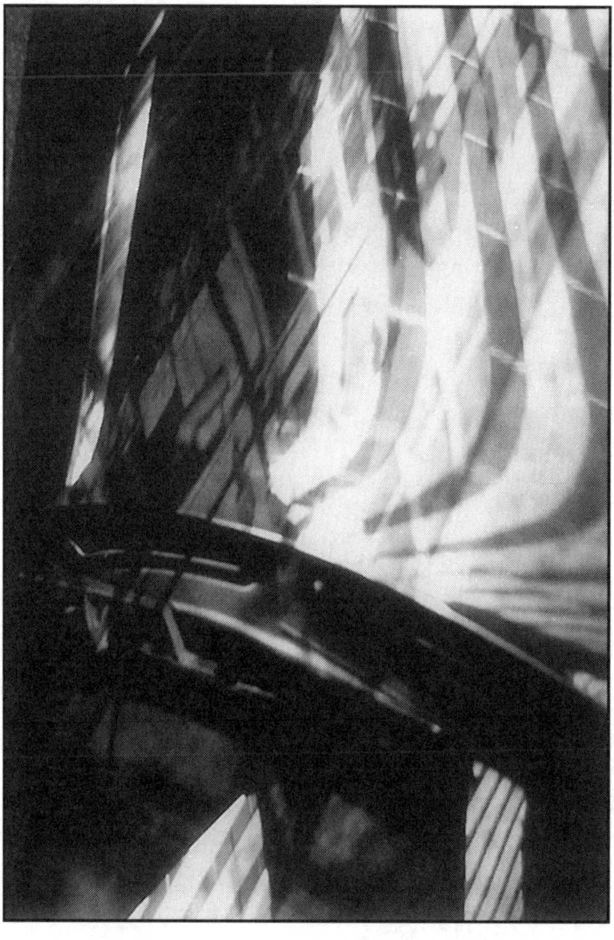

Chapter Thirteen
GETTING CLEAR ABOUT WHERE WE ARE GOING: RESULTS-ORIENTED ACCOUNTABILITY AS A TOOL FOR SYSTEM REFORM

Sondra G. Stein
National Institute for Literacy
Washington, DC, USA

INTRODUCTION TO THE ISSUES

Adult basic education services were first funded by the USA government as one of the fronts in President Lyndon Johnson's War on Poverty. The anti-poverty view of adult literacy and basic skills as a necessary and integral component of community strategies for empowerment of individuals and social, civic and economic development of the community, has persisted in many local communities over the nearly 30 years since this war officially ended. At the federal and state level, however, the prevailing view of adult literacy and basic skills has supported a more traditional school-based approach to adult education.

This school-based view of adult literacy and basic skills as segregated from the rest of life has had wide-reaching and mostly negative impacts on the quality and effectiveness of literacy and basic skills services available to adults in communities across the country. At the policy level we see its impact in the failure of politicians in both executive and legislative branches of government, at both the state and federal level, to recognize and support literacy and basic skills as an integral part of their own human investment strategies.

This failure to take into account basic education needs of key populations has short-circuited otherwise well-planned and well-intentioned human investment strategies — particularly in the area of welfare-to-work. It has also meant that the resources available for adult literacy and basic skills have always come from smaller, "discretionary" pools of funds. As a result, resources have never been sufficient to build the foundation necessary to achieve these broader social and economic goals.

Administratively, the accountability structures established by federal and state bureaucracies that fund adult literacy and basic skills also have supported this segregated, school-based view of adult literacy and basic skills. Most programs have not been held accountable for results — but rather for services delivered — for the number of adults who attend classes for a given number of hours. Multiple choice tests like the Test of Adult Basic Education (TABE) or the California Achievement Test (CAT), that were not normed on adult populations and have little relation to how adults perform in every day life, are the outcome measures widely used by federal and state bureaucracies.

This clear disjuncture between what programs feel is important for the adults and communities they serve, and what bureaucrats hold them accountable for, has resulted in a classical bifurcation between programs and funders, with programs having strong community mandates openly disdainful of the "values" of their funders.

This split has intensified in the recent period of diminished public resources. Increasingly, the message state and federal adult education administrators hear from governors and legislatures is that funding is dependent on results. Increasingly, available resources come with strings to "help move public aid recipients off the public dole" or to "help the underemployed and unemployed get the skills they need to work". State and federal adult education administrators and the programs they fund are unprepared for this shift in funding policy. Programs with a history of being held accountable only for seat time, are unprepared, unable and often, unwilling, to meet these new demands.

On the other hand, community-based and other contextualized

literacy programs that have practiced their own forms of results-oriented accountability, reject these new demands as being narrowly short-term, and counterproductive to the long term benefits of the community. Where public policy defines the problem (and the solution) in terms of "getting people off welfare", many adult educators — especially community-based educators — define the problem/solution in terms of "ending poverty and marginalization of the poor"; where public policy defines the problem as "ending teen pregnancy" or "ending single parent families", community educators talk about strengthening family and community resources.

This divergent discourse on the goals of adult literacy and basic education is surfacing at centre stage in the policy arena as policy-makers at every level begin to understand that the failure to measure results is a byproduct of a deeper failure of vision — of the lack of a consensus on what adult literacy programs ought to do, on what kind of impact a quality literacy program should have on the adults and communities it serves.

Fortunately, over the past decade a movement has begun to reframe the relationship between literacy and other state goals at a policy level. Fuelled by a changing world perspective as well as by the changing policy and fiscal environment, this movement is slowly effecting a "paradigm shift" in how bureaucracies think about programs, results and customers. Like the movement within the private sector to push decision making further and further down the line, this shift has great potential to realign decision making relationships between programs and funders, with groups of agencies operating under principles of shared accountability at the state and federal level giving greater decision making authority to local communities by holding them accountable, as a community, for achieving agreed upon results. Such a shift can make an extraordinary difference for adults and communities. There is potential here for real empowerment and real development in accordance with a common vision of what change and development will mean.

It is the purpose of this paper to explore this movement, within the area of adult literacy and basic skills, with special emphasis on two initiatives launched by the National Institute for Literacy (NIFL) in 1993 with the intention of developing the consensus, the knowledge, the technology and the will to measure our progress as a nation towards the National Adult Literacy and Life Long Learning Goal. Providing the Institute's rationale for developing the Performance Measurement Reporting and Improvement Systems (PMRIS) Initiative and what has become known as the Equipped for the Future (EFF)

Initiative, we will then turn to a more in-depth exploration of the ways in which these two initiatives are beginning to contribute to creating a more supportive institutional context for sustainable local development both directly, in the states and localities where they are operating and, indirectly, through their impact on the broader policy context.

DREAMING OF THE MILLENNIUM: THE PRESIDENT AND THE GOVERNORS SET NATIONAL EDUCATION GOALS

While national education and industrial policy has been a powerful factor in the economic and cultural development of many industrialized nations, in the United States education policy has been vigorously defended as the province of the states. This began to be challenged in the 1980's, as changes in technology, immigration patterns, and most of all, a much more competitive global marketplace, brought home to state and national leaders that the weaknesses of our education system made the USA, in the words of the Report that launched the current round of school reform, *A Nation at Risk*.

> The people of the United States need to know that individuals in our society who do not possess the levels of skill, literacy, and training essential to this new era will be effectively disenfranchised, not simply from the material rewards that accompany competent performance, but also from the chance to participate fully in our national life.[1]

By 1989, the President and the 50 Governors of the United States came together to set education goals intended to "energize public opinion and ongoing education reform efforts [...] to rebuild our education system so that it is among the best in the world."[2] While the idea of *national* goals for education is once again (in 1996) politically suspect, the goals agreed to by the President and Governors, and affirmed by the Congress in 1993 do, in fact, represent a continuing consensus of what Americans expect of their public education system.[3] The trick has been figuring out how to get there, both in terms of developing consensus on what those goals mean, and putting in place a system to reach them.

A plethora of public and private organizations have taken on these tasks for the public education system for school-age children (5-18 years, in the USA). Governors and state legislatures, egged on by coalitions of business leaders concerned about educating the future workforce, have established large scale school reform efforts. Professional organizations have led efforts to develop comprehensive voluntary content and performance standards, defining what it is students need to know and be able to do when they graduate from school if the nation is to achieve these goals.

Until 1993, when the NIFL launched what has become known as its *Equipped for the Future (EFF) Initiative*, there was no commensurate effort to address these issues for Goal Six, the National Education Goal that focuses on Adult Literacy and Life Long Learning. Goal Six reads:

> By the year 2000, every adult American will be literate and will possess the knowledge and skills necessary to compete in a global economy and exercise the rights and responsibilities of citizenship.

While there has been grave concern about the number of adult Americans who lack the requisite skills and knowledge to achieve these objectives, the consensus has been that the best way to address the problem is to fix the K-12 system, thereby reducing the number of young people who arrive at adulthood without the necessary skills. Rather than challenge this basic assumption, policymakers have tended to discount the results of the 1992 National Adult Literacy Survey, which found that nearly half of all USA adults — 90 million — lacked the level of skill associated with "success" in the global economy.[1] We are beginning to understand that preparation for the 21st Century will require that adults *regularly* update and upgrade their knowledge and skills. However, there has not yet been national acknowledgement that fixing the K-12 system (while it may ensure that young people get a better foundation) will ensure that adults will have the skills and knowledge they need throughout their lives to adapt to changes in technology, science and politics. Only a systemic, systematic approach to the delivery of adult literacy and basic skills will enable us to address these continuing, lifelong education needs.

The publicly supported adult basic skills system in the USA does not now provide this systemic approach. It is widely conceived as a second chance system for immigrants and those that have somehow fallen through the cracks, and described by most adult practitioners as a step-child of the K-12 system. This metaphor alludes to two characteristics of the system.

First of all, in more than two-thirds of the states, adult primary and secondary education is administered by the state agency that has, as it's first priority, primary and secondary education for traditional school age children. Second, the resources allotted to adult education are comparatively minuscule. In Massachusetts, for example, in a year when the number of adults without a high school diploma exceeded the number of school age children, the per capita expenditures averaged $215.00 per adult receiving services compared with $3,000 to $5,000 per child enrolled in school. Taken together, these two factors produce a system that is more than 80 per cent staffed by part-timers and volunteers. And while this system offers students an average of only six hours per week of instruction, it uses a curriculum based on the academic curriculum for children attending school 25 hours per week.

Under these conditions, it is not surprising that a three year evaluation study commissioned by the Federal Department of Education revealed that most programs were singularly ineffective in retaining students long enough for them to show progress on any standardized tests of learning gains.[5] Nearly a third of those who enrolled in classes, dropped out after less than 12 hours of instruction. Given these typical system results, it hardly matters that the system "serves" less than five per cent of adults in need.

An increasing number of adult education practitioners and researchers have attributed these failures of the adult basic education system to the extension of the K-12 model to adult education. Cognitive psychologists have questioned the usefulness of traditional school-based learning for students of any age, based on four key differences between in-school and out-of-school learning and mental activity: 1) the nurturing of individual cognition in school versus the reliance on shared cognition outside; 2) the valuing of pure mentation in school (what one can do without "external crutches") versus the need for expertise in manipulating physical and intellectual tools (including books, calculators and computers) outside of school; 3) training in symbol manipulation in school, versus reasoning about real things and situations outside of school; and 4) generalized learning in school (supposedly to aid transfer or portability of skills), versus the need to develop and hone situation-specific competencies outside of school.[6]

Evidence from contextualized adult education programs like workplace and family literacy programs confirms that those programs in which learning is related to real life needs and goals, and enables learners to develop familiarity and facility with tools and institutions they need to use in "life" are more successful at motivating adult students to persist in education until they achieve their goals. Since, however, state and federal administrators of adult education-related funds continue to rely on school-based measures for reporting purposes, there has been little incentive for practitioners to experiment with such contextualized approaches to learning. The system has not been set up to reward success despite increasing pressures to show success or lose funding.

The National Institute for Literacy launched its two results-oriented initiatives in this context, hoping to stimulate a rethinking of the goals and mission of adult education that would lead to reform at every level of the delivery system. The first of these, our **Equipped for the Future** (EFF) Initiative, was intended to begin the process of building a broad consensus on **what the national adult literacy and life long learning goal meant**, and **what adults would need to know and be able to do to achieve it.**

The second, inelegantly but descriptively titled **The Performance Measurement, Reporting and Improvement System** (PMRIS) initiative, was designed to assist states in establishing accountability systems for their adult education and training programs that looked at real world results instead of school-based process or progress measures (seat time, scores on tests), and linked the outcomes of these programs to state policy goals. Taken together, the two initiatives create the conditions for reframing how policymakers, educators and the general public think about adult literacy and basic skills education.

By shifting the discussion from a focus on process to a focus on results, the PMRIS initiative establishes the foundation for a discussion of what results are important. By starting with adult learners' own definition of what results matter, EFF broadens and enriches the discussion, making possible a definition of program results that make a real difference in learners' lives.

LITERACY FOR WHAT: CREATING STATE ACCOUNTABILITY SYSTEMS

The PMRIS initiative focused on building this new consciousness about literacy at the state policy level. The initiative was designed to raise the political visibility and the budgetary viability of adult literacy by making explicit the connection between building adult literacy and achieving other policy goals that were more central to most governors' political agendas — including economic development, decreased crime, family stability. Taking seriously Congress' vision of the NIFL as a convener across government agencies, the NIFL offered grants to Governors, rather than to state education agencies, inviting them to work with us to establish a single interagency accountability system in their states that would provide clear, easy to understand reports of the results — in terms of real world impacts — of adult education and training programs. We envisioned these systems as not only providing evidence of what the public was getting for their investment in these services, but also as providing the information necessary for continuous improvement of policy and programs.

In response to the tight fiscal environment of the 90's, many states were already engaged in legislatively-mandated efforts to streamline bureaucratic functions, cut through red tape for customers, and show legislators clear results for investments. Our grants attempted to involve adult literacy and basic skills programs in this broader effort. By engaging state policymakers from across the entire human resource spectrum (job training and employment security, health and welfare, corrections, and parent education) in a project that required them to articulate the specific ways in which literacy programs could contribute to the goals of their agencies, we hoped to encourage the development of stronger linkages between adult literacy programs and these other human resource programs. We believed that once state agencies reached agreement on outcomes of literacy programs that would make a real difference in terms of achieving broader state goals, it would be possible (and necessary) to shift the focus to the conditions and resources necessary for literacy programs to achieve these goals.

If, for example, a stated outcome of literacy programs was that adults leaving literacy programs would possess the knowledge and skills necessary to enter and maintain employment, did it make sense to invest a level of resources that supported no more than four to six hours of instruction a week? At that rate, it might take an adult years to achieve the desired result. If adult literacy programs were to achieve real results in real time frames, they would need resources akin to those invested in public primary, secondary and post secondary education. Through building a clearer understanding of the importance of literacy as a foundation, and the requirements for literacy programs to do their job, we hoped that the PMRIS project would help create a climate that was supportive of continued and increased investment in adult literacy despite the tightening fiscal environment.

GETTING THERE

In December, 1993, the NIFL officially launched the PMRIS initiative by convening policy teams from five states — Alabama, Hawaii, Kentucky, New York and Tennessee — that had been awarded grants for a four day Policy Academy.

During the Academy, each team worked with a "coach" to begin the strategic planning and implementation process they would continue back home. They began by articulating a shared vision for a preferred future for the state, and identifying the key human resource policy outcomes the state needed to achieve in order to attain that vision. Then the team focused on the question of «What kind of results would literacy programs need to achieve as a necessary — if not sufficient — condition for achieving those outcomes?»

According to the PMRIS design, states would begin to hold programs accountable for achieving these real world results. They would develop and put in place new performance measures appropriate to showing progress toward these results; and programs would be expected to collect the data necessary to show progress against these measures. These changes would provide an incentive for programs to focus teaching and learning activities on helping learners achieve these real world results so that they could demonstrate progress and success to their funders.

The process of implementation and degree of success differed from state to state, depending on a combination of several key factors: 1) the political culture of the state, including the history of collaboration between agencies at the state level, and between levels of government (federal, state and local); 2) the lead agency for the project, and its credibility as an honest broker across government; 3) the credibility, intelligence, good will and ability to negotiate government systems of the key staff working on the project; and 4) the political will to make it happen.

In several states, these factors combined to keep the project from moving from the conceptual to the practical level. In two states, for example, where there was little history of interagency collaboration at the state level, a change in the governor just as the project was ready to move from conceptual agreement to testing out the new system essentially brought an end to real progress. While key players waited to see what the new governor would do, the political will for change temporarily stalled, and the project staff at the lead agency did not see themselves in a position to move ahead on any of the systems change issues.

In both of these states, project staff retreated to focus on technical matters related to the collection, management and sharing of data, and the political focus on real world impacts got lost. In neither state was there an effort to engage local constituencies in a way that could bypass the political stalemate and move the project forward. As a result, in these states there was no progress in implementing an accountability system that could make a difference in how people think about adult literacy and basic skills or in how adult education services were delivered. The conceptual system design work completed by the project staff may find a place in future efforts to develop results-based accountability systems, but for now, the projects in those states can be said to have produced much paper and few changes.

The situation was very different in the third state where there was a change of governor. Here the initial project design included a dialogic process between the state interagency team and three "local research sites". Teams at these local sites tested out the on-the-ground workability of ideas for building a new outcome-based interagency accountability system and gave continuous feedback that shaped the design of the system. In each site, the local team engaged in their own strategic planning process: identifying common goals for the full range of adults seeking services in that area; identifying barriers that currently stood in the way of adults achieving those goals; identifying what those adults would need in order to get past those barriers and achieve those goals; and then assessing the strengths and weaknesses of the existing delivery system in relation to those needs.

Understanding common needs and goals

Beginning with this common understanding of common needs and goals, local providers talked together about how an interagency accountability system could help them overcome barriers, and offer more effective services. They also identified what other assistance they would need to help more people in their communities achieve the goals identified. Project staff and state team members relied on this information in designing key system elements, including policy outcomes, program outcomes and performance measures, and the information system for collecting, sharing and reporting results. Priorities identified by local providers — electronic sharing of client information, for example, so that an individual seeking services would not have to fill out multiple copies of the same forms but would have a "travelling client record" to facilitate referral — were prioritized at the state level to assure local provider buy-in to the new system.

The fruits of this multi-level project design became clear when progress at the state level halted due to a change in both the Governor and the governing party. While the state policy team here was also brought to a standstill, the project staff had support and encouragement from the local teams to move forward on piloting some aspects of the new system, including the electronic sharing of data. They also had political support from these local teams in lobbying the new administration to continue the project. *The combination of actual demonstration of good results on the ground with political support resulted, a few months later, when the dust of party-shifting had settled, in the project re-emerging with credibility with the new administration.*

Will electronic data sharing help?

My narrative so far has emphasized the pragmatic value of this dialogic (top-down/bottom-up) process in saving the state project, and in making the project worth saving. As the new administration moves forward, continuing to invest in it, the project will make a real positive difference in what happens. The electronic sharing of data — already in place in four pilot sites and ready to expand across the state — has simplified the bureaucratic maze that confronts adults seeking services and has decreased the paperwork that overwhelmed local program staff. Adults are now directly able to find the services they seek. And teachers now have more time for teaching and meeting the needs of adults in their communities.

Local programs are also beginning to use this new electronic information system to collect new data about results that matter. While there continues to be nervousness among practitioners about the impact of a new, still unknown accountability system, this is somewhat mitigated by the positive impact of the process and results so far. Practitioners can see their ideas reflected in the policy and program outcomes adopted by the state team, and they continue to have an active role in trying to figure out what measures to use and what data to collect in order to measure their progress toward achieving these goals. In the next year, as the system gets implemented as part of the state's welfare reform initiative, we will all have the chance to see what happens as this dialogic process becomes subsumed in the ordinary state machinery of grantees reporting results to the funding agency.

Will measuring progress and reporting success using the new results help programs in telling their story? Will it bring the resources they need to do their job better? Or will programs be held accountable for results they can't achieve due to factors beyond their control — like the lack of child care or good jobs in the area? Will state agencies implementing the new system enable communities to take these environmental factors into account by continuing to work with communities as a whole system, or will they pit program against program to see who can produce the best results? In short, will the new system be used as a tool for continuous improvement, for enabling local communities and the state to work together to assure the best possible results for the adults in the community or will it simply be a way of pushing programs to produce more for less? Both results are possible.

While the story is unfinished, the story line so far is promising. It appears that taking an outcomes-based approach to accountability can make a difference, as long as local communities are directly involved in the process of deciding what results matter. Being involved in the process has been, in itself, a benefit to local communities since it has served as a vehicle to bring a broad spectrum of local agencies and service providers together to focus on common goals — to get clear for themselves on where they are going, so they can chart a better course for themselves to get there.

A NEW STARTING PLACE FOR FUTURE SYSTEM REFORM: THE CUSTOMERS

Whereas NIFL's state accountability project began with a traditional "top-down" approach to system reform, the Equipped for the Future (EFF) Initiative was designed to engage the broadest range of adult literacy constituencies from the beginning. Starting with the customers of our system — adults seeking to build stronger literacy and basic skills — we hoped to build a consensus, constituency by constituency, stakeholder group by stakeholder group, of what the results of our programs should be and how they needed to be changed to get there.

At the same time that the state teams from Alabama, Hawaii, Kentucky, New York and Tennessee were meeting at the Policy Academy to think about visions and policy and program outcomes, NIFL was getting ready to send out an invitation to learners all across the country to join us in developing a clearer definition of the Adult Literacy and Life Long Learning Goal. The invitation letter read:

> Since 1990 we have had a National Goal for Adult Literacy and Life Long Learning in the United States [...]. This year the National Institute for Literacy and the National Education Goals Panel are trying to define this Goal more carefully so we can measure our national progress toward its achievement. We need your help to make sure that *the definition we come up with matches adult learners' experience of their journey to literacy and full participation in our nation's economic and civic life.*[7]

More than 1500 adults, studying in 151 programs in 34 states and the Commonwealth of Puerto Rico, wrote to tell us what they thought. They were teen parents, grandparents, and single adults looking forward to raising a family. They were first, second and third generation Americans, immigrants from Eastern Europe, the Middle East and Mexico, refugees from Southeast Asia, Latin America and the former Soviet Union. Used to being treated as if their voices didn't count, they frequently began their letters by "expressing [our] surprise and gratitude for the chance to respond to this very important subject. [...] I hope our voices will be heard now that we are being asked our public opinions".

The four key purposes for literacy

The 1500 voices spoke with astonishing unanimity. In the field of adult literacy it is common for practitioners and administrators to reject the idea of a national goal for literacy programs on the ground that we need to be responsive to the *multiplicity* of adult learner goals. While the adult learners in our study wrote about specific learning goals — like getting a GED or learning to read to their children — these goals were universally discussed in relation to four broader themes.

As our research progressed, we began to think about these themes as **fundamental purposes** for literacy, since they were the motivation for adults to acquire new knowledge and build stronger skills. These purposes are:

- **Access**: *the need to have access to information and orient one self in the world.*

- **Voice**: *the desire to give voice to one's ideas and opinions and to have the confidence that one's voice will be heard and taken into account.*

- **Independent Action**: *the desire to solve problems and make decisions on one's own, without having to depend on someone else to mediate the world.*

- **Bridge to the Future**: *the need to keep on learning in order to keep up with a rapidly changing world.*

When we rewrote the National Adult Literacy Goal to include these purposes, we found that we had the start on a goal that was, in fact, much more specific and measurable — that could provide a guide for teaching and learning:

> By the year 2000, every adult America will be literate and will possess the knowledge and skills necessary to orient oneself in a rapidly changing world, to find one's voice and be heard, and to act independently as a parent, citizen and worker, for the good of one's family, community and nation.

As we reflected on our findings, discussing them with colleagues at every level of the adult education and training system, a consensus began to emerge that these four purposes were descriptive of more than the adult literacy end of the adult learning continuum. **They described the motivation for continued learning for adults at every level of education**. As such, they seemed to provide the core for an adult — as opposed to a child-centred approach to education. Furthermore, since each purpose seemed to integrate both the cognitive (the knowledge or skill desired) and the behavioural or active (the changed behaviour desired) dimensions of learning, the purposes seemed to provide the basis for a new theoretical approach to adult learning that would enable us to account for the interaction of affective, cognitive and motivational factors in determining how, what, and under what conditions adults learn.

We were very excited about the potential significance of these findings. In July 1995, we released the report of our research at a national meeting of adult learners. We called the report *Equipped for the Future: A Customer-Driven Vision for Adult Literacy and Lifelong Learning* to emphasize that its findings were based on the voices of our customers. If the field was serious about meeting learner goals then we needed to listen to these voices, and use them as a starting point for rethinking what we teach and how we define and measure success.

STANDARDS-BASED REFORM

In order to create opportunities for people to think about and discuss the ideas in *Equipped for the Future,* we announced a program of planning grants that would provide encouragement and resources for organizations to engage teachers, learners, administrators and policymakers in thinking about and discussing the implications of this new vision for our field. The parameters we defined for the planning grants put EFF, along with national efforts to achieve the other goals, on the path of standards-based reform.

Standards-based reform is part of the quality movement. *It assumes that once you know what your customer wants, you continuously adjust all your systems to assure that you get there as effectively and efficiently as possible.* The eight national education goals were assumed to reflect the national consensus of what results we wanted from our education system. The next steps in the standards-based reform process were, for each goal, to engage key customers in developing content standards that articulate what students need to know and be able to do to achieve the goal, to develop performance indicators identifying how achievement of the content standards will be demonstrated, and to develop performance standards identifying the levels of achievement considered "good enough."

This consensus on what the results of the system should be serves as the starting point for system reform. The standards are adopted and teachers begin the task of figuring out what new curricula and teaching approaches are necessary to achieve these standards. System results are assessed regularly: are more students leaving the system with the knowledge and skills defined by the standards? If not, system workers and managers try to identify what other changes can be made in the teaching-learning process.

REFORM IS A JOURNEY AS WELL AS A DESTINATION

While it is surely true that you cannot get where you are going if you don't know where it is, it is also true, in system reform, that the road you take will determine whether you have any chance of arriving at your destination.

Over the five years that the National Education Goals had been in place, the Federal Government had supported the development of standards for all of the academic disciplines in K-12 education: maths, science, geography, history, social studies and English Language Arts. In most cases, the actual standards development work had been carried out by professional teachers' organizations. The government had also supported the identification, by unions and industry associations, of skill standards for workers in 22 industries including retail trades, hospitality, electronics, chemical workers, etc. As NIFL studied the public reception given these various standards we became clear that, here too, involving key constituencies throughout the process was critical to success. The broader the involvement of customers, the more likely it was that the standards would be an accurate reflection of what students, or workers, in the case of skill standards, needed to succeed in the real world. The broader the involvement of teachers and other stakeholder in the education system, the more likely it was that the standards would actually be used to drive teaching and learning in schools.

At the NIFL, we felt we had a good customer base for our standards-based system reform effort. Since our framework of four purposes and three adult roles (parent, citizen and worker) had come from the adult learners who were the customers of our system, we felt confident that it accurately reflected their perception of their needs. Our goal was to use this planning grant process to see how other customers and constituencies would respond to this framework, and to see whether teachers and other adult education professionals who were invested in the existing system would respond to this new approach to defining the results of the system.

The eight organizations that were awarded planning grants in October, 1995 became our partners in figuring out how to build broad investment in a common set of results for adult literacy and basic skills and how to undertake a nationwide process of system reform to achieve those results.[8] As we approach the end of this planning grant year we feel confident that we not only have a destination worth aiming toward, but we have mapped a good route to get there. Transcripts from focus groups and discussions with members of the Working Groups of the eight grantees confirm that adult learners, practitioners, and some key stakeholder groups are excited about the way the EFF purposes define the goal of adult literacy and basic skills education. It "fits" their experience of the real needs of adults. Further, the data collected through these focus groups, inquiry projects, and other grantee research activities, has actually begun the process of building content standards that directly reflect what adults need to know and be able to do to fulfil their responsibilities as parents, citizens and workers.

The planning grant year has affirmed that there is broad interest in reorienting the literacy system to achieve real world results. Over the next year our task is to describe both what those results are, and the process we used to define them in such a clear and compelling way that both the approach and the result make sense to all the constituencies and publics that are invested in the adult education enterprise. The challenges, as we understand them, are formidable. To date, the standards movement has focused solely on the cognitive dimensions of learning. Though there is broad recognition that this approach to what students need to know and be able to do leaves out or marginalizes the key affective and motivational dimensions of learning, no one has yet figured out how to combine them in standards. To think that we can do so seems, on some days, Quixotic. And yet, the voices of adult learners continue to affirm how important this effort is.

Not only are we trying to define the as yet undefined, we are also trying to do it in an open, collaborative way, engaging the full range of adult education constituencies, many of whom will be invested in the known, in the ways we do things now. Lillian Smith, one of the great thinkers of the USA Civil Rights movement in the 1950's and '60's wrote:

> It is important that we remember that when a man gives up something [...] he is not going to feel good unless he has something equal or better returned to him. This is the bargain which each human being makes with his own personality; this is the bargain a man makes with his family, his government, his culture, and even with his religion. These are the terms of real and lasting peace, whether it be peace of mind or soul, or peace between nations classes, or races.[9]

Will we find the right terms to make a good bargain? Will we find a way to bring our public definition of program results in line with the four purposes?

CONVERGENCES AND NEGOTIATIONS

What have we learned from the past three years of work on these system reform initiatives? The most important learning for us is that a shared vision of a preferred future is a powerful impetus for system reform. In the PMRIS initiative we saw how state agencies and local organizations alike could break out of the bureaucratic silos that keep them from working effectively together when they focus on defining common goals for their common clients. This focus on common goals enabled them to think about how each of their organizations and systems contributed one piece toward this common goal: they could begin to define common policy and program goals for that system, taking on shared responsibility for results, and investigating ways they can reallocate resources among themselves to make it more likely for adults to achieve those results.

EFF focuses on the individual learner's stake in these broad policy and programs goals. By starting with what adult learners said they needed to know and be able to do to achieve the broad policy goals of a productive workforce and an engaged citizenry, EFF builds a bridge to link policy to practice and practice to real world results. Over the next year, as the EFF initiative engages a broadening circle of constituencies in contributing their perspectives to the EFF framework of purposes and roles, we will aim to make that bridge sturdy enough to hold the weight of the adult literacy system. If we are successful, and the EFF framework represents the convergence of adult learner perspectives with the goals of policymakers, then the content standards and performance indicators we develop will provide a framework for adult literacy instruction and assessment that leads to success as both policymakers and practitioners define it.

Doing our job right is the key. For a vision of a preferred future to become an impetus for system reform, that vision must be widely shared. It must speak to the real needs of diverse constituencies. And that can only happen if those communities are involved in the process of shaping and refining both the vision and implementation of that vision through the kind of dialogic, consensus-building process we described above.

It is also true that the dialogic process is, itself, about change. In engaging teachers and learners, administrators and policymakers, legislators and other stakeholder, in thinking and talking with each other about what the results of the system ought to be and how we are likely to get there, we are actually beginning the journey to reform. It is a journey that may just assure that all of us end up better equipped for the future.

Notes

1. National Commission on Excellence in Education, 1983 *A Nation at Risk: The Imperative for Educational Reform*. Washington, DC: USA Government Printing Office.

2. National Education Goals Panel 1993. *The National Education Goals Report: Building a Nation of Learners,* Volume 1: National Report. Washington DC: USA Government Printing Office.

3. While the President and Governors agreed to Six Goals in 1990, the Congress added two more when they passed Goals 2000: Educate America Act, in 1994. The Eight Education Goals are: By the Year 2000:
(1) All children in America will start school ready to learn.
(2) The high school graduation rate will increase to at least 90 percent;
(3) American students will leave grades four, eight, and twelve having demonstrated competency in challenging subject matter [. . .];
(4) The Nation's teaching force will have access to programs for the continued improvement of their professional skills and the opportunity to acquire the knowledge and skills to instruct and prepare all American students for the next century;
(5) USA students will be first in the world in mathematics and science achievement;
(6) Every adult American will be literate and will possess the knowledge and skills necessary to compete in a global economy and exercise the rights and responsibilities of citizenship;
(7) Every school in the USA will be free of drugs, violence [...] and will offer a disciplined environment conducive to learning.
(8) Every school will promote partnerships that will increase parental involvement and participation in promoting the [...] growth of children.

4. Irwin Kirsch, Ann Jungblut, Lynn Jenkins & Andrew Kolstad 1993. *Adult Literacy in America: A First Look at the Results of the National Adult Literacy Survey.* Washington, DC: USA Government Printing Office.

5. Malcolm B. Young, et al. 1993. *National Evaluation of Adult Education Programs.* Washington DC: Development Associates, Inc.

6. For more discussion of these ideas see Lauren Resnick 1987, *Learning in School and Out;* Sue Berryman 1989, *Education and the Economy: A Diagnostic Review and Implications for the Federal Role;* and Sylbia Scribner 1988, *Head and Hand: An Action Approach to Thinking.* All three papers are publications of the Institute on Education and the Economy, Columbia University, New York.

7. For the full text of this letter, as well as a complete report of the research see Sondra G. Stein 1995. *Equipped for the Future: A Customer Driven Vision for Adult Literacy and Lifelong Learning.* Washington, DC: NIFL

8. The organizations included three local initiatives — one organized through the Mayor's Office, one through the public schools, one through the Community College District — two statewide organizations, one multi-state initiative, and two national organizations whose mission was closely linked to the

purposes of this initiative.

9. Lillian Smith 1978 "Ten Years from Today", *The Winner Names The Age*. New York: W.W. Norton Company.

Chapter Fourteen
«THIS IS A SCHOOL. WE WANT TO GO TO SCHOOL» INSTITUTIONAL SOCIAL RESPONSIBILITY AND WORKER EDUCATION

Sheryl Greenwood Gowen
Georgia State University
Atlanta, Georgia, USA

A SENSE OF SOCIAL RESPONSIBILITY

In the current climate of corporate down-sizing, dwindling wages, and shrinking benefits for workers, the belief that employers should be held at least partially responsible for the quality of life of their employees and the communities in which they live has emerged as a popular theme in American political debate.

In the first three months of 1996, for example, the *New York Times* featured several editorials and letters which addressed the extent to which employers have any social obligations other than to their shareholders and the bottom line. On the one hand, conservatives like William Safire argue that corporations have no obligations other than to turn a profit and remain competitive. On the other hand, more liberal public officials like Labor Secretary Robert Reich maintain that the corporations must address the educational and human needs of their workers. Reich has even proposed corporate tax breaks to those companies that recognize a social responsibility to their employees and the community. He argues that corporations should not be blamed for any perceived lack of social responsibility because these corporations are organized within and by a culture that has expected, indeed rewarded, a profit-only mentality. "[...] Corporations and their top executives [...] are behaving exactly as they are organized to behave. If we want them to put greater emphasis on the interests of their workers and communities, society must reorganize them to do so."

This basic unwillingness to accept mutual responsibility for the common good is America's most recent deal with the devil. In exchange for continued economic domination, profit is placed above people, product above process, competition above community.

The ways in which the country has approached the issue of worker education illustrates this general cultural pattern. Until quite recently, workers have been seen as expendable commodities. Relatively speaking, very few resources have been invested in educating the workforce or in enhancing educational levels for the majority of the worker population. Rather, like America's monetary wealth, its educational resources have been concentrated on managers rather than entry-level workers. On the other hand, training, which differs considerably from education, has been reserved for the vast majority of workers who have little or no post-secondary education. This training has focused on work-related skills, has been very short-term, and has been designed to enhance productivity rather than individual or community development.

But the fact that corporate social responsibility is now addressed in the public arena indicates that values and beliefs about the common good may be in question. One indication of change are the local worker education projects that have been launched across the country, quietly and outside of public awareness or debate. In this paper, I will describe one such program, which is grounded in a strong sense of institutional as well as personal social responsibility to workers and their communities. I will argue that successful programs of this kind rely not on institutional policy, but on the basic human spirit of key individuals within the institution. It is my position that American institutions seem unable to assume moral character of any kind. Rather, they are a direct expression of the culture in which they are situated as well as the beliefs of those key players who implement the policies and make the day-to-day decisions on the management and distribution of resources.

"WHAT CAN WE DO FOR YOU?"

The program I wish to discuss is situated in a large, urban, public university in the southeastern United States. Most importantly, the program, unlike many others, was not developed in response to any particular tax incentive, institutional policy, union initiative, funding priority, or governmental regulation. The conditions under which it occurred included an economic crunch and a massive reorganization that left many faculty and staff out of work or forced into early retirement and it has occurred because of the social consciousness of a number of key players in the institution as well as the patience and persistence of the workers.

In 1988, Bayside University experienced an especially difficult "reorganization" and the fear and pain that are inevitable from such a deep incision. In addition, the state legislature allocated no money for pay raises for staff (although faculty still received merit pay raises that year). One group most affected by this were the physical plant employees, who are some of the lowest-paid and least-educated employees at the university. In many American institutions, those employees who maintain a workplace tend to be invisible to the other, more privileged workers, and it is true at Bayside University as well. There are two universes operating within the same physical space. One consisting of faculty, students and more well-positioned staff while the other is given over to those who serve and clean up after the first group.

In an effort to soften hard economic news to the most economically vulnerable of employees, the president of the university met with staff and explained, "We can't give you raises". He could have stopped at this point, but he chose to ask what proved to be a pivotal question, "What can we do for you?" This question could have been perceived as a rhetorical ploy, but by at least one employee it was answered with all of the seriousness with which it was intended. A custodian spoke up and said, "This is a school. We want to go to school". A simple statement, heavy with irony. While the university was a centre for education, it offered that education only to "paying" students — learning was not a human right, but rather a commodity to sell in the marketplace.

The president, in the first of many acts of individual social responsibility, recognized the injustice of this commodification, and in a meeting later with his top administrators, declared that it was "inexcusable" that the university offered education courses to everyone in the state but did nothing to offer education to its own employees. The rest of the administrators at that table that day seemed never to have considered such a thought. Thus, from the beginning, this program was conceptualized as an institutional social responsibility and an employee benefit, not an effort at remediation or a way to increase productivity and reduce costs. If the classes had been designed as a remediation effort and had employed traditional testing or even alternative forms of evaluation, it is unlikely that many workers would have participated. Even without these efforts at "accountability", developing the trust necessary to create an effective learning environment took several months.

Many of the costs related to the program were met by using already existing resources, and thus the actual monetary outlay was quite small. For example, the Cooperative Learning Lab donated classroom space and the Department of Learning Assistance donated technical support.

The curricula/pedagogy

The program employed was designed to give learners the agency to develop their own notions of what literacy meant to them and what skills they wanted to improve. It also allowed them the control to decide how the new skills would be applied either at work or in their personal lives or in their communities. The program was developed according to principles of cooperative learning, and a humanized, pragmatic curriculum, with an emphasis on "connection, circles or chains of caring" and of teaching as a "moral enterprise" (Kazemek, 1986:23-24). The teacher, Carol, placed caring in the centre of her teaching and consistently encouraged the group members to care for one another.

One of Carol's goals was for students to grow in the acquisition of knowledge and the enhancement of skills within an ethical or moral framework. The donated space, materials, and, instructional support from members of other academic units across the university also modeled this collaboration and caring. The physical structure in the learning lab also allowed a collaborative use of space, with large tables, comfortable chairs, carpeting, plants, and art work. Most importantly, there was never any testing required by administration to measure improvement. Rather, the measure of the success of the program was how many employees attended the classes and whether or not the employees considered the classes beneficial.

The outcomes of this program have been profound. Many workers have begun to "see" themselves as people with hope, with some agency in their working and private lives. In the following section, I will discuss in detail one of the most compelling and unintended outcomes of the program and consider why a more critical approach to worker education may not have had the same consequences.

THE PROGRAM

In planning this program, Carol worked from a critical pedagogical base. She has been concerned with issues of social justice and worker exploitation for much of her working life. Her goals have always included a critique of the power relations in the workplace. While she did not consider herself a radical critical pedagogue, much of the critical literacy discourse informed her practice.[1] After six months of classes, however, Carol learned that her presumptions about critical literacy were not well-received by the women participating in this class. They were offended with Carol's attempts to develop a "critical literacy" that examined the political aspects of workers' lives. In addition, learners did not think of literacy as socially constructed, but rather as something one acquires in isolation and in silence.

Several incidents have drawn Carol and I to these puzzling conclusions. First, we both assumed that, after the workers' initial shyness, talking informally in class would be a relatively comfortable thing. But even though the physical space invited communication through the arrangement of tables and chairs and through the instructional materials, the class participants remained unusually silent. They seem unwilling to talk in groups and often whispered or simply did not talk at all, but worked intently and quietly on whatever assignment was devised for them. A few of the women were so timid in class that they rarely looked up from their work and did not look at anyone directly. Eyes remain lowered at all times. The «group» activities were done by individuals. Given the chance, each woman would prefer to work in a room by herself. For example, the Learning Lab has four break-out rooms for tutoring. Many of the women in the class would move off into those small tutoring rooms to work alone or sometimes in pairs. Others would stay in the main room, but would consistently work alone.

The literature also suggests that collaborative literacy work is a political act and that a critical understanding of one's life emerges in a collaborative literacy program. Carol tried gently to move in the direction of a critical literacy, but her attempts were rejected. A case in point: one night a new employee came to class and began a discussion about some unfairness that she believed could be corrected if her coworkers would get together and go as a group to the assistant manager. Carol saw this as a good opportunity to elicit some writing on a subject that would interest all of them and to begin to look at ways to use literacy to improve their working conditions.

Looking back, Carol now describes this as "the BIG mistake". Her efforts were seen by the other women in the class as a great breach of trust. They all stopped coming to class for a few meetings, and when they did begin to come back one of the women explained that Carol had overstepped her bounds with them. This worker explained that the class members did not want to bring up anything controversial about work and that someone in the class would report to supervision what went on in class. They each had too much to lose. They didn't see it as Carol's place to bring up controversy. Instead, they wanted the class to focus on non-work issues. They wanted a safe haven for learning, and they didn't want that safe haven to become politicized.

In the first few months of class especially, words seemed to be of little interest to the class. They were much more interested in improving maths skills, hand writing, and spelling than they were in improving reading or writing ability. During that time, Carol described the class as "not a particularly safe place to be" for the workers.

By the end of the first six months, Carol and I had learned a great deal about what seemed to work and what didn't seem to work in the class. But we were puzzled by what we had learned. We knew that our own assumptions about women and literacy were limited, but we weren't sure why. Carol discovered quite by accident, however, that at least three of the women in the class have been silenced by the secret of sexual abuse or domestic violence. When Carol made this discovery, she realized that some of the behaviours and beliefs that she was so puzzled by in the class are similar to the ways abused women's behaviours and epistemologies are described in the literature (described in detail in below). I suggest that the initial rejection of a critical curriculum is perhaps not unusual for abuse survivors. While the literature shows us (Fingeret, 1983; Gowen, 1992) that poor, low-literate women can be strong and smart and competent, there is a place where illiteracy, economic dependence, and abuse intersect. The following section describes three women who have been living in that intersection.[2]

THREE WOMEN, THREE SECRETS, THREE STORIES

The stories of abuse all came out as class members wrote in their personal journals, which Carol has used since the beginning of the classes. Carol has read and responded to these journals only when the women in the class have wanted to open a written dialogue. She has encouraged but not forced this dialogue, and many of the women in the class did not initially want to share what they had written with anyone.

The story of Ms. Colbert

Ms. Colbert is a good example. She began writing in her journal, held it very privately, and said that no one could look at it. Several months went by with Ms. Colbert writing in her journal privately and quietly. Then one day, Ms. Colbert told Carol that she wanted to share what she had written with her. The story in the journal was about Ms. Colbert's sexual abuse as a child by her stepfather and her mother's refusal to protect her. She finally was rescued by her grandmother. As the teacher pointed out, "It was finally a story of love and support". During all the months of private work in her journal, she had been writing the same story over and over, improving it and making it more explicit with each revision. When the teacher eventually read the story, she suggested to Ms. Colbert that her story might have real value to others and asked her if she might want to share it.

Finally Ms. Colbert wrote it anonymously for the literary magazine (called a newsletter) that Carol publishes for every one in the Physical Plant. Ms. Colbert also began writing poetry as she continued writing her story and she even began publishing her poetry in the "newsletter" under her own name. Then she became interested in maths, and figured out that she could move out of public housing and into an apartment in a much better school district for only $2.00 more a month rent. And she kept on writing her story. She began to talk to Carol about all of this, but it took months of writing and establishing trust first. These conversations were always private. No one else in the class knew about the abuse until she published her story in the newsletter, but then it was still a secret of sorts because the writing was anonymous. When she and the teacher talked about goals, she finally explained that "Before I didn't have any goals. The secret took up all my space for goals. Now I don't have a secret and I have goals".

The story of Ms. Lawson

The second woman's story came out first in journal writing as well. Ms. Lawson wanted to write for the newsletter, and her written stories were, according to Carol, "about Thanksgiving, Martin Luther King, and loving everyone". Then out of the blue came a long essay about living with an alcoholic. Ms. Lawson also decided to publish her story anonymously in the newsletter rather than discuss it in class. She continued to write in her journal about her husband and his personality with and without alcohol. She wrote that it was getting worse. She wrote that throughout the entire time in the class her husband resented her going to school. She made up lies about the class and never studied at home.[3]

Then one day she wrote that she was filing for divorce, and had a lawyer who was having papers served on her husband. Her husband told her that he would kill her if she ever divorced him. She doesn't think that he will, and she does not want to lose her house by moving out. She is, as this chapter is being written, in the most dangerous time in her relationship with her husband. It is that point at which the woman has something in print — divorce papers, a restraining order, an arrest warrant — that she is in the most danger of being hurt or killed by an enraged partner who sees the piece of paper as the ultimate denial of what he believes is rightfully his.

The story of Ms. James

Ms. James wrote in her journal that she wanted to write her autobiography some day. Carol encouraged her to start and she did. Of the three women I am discussing, Ms. James was the most ready to tell her secrets when she came to class and was most willing to share these secrets with Carol. In her autobiography she has written three stories of abuse: her father abusing her mother, her first marriage to an alcoholic, and her second marriage to an abuser. She would read and write these stories, then read them over again, and then talk with Carol about her husband's anger and her place in life. While doing maths in the class, she figured out that she could refinance a house she owned in another part of the state, buy a condominium and move out. She did all of this secretly and moved without telling her husband anything. She is doing well, taking a computer class, and continuing to work on her autobiography. Recently, one of her essays was published in a nationally distributed magazine for new readers, along with her picture. Ms. James is the most public of the three women about her abuse. Here is what she has written:

> This is a story about a woman who was very lonesome. She was having lots of problems at home. Her husband was very mean. He would beat her and call her names and made her feel like dirt. She stopped caring for herself like she should. She felt as though she wanted to commit suicide. That woman was me. I started to see myself in a different light when I had a certain accident. I fell in the middle of the street. Cars were coming. They missed me by a hair. As I was lying there a young police officer came to my aid and helped me up. He also helped stop the cars to prevent me from being hit. After that day I started to look at life differently. I thought all men were thoughtless and hateful but this young man proved to be a loving, kind human being who always was willing to help in any way he could. I have never told him how much I appreciated him. But some day I will. I see him every day. And he always has a smile. Just seeing his smile is like a sun shiny day to me. When I am unhappy his smile makes me smile. I know one day he will make a wonderful husband. As for me I am gaining confidence in myself and I am not so lonesome because I know life can be just as radiant as his smile.

This story illustrates an important point. Ms. Lawson does not attribute her "conversion" to literacy, but to the kindness of a stranger, ironically, a man. I do believe, however, that the role the literacy class has played is in allowing her the opportunity to write her story is significant. As Judith Lewis Herman has observed in *Trauma and Recovery*, inventing a language to express the unspeakable is a necessary step in healing from trauma. "The ability to tell your story — to speak your own mind — is the best antidote to powerlessness" cited in (Miller, 1994:11). The literature on narrative as a teaching and research strategy is already substantial (e.g. Bruner, 1986; Britton & Pelligrini, 1990; Carter, 1993; Chafe, 1990; Cooper, 1992; Paley, 1990; Sarbin 1986; Witherell & Noddings, 1991). A more intentional use of it in workplace literacy classes might help move those women who have been silenced by abuse into a stance of self-as-knower and maker-of-knowledge.

Ms. Lawson has recently told Carol that there is another woman in the class that is in an abusive marriage. This woman is very private, rarely sits with anyone and will not write at all. If asked to write a little, she says she has nothing to say. Instead, she reads newspapers and does worksheets that Carol provides for her. She keeps coming to class, but she has not moved in the ways the three other women have. Recently she has started asking Ms. Lawson why she left her husband. We wonder if she, too, will start to write about abuse in her journal.

IMPLICATIONS FOR LITERACY PROVIDERS

The stories described here are anecdotal and I do not claim that they are generalizable. But I do believe that they surface an important issue that has not been formally addressed in any consideration of workplace literacy policy or practice. However, if we look at the statistics of abuse, we realize that in any workplace class for working poor women, there is a strong possibility that some of the participants might be abuse survivors.

This is a research question that clearly deserves more attention. If a woman is a victim of domestic violence, then her reasons for enrolling in a literacy class and the changes that occur in her life as a result of becoming more literate are fundamentally different from the those of women who are not abuse victims. On the other hand, the abuse victim's reasons for not participating in literacy classes are also important to consider in designing both policy and delivery of services, especially in the workplace.

WOMEN AND ABUSE

In the United States, approximately one in three women will experience some sort of domestic violence (American Medica Association, 1992). Most of these women will survive the abuse physically, but their healing will take time, and the trauma and the healing will shape the quality of these survivors' homes, their families, and their work. Health and Human Services Secretary Donna Shalala claims that, "Domestic violence is an unacknowledged epidemic in our society" (Smolowe, 1994:20).

But the consequences of spousal abuse as well as childhood sexual abuse are rarely considered in the literature on worker education programs. When employees seek help for these very difficult situations, they logically turn to Employee Assistance Programs, where available. Given the high number of women who have survived/are surviving sexual or domestic abuse and the ways these experiences and the healing process shape and are shaped by education, it is imperative for policy makers to systematically consider how literacy programs might allow for advocacy for women as they heal from these abuses.

Most importantly policy makers must realize that women abuse survivors are likely to be participants in worker education programs, especially those designed for front-line, hourly-wage earning, low-skill workers. This is specifically because the two factors that put women most at risk of violence are low education and low wages — the very segment of the workforce that is described as most in need of additional training. Moreover, those women who have lower incomes and who have less job and economic security are not only more likely to be victims of domestic violence, but that violence is also likely to be more frequent and more severe (Arias, 1988).

Finally, women with few viable economic alternatives and with little access to community resources are also more likely to remain in abusive relationships and to maintain negative images of themselves (Haussman, 1981; Belenkey, Clinchy, Goldberger, & Tarule, 1986). And when women gain the education and skills to break out of abusive situations, they are likely to experience escalated forms of abuse, derision, or even death. For these reasons, working with women survivors requires special skill, sensitivity, and an awareness of the sometime fatal consequences of literacy and empowerment.

Of course, not all abused women are "silent", undereducated, and underemployed. On the contrary. Domestic violence occurs with frightening regularity across all levels of education and job status. What appears to differentiate those abuse survivors who are successful in education and the job market from those who are not, is the level of access to substantial support systems in their communities, such as good education and therapeutic facilities, or even significant family material resources. These young women tended to develop cognitively into women who perceive of themselves as knowers and producers of knowledge. Thus the effects of domestic violence appear to be mediated by community and educational resources. Those women who are least likely to have these resources at their disposal are most likely to remain silent selves, unable to tell the secret of their abuse, and isolated from the support systems they need to begin to heal.

Alternative forms of adult and workplace education have tended to emphasize collaborative learning groups that encourage learners to take control of their literacy learning through developing voice and action. This can be seen most clearly in the "critical literacy" for personal and political transformation espoused by Freire (1973) and his followers (e.g. Giroux, 1984; Lankshear & McLaren, 1993). But this critical model is not without its problems. For one thing, it's emphasis on actively engaging the word and the world is at odds with America's rather narrow prescriptions about femininity (see Kierstead, D'Agostino, & Dill, 1988; Long, 1989), making critical literacy a conflicting path for many women. This is crucial to our understanding of women's (and men's) attitudes and beliefs about literacy acquisition because sex-role identity is closely linked to measures of self-esteem (Robinson-Awana, Kehle, & Jensen, 1986).

Kazemek pointed out in 1988 that up until that point, there has been no ethnographic or case study research to consider the effectiveness of a collaborative approach to literacy education for women. The program described above has given us the opportunity to carry out such research over an extended period of time. What we must conclude from our experiences is that while collaborative and critical approaches to literacy education might be quite appropriate for many women, they might not provide a good starting point for women who have been silenced by violence and abuse and whose goals are circumscribed by secrets that "take up all the space".

REFLECTION ON KITCHENS AND ON LITERACY CLASSES

Ms. Taylor, a supervisor at the university who left her husband and got her GED years ago, is testimony to the fact that while literacy can change a woman's life, it also has its costs. When Ms. Taylor came to work at the university, she had no education, an abusive husband, and three daughters. She decided that in order to get ahead she would need a GED, but when she set out to get one, her husband started to beat her. She was able to divorce him and move on with her education.

Not all women are so lucky. About two years ago a young woman with two small boys and a "live-in man" came to a GED program at a local technical school in the metro-Atlanta area. She was very bright and wanted to get her GED, but the closer she got, the more her man beat her. She confided all of this to her teacher, who encouraged her to get her man to come with her to classes, but he refused and the beatings escalated. Finally she got tired of it all and shot him one night. She is now serving time for murder and her children are in foster care. She does have her GED, but she has 12 more years of time to serve as well.

Still another story: During the break in a GED class at a community college in New York, several women got together and started talking about their men beating them. They were all tired of it and frightened, too. To help one another, they started a support group for battered women. One of the women's ex-husbands found out about it and when he later returned and raped her, he told her, while he was raping her, that he was doing it because of her GED class support group. We are sobered by these stories. They force us to reflect upon the particular consequences of literacy for women who are poor and undereducated and who are caught in abusive relationships. We realize how different our assumptions are about literacy's power to change lives. Change is never easy and true power is dangerous as well as liberating.

The life-changes that have occurred as a result of this learner-centred project are remarkable and important. The program cannot be easily replicated, however. In the United States, at least, a program like this requires key individuals within institutions who are willing to think beyond cultural norms about institutional as well as personal responsibility to workers and to communities and who are also willing to take risks. There is no hope of the proliferation of this model through legislative action, or tax incentives, or mandates. The changes called for are more basic, more profound, and more risky. Only when more Americans recognize the inherent benefits of educating all members of society will our nations' corporations and institutions exhibit a true sense of social responsibility.

Notes

1. See, for example, Lankshear & Lawler 1989; Bee 1993; Lankshear & McLaren 1993; Rockhill 1993.

2. It is important to remember that women who have been sexually abused as children and women who are currently in violent relaionshps are treated quite differently in the clinical literature. We combine them inthis discussion because they each were silenced by their experiences and unable to move towares more academic work until they had dealt with their secrets.

3. We believe that this is a significant aspect of a workplace literacy program that is delivered on work time at the workplace. It offers those who need it complete confidentiality. They can take the classes and develop their skills without the abusive partner ever finding out the

References

American Association of University Women, 1994. *Shortchanging girls, shortchanging America*. Washington, DC: Author.

Arias, I. 1988. Economic, social, and psychological resources as predictor of victimization. Paper presented at the Annual Meeting of the Society for the study of Social Problems, Atlanta, GA. August 21-23.

Bee, B. 1993. Critical literacy and gender. In C. Lankshear & P. McLaren (Eds.), *Critical Literacy: Politics, praxis, and the postmodern*. Albany, NY: State University of New York Press.

Belenky, M. F., Clinchy, B. Goldberger, N. & Tarule, J. 1986. *Women's ways of knowing*. New York: Basic Books.

Brownmiller, 1984. *Femininity*. New York: Linden Press/Simon & Schuster.

Britton, B., & Pelligrini, A. (Eds.. 1990. *Narrative thought and narrative language*. Hillsdale, NJ: Erlbaum.

Bruner, J. 1986. *Actual minds, possible worlds*. Cambridge: Harvard University Press.

Carter, K. 1993. The place of story in the study of teaching and teacher education. *Educational researcher*, 221), 5-12, 18.

Chafe W. 1990. Some things that narrative tells us about the mind. In B. Britton, & A. Pelligrini, (Eds). *Narrative thought and narrative language*. Hillsdale, NJ: Erlbaum.

Chodorow, N. 1978. *The reproduction of mothering*. Berkeley: University of California Press.

Cooper, P. 1992. *When stories come to school: Telling, writing, and performing stories in the early childhood classroom*. New York: Teachers and Writers Collaborative.

Fingeret, H. A. 1983. Social network: A new perspective on independence and illiterate adults. *Adult Education Quarterly*, 33, 133-146.

Freire, P. 1973. *Education for critical consciousness*. New York: Seabury Press. Glasgow.

Gilligan, C. 1982. *In a different voice*. Cambridge: Harvard University Press.

Gilligan, C., Lyons, N. P., Hanmer, T. J. 1990. *Making connections: The relational worlds of adolescent girls at Emma Willard School*. Cambridge: Harvard University Press.

Gooden, C. R. 1993, summer. Diversity with style - learning style that is! *Kappa Delta Pi Record*, 29(4), 129.

Gowen, S. G. 1990. Measuring women into silence/hearing women into speech: Beliefs about literacy in a workplace literacy program. *Discourse & Society*.

Gowen, S. G. 1992. *The politics of workplace literacy: A case study*. New York: Teachers College Press.

Herman, J. L. *The aftermath of violence: From domestic abuse to political terror*. New York: Basic Books. N.D.

Kazemek, F. 1988. Necessary changes: Professional involvement in adult literacy programs. *Harvard Educational Review, 58*,464-487.

Kierstead, D., D'Agostino, P., & Dill, H. 1988. Sex role stereotyping of college professors: Bias in students' rating of instructors. *Journal of Educational Psychology, 80*(3), 342-344.

Lankshear, C. & Lawler, M. 1989. *Literacy, schooling, and revolution*. London: Falmer Press.

Lankshear, C. & McLaren, P. 1993. *Critical Literacy: Politics, praxis, and the postmodern*. Albany, NY: State University of New York Press.

Long, V. O. 1989. Relation of masculinity to self-esteem and self acceptance in male professions, college students and clients. *Journal of Counseling Psychology, 36*(1), 84-87.

Miller, M. V. "Surviving Anne Sexton", *New York Times Book Review*, p. 11 Section 7, November 20, 1994.

Mulqueen, M. 1992. *On our own terms: Redefining competence and femininity*. Albany, NY: State University of New York Press.

Noddings, N. 1991. Stories in dialogue: Caring and interpersonal reasoning. In C. Witherall & N. Noddings (Eds.), *Stories lives tell: Narrative and dialogue in education* (pp. 157-170). New York: Teachers College Press.

Paley, V. G. 1990. *The boy who would be a helicopter: The uses of storytelling in the classroom*. Cambridge: Harvard University Press.

Robinson-Awana, P., Kehle, T.J., & Jensen, W.R. 1986. But what about smart girls? Adolescent self-esteem and sex-role perceptions as a function of academic achievement. *Journal of Educational Psychology*, 78(3), 179-183.

Rockhill, K. 1993. (Dis)connecting literacy and sexuality: speaking the unspeakable in the classroom. In C. Lankshear & P. McLaren (Eds.), *Critical Literacy: Politics, praxis, and the postmodern*. Albany, NY: State University of New York Press.

Sarbin, T. 1986. The narrative as a root metaphor for psychology. In T. R. Sarbin (Ed.), *Narrative psychology: The storied nature of human conduct*. New York: Praeger, pp. 3-21.

Smolowe, J. July 4, 1994. When violence hits home: The Simpson case awakens America to the epidemic of domestic abuse. *Time*, 18-25.

Chapter Fifteen
FACING TRAINING AND BASIC EDUCATION: ONE UNIONIZED WORKPLACE EXPERIENCE

Jorge Garcia-Orgales
Doris Marshall Institute
for
Adult Education and Action
Toronto, Canada

In the last decade, people involved in basic education and training in the workplace in Ontario, Canada had to deal with a series of questions to guide their work. Are people moving into "bad jobs" because they do not have the literacy and knowledge necessary for "good jobs?" Is the economy of Ontario suffering in "competitive" terms because workers are not properly trained to compete? Is it the responsibility of the state, the employer or the individual worker to improve workers' skills? Are skills and literacy training a right of the individual or a support to a competitive economy? While these questions address the livelihood of workers, they do not deal with the most fundamental problem of power relations workers face in the workplace and in society, as individual workers and as a community.

An effective social policy on basic education and training that addresses the needs of employed, employable and unemployed workers, needs to go beyond basic economic requirements and concentrate on increasing workers' expertise not only as producers, but also as consumers and citizens of the society.

This article[1] looks at the experience of labour-side members of a Joint Workplace Training Committee that has promoted, negotiated and monitored the delivery of basic education and training for the last five years in Schneider Canada, an electrical plant in Toronto. The Joint Workplace Training Committee considered in this paper is part of the Sectoral Skills Council in the Canadian Electrical/Electronic Industry. The Sectoral Skills Council is supported by federal and provincial governments, a manufacturers' association and several unions representing workers in the sector.

In the experience of the labour-side members of the Joint Workplace Training Committee, a well-crafted set of union goals allowed workers to use the opportunity to improve their relationships in the community, as well as their working conditions. Still, the positive results achieved were not sufficient for the other parties, governments and employers, to consider their goals accomplished. For the other parties, a well-crafted union agenda challenged their power in the community and in the workplace and, as such, their support of the project weakened. Both parties, governments and employers, would prefer a more traditional relationship in which governments fund employers to organize and deliver only job-specific training.

LABOUR'S TRAINING AGENDA

In the mid 1980s, Canadian trade unionists, like the rest of society, had to cope with a declining economy, loss of jobs, opening borders and an influx of new technology and new management models. Those changes created turmoil in the labour market as well as in the workplace. Workers who believed they had a job for life found themselves unemployed and underqualified (in the estimation of labour market analysts) to find a job in the "new" economy. At the same time, employed workers saw the implementation of new management techniques and the investment in new equipment as a challenge to their skills and job security. The labour movement — the voice of workers at the policy level and at the workplace level — got deeply involved in finding solutions to those concerns.

Basic education and training were an important area in the set of proposals that formed the labour agenda for this time of changes. It is important to underline however, that labour did not consider basic education and training to be the solution, or even the most important part of a solution, to the structural changes occurring in the economy. In fact, labour systematically denounced those who centred all their attention on the education of workers as a solution, clearly pointing out that better skills do not create jobs and a better economy. Better skills are utilized and flourish in times of full employment and consumer spending. Consequently, labour has fought for a job creation strategy as a first priority. They saw education and training as *part* of that policy. Job creation and wealth distribution were the central issues in labour's agenda to manage change in the new economy.

Still, inside the labour movement, there were three positions on how to address basic education and training:

1. **Training as a right**: Advocates of this current of thought understood training as a basic right of citizenship, and as such, it should be democratic and equalitarian in its practice. They particularly disliked the kind of training in which management got most of the allocated training money, and the little bit that did go to workers went to tradespeople. A regular assembly-line worker would not get training or basic education at the workplace.

2. **Labour-management cooperation:** Advocates of this trend were searching for better ways of labour-management relations. They believed that training was one of the issues in which both parties had a common interest. They saw training as one of the ways to build positive labour-management relations, helping the industry survive and prosper. They could have pushed other issues like ergonomics or equity to build cooperation, but they decided on training.

3. **Building training:** These people were not worried about jointress, or government money, or where training came from. They had a very pragmatic approach. They were interested in increasing training. They thought training would be a tool for equity and advancement in the workplace.

The three trends of thought resulted in a very clear document about education training that was approved by the Ontario Federation of Labour at its 33rd annual convention in November, 1989. The following principles were established:

> We want training that equips workers to have more control over their jobs and their work lives, builds on workers' existing capabilities, prepares workers for what they want and need to know now and in the future, puts workers in a better position to shape that future and starts eliminating job discrimination based on gender, race or ethnicity.
>
> We also want training that leads to good jobs. We know training only makes sense when it is part of an economic strategy for full employment, for the creation of jobs and for a labour process which relies on

workers' skills rather than one which tries to dispense with the skills and the workers.

The key elements of a labour view of training are:

1. Training is a right.

2. Training is a tool for greater equity.

3. Training is a fundamental part of the job.

4. Training rights include the opportunity, through paid educational leave, for workers to upgrade themselves to achieve a high school education.

5. The content of training must be geared to workers' needs as they see them and must be developmental.

6. Workers and their unions must have a central role in determining, at all levels, the direction of training.

7. Training for employed workers should be funded by a new training tax on employers.

8. Training for displaced workers and people wishing to enter or reenter the labour force should be funded out of general revenue.

9. Training programs must be carried out in conjunction with public educational institutions in which labour has a much more significant voice.[2]

D'Arcy Martin, in his book *Thinking Union*, summarizes the situation at the time in the following terms:

At this time both training users and providers were experiencing a mounting dissatisfaction with the existing relationships around training. For many individual learners, the system of training opportunities had become too complex and too uncertain in its link to meaningful and well-compensated jobs in an increasingly volatile labour market. Employers were complaining that the system was not satisfying their needs for a flexible, motivated workforce capable of sustaining the "competitive advantage" that was seen as crucial for survival. For labour, the system was elitist, fragmented, and filled with dead ends. Social action advocates had a completely different fix on things: they thought it was time to use training to address systematic barriers of exclusion and marginalization in the workplace.[3]

Labour movement representatives understood their position of power relative to others in society when having to deal with the realities of the economic change. They were not powerful CEOs or state advisors who could use money or power to bend the agenda in their favour. Neither were they the marginalized, under-represented pariahs of the political arena: they were not homeless or native people, part-time service workers or single mothers on welfare. The labour movement did have some formal recognition in some initiatives at the federal and provincial levels of governments, but no real power or voice to generate support for their ideas.

At the workplace level, unions had a bit more power through collective agreements. But, the conversation at the workplace level was insular, centred on the needs of a particular office, plant or business, with no or very little opportunity to influence a larger arena. The sectoral arena was a different opportunity to be explored. Unions hoped they could shape economic and social strategies around restructuring at the sectoral level.

But the labour movement knew that "you need two to tango": they needed management support. Management, on the other hand, needed union support to be able to implement the changes in management techniques and in equipment that they considered indispensable to their companies' survival and prosperity. In a sectoral structure, management could work with unions in a different manner. Also, through those sectoral bodies, they would be able to gain access to government funding that would not be available for management-only enterprises.

THE SECTORAL SKILLS COUNCIL

The idea of sectoral councils had a particular development in the electrical and electronic industry in Canada. The electrical and electronic industry is quite important in the manufacturing sector of Canada's economy. It employs ten per cent of the manufacturing workers, it has a very high investment in research and development, it ranks very high in exporting products, and it is a major producer and consumer of micro-electronic technology. In 1988, the industry association and relevant unions formed the Joint Human Resource Committee to address the sector-wide issues of training, retraining, technological change and adjustment. The committee produced a significant study: *Connections for the Future*.

According to David Wolfe and D'Arcy Martin,

> ... the result of that study, *Connections for the Future*, revealed that the industry suffered significant job losses during the first recession of the 1980s, but subsequently grew at twice the rate of general manufacturing in Canada (Canadian Electrical and Electronics Manufacturing Industry, 1989). By 1987, employment levels had surpassed their previous peak. However, the net result of the restructuring was a significant change in the occupational and skill mix of the workforce. At the root of the change was a dramatic shift between the proportion of production jobs and the number of white-collar, salaried ones. The job categories that grew the fastest were those with higher professional and technical qualifications. At the same time, a new configuration of skills requirements was emerging within the smaller production workforce, resulting from the general shift toward those occupations with higher skills levels. The effect of these changes was compounded by the declining pool of new labour market entrants for the industry to draw upon. The human resource study also suggested that the existing post-secondary educational system was not providing sufficient graduates to meet the skills requirements of the industry. For its part, the union was concerned that its members were going to lose their chance at the higher skilled jobs in the industry without access to better training opportunities. Through their involvement with the study, key segments of both management and labour came to the view that they must retrain and redeploy the existing workforce to meet future skill needs.[4]

This led to the formation of the Sectoral Skills Council in July, 1990.[5] A key aspect of the council's organization is parity between management and unions at all levels. Six members per labour and six per management form the steering committee. Although a large number of non-unionized workplaces belong to the council, management has to allow the unions to make decisions in those cases.

The Sectoral Skills Council signed separate agreements with the Ontario Ministry of Skills Development, and Employment and Immigration Canada for the provincial and federal governments to provide funds to the council. The funding is set at one per cent of the wage bill for each of the participating workplaces. The cost of the fund is shared between private sector employers and the two participating governments. The council is designed to operate nationally but, until July, 1996, is only operational in the province of Ontario.

The Sectoral Skills Council is a highly decentralized structure. The planning, monitoring and control of training is done at the workplace level by a Joint Workplace Training Committee. When the decision to participate in the fund is agreed upon by a union and management, a committee is formed using parity as a rule. Both chairpersons (management and union) sign the training applications to be considered for funding. Each Joint Workplace Training Committee has control of the training activities in their workplace. Each workplace's fund is controlled by the council. Each workplace fund consists of contributions from the workplace and matching government funds.

Up to May, 1996, we have the following facts about the Sectoral Skills Council:

- There are 155 companies participating;
- There are seven unions representing workers;
- There are 52,349 members with rights to apply for training;
- In 1993, the number of trainees was 3,481;
- In 1994, the number of trainees was 17,409;
- In 1995, the number of trainees was 38,781;
- In 1996, up to May, there were 18,380 trainees;
- The training expenditures in 1993 were $1,650,000; in 1994, $5,500,000, in 1995, $7,850,000, and up to May, 1996, $4,133,192.

The agreement between the parties was that training provided was to be portable, equitable and incremental. By portable, the parties understood that training would be oriented to the industry and not exclusively to the workplace. This way workers would increase their freedom to move to another job in another company when there was an opening, or if their plant closed. "Equitable" meant the opportunity to be trained or to improve education levels would be given equally to every member in the workplace. "Incremental" training meant the training provided would be new and on top of any training that the company or the unions were providing already when they joined the council.

The actual training supported by the fund is distributed between three different categories. The distribution of the training funds attempts to balance priorities between the needs for job-related training, education and group activities. The three training categories are:

- **Type I**: job/skill updating/upgrading, constituting 62 per cent of the fund expenditures;
- **Type II**: general education/training, constituting 20 per cent of fund expenditures; and
- **Type III**: employees' group-directed training, constituting ten per cent of fund expenditures, for a total of 92 per cent. The remaining eight per cent of the fund is set aside to cover administrative costs.

The types of training allowed by the fund was a recognition of the different needs of the parties represented, as well as a guarantee that every interest would be safe and protected from the others. The *Type I*, job-specific training represented the main interest of employers: their need to improve the ability of workers to perform on the job. The Type *III*, group training represented the desire of the unions to have some money allocated to collective training. And finally, *Type II* training recognized the right of individual workers to decide to learn something that might or might not contribute to their immediate job skill, and might or might not involve something related to the union.

AT THE WORKPLACE LEVEL

A union member of the Joint Workplace Training Committee at Schneider Canada, said: "We got involved because we believed that this training will be worker-driven meaning that this local union and the joint training committee will be able to have education and training done to benefit workers; that management won't be choosing who gets trained any more. Everyone will be given training".

This workplace employed almost 500 workers when it first joined the council. After many lay-offs and a change in ownership in June, 1996, a bit less than 400 workers were employed at the plant. The workers call themselves "the United Nations" because of the number of languages and nationalities found in the workplace. A mix of West Indians, South Asians, Latin-Americans, Portuguese and others from different origins form the workforce. The average length of employment in the plant is 15 years, with a large group of workers that has been in the plant for the last 20 years. Most of the workers have not finished secondary education, and a good number of the immigrant workers do not have primary education. Also, speaking, reading and writing English is a problem for an important number of people. Most of these workers did not think of going back to school or having any form of education as a valid alternative for them.

The union leadership at the workplace level made the decision to join the council very quickly, and for two main reasons:

1. **To democratize the process by which training was provided**. "In the past", according to a union member on the committee "what happened with training in the workplace was that management went out there and chose who they wanted to train. Maybe because of the colour of your eyes or because you were related to somebody, or something like that, you would get training. You would be given, or not given training regardless of how long you have been working here or how much ability you have demonstrated in the past. The workers here, they may not be able to express themselves in English, but they have done the work very well and for a long time. That showed us that these people could be trained; they have the brains. All they need is training in a manner that recognizes their experience and their abilities. That was the main reason that we had to get involved in basic education and training in the workplace". The other reason was:

2. **To increase the general level of the education in the workforce to facilitate the transition to new jobs or to the use of new technologies.** "The outside pressure moved people to take courses", the union member continued. "There was a general interest in a small number of people, but not so much geared toward work as geared to general knowledge. But as the pressure grew, especially with the job changes, people realized that in order to keep this job, or to get a job in some other place, they had to have a little bit more than just a body; they have to have some sort of skill that you can take with you, something that you can demonstrate".

Management had their own agenda in supporting the union position. They understood that new computerized technology and quality controls would require the workforce to be able to read and write English more fluently. Management's decision to implement ISO 9000[2] had an important impact in their decision to participate. In ISO 9000-certified workplaces, workers are supposed to follow strict guidelines on how to perform their jobs, step by step. They have to be able to record performances and show auditors that they are following the proper procedures.

While both parties agreed on the need to tap into the fund to obtain new funding for training, there was a subtle difference in what kind of training was necessary in the plant. The employer's representatives were interested in getting workers prepared to perform with computerized machinery in a modern management setting. On the other side, the union's representatives were interested in giving their members a chance to improve their basic education at the workplace without incurring any cost of their own.

The union did not consider the demands of the employer selfish or out of the range of requiring knowledge necessary to improve skills at the workplace. On the contrary, the union believed that, in a large way, its members' job security depended on their ability to fulfil company requirements. The union insisted, however, on the need to improve basic education levels before moving into training in new technology. The union asked for improved reading, writing and computers skills as the starting point.

The union representatives explained:

> We saw changes coming with the new technologies. We knew that you will need to read and write a lot more. We wanted to build up that training from the bottom, instead of going right to the people who are more educated and offering them more skills. We tried to nail the training at the bottom. We wanted to bring the people at that bottom level up to a level in which at least they would be able to compete with those most educated people on the jobs, or in the training that the company will be bringing in. Let's all be on a level-plain field; let's all have the same opportunities.

At the end of the process both parties agreed on the need to start improving basic skills. They also agreed on an open process to invite members to participate in training. Everybody would be invited to apply for training, but nobody would be compelled to take training. The Joint Workplace Training Committee would make every effort to facilitate workers' application for training. The company and the union made a joint presentation to employees about the training fund. Facing a large number of people with English language problems, or who had been out of school for a long time, the Joint Workplace Training Committee created an application form that had a box to mark if a worker needed any kind of help in filling out the application. Workers were presented with a large sample of the form, and told to put their name and mark the box if they had any doubt. Contacted later by members of the Joint Workplace Training Committee, most workers preferred to talk with union representatives on the training committee, instead of management.

Both labour and management recognized that the company would greatly benefit from the improved abilities of the workers, and so the company should support the training beyond just using the fund money. The company agreed to pay workers' salaries when they were taking training without claiming that expense to the fund and the union agreed to organize training in a way that would minimally disturb production.

UP-TO-DATE RESULTS

The training started in February, 1992. The first year very little money was spent because the contributions were just starting to build a sizeable pot. Training expenditures grew over the years to reach more than $90,000 in 1995. The following table shows the number of people trained and the courses taken:

- English as a Second Language (Basic) — 61 participants
- English as a Second Language (Intermediate) — 45 participants
- English as a Second Language (Advanced) — 30 participants
- English/Maths Upgrade — 10 participants
- Introduction to Computers — 88 participants
- Blueprint Reading — 70 participants

Most of the training was classified under *Type I*. Although English as a Second Language could be considered *Type II* "general education" training, the union was able to negotiate all the courses above mentioned as "job specific" using the link to new technology usage and quality control at the source techniques. Money spent sending union representative to courses and conferences about training need was classified as *Type III* "group training".

The union leadership considered their achievements as important. They said:

> Today most of the people who could not speak or read English five years ago can do it. Most of them are at intermediate level, some of them at advanced, and some still at basic level.
>
> Somebody came to me some time ago. She said to me: "I cannot read or

write, am I OK to go to this course?" The other day she came to me and said: "You know, I did not realize how much I was actually missing. My son is bringing papers from school and I am able to read them and understand them now. I don't need my son reading the papers to me in my own language". She feels more fulfilled at home.

We had a case with an Asian lady. All her kids are in university. She was attending English as Second Language classes in the high school of her neighbourhood, but classes were Saturday morning when it complicated her family life, shopping, etc. We got her into one of our classes in the plant, just as part of her working day. She told me: 'It is not that I couldn't speak English. It was insecurity. I was afraid of doing mistakes. Now, not only do I work better and I can ask questions when I do not understand something, I can understand my kids when they talk about university'.

Still, there were stumbling blocks that made the project move slower than was expected. Between 1993 and 1994, training was suspended for seven months because of disagreements between union and company representatives. The company was asking that salaries be paid from the fund, instead of covering salaries themselves. The company said that, since it was an allowed expenditure, they would like to charge them to the fund. The union was saying that salaries were the largest expenditure and charging them to the fund would drain it very quickly. After a seven-month pause, the company agreed to continue paying the salaries of workers taking courses.

Another disruption to training was a series of layoffs caused by the downsizing of the company. In some cases workers who stayed in the plant were moved to other shifts. Some of these workers had to suspend their attendance in classes. In turn, some classes could not find enough people at the level in which the class was functioning to replace the ones gone. Due to small numbers of attendees, some classes were cancelled and rescheduled. Similar situations happened when the company would shut down the plant due to lack of production. Classes needed to be cancelled and rescheduled later, at the re-opening of the plant.

Contrary to all expectations, the Joint Workplace Training Committee had to start giving courses on English as a Second Language at a level below the basic level in the last months. After several years, some workers came forward to ask for very basic education. A member of the committee said:

You know people really well. You know them for periods longer than 20 years. You speak to them every day. You walk alongside them and, suddenly, you know that they cannot read or write English. They perform their jobs at a high level and, still, they cannot read or write. Probably there are more workers out there who have not come forward. There are workers there who have educated kids. Some even have lawyers and doctors in their families. It takes a lot of courage for somebody like that to come forward and say, 'I cannot read and I want to learn'. These cases are handled on a one-to-one basis. It is a very delicate situation. They made the first step. They told us. Now the committee, we, the union, has to keep their interest alive and give them what they deserve: an education.

IS THE FUTURE PROMISING?

Even though most of the achievements of the Sectoral Skills Council, both at the general level and at the workplace level, could be considered very important, the future of the council is not secure. Changes in the political climate in the federal and provincial governments, as well as a strong move to purely skill-oriented training on the part of management, have made trade unionists fear that the council could disappear or dramatically change its path. Still, they have some hopes that some other avenues could open to keep the council in operation.

The federal government agreed to renew the Sectoral Skills Council's funding until 1997. Meanwhile, the federal government announced its intention to transfer the responsibilities for job training, with the funding mechanisms, to the provinces.

In 1995, the New Democratic Party (social democratic) lost the provincial elections to a Conservative majority creating even more insecurity at the provincial level. The NDP government had strongly believed in the need for bipartite structures to tap into labour inventiveness to promote progress in the marketplace. The Sectoral Skills Council was one of its most clear examples that it could work. The new government does not consider labour an asset to the economy and, as such, it is not interested in making bipartite bodies part of its agenda. At the time this article was being written the provincial government already communicated to the council their intention of not renewing the funding. They are allocating some funds for the council to wind up their operations. The government recognizes the excellent results achieved by the council. Still, it prefers to look for other opportunities to pursue their agenda in education and training.

At both the industry and workplace levels, management is

aggressively pursuing its agenda on training. The Sectoral Skills Council grew in the last two years to incorporate more than 150 plants in its ranks. About two-thirds of those plants are not unionized, making unions weak in their claim to be the workers' representatives on the council. Besides the number of non-unionized workplaces present, management is confident that a conservative government — with its agenda of fiscal restraint and competitiveness — would support their side in any internal struggle for power in the council.

Conservative tendencies are moving to the workplace, making management more assertive in their request for job-specific, skills-oriented training. A union representative said:

> Today, things are changing. Management is equalling training with value. If this person gets this training, what value will she or he bring to the company? We cannot simply say this person will be able to function more efficiently because she or he will be able to read properly, or do basic addition and subtraction. They do not see that as important. We have to be able to demonstrate the dollar value. They want to know that if we spend X number of dollars on training, they will increase their productivity in X number of dollars.

Still, it is at the workplace level that the project has better chances of survival. That is where management realized, and unions proved, that they could mobilize and organize workers to improve their ability to perform through training. Possible changes would be necessary, but there is a reasonable hope that the Sectoral Skills Council and the Joint Workplace Training Committees will survive.

REFLECTIONS

Training vs. basic education

Management, unions and education circles tend to use the terms "training" and "basic education" interchangeably, but two very different concepts seem to be covered in the debate. One side of the debate promotes the improvement of *skills* necessary to perform more competently. Some of the defenders of this concept will even go to the extreme of talking about *people skills* to refer to communications and relationships. This concept centres all the learning processes on adapting a participant to an established body (it could be a workplace or a neighbourhood), and functioning according to pre-established rules, and is more commonly found among the promoters of job-specific courses.

On the other side of the debate, the important achievement is the development of *values, attitudes* and *convictions* that help individuals feel stronger in defending their rights. This group sees the learning process as an opportunity to advance those rights., and the promoters of basic education schemes agree.

The economic model of "global competitiveness" promotes open trade, privatization of government functions, deregulation, downsizing and large unemployment. Labour force (employed and employable) insecurity is built in as part of the model. In the training/education field, this insecurity is playing a role at four different levels.

First, it is dramatically changing the rhetoric that grew out of the fight for literacy and the "Literacy Year" of the United Nations. In that discourse, basic education was a social entitlement and was expected to be supported by public funding. The direction of privatization/transferring of training and the deregulation of delivery agencies opposes such discourse. Instead, training becomes a commodity to be acquired in the market by those who can afford it.

Second, since employed workers are increasingly worried about their future, they themselves feel a need to improve their *skills*. Job-specific training in new technologies and new management techniques look like a life jacket in a stormy sea. Any suggestions about improving citizenship rights through education seem idealistic and non-practical and, as such, do not have strong support.

Third, in the "competitiveness" model, the whole education system is being oriented to provide updated employees to the corporation. Partnerships between university or community colleges and corporations or manufacturers' associations — to develop curriculum that fits industry needs — are becoming commonplace. And it starts earlier. Even young students are changing from learning about what they are interested in and then finding a job in that field, to learning about what could lead to a job, even in fields they are not interested in.

Fourth, unemployed workers are being sent from skills-training course to skills-training course in a process where the victim gets blamed for not finding a job that does not exist. Attached to this victimization on the part of society, the unemployed feel their self-confidence and their value as citizens diminished. After so much training the individual unemployed worker feels there must be something wrong with "me" if a job cannot be found.

In society and individually, the discourse of the "competitiveness" model generates support for the vision of basic education and training mentioned above. And the economic model and the vision of basic education and training reinforce each other. If the model was changed to one of full employment and job security, the support by individuals and institutions to the vision of basic education and training would be very difficult to achieve.

Results vs. ideology

The present state of insecurity of the Sectoral Skills Council shows that the right-wing agenda promoted by the neoconservative governments is based in ideological prejudices instead of measurable results. The neoconservatives governments get elected on a platform of improving the economic state of the country or province by openly embracing the free market economy. To be able to succeed in that free market economy, the neoconservatives said, the workplaces must be prepared to compete nationally and internationally. To successfully compete, they continue, the work force must be highly trained and motivated. With a highly trained and motivated work force, they concluded, workplaces will improve productivity and quality and reduce costs making them prosperous and good corporate citizens.

The results achieved by the Sectoral Skills Council are in accordance with the neo-conservative agenda. The workers have been improving their qualifications and feeling more integrated to their workplaces. Also, because of the matching formula, the corporations have been saving money that, it is presumed, would be invested in new equipment. From the business perspective the decision of the provincial government to cancel the funding to the council is contradictory with its platform.

That contradiction gets clarified when you take into account the hate those neo-conservative governments have to any community based organization. The unions, because of their organized number of members and their political clout, become the main target to be dismantled by the right wing governments. Legislation supporting workers' rights gets revised, devolving control to the corporations. Organizations, supported by the government, in which unions have a voice are dissolved or discredited as inefficient.

The Sectoral Skills Council is a victim of an ideological war that does not consider results important in order to make decisions.

Other workplace experiences

This article is based on the Sectoral Skills Council fund in general, and the specific experience of one workplace in which the results, from the point of view of promoting basic education, were successful. The tendency at other workplaces is towards more "business-oriented" results. A general acceptance of the need for companies to be "competitive" to stay in business and, as a natural consequence, to provide job security for workers, has made union representatives on the Joint Workplace Training Committees more accepting of job-specific training.

From statistics presented by the Sectoral Skills Council the "Professional Upgrading/Technical Upgrading" categories have been increasing in their use of the fund. In 1993, 53% of the fund was utilized this way. In 1994, this use increased to 58% ; in 1995, it reached 75% of the fund and by May, 1996, it was using 79% of the fund.

On the other side, the "Basic Skills" category has been declining in use. In 1993, 11% of the fund was used for this category. In 1994, it increased to 13%; in 1995, it decreased to 8%. By May, 1996, it had decreased again to 4% of the use. The "General Technology Skills" category has remained around 4.5% over the life of the fund.

The "Group or Interpersonal Skills" category has also been declining in use: in 1993, it used 15% of the fund; in 1994, 11.5%; in 1995, 10%, and in 1996 (May), 8%.

Part of the shift in the direction of training could be due to the lack of capacity on the part of the national union to support and guide the labour representatives on the local Joint Workplace Training Committees. To deal with this, the Communications, Energy and Paperworkers Union developed a course called "Facing Training" to prepare labour representatives on training committees.

The "Facing Training" course covers everything from general labour principles on training, negotiating training with management, and how to choose training providers who would utilize progressive adult education methodology. The course has been presented once a year, and some committee representatives have been using the course as a vehicle to exchange experiences, information and do networking. In the interval between the courses, however, staff time dedicated to monitoring the kind of training being delivered at the workplace level has been minimal.

Using the Opportunity to Advance Basic Education

Participation on the Sectoral Skills Council and on the Joint Workplace Training Committees has allowed national and local labour representatives to know better the needs of workers in the area of basic education. The interest of individual members, however, has not been great.

At the national level, the experience has allowed unions to negotiate training principles that they support. Results may be uneven in their application in different workplaces, but the promotion of progressive adult education principles has been achieved. Also, the opportunity to have the union involved in a different arena other than collective bargaining provided the leadership and staff with a very important experience.

At the workplace level, a new awareness of members' needs could be highlighted. Labour representatives on Joint Workplace Training Committees know now that their members are sometimes very clever about hiding that they only have very basic education. That knowledge is allowing the union to address new areas of concerns, and the active participation on committees is showing the local leadership that something can be done about it.

The individual reaction to the fund is showing that "basic education" is defined by the recipient and not by the provider or promoter. In most of the workplaces, the *Type II* "General Education" allocation has been not used in large numbers as expected. Workers who have no education are not using the opportunity to acquire one, but those who already have schooling are using the fund to improve their education.

The union representatives we interviewed stated clearly that the most important reason for people's participation was their fear of losing their jobs. They believe that, without the external pressure of economic changes, most people would not engage in the learning process. Some other experiences show the same tendency. In several workplaces where workers were reluctant to participate, the announcement of a plant closure or downsizing caused a stampede of applications. Workers would request everything from finishing Grade 12, to computer literacy, to upgrading in reading, writing and maths, and to upgrading their technical skills.

This tendency seems to show that recipients and not providers or promoters of basic education/training are the ones defining needs in the learning process. Still, the representatives recognized that the role of the education/training promoter should be better developed to encourage workers to take advantage of the fund.

Building links between ourselves and with the community

A clear success of the Sectoral Skills Council is seen in the improvement in relations between unions themselves, and the new relationship between unions and the public education system.

In a large sector of the economy like electrical and electronic manufacturing, it is quite common to find more than one union representing workers. Different approaches on dealing with management, and sometimes conflicts about which union has the right to represent which members, has meant that, while unions may be linked through the national bodies of the labour movement, they are not necessarily together at the industry level. Having seven different unions on the Sectoral Skills Council required a collective approach by all. In the process of developing that collective voice, a series of barriers were removed.

When there were disagreements on issues, they were ironed out before they were presented to management, creating a culture of working together. Similarly, in the last two years, the "Facing Training" course — originally developed by Communications, Energy and Paperworkers Union — has been offered to representatives on Joint Workplace Training Committees for all the unions. The other unions suggested changes to the original course and it was updated to make it a collective tool of union training. At the same time, networking among workplaces represented by different unions became more common; they exchanged names of training organizations, curricula, experiences in the application process, success stories and techniques to deal with management.

Another aspect of building links has been the practical relationship developed with educational institutions. In the past, the labour movement supported public education as the way to guarantee the right of workers' access to a good, fair and free education system. They made that view quite clear in their political activities. The Sectoral Skills Council has allowed for the creation of a relationship with the education system. A large system of relationships was developed, from the participation in general task forces as members of the council, to direct buying of services by the committees. Also, the support for community education by the unions helped build the link between the established education system and community-based educators.

Equality for all

The decentralized structure of the Sectoral Skills Council has meant a very uneven result in the nature and quality of the training provided.

The formula of the council passing the control over training directly to the workplaces — to those who "should know what is needed" — has provoked disparity at different levels. Training courses vary from "CTI Cryogenics Cryopump" and "Understanding North American Free Trade Agreement Regulations", to "Basic English" and "Computer Literacy" in different workplaces. Also, in some workplaces, training was oriented to vary basic levels, at the expense of the most advanced workers. While in other workplaces, improvement was seen in those who were already better prepared, leaving the basic level to be pursued by the individual workers on their own.

The lack of central control and/or a system to evaluate and monitor the training delivered at the workplace level seem to be the main reasons for the unevenness. Although everyone agrees that training supported by the fund should be "portable, incremental and equitable", without a measurement system or a central monitoring body, this can mean different things. In many cases these categories are interpreted differently by different players.

Beyond "bread and butter" unionism

The labour movement has always seen its role at two levels in society: as representatives of their members at the workplace level, fighting for benefits, wages, input, etc., and as the voice of working people in society, fighting for a just distribution of wealth and fair political participation. The labour movement prioritized the first aim (members' improvement) over the second (societal representation) by setting its agenda around bargaining with individual corporations. This approach benefited union members tremendously. From much better wages, to protection to working conditions, unionized workplaces surpassed non-unionized ones, but at the same time created its own problems.

First, it divided the working class into two categories, those protected and those not protected by unions. Using that fact, the right-wing propaganda pitted workers again workers, saying to non-unionized workers that unionized workers were lazy, and made too much money thanks to their unions. Following that argument, they would say that, because unionized workers made too much money, companies cannot compete; because companies cannot compete, they close, because companies close, the economy is dismal and, because the economy is not working, they — the non-unionized workers — cannot find any decent paying jobs. At the same time, their argument to unionized workers is as follows: Because the union is too rigid, the company cannot compete in the marketplace, therefore they will close and go to non-union workplaces — in the same country or abroad — to get a cheaper workforce.

The focus of unions on "bread and butter" contract issues also distanced union members from the marginalized in society: homeless, welfare recipients, native people, etc. The income and living conditions of full-time, unionized workers is far above those of members of the marginalized groups. The right-wing discourse of individual responsibility as the measurement of success caught many unionized workers minds, and they ended up blaming marginalized people themselves for their low status in society.

As labour academic Elaine Bernard writes:

> There has always been a tension within unions between servicing members and fulfilling the wider social mission of labour to serve the needs of all working people, whether they are organized or not. It is becoming increasingly clear in today's political environment that unions need to do both. Unions, like any organization, will not survive if they do not serve the needs of their members. But unions will not survive and grow, if they only serve the needs of their members.[8]

Enlarging their mandate to represent all working people in society would mean unions need to participate in the political arena to stop governments from submitting to the will of large corporations. They would need to enlarge the recognition of civic rights of the individual, and fight to improve minimum standards that society provides for all. Also, they would have to expand their mandate for bargaining, and the terrain in which that bargaining is held.

Similarly, unions pursuing a larger agenda than collective bargaining issues — moving into industrial and social democracy as the final goal of their activities — would put basic education at a more important level than they have it at this point; simply linking basic education to job security and job training when evaluating their aims.

CONCLUSIONS

The case study highlighted in this article shows the ample possibilities of basic education delivery at the workplace level as a tool to democratize education and improve citizenship. As a union representative said:

> When you hook a person to education, when a person can read a paper, you are not giving them just a tool to do a job. You are giving them a possibility to inform themselves, to be able to have an explanation about why they would support a candidate in elections, to be able to tell the people who are governing them, at any level, what their expectations are.

On the other side, the decentralized scheme and the focus on job-training — due to government funding and employer participation — has made that opportunity go unexplored in many cases.

A government training policy that equally promoted job qualifications for full employment with education as social entitlement would create a social environment, and a funding strategy, that would help balance the system. Employed, employable and unemployed workers' need for a job and a living wage — and to be active participants of a democracy — should be an integral part of that policy. A policy oriented only to job-specific training sees workers solely as producers, as attached to the piece of machinery that they operate or could operate. A larger policy, recognizing education promotion as its base, would increase the participation of workers as creative participants in a society pursuing progress and fairness.

The decision of governments to develop and enforce a training policy, that promotes full employment and the right of the individual to a lifelong learning environment, is not based on experiences or concrete results. Instead it is based in ideological understandings of their roles and the constituencies that they serve. In that sense, it is idealistic to expect that neo-conservative governments would support progressive policies in education and training. In the education environment created for neo-conservative governments any rights gained in the past would be challenged and must be defended. As well, any improvement in the allocation of resources to be managed by the communities would be obtained after a long and painful struggle by the progressive forces.

Notes

1. This article is based on collected statistics and interviews. The author thanks the following people for agreeing to be interviewed: Gary Ramos, Brian DeCastro and Mahadeo Ketwaroo-Nanoo, members of the Joint Workplace Training Committee at Schneider Canada and of Local 521 of Communications, Energy and Paper Workers Union of Canada (CEP); Paul Heath, member of the Secretariat of the Sectoral Skills Council, and D'Arcy Martin, Education Representative of the Communications, Energy and Paper Workers Union. Also, special thanks to Lorraine Endicott for editing the article.

2. From *Education and Training*, Document 5, 33rd Annual Convention, Ontario Federation of Labour, November 20-24, 1989.

3. Martin, D'Arcy 1995. *Thinking Union: Activism and Education in Canada's Labour Movement* Toronto:Between the Lines.

4. Wolfe, David & Martin, D'Arcy 1996. *Human resources think for themselves: the experience of unions in the Sectoral Skills Council*. In *The Emergence of Sectoral Councils in Canada*.Eds., Andrew Sharpe and Morley Gunderson, University of Toronto Press.

5. Participants included the Electrical and Electronic Manufacturers Association of Canada (EEMAC); the Communications Workers of Canada (today the Communications, Energy and Paper Workers Union of Canada (CEP), the International Brotherhood of Electrical Workers (IBEW) and the United Steelworkers of America (USWA). Some other unions joined the council later: the International Association of Machinists and Aerospace Workers (IAM), the International Federation of Professional and Technical Employees (IFPTE), the Canadian Auto Workers Union (CAW) and the Labourers International Union of North America (LIUNA).

6. The International Organization for Standardization (ISO) is a world wide federation of national standards bodies, based in Geneva, Switzerland. In 1987, the ISO first published the ISO 9000 series of international standards for quality management. The ISO 9000 standards actually originated from the quality standards of the U.S. Department of Defense in the late 1950s, known as MIL-Q9858.

7. In English-speaking Canada, courses on the English language are commonly called "English as a Second Language", disregarding the knowledge that many immigrants have been speaking and writing many languages from their original country or area of the world in which they used to live.

8. Bernard, Elaine, 1996. *Why unions matter*, Harvard Trade Union Program.

Chapter Sixteen
LITERACY, THE INSTITUTIONAL ENVIRONMENT AND DEMOCRACY

Serge Wagner
University of Quebec at Montreal
Montreal, Canada

THE QUEBEC EXPERIENCE[1]

> We should not judge education only in terms of efficiency and social well-being. Equally important, if not more so, is the role of education in making people capable of appreciating the culture of the society and of playing a part in it and, thereby giving each individual an assurance of his or her own value. J. Rawls

In a fundamental text, *Theory of Justice*, John Rawls (1987) suggests that social justice must rest on a virtual contract, founded on principles of equity that do as much as possible to promote equality between citizens and apply to the basic structure of the society and its institutions. Moreover, some social institutions, such as education, are tied, *inter alia*, to a "remedial principle"[2] that requires them to compensate for inequalities of birth and social conditions.

When applied to adult basic education, such a concept demands that it compensate for inequalities of social background and for inequalities that may have built up since initial education. Basic education provides the adults in question with a "second chance" only if it enables them really to "catch up" with those who are unequally ahead of them and, above all, to realize their full capacities. The adult basic education system will therefore be judged to be fair if it is an instrument of inclusion rather than exclusion. The aims that Rawls sets for education in general are related to those of the literacy-conscientization movement brought to the fore by Paulo Freire, still relevant today, in common with our notion of citizenship.

According to the perception of justice as equity, adult basic education in Quebec appears overall to offer little or no justice. This can be explained by a number of factors, including the inadequacy of resources allocated to it and its growing subservience to certain major social policies that discriminate against marginalized populations. Such policies have led to a reconfiguration of adult basic education, henceforward characterized by a two-fold phenomenon: a decline in global thinking, and a re-emphasis on the individual, the local and the particular, accompanied by the emasculation of any socio-political dimension.

There has been a shift towards "micro" social aspects of basic education at the expense of a wider vision of its purpose. The new institutional environment thus created shows up the dangers and limitations of "micro" approaches, that too often take an isolated, narrow, "functional" view that obscures or actually supports the general injustice of the system. It shows the necessity of focusing attention once more on socio-educational policies and the basic education system.

The assessment of Derouet (1989:18) on the dangers of "an ethnology that favours the mundane and the banal at the expense of formalized social and more classically political relationships" seems especially relevant, and we agree with the necessary link that he proposes to re-establish between the particular and the general: "The same definitions of justice, equally political and equally general, are valid both for what appear to be very simple situations and for the most complex educational program".

Our somewhat pessimistic vision of the Quebec experience has to be mitigated by three factors. First, Quebec has opened a public system of adult basic education, that has enabled some people to acquire useful skills. Second, the recent nature of the field of intervention provides reason to believe that it will be more fertile in future. Third, numerous institutional environments have gaps that make it possible for innovative practices to emerge that do reflect community reality, the interests of the target populations and social solidarity.

Having established the issues, we shall approach literacy from the angle of policy and practice by examining how the present institutional environment has arisen out of the dynamics of a singular conjunction between the field of education and dominant socio-economic forces. As will be seen, this situation raises questions of equity. And finally, we shall try to identify some directions for the renewal of literacy.

The general context: an inequitable basic education system

Quebec, the only majority French-speaking society on the North American continent, contains over seven million inhabitants, of whom almost six million are French-speaking. Having long been affected by a linguistic division of employment that placed its majority at a disadvantage, the Quebec society engaged at the beginning of the 1960s in a "quiet revolution". In education, there was a considerable reform: a Ministry of Education was (finally) created in 1964, and a network of adult basic education was set up in each school district in Quebec.

But the reform movement, inspired by social democracy, slowed down after the crisis of the 1980s and the rise of neoliberalism: the equalizing function of the state was called into question, the social security net that had been introduced to protect the most disadvantaged was cut back, and so on. The economic situation in Quebec that had improved throughout the 1960s and '70s, deteriorated as a result. The new economic strategies had the effect of "increasing unemployment, underemployment and poverty" (Noël, 1994). Under the influence of the American "dual" model of society, the polarization between the poor and the "others" tended to increase.

In education, any progress achieved has not yet closed the gap serparating Quebec from the rest of the Canadian population. This gap is seen in average length of schooling and in the level of literacy. Three surveys on the reading and writing abilities of Canadians have in fact placed the Quebec population among the lowest of the provinces (Southam News, 1987; Statistics Canada 1989, 1996). Almost 900,000 Quebec adults (19 percent) have reading abilities that are too limited to meet the needs of reading in everyday life.

One key aspect of the education system reveals the lack of equity in the areas that we have been discussing. That is the proportion of pupils obtaining a certificate of secondary education (corresponding to eleven years of schooling), which has long been considered a minimum requirement for socialization and labour market entry and will, it is thought, be required for the majority of the jobs to be created between now and the year 2000 (Lafleur, 1992).[3] Quebec schools are slipping even in their achievement of this goal: between 1985 and 1992, the proportion of pupils in one cohort leaving ordinary schools without a secondary certificate has gone from 29 to 35 percent (MEQ,

1995a). In adult education, the system is proving even less effective, since hardly 25 percent of dropouts succeed in obtaining their secondary certificates through it (Moreau, 1996).

School failure is made more serious by the fact that it affects individuals from disadvantaged backgrounds (Beauchesne, 1991). It combines with poverty to form one of the factors leading to the "spiral of exclusion" (Moreau, 1996: 12). Educational institutions are therefore very poor at meeting the "remedial principle", in providing a real "second chance" and in combating the negative effects of the accidents of birth and social position. In fact, it is the whole of the educational resources of the society that are inaccessible to disadvantaged people. In 1991, for example, only six percent of adults with less than eight years of schooling took part in any adult education activity, compared with 53.2 percent of those who had enjoyed post-secondary education (Doray & Paris, 1995). These general data should be kept in mind for a true appreciation of adult basic education.

LITERACY IN EDUCATION

The field of adult literacy is a composite marked by major recent changes that have affected its orientation within the education system. From the point of view of equity, provision appears to be "performing" poorly, as it still inaccessible and seems to reinforce rather than combat "exclusion".[4]

A policy that is split between a twofold provincial network

In the mid-1960s, adult basic education was handed over exclusively to the school boards,[5] under the coordination of the Ministry of Education. Literacy was theoretically part of basic education, but there was no analysis of the major problem of functional illiteracy, that affected the adult population. The problem was discovered by the arrival of illiterate adults in the school network, through the involvement of popular education agencies that followed an approach based on the literacy conscientization of Freire, and through the activities of some "first line" interveners in the Ministry of Education and some school boards. The field of literacy however, never developed its own policies, as was the case in some countries or societies;[6] rather, it was made up of a mixture of various legislative and political measures that often went far beyond literacy in the narrow sense.

The most original element of policy in the different measures that made up the field of literacy was probably the existence of a twofold network, as the monopoly of the school boards was breached during the 1970s, when the popular organizations succeeded in having their work recognized and (partly) subsidized. But government indecision provoked a contradictory twofold effect. While it encouraged local initiative, it also led to insecurity in both networks, the complementarity and relative weight of which were never agreed.

It was the *school boards* that had the larger budgets and hence carried out the greater volume of literacy activities. Literacy essentially meant the first years of general education leading to a certificate of secondary education (in theory more than in reality because of the high rate of dropout). Until the mid-1980s, a number of school boards tried to renew their intervention by seeking to distance themselves from the "school model". This (central) initiative gave rise in the regions to a vast action-research movement. Under the leadership of a development team, a provincial *Experimental Plan* (1980-1984) was carried out, involving most of the school boards (Wagner & Grenier, 1984). Moreover, an interregional literacy team was set up in 1982, to bring together the local educational bodies into "regional boards" that would launch coordination initiatives and action-research.

From 1984, however, the Ministry of Education appeared gradually to abdicate its leadership, largely reintegrating literacy into the bosom of adult general (academic) education. In 1989, the new Public Education Act drew adult education further into the structure of ordinary education. Paradoxically, the Act granted each adult the right to free basic education up to the secondary education certificate — which entailed a considerable increase in enrolments. But second thoughts meant that what was granted in law was refused by administrative means: the budget for general education was reduced.[7]

Literacy enrolments in school boards, by type of education

YEAR	FULL-TIME	PART-TIME	TOTAL*
1988-89	5,225	10,908	16,201
1989-90	8,001	13,804	21,806
1990-91	12,318	17,001	29,319
1991-92	19,111	14,409	31,852
1992-93	14,434	12,744	25,737
1993-94	11,811	12,349	22,783
1994-95	10,232	11,444	20,109

* *Some individuals may have enrolled full-time and part-time in the course of the same year. (Source: MEQ)*

But the decline was greater than the statistics show, as the Ministry gradually abandoned its expertise and leadership in literacy. It thereby ended the *Experimental Plan* in 1984, dismantled the development team that had run it, and abolished the literacy research programme. Further, the *Alpha* biennial research publication project that had enabled innovative local experiences to be disseminated to all areas, became internationalized from 1986, thus losing its function as a catalyst in Quebec. The special activities connected with International Literacy Year (1990) seem to have disguised the actual decline, which accelerated from 1991. The last large-scale provincial seminar on literacy — inauspiciously called ''Literacy Break'' (*Pause alpha*) — was held in 1992. In 1993, the Ministry ceased to fund the regional literacy boards, and in the following year, it ended 13 years of publishing the journal *Alpha-liaison*, which then had 2000 subscribers. In effect, provincial energy seemed to be directed essentially towards the experimental tailor-made literacy education program (MEQ, 1986) that was then set up in all school boards. This program leaves much of the initiative to local projects.

As for residual research activities, these were monopolized by the statistical analyses of the populations enrolled in the school boards (Roy 1990; Roy, Mastriani & Gobeil, 1991; Roy, & Mastriani 1993; Roy, 1996), which added nothing to the outcome of education itself or to its effects from the point of view of equity. They were part of the functionalist view of an institutional field focusing on ''teaching hours'' and ignoring the socio-educational issues at stake.[8]

In sum, the whole of the literacy system appeared to be concerned exclusively with the functioning of the system. ''The recruitment of the clientele (*sic*) remains one of the major obstacles to the development of literacy,'' the inter-regional team observed, which meant that it had to allocate ''resources periodically to tracking [people] down (*sic*) and recruiting [them]'' (EIA, 1996:17). The ''clientele'' was in some way the raw material of the ''literacy machine'', which consumed many of its members, losses being considerable: over half the people enrolled for a given year did not re-enrol in the following year (Charest & Roy, 1992).

Since the political authorities refused to adopt a literacy plan, the leaders of the institutional ''literacy movement'', state officials and school boards had to be careful in what they said and did as their room for manoeuvre and freedom of expression were more limited than in the popular network. They were driven into a defensive position and attempted to defend what had been achieved, lamenting the fact that they had to ''provide literacy under unstable conditions''. Because they felt that "they were not listened to", they adopted "a clear policy of overcoming illiteracy" (EIA, 1996).

The *network of popular groups*, unlike the school boards, devoted itself exclusively to literacy. But, like the school network, it was monopolized by the struggle to survive and It also found it difficult to design a literacy project that really differed from what the school boards did.

At the outset, the network of popular literacy groups took a militant sociopolitical stance, largely inspired by the "Freirean" perspective (Wagner, 1974; Miller, 1987), and sought to see literacy as part of the perspective of individual and collective advancement adopted by the Quebec popular education movement. That contrasted strongly with the charitable orientation of the Anglo-Quebec or Anglo-Canadian "community" groups. The successes of the movement then rested perhaps more on the breakthrough it made among marginalized populations (that schools hardly reached) than on its literacy work itself. Moreover, several of the organizations associated with it were also characterized by a democratic structure: learners, who were not defined as a *clientele*, were invited to join in democratically managing them. Life in the popular literacy organizations allowed a number of learners to enjoy, perhaps for the first time, an enlarged experience of citizenship.

But in the second half of the 1980s, the popular movement had serious difficulties in maintaining and implementing its platform when resurgent neoliberalism made every proposal with a social dimension seem obsolete. Besides, the reality of illiteracy and the content of literacy appeared more complex than the simple literacy-conscientization dichotomy suggested. The radical discourse of popular groups became weaker, and they found it increasingly difficult to distinguish themselves from the school boards since some of the latter successfully adopted "popular" strategies of outreach and recruitment in disadvantaged areas while talking more in terms of the community. The respective particularities of the two networks were reduced.

In effect, the "academic approach" infiltrated in various ways the projects that were thought of as popular, thereby helping to inhibit their "alternative" choices. First, some school boards set up "popular" literacy organizations when they saw that the Ministry program of popular literacy meant additional funds, and was more flexible than the provincial rules by which they were governed.[9]

Second, the "academic approach" also penetrated some groups that had continued working independently. In several regions, for example, coordination mechanisms helped to bring about a rapprochement and a division of responsibilities between "popular" organizations and school boards. Further, because of the limited funding of the government program, some groups had, in turn, to establish service contracts with school boards. Moreover, in order to obtain funding for teaching hours in certain programs, some bodies had compulsorily to take on teachers and to use the literacy program of the Ministry of Education.

The loss of particularity between the two networks was at the expense of the popular literacy network, as this could only really exist if its members were working towards a goal different from that of the institutional network. Historically, it was the Association of Quebec Popular Literacy Groups (*Regroupement des groupes populaires en alphabétisation du Québec*, RGPAQ), founded in 1980, which had been the vector of the popular movement. But in the second half of the 1980s, the RGPAQ and its member groups were taken up with the struggle for their survival; and as a result of "academic" infiltration, the particularity and legitimacy of popular literacy declined. Already in 1995, only 37 groups were members of the RGPAQ, while 25 groups preferred to join the Inter-Regional Literacy Group, under the leadership of the academic sector.

In 1995, the popular network nonetheless obtained some improvement in the "Independent Popular Literacy Support Program" (*Programme de soutien à l'alphabétisation populaire autonome*) and a 104 percent increase in its budget. But the way the decision was taken was typical of the management of literacy: it was simply announced in a ministerial press release that took the additional funds required from the general education budget for the school boards. The increased activities of the popular network thus entailed a corresponding reduction in the budget for school-based basic education. Paradoxically, the expansion of the *program* of popular literacy threatened to weaken still further the popular *movement*. In 1996, for instance, only 37 percent (48 out of 130) of the "popular" groups were regular members or sympathizers of the RGPAQ.[10]

The loss of particularity of the popular literacy projects helped to reveal their true nature in the eyes of government. In the context of the present economic crisis, governments have subsidized a number of community initiatives that enable "essential services to be provided at reduced cost by transforming unionized jobs into non-unionized jobs" (Fontan & Shragge, 1996b). That is exactly the interpretation that can be placed upon the action of the Minister of Education, who subsidized the expansion of the popular network from the adult general education budget for the school boards. When it is not hiding behind a democratic project, the new "social economy" sector is helping to "dualize" society by establishing a second-rank sector for second-class (marginalized) citizens. It is also remarkable to find, in some popular literacy projects, learners and teachers who are on the same "employability" programs: the former enrolled in one of the training elements, and latter in a labour market entry element.

"Back to basics" literacy

As the difference between the two networks diminished, it is right to wonder whether one of them was not a victim of "back to basics literacy".[11] The emerging institutional environment tended to ignore the antecedents and consequences of literacy, and to eliminate all controversial aspects, including questions associated with social justice. The same institutional environment of literacy seems, in fact, to exhibit a disproportionate fixation with literacy as such, and its educational dimensions. A summary of titles of articles that have appeared in three periodicals devoted to literacy[12] clearly illustrates the gradual disappearance of politics in favour of education.

Over the years, the content of practice has nonetheless evolved, and new questions have appeared, such as family literacy and employment-related literacy. Several of the writings referred to below on "particular populations" also address these two issues. However, many documents ignore political aspects and remain confined to a methodological perspective. Family literacy is a good example: its content was first fixed in the United States, and it often tended to make (poor and single) mothers responsible for their own literacy and that of their children by saying nothing about the injustice of their social conditions and the lack of policies relating to child care, education and social security (Wagner, 1994; Roy & Tremblay, 1994).

Typology of articles on literacy in three periodicals
(number and %)

	Collection Alpha 1978, 1980 1982, 1984, 1986	Alpha-liaison 1984-1992	Le Monde alphabétique Nos. 1-17 1991-1995	TOTAL
Politics, organization, guidance and research	18 - 30%	26 - 14%	15 - 12%	59 - 16%
Sensitization, recruitment and prevention	1 - 2%	11 - 6%	7 - 6%	19 - 5%
Approach and methodology	10 - 17%	90 - 49%	38 - 31%	138 - 38%
Particular populations	12 - 20%	40 - 22%	26 - 21%	78 - 21%
Teachers	1 - 2%	6 - 3%	8 - 6%	15 - 4%
Learners	0 - 0%	1 - 1%	14 - 11%	15 - 4%
Descriptions of experience	18 - 30%	8 - 4%	13 - 10%	39 - 11%
Other	0 - 0%	0 - 0%	3 - 2%	3 - 1%
TOTAL	60 - 100%	182 - 100%	124 - 100%	366 - 100%

Democratic alternatives

The new institutional environment introduced since the mid-1980s thus favours an apolitical "back to basics" view of literacy that leaves the responsibility for reconstructing the question to each local project so that it can better reflect social concerns. Some "micro-projects" do so, by trying to take into account not only the educational aspects of literacy but also its economic, social, political and ethical aspects. A few examples may be given:

1. The forum "A Society without Barriers" (*Une société sans barrières*), aims to encourage illiterate people to exercise their rights in society. Illiteracy is seen less as individuals' own failing than as the result of obstacles put in their way by society and its institutions. And literacy is regarded from the standpoint of "five rights recognized as valid for the whole of the population, which illiterate people often find it impossible to exercise. These are the right to full participation in democratic life, the right to accessible services, the right to information, the right to work and the right to learn" (Bélisle, 1991:11).

2. We referred above to the importance of the certificate of secondary education, and to the large number of young people and adults who do not succeed in obtaining it. A project launched by an organization in the social economy, the Alliance for the Economic and Social Renaissance of Southeast Montreal (*Regroupement pour la relance économique et sociale dans le sud-est de Montréal*, RESO), which works in one of the poorest areas of Quebec, has achieved remarkable results.

In 1991, a group of 83 recipients of unemployment insurance or social security assistance (half of whom were at presecondary or literacy level), joined a school board's general education program. After 52 weeks, the results were spectacular (especially if they are compared with the generally poor performance of the education system): 52 obtained their certificate of secondary education, 12 reached the penultimate level of secondary schooling, a total success rate of 77 percent; 87 percent of those who finished started vocational education. The experiment was repeated in the following years with a success rate that ranged from 71 to 80 percent (Soutière & Gareau, 1996:6). By way of explanation for the high degree of success in reversing the school failure rate, those running the project pointed to a number of administrative and educational measures, and particularly to "ongoing support in the environment in which they live and to which they belong" .

3. Another notable micro-project, also linked to the social economy, is the educational dimension of the *Chic resto-pop*, a community restaurant that largely serves marginalized young adults with little formal education and no certificate of secondary education. The project provides jobs for some worker-trainees, and an education program for others: either vocational training in catering, or a remedial academic program devised by the *Chic resto* in collaboration

with a school board. Although the evaluation of the educational dimension is not yet completed, the overall data for the worker-trainees who have left the project are intriguing: 46 percent say that they have seen their situation improve, while 54 percent state that this interlude did not necessarily lead to an improvement (Fontan & Shragge, 1996a).

One of the interesting aspects of the experiment is that it includes education in a multidimensional project of socialization and labour market entry, closely linked to community life, and that the frontier of exclusion can therefore be crossed. Moreover, the project has done a remarkable amount of work in social communications, whereby the team running it and the trainees, most of whom had little previous schooling and were excluded, have demonstrated that they have something to say, and to sing about, and that they can do so using a range of instruments of communication: film, sound recordings and print (Prud'homme et al., 1995).

4. While literacy workers often state that learners already possess their own load of experience and knowledge, but that the latter frequently find it difficult to identify these, which is an important aspect of education. The project "Our Strong Skills" (*Nos compétences fortes*, Bélisle, 1995) does offer an approach that enables people who "find writing completely or largely alien" to recognize their skills, and to have them recognized. So as to circumvent the written word, which is the compulsory way of having learning recognized, the approach suggested favours oral and audiovisual communication.

The project therefore aims to increase self-esteem among completely or functionally illiterate people, a benefit that is too often socially denied them. Among the generic skills identified are a sense of responsibility and of organization, and the abilities to contact others, to learn from experience, to get by and have confidence in oneself.

Literacy Outside Education

The considerable growth in the number of people enrolled in literacy between 1988 and 1991, and then its decline from 1992 onwards, can largely be explained by factors external to the activities of the two networks. The conceptual framework and the institutional environment of adult (basic) education are now determined less by educational than socio-economic forces. That is partly a result of the decision by the Government of Quebec, in 1984, to remove the management of adult education policy from Education, whose role has henceforward been reduced to a "mission to service the labour force development agencies" (MEQ, 1984:47). The weakening of the role of the Ministry of Education led, in 1989, to the dismantling of its Directorate General of Adult Education (DGEA), a section of which nonetheless remained as an educational extension service. But literacy has retained, or even increased, its power of attraction (Hautecoeur, 1996), especially because the Federal Government takes an interest in it, and because the federal and provincial authorities governing economic policy have initiated a set of measures for certain marginalized populations (that are illiterate or have little schooling).

Federal and provincial specialization

The retreat by the educational leadership of Quebec in the field of adult education since 1984 has not been felt so strongly in literacy because the Federal Government has filled the gap to a certain extent. Education is under provincial jurisdiction, but the Federal Government has intervened in adult education since the early 1960s (from the standpoint of labour force training), and specifically in literacy since 1989, when it armed itself with a policy on the issue and set up the National Literacy Secretariat (NLS).

The partial retreat by the Province, and the Federal advance, has led to specialization in the functions of the two governments, the former taking on the day-to-day management (teaching hours), and the latter laying down guidelines and subsidizing research and development: public awareness, development of teaching materials, improving access, co-ordinating information, research, pilot projects, etc. The Federal Government has thus played a key role in launching "literacy in the workplace" and "family literacy" projects.

The process of reconceptualizing the field of literacy also illustrates the respective leadership styles of the two governments. At first, the Government of Quebec attempted to reduce the importance of literacy (Maheu & St-Germain, 1984), thereby perpetuating the position of its elites, while the Federal Government adopted a more inclusive approach based on the handling of written information (Statistics Canada, 1989), devised by the Americans (Kirsh & Jungeblut, 1986), which nonetheless minimized ethnolinguistic differences. Then the Government of Quebec thought again and produced a study specifically on the situation in Quebec, based on the federal data, perspective and methodology, which led it to deny the existence of an illiteracy problem peculiar to French-speaking

Québécois. This, even though the gap between French-speakers and English-speakers was significant (Roy & Gobeil, 1993:31).

Furthermore, the Federal Government's literacy policy paid significant attention to economic aspects. This attitude that was already present in the creation of the National Literacy Secretariat (State Secretariat,1987), gained in strength even though the federal intervention did take social and community aspects into account. Several of the research studies sponsored by the NLS helped to re-orient provincial practice towards a more economic perspective. The systematic "telescoping" between literacy and the economy[13] culminated to some extent in the international survey of adult literacy (OECD and Statistics Canada,1995), the title of which is itself revealing: *Literacy, Economy and Society*.

It was also the Federal Government that introduced the notion of partnership into the field of literacy (NLS 1990), thereby helping to bring the field out of the "enclave" of education and to widen the circle of organizations with an interest in the subject. But the principle of partnership sometimes had the effect of eliminating any perspectives that were too radical — since it was necessary to reach agreement between all partners — and of obscuring the responsibility of the state for the basic education of its citizens.

Lastly, the federal intervention gave rise to a certain convergence between the federal and provincial authorities that opened the way for the two networks to work independently, and this was exploited particularly by the "popular" network.

Social and economic policies

In Quebec, and throughout Canada, adult education (and hence literacy) is greatly influenced by government social and economic policy, particularly since the start of the move from *passive* income-support measures to *active* work creation schemes, as recommended by the OECD. This perspective often leads to adult education's being given an instrumental role, as the aim is less to respond to the educational needs of adults or to attain better equity, than to find an "economic" solution to the various problems of labour market entry and social dependency. These policies, at first devised for the "active labour force" in the mid-1960s, embraced the "inactive" population (especially those in receipt of social security assistance) following the crisis of the 1980s and the weakening of the welfare state. The importance of literacy in the context of these policies was thus related to the number of people with low levels of schooling who were targeted for socio-economic purposes.

The period from the mid-1960s to the early 1980s was optimistic: it was a high point in the creation of the Canadian welfare state. During this period, the aims of labour force training and adult education policies tended to become confused. The federal and provincial governments adhered to the theory of human capital, according to which an expansion in labour force training leads to a global improvement in the economic situation and in employment (Dandurand, 1983; Paquet, 1993). The human capital theory partly explains the convergence between the federal labour force training and recycling policies and the Quebec policy of expanding the adult education system.

But the rise of neoliberalism in the 1980s led to a questioning of policies of general, widely accessible education. A neoliberal counter-argument emanated from the Federal Government that rethought its labour force training strategy in the early 1980s. The human capital theory was henceforward deemed to produce inadequate "economic" returns. According to the Dodge Report (1981) in particular, a number of needs could be better met by initiatives directly tied to employment. In an attempt to make vocational education "more suited to the needs of the labour market" (Hunter, 1993:387), the Federal Government reduced its grants to workplace education in favour of shorter activities that were open only to target populations in difficulty. These activities often took the form of "employability" schemes in which it was thought that positive attitudes at the workplace and some low-level skills could be inculcated more quickly.

A number of models were used: (1) (short-term) training, (2) a (subsidized) process of (re-)entry into employment, and (3) a mixture of training and labour market entry (Dodge et al. 1981). The meagre concern for equity seen in such schemes was reflected also in the recommendation to "reduce the funds ...allocated...to the acquisition of non-specialized skills and to increase the resources devoted to the acquisition of highly and semi-specialized skills" (idem: 195). Adult education was thus engaged in a process of "dualization" that helped to increase the gap between the "haves" and the "have-nots', the former having access to certificated training and the latter being relegated to short-term uncertificated training and employability schemes (Paquet, 1993; Trudel et al., 1994).

Then, in 1984, the Quebec Government withdrew from the education sector responsibility for its adult education policies, and socio-economic agencies benefited from their considerable freedom to take over the field and impose their own aims, pursued among "well-targeted" populations: immigrants, social security recipients, the unemployed, young dropouts, etc. That decision explains how it was possible to develop literacy activities in the absence of any adult education policy.

But the categories into which people were put by the socio-economic agencies created divisions, and a peculiar assessment of the problems experienced by the people in question. It would not be accurate to suggest that the socio-economic policies of the last few decades were devoid of all preoccupation with social justice and education, but it has to be said that these often took second place. It is thus easier to understand how a committee of enquiry set up by the Government of Quebec should have felt it necessary to state that "literacy and adult education are not only questions of employment and employability", adding that "literacy and the education of the entire adult population is a fundamental aim of citizenship adopted by societies far poorer than Quebec" (Bouchard, Labrie & Noël, 1996:219).

The slide back to "basics'

The spread in recent years of policies favouring socio-economics, have radically affected the institutional environment of activities among vulnerable populations. While they have enabled interesting "micro-projects" to appear (a few examples were given above), they have also resulted in divergence from the aims of education and social equity that they were supposed to achieve. We shall give a few illustrations that raise doubts as to the justice of some measures and policies.

- **Compulsory literacy**. One of the traditional features of adult education (and literacy) is the high degree of motivation of its participants, but in recent years there has been a dramatic change in this situation. Adult education services have been obliged to accept adults who had little motivation or were forced to become literate.

  First, thanks to the flexibility of legislation, many of those in charge of ordinary education literally expelled thousands of young people in difficulty into adult education, telling them that they would find it easier to obtain their certificates of secondary education there. It is clear that the intended aim was to make the task of ordinary education simpler. Second, some social programs, among them "Remedial Academic Education" (*Rattrapage scolaire*) and "Return to Study for Heads of Single-parent Families" (*Retour aux études pour les chefs de famille monoparentale*), are measures that are compulsory or offer incentives to join adult education: bonuses or special payments given to social security recipients who agree to enrol, various penalties for people who refuse to return to study, and so on.

The two practices of "managing" populations in difficulty often pay little regard to individuals' dignity, or even their integrity. For all that, the influx of unmotivated adults harms the atmosphere of learning, and many teachers who cannot cope find themselves obliged to take courses in "class management (and discipline)".

- **Forbidden literacy**. While return to studies is all but compulsory for some people, it is forbidden to others! Such a prohibition is written into the Remedial Academic Education (RS) program that is open only to persons who left school more than 24 months before. The people who designed it wanted to avoid young people being tempted to give up studying in ordinary education and dropping out of school to receive social security assistance and then to take advantage of the RS program, with its grants. This attempt to avoid abuse has penalized a significant section of jobless young people with low levels of schooling who need to return to study to make it easier for them to find jobs.

- **Minimum literacy**. One of the surprising effects of some literacy programs is that they do not guarantee the literacy of the people concerned. This is expressly the case of the "Linguistic Integration Program for the Illiterate Clientele" (*Programme d'intégration linguistique adapté pour la clientèle analphabète*, see MCCI, 1991), an element of the Government of Quebec's policy of integrating new immigrants. Since it has been decreed that the number of hours of language education is to be the same for all immigrants, it has been necessary to reduce the aims of the program for the illiterate "clientele".

  Their education is therefore largely devoted to learning oral communication in French, reducing the learning of the written word to "overall survival" (p.1). It is often called "survival literacy". Similar administrative and educational measures serve to widen the gap between immigrants who had an education in their mother tongue and illiterate immigrants, at the very outset of their integration into the country. This helps to bring about different classes of citizenship and obviously flouts the principle of remediation referred to above.

- **Non-literacy**. Some so-called "employability" programs that accommodate a large number of adults with little or no schooling are another variety of problem program. The content of these programs results from a combination of social and educational policies, the educational aspect of which is sometimes tenuous or non-existent. Frequently, the time given to education is not sufficient to deal with gaps in basic education, while all that is done is to inculcate a few immediate skills associated with a particular job.

What is worse, the "employment" aspect often has serious omissions. A majority of the beneficiaries of these programs are in fact often directed towards temporary, poorly paid jobs that they lose, in three cases out of four, when the government employment subsidy comes to an end (Bouchard, Labrie & Noël, 1996: 79). After a run around one of the new circuits of exclusion, the majority find themselves back where they started, but a bit more disheartened, abused and stigmatized.

CONCLUSION: THE NEED TO RETHINK LITERACY

In Quebec, society does give some recognition to the field of literacy. Illiterates are now one of the legitimate and socially recognized categories of vulnerable populations — together with other educational and social categories such as school dropouts, the poor, the unemployed, recipients of social security assistance, female heads of one-parent families, etc. There is no question but that progress has been made in literacy, action has been taken, and expertise has been acquired in various places. But the field is faced with a problem environment and a lack of institutional support, which means that responsibilities remain on an individual, local level, obscuring its political and structural weakness. Major inadequacies are to be found, particularly in the awareness of the phenomenon, in the orientation and direction of its policies, in the coherence between literacy activities, and in the distribution of initiatives. Furthermore, the links between literacy and basic education activities, and some socio-economic measures, are seen to be problematic.

Such problems can only be resolved by creating the time and space for discussions between the different partners involved: political (educational and social) agencies, service organizations, research institutions and, of course, representatives of the target populations and learners. A few directions for rethinking collective action may be sketched out.

Understanding of illiteracy and literacy

The phenomenon at issue is still perceived in a rather one-sided, "back to basics" way. Public attention has been fully taken up by the equation between illiteracy and literacy that has paradoxically, not been explored very deeply. The real effects of illiteracy are, for example, still little known, as are those of literacy teaching and learning. And little interest has yet been shown in the fundamental question of literacy itself, or in the mechanisms and channels of social communication used by persons with little or no literacy, for example. Further, a more accurate assessment of the phenomenon can only be made if the essential partners who are generally kept out are in fact drawn in: ordinary education, libraries and cultural institutions, those who work in social communication with citizens, etc. Finally, as the understanding of a phenomenon such as literacy is an open question, it is important that research should be able continually to enrich policy and practice.

The need for results

Some years ago, the literacy agencies were publishing texts by learners (that were almost incantations) which magnified the effects of literacy learning. That is all very well, but attention should also be paid to reports of failure. Above all, individual reports, positive and negative, are not enough: they have to be part of a broader evaluation of the results achieved, notably with regard to the justice of policy and practice, and of the real changes that these bring about in individuals' lives. Management accounting in teaching hours and the number of places is necessary but inadequate. Central and local providers do have to be accountable for their actions. In consequence, it would be of benefit to introduce evaluation mechanisms (that are rigorous but flexible and include qualitative aspects), and to use them more widely where they already exist.

Coherence between education and socio-economic policies

A whole range of measures and policies are currently addressed to the vulnerable populations (including "illiterates"), but they seem at the same time overlap one another, without any real co-ordination. We should make use of what we have learnt in the last decade — the complexity of social phenomena, and the need for better integration and harmonization of different policies addressed to the same populations. Some of the examples given above on the divergence of pure literacy demonstrate the requirement to reconcile socio-educational, social and socio-economic policies rather better. Lastly, literacy must be accorded the resources that match its objective importance in society. For example, a "literacy" sector founded essentially on unpaid voluntary or temporary work, and the human resources of unstable organizations, will not have a long-term impact. Moreover, a balance has to be found between the activities of literacy as such and those of research and development.

Between "micro" and "macro": obligation and balance

In social policies, including literacy, there is still an imbalance between a common direction and local autonomy, between the initiatives of the state and those of the civil society. A central impulse must be given that does not stifle local initiative; resources have to be more suitably split between the centre and the periphery. Similarly, co-ordination and networking have to be encouraged and stimulated without necessarily being imposed. And bureaucracy must never crush creativity! In fact, any literacy policy should be part of a policy of institutional support rather than administrative centralism, entailing a rational devolution of responsibilities in the interests of democracy and effectiveness.

(Re)introduction of social equity

Much policy and practice, being circumscribed by management mechanisms, has perhaps lost sight of the fundamental aims to be pursued. There is no reason for the existence of any policy or practice unless it produces justice, helps to increase social equity and genuinely guarantees the right to education. Adult literacy makes no sense unless it helps to reduce poverty, inequality and exclusion, and as a corollary, brings about greater citizenship and democracy. Ideally, literacy classes are, for learners and teachers, a laboratory for the learning and exercise of democracy. The primary aims of literacy need to be clearly identified and targeted.

The measures suggested are merely sketched out, but they seem to be ways of thinking globally while acting locally — to quote from the Brundtland report on the environment — in the context of a more equitable basic education system.

Notes

1. Stephane Ratel & Carole Choronzey, of the Education and Literacy Research Laboratory of UQAM, helped with the documentary research and the making of the two tables. Also, Professor Marc Turgeon of UQAM and Sylvie Roy, Researcher at the Ministry of Education, made helpful comments on the text. The text concentrates on the situation of French-speakers and speakers of other languages in Quebec, leaving aside the position of English-speakers and speakers of native languages.

2. According to Rawls (1987), the remedial principle is applied when certain institutions practise positive discrimination among disadvantaged populations: "... in order to treat all people equally, to offer true equality of opportunity, society must devote more attention to the most deprived in terms of natural gifts and those most disadvantaged socially by birth, The idea is to correct the influence of cinrcumstances in the interest of greater equality" (p. 131).

3. If there is a plentiful labour supply, some employers demand qualifications higher than those required for the task. Such discriminatory selection, termed "credentialism", is particularly common among populations with low levels of schooling.

4. Over recent years, lliteracy activities are said to have reached less than 5% of the target populations (EIA 1995). Moreover, the number dropping out is very high, which increases the feeling of personal failure among some adults. Some of them only have time to discover an additional problem, illiteracy. Some people then speak of a process which "creates illiteracy".

5. The other Canadian provinces generally leave the field open to the initiatives of different agencies (community colleges, school councils and community organizations).

6. The Government did not follow up the suggestion made by the Commission on Adult Education (*Commission d'etude sure la formations des adultes*, 1982) of conducting a literacy "mission", or a similar proposal made by the Higher Council of Education (*Conseil superieur de l'education*, CSE 1990). That contrasts with the actions of the two provinces neighbouring Quebec, New Brunswick and Ontario, which adopted explicit policies.

7. The limited access to education for adults who are illiterate or have little education is discriminatory, since there are quotas for enrolments only for adults attending school boards and colleges (CSE 1994). The universities receive subsidies for all the students (young and mature) that they can

accommodate, even though there is no law guaranteeing (adults) access to university education.

8. On the basis of "input-output" accounting, three indicators of success have been indentified: hours of literacy, annual attendance, and percentage of leavers (Roy & Gobeil 1993). Research projects have in fact led to notable advances in the prevention of illiteracy, services to speakers of other languages and success in literacy. But as they are not part of an overall plan, they do not feed into "grassroots action".

9. Moreover, the popular literacy agencies were not tied by the collective agreements of the education sector that enabled them to take on staff at low cost.

10. The popular movement nonetheless tried to find a new internal coherence, particularly through an ambitious program of self-training, independent publications, greater coordination between groups and the adoption of a literacy policy (RGPAQ 1996).

11. One example of the concentration on "back to basics" literacy is the title of the journal published by the RGPAQ. This was initially entitle *Alphabetisation poplaire* in 1981, but when it was relaunched in 1990 after a lapse of a few years, it was given the anodyne title *Le monde alphabetique*.

12. The methodology, inspired by Bardin (1996), consisted of classifying each article in accordance with descriptors representative of each article.

13. Doray and Richard (1996) used the expression "telescopic translations" to describe the process of establishing discussion links between certain economic problems and investments in education. The "economy-literacy/basic education" telescopic translations obviously bore fruit because they started to appear in the comments of those concerned with the economy. Illiteracy was hence once again identified as one of the major obstacles to Canada's economic competitiveness (see, for example, CEC 1992).

References

Bardin, L. 1996. *L'analyse de contenu*. Paris: Presses universitaires de France.

Beauchesne, L. 1991. *Les abandons au secondaire: profil sociodémographique*. Quebec: Ministry of Education.

Bélisle, R. 1991. *Une société sans barrières, forum pour favoriser l'exercice des droits des personnes analphabètes dans la société. Compte rendu du forum suivi de fiches pratiques*. Montreal: Institut canadien d'éducation des adultes, Centrale de l'enseignement du Québec, and Regroupement des groupes populaires en alphabétisation du Québec.

Bélisle, R. (ed.) 1995. *Nos compétences fortes. Manuel des animatrices et des animateurs*. Montreal: Institut canadien d'éducation des adultes.

Bouchard, C., Labrie, V. & Noël, A. 1996. *Chacun sa part. Rapport de trois membres du Comité externe de réforme de la sécurité du revenu*. Montreal: Ministry of Employment and Solidarity.

CAS. 1989. *Deux Québec dans un: rapport sur le développement social et démographique*. Boucherville: Gaétan Morin.

CDEACF & FORA Centre. 1995. *Catalogue francophone canadien de documents d'alphabétisation*. Montréal, Sudbury: Centre de documentation sur l'éducation des adultes et la condition féminine, Centre franco-ontarien de ressources en alphabétisation.

Charest, D. & Roy, S. 1992. *Départs et abandons en alphabétisation*. Quebec: Ministry of Education.

CSE. 1994. *Vers un modèle de financement en éducation des adultes*. Quebec: Conseil supérieur de l'éducation.

Derquet, J.-L. 1989. L'établissement scolaire comme entreprise composite. Programme pour une sociologie des établissements scolaires. *Justesse et justice dans le travail. Cahiers du centre d'études de l'emploi* (33): 11-42. Paris: Presses universitaires de France.

Dodge, D. et al. 1981. *The evolution of the labor market in the 1980s. A report of the Study Group on the Evolution of the Labor Market*. Ottawa: Employment and Immigration Canada.

Doray, P. & Paris, L. 1995. *La participation des adultes à l'éducation au Québec en 1991*. Montreal: UQAM, Institut canadien d'éducation des adultes.

Doray, P. & Richard, D. 1996. Les relations économie/éducation comme processus de traduction: le développement des politiques de formation des adultes au Québec. Paper given at the symposium on adult education at the conference *Recherche en éducation et en formation*. Montreal, September 1996.

ECC. 1992. *A Lot to Learn — Education and Training in Canada*. Ottawa: Economic Council of Canada.

EIA. 1995. *Mémoire. Etats généraux de l'éducation*. [Quebec]: Equipe interrégionale en alphabétisation.

EIA. 1996. *L'équipe interrégionale en alphabétisation. Document d'information*. [Quebec]: Equipe interrégionale en alphabétisation.

Fontan, J.-M. & Shragge, E. 1996a. The Chic Resto-pop. The reaffirmation of citizenship through socially useful work. In Hautecoeur, J.-P. et al. *Alpha 96. Basic Education and Work*, 339-360. UNESCO Institutue for Education, Hamburg: Culture Concepts Publishers, Toronto.

Fontan, J.-M. & Shragge, E. 1996b. L'économie sociale: une économie pour les pauvres? *La Presse* (Montreal), April, p. B3.

Government of Quebec. 1994. *Régime pédagogique applicable aux services éducatifs pour les adultes en formation générale*. Quebec.

Hautecoeur, J.-P. 1996. Is literacy "a good deal"? A critique of the basic education debate in Canada. In Hautecoeur, J.-P. et al. *Alpha 96. Basic Education and Work*, 57-77. Culture Concepts Publishers, Toronto; UNESCO Institute for Education, Hamburg.

Hunter, J. 1993. *Employment: A Challenge. Federal employment policies and programs, 1900 to 1990*. Hull: Public Affairs, Government of Canada.

Kirsh, I. & Jungeblut, A. 1986. *Literacy: Profiles of America's Young Adults (Final Report)*. Princetown NJ: National Assessment of Educational Progress.

Lafleur, B. 1992. *The Costs of School Dropout for Canada*. Ottawa: Conference Board of Canada.

Maheu, R. & St-Germain, C. 1984. *L'analphabétisme au Québec: résultat d'un sondage. Etudes et analyses*. Quebec: Ministry of Education.

MCCI. 1991. *Programme d'intégration linguistique adapté pour la clientèle analphabète*. Quebec: Ministry of Cultural Communities and Immigration.

MEQ. 1984. *Un projet d'éducation permanente. Enoncé d'orientation et plan d'action en éducation des adultes*. Quebec: Ministry of Education of Quebec.

MEQ. 1986. *Guide de formation sur mesure en alphabétisation*. Quebec: Ministry of Education of Quebec.

MEQ. 1995a. *Indicateurs de l'éducation*. Quebec: Ministry of Education of Quebec.

Miller, L. 1987. Les pratiques dans les groupes populaires d'alphabétisation québécois. In *Literacy in Industrialized Countries "A Focus on Practice"*. Toronto: ICAE.

Moreau, L. 1986. *La pauvreté et le décrochage scolaire ou la spirale de l'exclusion*. Quebec: Ministry of Income Support.

NLS. 1990. *Partners in Literacy. National Literacy Program*. Ottawa: National Literacy Secretariat.

Noël, A. 1994. Le chômage en héritage. In Gagnon, A.-G. et al., *Québec: Etat et société*, 421-431. Montreal: Québec-Amérique.

OECD. 1996. *Learning at any age*. Paris: Organization for Economic Co-operation and Development.

OECD and Statistics Canada. 1995. *Literacy, Economy and Society: Results of the first international survey of adult education*. Paris: Organization for Economic Co-operation and Development; Ottawa: Statistics Canada.

Paquet, P. 1993. L'évolution des politiques canadiennes et québécoises de formation des adultes depuis 1960. In Dandurand, P. et al., *Enjeux actuels de la formation professionnelle*, 225-258. Quebec: Institut québécois de recherche sur la culture.

Prud'homme, P. et al. 1995. *Le Chic Resto Pop*. Montreal: Fides.

Rawls, J. 1987. *Théorie de la justice*. Paris: Seuil.

RGPAQ. 1996. *Plan d'action en alphabétisation*. Montreal: Regroupement des groupes populaires en alphabétisation.

Roy, S. 1996. *Population inscrite à des activités d'alphabétisation dans les commissions scolaires du Québec: portrait statistique 1994-1995*. Quebec: Ministry of Education.

Roy, S. 1990. *Population inscrite à des activités d'alphabétisation dans les commissions scolaires du Québec: portrait statistique 1988-1989*. Quebec: Ministry of Education.

Roy, S. & Gobeil, I. 1993. *Les capacités de lecture des Québécoises et des Québécois: résultats d'une enquête canadienne*. Quebec: Ministry of Education.

Roy, S. & Mastriani, L. 1993. *Effectifs scolaires des services d'alphabétisation dans les commissions scolaires du Québec: Statistiques pour 1991-1992*. Quebec: Ministry of Education.

Roy, S., Mastriani, L. & Gobeil, I. 1991. *Population inscrite à des activités d'alphabétisation dans les commissions scolaires du Québec: Statistiques pour 1989-1990*. Quebec: Ministry of Education.

Roy, S. & Tremblay, H. 1994. *Prévention de l'analphabétisme et alphabétisation familiale. Document 1: notes et réflexions à partir de trois conférences*. Quebec: Direction de la formation générale des adultes; Longueil: Commission scolaire Jacques-Cartier.

State Secretariat. 1987. *Working Document on Literacy. Final Draft*. Ottawa: State Secretariat of Canada.

Southam News. 1987. *Illiteracy in Canada. Survey Report*. Montreal: Innova Group.

Soutière, M. & Gareau, J.-M. 1996. *Dans le Sud-Ouest de Montréal, des chômeurs passent du primaire au diplôme d'études secondaires en un an!* Montreal: Regroupement pour la relance économique et sociale dans le Sud-Ouest de Montréal.

Statistics Canada. 1996. *Reading the Future: A Portrait of Literacy in Canada*. Ottawa: Statistics Canada.

TREAQ. 1995. *La formation des adultes dans les commissions scolaires. Mémoire présenté à la Commission des états généraux sur l'éducation*. Sainte-Foy: Table des responsables de l'éducation des adultes dans les commissions scolaires du Québec.

Trudel, L. et al. 1994. *Apprendre à l'âge adulte. État de situation et nouveaux défis*. Montréal: Institut canadien d'éducation des adultes.

Wagner, S. 1974. Alphabétisation et domestication. Expérience du Carrefour d'éducation populaire de Pointe Saint-Charles. *Discussion sur l'alphabétisation*, Winter 1974: 663-675.

Wagner, S. 1994. Alphabétisation et libre-échange. *Alpha-liaison* 14 (1): 24-25.

Wagner, S. & Grenier, P. 1984. *L'alphabétisation institutionnelle au Québec, un aperçu préliminaire*. Quebec: Ministry of Education.

Chapter Seventeen
MAKING UP FOR LOST TIME: RESCUING THE BASICS OF ADULT EDUCATION

Enrique Pieck
El Colegio Mexiquense
Toluca, Mexico

> [...] Listening to what the popular sectors want from adult education, may help the education system to make a real contribution to the betterment of their quality of life (García Huidobro: Los cambios en las concepciones actuales de la educación de adultos).

Introduction

Adult education began to flourish in the early 40s with a handful of promises for the marginal populations: developing rural areas, meeting specific needs in isolated regions, linking education and work, encouraging participation, etc. In short, helping to improve people's living standards, reaching those unreached and neglected by the formal education system and trying to respond to their particular expectations and circumstances. From its early emphasis on community development to the notion of functional literacy as a means of contributing to the industrialization and agricultural modernization processes in some Latin American countries, programs have remained far from delivering their basic promises. As La Belle (1986:265) points out, "[...] given the complexity of human experience and the evidence to date, the power of nonformal education to achieve such social benefits remains an article of faith".

By the 1970s most Latin American countries had adopted adult education and recognized it as an important part of the educational scene. Legislation was adopted to regulate its activities, financial resources were allocated, many programs were implemented by a number of institutions in every country, and there was a continuous growth in the number of people participating in this activity. Despite this fast development and "enthusiasm" most adult education programs continued to be remedial in nature (Buttedhal, 1989). Latin American countries, as Gajardo (1985:76-77) points out:

> [...] are still far from having established national systems of adult education capable of performing diversified and flexible activities that can respond to educational demands of various groups, and of combining strategies that attend to their particular needs and interests.

Research carried out along these years have shown the limited outcomes of programs, the small size of the clientele, and how unrealistic it is to expect adult education activities to have an impact on basic social structures (La Belle, 1976). Even earlier Coombs's (1976) expressed faith in nonformal education1 admits words of caution concerning the always slow process of progress and change. Some other authors, like Bock and Papagianis (1976; 1983), have looked at other limitations of the impact of nonformal education credentials on its students, and its allocation function in terms of socializing learners into accepting an inferior status in the social and economic system. Nonformal education seems to be trapped in the same web of social constraints as formal education (Evans, 1983:274).

In the face of so many failures since the 1940s and so many institutional experiences that have not significantly improved living conditions for people in marginal areas, there is a strong need to look at different strategies, learn from other methodologies, and take people back to the centre of a new educational agenda. Many have emphasized the need to look into the "black box" and take into account the participant's perspective (Martinic, 1988; Schmelkes and Street, 1991; Pieck 1991; 1993; 1995; Silva, 1996), showing that although in the end the benefits are limited, community education programs are very significant and meaningful for those who live in marginal and isolated places. These findings shed light on developing strategies aimed at people's needs taking into account their everyday life.

WHY A CHANGE?

The concern for a new educational strategy for the adult population living in marginal rural and urban areas and for a reassessment of the notion of literacy, stems from a set of key considerations: the poor impact both governmental and non-governmental adult education programs have had on improving people's living conditions, and increasing poverty levels in most under developed countries.

Adult education in Mexico, a deadend: how we got there? An overview

Within the field of adult education, the Cultural Missions Program in the early 1920s represents one of the most successful historical examples of State education geared towards marginalized populations in Mexico (Schmelkes, 1989:57). Cultural Missions developed an integrated conception of adult education, "[...] the most advanced thinking in Mexico and the actual application of social and educational theories *in situ*" (Sánchez, 1971:95). They were thought of as an instrument of nonformal community education developing cultural, educational, and self-employment activities where both children and adults were involved. Educational activity was intended to be a component of all social development projects, which would benefit the community. Their strategy was based on a team whose activity was centred in community needs and development.

Every Mission consisted of a team of teachers (missionaries) each with a specialization: a formal education teacher, a carpenter, a blacksmith, a veterinary, a recreation teacher, and a home economics teacher. They lived in the community for a period of two years. The program had its golden years in the first decades, then rural education became a secondary concern when rural areas were imbued with the emphasis on technical agricultural education within a new development strategy. This program continues to this day, although with less support than in previous decades, and with neither the spirit and social mystic from other days, nor relationships with the community development processes.

Many programs geared towards the marginalized population have been carried out. The development of adult education in Mexico has been continuous, and its importance has varied according to the social, economic and political circumstances. It goes from massive literacy campaigns and agricultural extension in the 1940s and 1950s, to the emphasis on rural development and technical education in the mid 1960s. Areas covered have included health, housing, nutrition, domestic activities, self-employment, rural development, basic education, and literacy.

In the early 1970s the educational policy started to offer continual formal support to adult education. Out-of-school education became part of the national education system and the struggle for wider literacy was regarded as a permanent activity, different from the emphasis on sporadic and spontaneously based literacy campaigns of previous years. In 1981, the National System for the Education of Adults (INEA) was created as the main institution in the field, with the aim of providing literacy and basic education to the adult population. Not until then did the State define its policy in this particular area.

Currently, a number of questions arise concerning the outcome of adult education programs. Recent years — a "lost decade" indeed — have demonstrated the limits and constraints of traditional conceptions and practices of adult education on improving people's living conditions and meeting their expectations. Adult education has turned into a practice irrelevant to the day-to-day needs of people living in marginal areas. Some studies have questioned if political rationality has proven to be far more important than technical rationality in the promotion of adult education (Morales and Torres, 1990).

Adult education has certainly not gained any significant ground within national education policy: not more than two per cent of the educational budget is assigned to these programs (Schmelkes & Kalman, 1995). So far the government has not shown any real concern for adult education, nor its potential role within the development processes. It has remained a "poor education for the poor". This situation is reflected in the level of teacher training; the lack of resources; traditional pedagogies; curricula *inertia* that does not take into account the big differences among young and adult population, local cultures, and the importance of gearing programs towards work opportunities; etc.

It is acknowledged today that advances achieved through literacy programs are an outcome of the growing formal education system, a fact that casts severe doubts about the efficiency of the INEA. The National Program for Literacy, launched in 1981, had a number of problems such as: ineffective central process; inadequate training for teachers; a rigid system in the face of the new demands of the target population; etc. (Morales & Torres, 1990; De Lella & Ezcurra, 1984). Unfortunately, low efficiency rates were the outcome of this ambitious program. Many commentators have maintained that INEA's work should be restructured because "[...] if certification rates remain the same — in 1988 only 52,000 primary education and 28,000 secondary education certificates were issued — it will take 400 years to do away with illiteracy in Mexico" (CEE, 1991:9).

Various aspects of **literacy programs** have been criticized. For example, some believe that these programs conceive of literacy as a technical activity and so do not guarantee a real and continuous use of written language. Others point out both a lack of coordination with other adult education activities, and no serious interest in writing skills or incorporating elements from local cultures when programs are addressed to indigenous populations (Schmelkes & Kalman, 1995).

In terms of **basic education**, it is recognized that these programs have little demand from the population. Problems stem from a lack of methodologies, irrelevant course content, improperly trained teachers; no links with people's everyday life and work opportunities; pedagogies that do not reflect the way people learn; and the imposition of an *official* culture that has little to do with the *people*'s culture. This has led to programs with a minimum impact and efficiency rates of only 32 per cent (SEP, 1996; Schmelkes & Kalman, 1995).

Community education deals with training for domestic activities and self-employment. It has been the most popular and encouraged among adult education programs. This is a sign of the major emphasis put on this area and demonstrates the government's interest in it. Community education programs are normally geared towards a wide range of the young and adult population, with more women participating due to the nature of the courses as material for starting workshops such as carpentry, electrical, metal working, in marginal rural areas is scarce. Community education programs provide — their way — labour training geared to marginal populations, although many of these courses have little to do with formal training, they do provide the basic knowledge and skills emphasizing self-employment.

The main problem faced by community adult education is that it is not considered to be an important educational strategy that could have a major role in society. As a result, community education has a marginal status, a lack of resources and support, a minimal curriculum, poorly trained teachers, little teaching materials and classrooms, etc.

Despite the marginal conditions in which these courses are taught they are meaningful and useful to the people living in marginalized areas. Courses certainly fall within the context of the community and are applicable beyond the formal objectives of the programs. Nevertheless, training rarely exceeds the basic needs and does not substantially impact family income or local development (Pieck, 1993). As some authors agree, this form of education, which is of utmost importance for marginal populations because it encourages economic activities, has yet to demonstrate its full potential, as well as propose alternatives for its shortcomings (Schmelkes & Narro, 1988:254). Despite the emphasis placed on strengthening the economic development processes, programs have been geared towards assistance measures that try to compensate for low socioeconomic levels through skills and knowledge that barely improve the living standards. Courses rather act to distract the population from its everyday occupations, seldom providing self-employment opportunities (Pieck, 1993).

Far from the experience of the Cultural Missions in the postrevolutionary stage (1930s), community education programs nowadays are neglected by INEA. Programs remain in a permanent *inertia*, developed by institutions that are not concerned with providing complementary support to the activities people engage in after taking the courses, nor have programs gone beyond the practice of a *non formal non-vocational education* (Jayaweera, 1979). The lack of political support is evidenced by the marginal conditions in which this type of education has to be carried out. In the past, people's activities and concerns formed the basis of the educational program (Cultural Missions). Now programs only offer a pre-established set of courses, with the hope that they can be useful to people living in marginal rural areas. Programs normally do not offer students the support to undertake an economic project, provide an updated curricula, or attempt in any way to become involved with community development proposals.

Alternative education: contributions and limitations.

As a different educational alternative, the emergence of popular education has been regarded as a reaction to the failures of conventional approaches to adult education (Latapi, 1988). It has been described as a strategy that is based on the reality of the deprived classes, intending to lead to a transformation of the living conditions of the poor, and implies a class perspective with an educational process based on people's participation, among other characteristics.

However, a number of difficulties have been pointed out concerning the implementation of popular education programs, particularly when it comes to encouraging communities' involvement and organization around the solution of their problems, that is, a concern about participation, with a number of authors reflecting on the foundations of popular education and its real outcomes in terms of responding to people's expectations. As a result there is consensus on the need for more knowledge about the way popular education contributes to developing people's capacity for communication and critical consciousness of social relations and processes, and how much it contributes to the emergence of alternative forms of social organization (Brandao, 1986:145).

Criticisms of popular education have mainly pointed to an excessive concern with the ideological and political, and to how the pedagogical characteristics and the content of the programs have been underestimated (Brouwer & Martinic, 1991:7). This has led to an over-ideologization process where education means conscientization *regardless of specific pedagogical processes concerned with skills acquired in order to meet immediate survival needs* (Rivera, 1991).

Some other authors have mentioned the need for a new theoretical and conceptual reevaluation that could go beyond the mere idealism and social commitment that has characterized previous attempts, particularly those of the 1980s. Some critics urge that an assessment is necessary of the link between educational programs and economic and productive projects, and the usefulness of these projects for local community organizations (Gianotten & De Witt; 1988). The need to have a project linked to participants' productive lives and potential, as a crucial reference for adult education, has come as a result of problems concerned with the lack of people's participation and interest in programs. It is assumed to have had an impact in terms of people's perception of tangible results in the short term and as a motivational starting point for further activities.

Unlike other Latin American countries, the development of NGOs has been a slow process in Mexico as a result of a political system that has tended to coopt almost every space of civil society. From the mid 1970s, a number of different non-governmental organizations started several programs geared towards marginalized areas, focusing on the organizing and support of social and productive projects in several regions of Mexico, especially in the rural sector. The impact of many of these programs is largely unknown. Some things can be said though: most of them have been implemented on the understanding that participation and people's basic concerns are to be taken as the basis of the project.

Despite its failures and difficulties, popular education's emphasis on the development of the identity and reorganization of popular groups in society and commitment to social change, makes it possible to conceive of it still as a real educational alternative to that of most conventional official adult education programs. Alternative educational experiences have served popular sectors throughout history; the new task is to find out how it can serve them in a better way (García Huidobro, 1994).

The Challenge: Facing Poverty and Social Exclusion

Nowadays Mexico is going through its worst social, economic and political crisis since the Mexican Revolution. Poverty levels have increased to unprecedented levels as a result of a neoliberal policy that has not been able to provide equal opportunities for society. Day by day larger sectors become excluded from the social, economic and political spheres. Wages have gone down to new levels: in 1990, 62 per cent of the employed population was earning less than twice the minimum salary. From 1984 to 1989, there was an increase from 19.5 to 23.6 per cent in the amount of people living in extreme poverty. This percentage increases to 42.1 per cent in the rural areas (Alarcón, 1994:135-136).

The crisis has put marginalized people in a corner where their traditional ways of facing survival needs are in danger of disappearing. Economic crisis leads inevitably to social exclusion. Unemployment and poverty result in people remaining outside of the social and economic mainstream and delaying them in their own learning process that is fueled by their everyday experience. It is through contact with meaningful everyday life that people are part of the social and political spheres. In countries like Mexico, this contact is everyday smaller.

Democracy becomes a must after sixty years of having a ruling political party that has blocked popular participation through a strategy where almost any social participation has to be chanelled through the corporativist apparatus. Lack of participation can be explained as Torres (1990:120) points out, as a result of a social system and a national culture that do not include participation as a basic component of everyday life. It is within this context that a new strategy for adult education programs in Mexico has to be envisaged.

In the face of economic crisis, both youth and adults in marginal sectors have had to resort to a wide assortment of *economic survival strategies*, to be found mainly in the wide field of the informal sector. What these sectors ask for is work opportunities and educational support in a context of unprecedented levels of unemployment and social inequalities. Adult education programs would have to take into account the broad range of activities people are engaged in if they want to meet the needs of this particular sector. Programs are challenged to provide people with the knowledge and skills that may help them face more effectively everyday life needs: training linked to self-employment and to people's social and economic survival strategies. Programs must reorient adult education towards people (needs and contexts), and return them to the centre of educational activities. What can the foundations of such an educational strategy be?

BASIC CONCERNS IN A NEW STRATEGY

Emphasis on basic needs and productive work support

The poverty in which large sectors of the society in developing countries live, calls for a *Basic Needs Approach*, one that "[...] corresponds to a broader and more meaningful conceptualisation (*sic*) of development in terms of its emphasis on poverty alleviation and reduction in income and asset inequalities" (Lisk, 1985: viii). Against this framework what is most needed for marginalized people is to meet their survival needs, anything else must come later. In this light there is an enormous challenge for the pedagogical processes to respond to both providing skills and meeting basic educational needs. Education must have a sense of immediate usefulness, and that means the development of effective competencies (skills, resources and information) that promote increasing levels of self-subsistence, methods for advantageous incorporation into the labour markets, and capacity to express an active voice in public decision making (Berlanga, 1995:719). This has implications as well in terms of the need for new orientations in institutional strategies.

Traditionally, emphasis has been placed on literacy and basic education as the main activities within adult education, regardless of the importance of community education (Garcia Huidobro, 1986). This emphasis on traditional education has led adult education to move away from strategies and methodologies that consider people's needs and the context of their realities as a major concern.

Understanding the pedagogy of the nonformal sector

A strategy linked to people's economic activities and projects must take into account the way people learn: their own pedagogies. It must be a strategy rooted in the experience of people, in the way people set up their projects. People from the marginal urban and rural areas have their own pedagogical process, therefore it is important to understand how transmission and reception of knowledge operates in these nonformal sectors. Many of the failures of so many programs could be explained by the symbolic violence exerted through the application of official pedagogies that have little relevance to the way people learn. The notion and practice of pedagogy in many informal sectors has a strong relationship with peoples' basic needs. Meaningful learning is accomplished to the extent that basic needs are met.. The everyday life of people from these marginal sectors sectors generates by itself a pedagogy that suits their basic needs.

Posner (1985), based on some of Bernstein's categories, makes a distinction between what he calls *local or operative knowledge* and *official knowledge*. The differences refer to: the practice of splitting areas of specialized knowledge, as opposed to the practice of relating knowledge and linking it to practice; the idea that learning is a solitary act, as opposed to learning in a group; a practice where the textbook is central for a learning based on past experience, as opposed to a practice where there is no text but multiple references to other texts in a continuous process of trial and error. Other differences include learning that takes place in a classroom or learning that takes place in everyday economic and social activities of life; the idea that knowledge and application are separated, as opposed to a practice where knowledge is to be applied and continuously self-tested. Other differences include the view that knowledge is viewed as something to be stored, as opposed to the idea that knowledge must be tested and used for solving and meeting needs; and private knowledge, as opposed to the practice and conception of knowledge as property of the group, something that is spontaneously shared.

Each type of knowledge represents two very different classifications of knowledge, with the *official knowledge* considered socially superior — the official system — that destroys, devalues and interrupts the informal system, instead of doing all it can to encourage and profit from it. The other type — peasants and small-scale producers' knowledge and the way they transmit knowledge, have been often neglected by official institutions, despite the efficiency levels at which these units operate.

The effect at the point of production, as Posner (1994) puts it:

> [...] is a disassociation between the rules of production and the rules underlying the organization of the social division of labour leading to a disassociation between the components of knowledge, its accessing and transmission which make the system efficient — in other words the well-known rural paralysis which leads to the demise of the rural community and in the urban informal sector the destruction of any possibility of association between the spheres of production and the social.

This highlights the need for an integrated strategy to mobilize and profit from local operative knowledge. Adult education could see the extent to which operative knowledge can be used as the basis for its organization and practices. There is a richness lying in people's everyday activities and survival strategies that must be rescued and profited from.

Rescue hidden literacies

From the preceding comes the need to rescue native and hidden literacies that have proven to be more successful for meeting their daily survival needs than basic education. The Alpha projects have documented a wide assortment of experiences and initiatives that challenge traditional meanings of literacy and call for a new assessment of the concept (Hautecoeur, 1996). This becomes important nowadays, when in the face of poverty conditions, people have resorted to use — and to learn — different kinds of knowledge. It is particularly important when this knowledge is continuously being devalued by a society that does not deem it worthy, nor does it fit within the dominant economic models, despite its enormous social value in terms of meeting people's needs and their capacity to enable local development.

In this light it becomes important to reassess the notion of literacy. Behind the connection between literacy and operative knowledge lies the idea of participation. In order to put in practice Freire's notion of literacy as "a form of cultural politics" (Freire & Macedo, 1987: xii), it is important to "take a risk" and start from people's participation, because the construction of such experiences (participation) within ongoing relations of power, as Giroux (1982) points out, "[...] provide them with the opportunity to give expression to their own needs and voices as part of a project of self and social empowerment".

The idea of participation then marks a difference in this new notion of literacy. Before the pedagogy becomes political, it must start from people's participation, in the many forms it takes, as a first compulsory step. Then literacy may become "[...] inherently a political project in which men and women reconstitute their relationship with the wider society" (Giroux, 1987: 6), a means for constructing one's voice as part of the wider project of possibility and empowerment (*Ibidem.*). That leads to take the notion of participation as crucial if programs wish to have a significant impact on the marginal population.

The importance of participation

A major lesson to be drawn from experiences carried out by NGOs, some of them based on the idea and practice of popular education, is the importance of people's participation, an inherent part of this educational strategy. Participation as a way of learning (self-didactics) entails letting people do what they feel they can do, respecting people's own ways of facing everyday needs in order to stress their role in social life and strengthen their own survival strategies.

Against this framework there is a need to support people's experiences of social participation, give institutional support so that people can put into practice what they know, carry and continue their own projects, and support them with successful training processes. Popular participation must be taken as a *sine qua non* for meaningful learning. It is important to acknowledge that people are eager to find spaces for participation, more than to learn how to read or how to write.

Some popular education experiences and governmental programs show the importance of regarding participation in its most elemental expression and not in social and political participation stereotypes. Participation is to be found in its economic expression, in people's everyday activities that have a clear meaning, a purpose and a high social and individual usefulness. Youth and adults in the marginal areas have their particular ways of participation, and these vary depending on the population characteristics, the nature of the context and people's needs. In this sense, it is important to value people in terms of their professional capacities (Chourin, 1996), where their activities — their objects — will be rooted within social and economic aims.

Participation is to be found in the way people give their own answer to their daily needs, in how they put into practice — in their own survival projects — native and traditional knowledge, in how they get together in order to get an education (building classrooms, cleaning, etc.); in how they meet the lack of public services (building roads, digging wells); in how they get together to organize traditional festivities; in the everyday economic activities they engage in (mechanic workshops, blacksmiths, bakeries, clothes-making).

Educational activity, besides linking people with the productive sphere, will accomplish an important social role in terms of its contribution in fostering social participation, a more active and stronger civil society where people practice their rights and have access to different codes and the promotion of equality. This can be observed in many experiences fostered by NGOs. It happens also in government sponsored programs, where people have been given the opportunity to carry out their projects.

MEETING LOCAL NEEDS : WHAT SOME NGOs CAN SAY

There are many examples in Mexico of groups and individuals trying to generate their own models and proposals in order to meet their basic needs within the context of social and economic crisis. In the Mexican context, the peasant revolt in Chiapas constitutes a landmark for the need to rely on participation strategies that may assume the knowledge and practices from indigenous communities, a different conception and practice of adult education. Nowadays the native groups show grassroots initiatives in terms of generating educational alternatives that may respond to their reality of long-time exclusion.

The experience of Chiapas

Chiapas, the most neglected area in educational, social and economic terms, is an example of educational proposals that try to take into account for the first time, cultural identities and ways of learning that people themselves envision as solutions to their social and economic problems, and that promote the strengthening of their group consciousness.

In Chiapas, groups of people gathered around an educational project, have made as their goal to spread, share and empower alternative experiences in education.[2] The purpose is to contribute to a pedagogical movement that can meet the needs of indigenous and peasant communities. This project understands alternative visions of education as a basic component on the road towards democracy. Therefore, a crucial element within the strategy is an attitude of **respect** as opposed to years of exclusion, violence, racism, disregard and despise for local cultures. The project underlines the need to broaden these cultural spaces and resources in order to make them flourish again.

Ethnic regional autonomy is considered as a condition *sine qua non* for giving a new answer to the educational quest. There is a need to set up mechanisms to assure local control of the human and material resources for education as the only way to guarantee that educational activities arrive in the communities, meet local needs, and respond to their cultural forms. Participation is encouraged in order to imagine and control educational actions. Every educational activity is consulted with the community for approval.

As part of the pedagogical strategy, the project acknowledges and fosters the use of different forms of learning, many of them typical of indigenous cultures — (watching, observing, example) as opposed to verbal language — and other strategies that represent a pedagogical patrimony that should be encouraged. In the same way, technical and professional training is an important part of the project and is carried out in ways that enrich community life and facilitate access to regional and national labour markets.

Indeed one of the most important expressed lessons of this process, is that people involved in the project dared to challenge their everyday way of conceiving of education, and were "forced" to renounce the idea of having everything planned and controlled.

Some communities have begun their own educational processes by getting together to build a school that meets both their values and traditions, and that allows them access to the content of national education. They are making up and giving way to their own idea of education, putting in practice their abilities to re-work their knowledge, choosing contents they feel are valuable and assigning levels to them.. They are building their school their own way. In Bhola's words: "[...] local cultures reinvent their curriculum" (1990).

The social and economic results that should develop as a result of the Chiapas strategy follows, to a certain extent, the basics of a different kind of education:

- a new conception of development based on the idea of local economy and community; that fosters new ways of handling natural resources and new kinds of productive and survival activities;
- the need to define educational activities as political activities and to develop the capacity to formulate welfare projects for improved living conditions through the consolidation of collective projects; and
- stimulate meaningful learning in order to value their own culture as the starting point for building a cultural identity (Berlanga & Márquez, 1995:720).

Another interesting experience has been carried out in Oaxaca[3], one of the poorest states in the country. There indigenous people from several communities, helped by a non-governmental group, got to work as managers of forest projects in their communities. People already knew how to cut trees, drag and carry logs, but knew nothing about numbers, documents, accountability. Taking advantage of people's own traditions and culture, an education project has developed upon a particular action-research strategy based on a *transfer-appropriation* methodology that is designed to transfer knowledge and skills to indigenous peasants with schooling levels that do not go beyond primary education.

Since the traditions in many communities involve "assigning charges" to people every so often, it was the community itself that periodically assigned people to follow a training course and occupy administration posts (embedded in the traditional notion of "community assignment"). In a 13-year experience, 81 forest community projects have been developed where peasants take care of the administration, accountability and auditing of their own projects.

Surely an accountant or business administrator would say it is impossible to teach accounting to peasants in a four-week course, or that they cannot take care of the management of their forest economic projects. In the words of the team involved in the education project, the lesson is that specific local necessities do not require much science or academic knowledge. Only basic minimal hands-on knowledge is needed for people to administer their own local projects. Sending peasants to the university besides being an unaffordable investment would mean professional training disconnected from the community environment and culture. As a result, their ideas about what should be done would more than likely contradict the real demands of the people from the community.

Servicios Educativos, A.C. (SEDAC) is another NGO located in the Valle del Mezquital in the state of Hidalgo, considered as one of the poorest regions in Mexico. The methodological model used by this experience is called "autodidactismo solidario" (self-didactics). The methodology is based on basic elements such as: group self-learning, exchange of experiences as intergroup support, group self-tutorship, group self-evaluation, collective planning and execution of activities The idea which guides this methodology is based on peasant participation in the programs so that this participation may be the source of a ***collective learning process***. SEDAC has fostered social and economic projects in different areas: housing, community shops, workshops and craft production cooperatives. A network of similar projects support each other by sharing their experiences, learning valuable knowledge needed to carry out their own projects (Pieck, 1996).

These examples, as many others, show the importance of starting from people's needs and self on-going projects, and taking into account their organizational and cultural features. The result of it has been community participation in *their* economic projects, a process that is taking place at a local level. These projects show new pedagogical strategies and ways to foster popular participation. Many lessons could be drawn from these experiences about how to change institutional environments so that they respond to their activities and strategies, to their on-going projects, provide complementary educational and financial support, encourage research lines, and help to solve specific problems faced by these institutions and projects.

SUPPORTING LOCAL INITIATIVES

What are the chances of fostering and spreading participation at the community level to have an impact on the structure of society? Chances are not great. Most adult education projects are small in size and seldom have achieved a significant impact on the social and economic situation of learners, neither have they had an impact at the level of national adult education policies. Evans (1983:293) makes it clear when he states that "[...] effective reform on a larger scale requires the development of administrative procedures that meet the dual needs of providing resources on a large enough scale while at the same time allowing enough autonomy and flexibility at the lowest levels to respond effectively to diverse local conditions".

A key issue in the institutional environment in order to sustain the development of local initiatives, is *decentralization* — the shifting of decision making and resources to the local level. In Mexico, this may not be an easy process since decision making has long been highly centralized and the institutional apparatus has been used to accomplish a very effective cooptation function. Decentralization entails a respect for local participation, the process that is now slowly beginning to emerge in Mexico and that can act as a potential counterforce to State cooptation. The Chiapas project, just mentioned above, is a true example of such a grassroots initiative. As García Huidobro (1986:36) underlines, "[...] the social and political richness or poverty of decentralization is directly linked to the richness or poverty of local organization".

The need to support people's projects calls for *an educational strategy linked to people's ongoing activities*. When it comes to develop training programs aimed to meet people's expectations and to rescue local knowledge, an "in-the-work training" strategy is needed. This clearly marks a difference with "on-the-job training" programs designed to meet training needs of people already working in the formal labour market. There is also a difference as well with "for-the-job training" schemes that have little relevance nowadays within a formal labour market where access to marginal population is severely restricted.

The needs-oriented supports to economic projects carried out by people in the marginal sectors, are seldom provided by adult education programs. Women working together to put into practice inherited traditional embroidery skills do not need a one-year course on clothing skills, but specific training on how to make shirts that do not shrink, that have proper sizes, new designs, etc., so that sophisticated and valued embroideries end up on shirts and blouses people can wear. There are many examples like these. Youth making tables who need specific techniques so they are durable; people carrying out a milking project who do not have the knowledge to advance into cheese and cream production; women who do not have the organizational skills to carry out a cooperative; etc. There are many examples of such projects being carried out in marginal areas.

Such needed projects demand a different orientation of providing adult education. Vielle (1995), within the context of Mexico, suggests the modification of the National Institute for Adult Education into an institution more concerned with providing people with the skills they need to continue performing their everyday activities: an adult educational institution making work the most fundamental need expressed among the adult population. Conceiving of this approach apart from an integrated strategy entails a risk of falling into a practice that has to do less with adult education than with training. This calls indeed for an integrated educational strategy where economic activities may be at the centre but not be the only ones.

The need for an integrated approach

To improve effectiveness means understanding people's needs. However, the question is how to connect both needs: the need for an education that provides effective competencies for economic survival and social and economic insertion, and the need for an education that provides the social equipment for action towards the strengthening of impacts at the local level. This calls for an integrated approach which, according to Berlanga & Márquez (1995:724), should offer:

- the promotion of a social conscience of group and community cultural identity;
- a relation with reality as an educational practice for the transformation of life, family and local conditions that could have an immediate impact on subsistence conditions and the recovering of productive activities; and
- not only technical and professional competencies but attitudes, values and skills that may facilitate their social and economic insertion.

The Centre for Rural Development Studies — CESDER (Berlanga and Márquez, 1995:728-730) is carrying out an interesting and promising educational model organized around four curricular axes: 1) a community educational economic project, as an educational strategy aimed to incorporate people into the work and production spheres; 2) work to improve production conditions and family welfare as a way to maximize education's usefulness for participants and their families; 3) a link with the community, achieved through community work, as a means to guarantee reflective processes that lead to compromise; 4) general educational knowledge that may enable the development of the previous curricular axis and facilitate access to further education. These curricular axes are organized as "practical interest centres", based on the relationship between production-education and work-education, taken as real commitments by the participants.

To follow the curriculum, participants have to perform labour duties in the community project, show the betterment of family welfare through the application of knowledge and skills acquired during the course, and perform community labour duties that demonstrate what has been learned. The curriculum thus entails an education-formation process strictly linked to production and work activities. This is a model where adult education goes beyond the mere educational rationale and conceives of it as a process which cannot be isolated from work and people's everyday economic activities.

In addition to having an integrated curricula, some authors call for *integrated institutional support*. In the words of Coraggio (1994:30):

> [...] it is necessary that new social policies, geared to "invest" in people, reorganize their national resources, not only through an unprecedented transfer of knowledge and capacities, but also in terms of basic means for everyday life, credit, lands, privileged access to markets and technologies, in the name of popular economy.

Domestic and self-employment courses carried out by community education programs provide a good example of the need for integrated institutional support. Even if the curricula does not have a direct link with work opportunities, people — due to their economic situation — profit and derive economic activities from what has been learned. Unfortunately, programs do not meet the expectations raised in participants from the courses, and so they do not provide any complementary support, nor are they linked with other institutions. Should courses be integrally supported they would certainly be more useful to people and would provide more solid opportunities either for people's ability to be employed or for carrying out their personal projects.

The irrelevance of educational content can explain the failure of many educational programs. Adult education can become trustworthy and prestigious in the eyes of society by providing an effective and high quality service (García Huidobro, 1994). The training experience in Oaxaca is an example of an effective adult education strategy linked to people's ongoing projects. The experience challenges traditional ideas about peasants" inability to learn accountability in short-term courses and taking care of their own projects. The project has shown so far it was possible. It is possible.

Against a framework of poverty and economic recession, adult education has the opportunity to foster people's social and economic incorporation, encouraging and strengthening local development. This calls for the *rescue of the productive side of adult education*, to go beyond the educational rationale of most adult education programs, and move towards demands derived from work necessities, production, and social and economic exclusion.

This is also related to the importance of *learners' diversity*, as opposed to universal educational models geared to traditional stereotypes of the adult population.. Diversity then is related to the association of knowledge with people's needs and expectations. Unemployed youth in marginal urban areas need a different education than those who live in isolated marginal rural areas. Women, being the largest group among the adult education clientele, especially in the rural areas, do not have programs that take into account their social and productive role in rural life. The example of Chiapas clearly illustrates that respect for people's own ways of doing things is crucial to the success of programs. All these aspects reflect diversity and show that one program does not suit all.

These ideas have been put forward on many occasions. Maybe, as Evans puts it, "[...] adult education should be viewed as a negotiated process that includes consciousness raising on the part of clients, policy makers, planners, managers, evaluators" (1983:343). This consciousness about a new adult educational strategy and a reevaluation of the importance of adult education within national education policies and about the role it plays in social and economic processes is imperative.

So far attention has been put on the need to rescue the individual and the community and the need to have a learner-centred strategy. Much has been experienced from an institutional perspective that has not been able to offer people answers to their everyday learning needs. Why not tackle the problem from a different perspective? Why not learn from alternative education experiences that, based on different methodologies and strategies, have been proven through adult education? Isn't it clear that programs have more possibilities to be successful when they start from people's expectations and meet their needs? Isn't it worthwhile to develop programs based on the way people learn instead of imposing pedagogies that interrupt people's own processes of receiving and transmitting knowledge? Is it not eloquent enough that a long chain of ineffective programs carried out over the years have only permanently altered a social reality instead of understanding that reality whose needs, contexts and social processes are different from institutional perspectives?

Notes

1. Both terms: *adult education* and *nonformal education* are used almost indistinguishably by a number of authors since many of nonformal education activities are addressed to the adult population and thereby are labelled by some authors as *adult education*.

2. This experience is carried out today by different people involved in a project called MECHA. Information provided in this section has been taken from (MECHA, 1995).

3. Taken from the experience of "*Asesoria Tecnica a Comunidades Oaxaquenas*" on training indigenous peasants as managers of forest community projects (Lopez Arzola, R. and J. Gongora, 1995).

Bibliography

Alarcón, Diana. 1994. "La evolución de la pobreza en México en la década de los ochentas", En *Frontera Norte* (México), Vol. 6, N° 1, pp. 133-140.

Berlanga, Benjamín &Ulises Márquez. 1995. Las escuelas rurales de formación para el trabajo: una opción educativa para la agricultura de pobreza. In Enrique Pieck y Eduardo Aguado (Eds.): *Educación y Pobreza: De la desigualdad social a la equidad*, México: El Colegio Mexiquense.

Bhola, Herbans S. 1990. *Alfabetización para la supervivencia y para superar la pura subsistencia*, Barcelona: UNESCO/OIE.

Bock, John & George Papagianis (eds.) 1983. *Nonformal Education and National Development*, United States: Praeger.

Brouwer, J. & Sergio Martinic. 1991. *Promotores comunitarios: sus aportes y dificultades*, The Hague: Bernard van Leer Foundation. Occasional paper, n° 4.

Centro de Estudios Educativos (CEE) 1991. "Editorial", *Revista Latinoamericana de Estudios Educativos*, Vol. XIV, n° 3.

Chourin, Michel. 1996. "From Trainee-Learner to Actor in an Alternative Economy", in Jean Paul Hautecoeur (Ed.): *Alpha 96, Basic Education and Work*, Hamburg: UNESCO Institute for Education/Toronto: Culture Concepts.

Coombs, Ahmed. 1976. Nonformal Education: Myths, Realities and Opportunities, *Comparative Education Review*, Vol. 20, n° 3.

De Lella, Cayetano & Ana María Ezcurra. 1984. "El Programa Nacional de Alfabetización. Una aproximación diagnóstica desde los alfabetizadores", *Revista Mexicana de Sociología*, Vol. XLIV, n° 1:39-65.

Evans, D. 1983. Participation in Nonformal Education at the Local Level. In John Bock and George Papagianis (eds.): *Nonformal Education and National Development*, USA: Praeger.

Freire, Paulo & Donaldo Macedo. 1987. *Literacy: Reading the Word and the World*, London: RKP.

Gajardo, Marcela. 1985. "Educación de adultos: de Nairobi a Paris", *Revista Latinoamericana de Estudios Educativos*, Vol. XV, nº 3:69-82.

Garcia Huidobro, Juan E. 1986. Educaçao de adultos: Necessidades e politicas, Pontos para um debate. In MEC/Fundaçao Educar/OEA/IICA: *Reflexoes Teóricas e Metodológicas sobre a Educaçao de Jovens e Adultos*, Brasil: MEC.

García Huidobro, Juan E. 1994. "Los cambios en las concepciones actuales de la educación de adultos. In UNESCO/UNICEF: La educación de adultos en América Latina ante el próximo siglo, Santiago, Chile: UNESCO/UNICEF.

Gianotten, Vera & Ton De Witt. 1988. Promoción rural: mitos, realidad y perspectivas. In A. Ooijens J. and G. Peer (eds.): *Educación Popular en América Latina, La Teoría en la Práctica*, Paperback nº 4, Holland: CESO.

Giroux, Henry. 1987. "Introduction". In Paulo Freire and Donaldo Macedo, *Literacy: Reading the Word and the World*, London: RKP.

Hautecoeur, Jean Paul (ed.) 1996. *Alpha 96. Basic Education and Work*, Hamburg: UNESCO Institute for Education/Ministère de l'Éducation du gouvernement du Québec and Culture Concepts Publishers, Toronto Canada.

La Belle, Thomas. 1986. *Nonformal Education in Latinamerica and the Caribean. Stability, Reform or Revolution*, USA: Praeger.

Latapi, Pablo. 1988. "Participatory Research: A New Research Paradigm?" The Alberta Journal of Educational Research, Vol. XXXIV, nº 3.

Lisk, Franklyn (ed.) 1985. *Popular Participation in Planning for Basic Needs*, England: Avebury.

López A., Rodolfo & M. Jesús Góngora. 1995. *Formación de campesinos indígenas como directivos de empresas forestales comunales (1982-1995)*. Paper presented in: Retos y perspectivas de la educación de adultos en México, México: Universidad Pedagógica Nacional.

Martinic, Sergio. *El otro punto de vista. La percepción de los participantes en la educación popular*, Chile: CIDE, documento de discusión, nº 31.

Morales, Daniel A. & Carlos A. Torres. 1990. *The State, Corporate Politics and*

Educational Policy Making in Mexico, USA: Praeger.

Osorio, Jorge. *Educación de adultos y democracia*, Editorial Popular, 1990.

Pieck, Enrique. 1991. *Hacia un perfil de la educación comunitaria en el Estado de México*, Revista Latinoamericana de Estudios Educativos, Vol. XXI, nº 3.

Pieck, Enrique. 1993. *The Social Function and Meaning of Nonformal Education. A Study of Official Community Education Programs in the State of Mexico*, PhD. Thesis, London: Institute of Education.

Pieck, Enrique. 1995. "Reproducción y resistencia. Algunas implicaciones del proceso educativo desde la perspectiva del participante." En Enrique Pieck y Eduardo Aguado (Coord.): *Educación y Pobreza: De la desigualdad social a la equidad*, México: UNICEF/El Colegio Mexiquense.

Pieck, Enrique. 1996. "Education in the Service of Economic Survival". In Jean-Paul Hautecoeur (ed.): *Alpha 96. Basic Education and Work*, Hamburg: UNESCO Institute for Education/Toronto: Culture Concepts Publishers.

Posner, Charles. 1994. *The informal sector and educational reform*.

Rivera. 1991. *Educación étnica y modernización*.

Sánchez. 1971. *A Revolution by Education*, USA: Greenwood Press.

September 1996. *Programa de Desarrollo Educativo, 1995-2000*.

Schmelkes, S. & Judith Kalman. 1995. *La educación de adultos: estado del arte. Hacia una estrategia alfabetizadora para México*, México: INEA.

Schmelkes, S. & Luis Narro. 1988. Adult Education and Training in Mexico. *The Alberta Journal of Educational Research* (Canada), Vol. XXXIV, nº 3, pp. 246-258.

Schmelkes, S. & Susan Street. 1991. Tres visiones en México: los funcionaraios, los usuarios, *Revista Latinoamericana de Estudios Educativos*, Vol. XXI, nº 1.

Silva L., Yengny. 1996. *Los alcances de la educación para el trabajo en los centros-taller nuclearizados: el punto de vista de sus participantes*, Tesis de Maestría, México: Universidad Iberoamericana.

Vielle, Jean Pierre. 1995. La educación de adultos centrada en el trabajo. In Oscar Zires (Ed.): *Necesidades educativas básicas de los adultos*, México: INEA.

Weinberg, Pedro Daniel. Educación de adultos y trabajo productivo. In UNESCO/UNICEF: *La educación de adultos en América Latina ante el próximo siglo*, Santiago: UNESCO/UNICEF.

Section Five

From Alternative Visions to Politics

Chapter Eighteen
BASIC EDUCATION: DEFENDING WHAT HAS BEEN ACHIEVED AND OPENING UP PROSPECTS

Jean-Paul Hautecoeur
UNESCO Institute for Education

"Education… one of the principal means available to foster a deeper and more harmonious form of human development and thereby to reduce poverty, exclusion, ignorance, oppression and war"

Jacques Delors, *Learning: the Treasure Within*
Report to UNESCO of the International Commission
on Education for the 21st Century, 1996

CREATING A NEW SPIRIT

The Delors Report to UNESCO opens with these few lines as an epigraph, calling attention to the late 20th century calamities that will not be solved by the utopias of the 21st. It reiterates the indispensable purpose of education in helping humanity to "progress towards the ideals of peace, freedom and social justice", while in other places it is seen above all as serving global competition and economic domination.[1]

"When… humankind is apparently hesitating between continuing headlong along the same path and resignation… there is, therefore, every reason to place renewed emphasis on the moral and cultural dimensions of education." Delors continues, taking the view that future globalization should be humane and enjoy a "new spirit" of intercultural cooperation. Beyond the remedial, curative mission of education, a mission of creating *lifelong learning within society* comes to the fore as a prerequisite of a new ecology of social interchange. The International Commission on Education for the 21st Century does in fact give priority to *learning to live together*:

> *Learning to live together*, by developing and understanding of others and their history, traditions and spiritual values and, on this basis, creating a new spirit which... would induce people to implement common projects or to manage the inevitable conflicts in an intelligent and peaceful way. Utopia, some might think, but it is a necessary Utopia, indeed a vital one if we are to escape from a dangerous cycle sustained by cynicism or by resignation.[2]

It is in this global context of the need for a new spirit in education, and in the footsteps of the Delors Commission that our questions about adult basic education in industrialized countries acquire a universal relevance. However, we are not speaking about "basic education" in the Commission sense, which sees it above all in the context of formal education as the beginning of a continuum of cycles of academic learning. We also speak little of literacy in our regions, where adults have for the most part received some schooling and are living in a written environment.

We use the term *basic education* in the pragmatic sense of improving individuals' and communities' skills in activities relating to adult life, without necessarily making any reference to schools or to vocational training, which would be limiting (see the Introduction). Literacy and communication activities can obviously be integrated into basic education. But they are not a prerequisite or an *a priori* priority. They become imperative if the context requires, and if people need and ask for them.

To us, basic education willingly takes part in this new spirit, which is an absolute necessity in the face of the deteriorating living conditions and social relationships in our regions, which are disturbingly called "under-developing". There are radical initiatives, often marginalized but also within institutions, that are seeking to prevent the spread of sheer madness, feelings of powerlessness, resentful and poverty-stricken subservience, the systemic destruction of the historical, cultural and genetic heritage, and so on. There are many experiences of liberated working, the alternative economy, community organization, local democracy, cooperative services, cultural development and neighbourhood ecology, showing a constructive coming together in solidarity, creativity, cooperation, relevant learning and collaboration on the part of governmental and non-governmental organizations.

Our task in recent *Alpha* publications has been to report on some of these experiences and to examine the learning and basic education practices used in them. We now have to look at them again in order to find out more generally how the meaning and practice of basic education have been transformed, and what expectations and requirements the different actors may have expressed with regard to suitable education policy and institutional environments.

Policy Matters

The questions from which the research team started for *Alpha 97* were as follows:

- In recent years, what changes have affected the relationship between the policies, institutional environments and local practices of basic education in the different regions? How are these to be evaluated?

- On the basis of these findings, how can an institutional environment of basic education be established that will encourage local initiatives and give them lasting development?

- How can educators co-operate to this end?

In order to relate these questions more closely to the desire to change habits of thought and behaviour, I refer to the dichotomy clearly formulated by Hanna Fingeret:

> The need to understand the nature of the problem is translated (in the USA) into the question: 'How many illiterate adults are there?' ... The political agenda is then framed in terms of insuring profit, productivity and international competitiveness rather then by enhanced quality of life...
>
> The central policy question that serves people with low literacy skills is: 'How can literacy development support communities in addressing their issues? How does change happen at the community level, and what role can literacy development play?'
>
> The relevant measures of success are not found on tests, but are

reflected in indicators of racism, poverty, sexism, educational equity, access to productive work and full participation as citizen in democratic communities.[3]

One decisive change over the last ten years has been that groups of citizens have taken the initiative at local level to resolve problems affecting them, and that community organizations have emerged in almost all areas of collective life. These events have occurred while most states have been radically altering their conception of how public services should be administered, often reducing them to the minimum and transferring responsibility to local groupings and voluntary bodies. There has been a change in the relationships between the civil society and the state and, conversely, between public authorities and citizens. There is still no clear horizontal and vertical delineation of the new democratic relationships between civil society organizations and public authorities. All this is taking place against a background of both growing dependency on, and an organized resistance to, the "single market".

This is the overall historical background to our questions. These are no longer posed as they were in the 1980s, when it was expected that the state would devise systematic centralized policies to provide public services such as adult education, with the consequent requisite budgets. We have taken note of the rights, responsibilities and imagination of individuals and their communities, which have been translated into action through "initiatives" in the economic, cultural, social and ecological fields. From now on it is at this level, at the grassroots and in practice, that new "policies" are designed and tried out, usually in the gaps between government programs. The latter are then considerably affected in turn.

This is the meaning behind the questions we asked above, and the direction of our research on the appropriate relationships which should be created in each local, regional and national context between citizens' organizations, intermediary organizations and the state. The old divisions between administrative sectors and professional fields are no longer taken as immutable. Nor are the privileges taken for granted which the cultural and political elites have established for themselves through a network of institutions given legitimacy by a one-dimensional view of history, conservative science and back-scratching laws. This is what has happened in Central and Eastern Europe; it is also the case in Western Europe and North America.

In this vast picture, the question arises of the place of different types of basic education (different types of learning and education suit different contexts), and of the profiles and roles of trainers, their status and training. These were — and still are relatively — clearly set out in the grade structure of formal education and even of adult education, which has gradually become integrated into it. They were already more fluid in the case of literacy work, which was often split between increasingly formalized basic education and popular or lifelong education, which was often "left" to the voluntary, unpaid sector.

In future, if the vision of *lifelong education within society* is to be achieved, it will be necessary to give strategic importance to basic education in its social context, as is done today with vocational training that is tied to the single market.

> The concept of learning throughout life is the key that gives access to the twenty-first century. It goes beyond the traditional distinction between initial and continuing education. It links up with another concept often put foreword, that of the learning society, in which everything affords and opportunity of learning and fulfilling one's potential... In short, 'learning throughout life' must take advantage of all the opportunities offered by society.[4]

CHANGES AND TENSIONS

Mythic power

The fortune of the literacy and popular education movements in the 1970s and 1980s was made largely thanks to mythology. In the last ten years, in Western Europe and North America, the three ideological pillars of these movements have been shattered: disastrous figures, mobilization campaigns and the struggle to eradicate illiteracy. One goal of militant utterances has been widely attained — agreement on the urgent need for literacy and basic education and, in consequence, for the universalization of these services in many countries. But the object of the earlier campaigns has vanished. There are still signs of it here and there, but its meaning and functions vary.

Literacy has become a key sign of post-modernism, the reality of which is to be found in paradoxical, heterogeneous virtuality, rather than in history or a sense of system.[5] It is also an emblem of new industrial cultures: exchange value in the global market, access to information highways, codes, the graphic environment, polymorphous skills, a means of treating and retraining deviants, a ticket to employability, etc. It is still recognized as the basis for completing an academic "career". It reappears as a conditional value of moral rectitude (J.-P. Hautecoeur, above). In reality, its mythic power is far from growing weaker.

Weak success

From a political point of view, it is recognized that this sector of education now has a high profile and that it has achieved priority status in many countries. It has been enshrined in its own laws. It has given rise to lasting arrangements that have absorbed earlier disparate staffs and organizations. It has carved out a place in universities, etc.

However, it is unfortunate that it is a sector which is still floating between ministerial jurisdictions: sometimes dealt with under schools, sometimes under lifelong education, sometimes culture and citizenship if there are disturbing social conflicts, and often drawn strongly to employment and the management of human resources. A destabilizing syndrome of being shuttled to and fro affects the security that has apparently been achieved. There is another lasting tension, between the autonomy of the new sector of the profession and the desire either to make it a special form of education or to see it diluted as part of the overall education system or a socialization and labour market entry scheme.

Moreover, dissident voices have generally lost out in favour of the institutionalization of adult basic education, the acceptance given to it by public opinion, its connotations of virtue and a manifest accommodation with conservative tendencies. Criticism has tended to be a mere digression from the consensus: the attraction of the market undermines any reminder of social democracy and rules out anything that threatens to cause dead losses.

Professionalization

The transformation of social movements into education and training systems has been accompanied by professionalization: standardization of entry and exit requirements, quality control, staff training, rationalization of costs, computerization, resource allocations, endogenous culture, performance indicators, bridges between systems, etc. The era of unpaid voluntary work seems to be no more. Its vestiges can be criticized if staff are still occasional or services are sub-contracted. There is increased pressure on basic education systems to be more effective and efficient according to macro-economic criteria. There is a noticeable tension between two models that coexist to varying degrees: that of one-to-one teaching, which relies on psychological proximity and does not work out the full economic cost, and that of human resource training or "active" management of large numbers.

Nonetheless, professionalization cannot be reduced to systemic standardization. Some countries have standardized their basic education systems (the Netherlands and Dutch-speaking Belgium), others have favoured a dual system, and still others have continued to allow a range of models and schemes. Tensions exist in each of these cases. A dual system tends to become unified (Quebec and Portugal) on the school model and to institutionalize sub-contracting. A decentralized pluralistic model (France and French-speaking Belgium) tends to accentuate the disparities in resources and quality of services. But the competition between educational organizations also leads, in the medium term, to a quest for quality and professionalization of services.

In reality, the dichotomy between unpaid volunteers and professionals is no longer relevant to the evaluation of the strength of an organization or the quality of its services. Many voluntary organizations have a hybrid structure in which there is much reliance on unpaid participation even though effectiveness criteria retain their over-riding importance. In alternative economies, non-monetary transactions and criteria of reciprocity and solidarity are recognized as preconditions of quality and resistance to the assimilation by the single market. On the other hand, professionalization can be seen as having possible undesirable corporatist and bureaucratic side-effects (N. Druine, D. Wildemeersch).

Dependence on the labour market

The major change that has occurred in basic education is obviously their dependence on the labour market, on economic competition and schemes to combat unemployment, instability and exclusion. Education has become an essential parameter of economic competitiveness in both specialized and unskilled jobs. Basic education has become a prerequisite of vocational training. Training in languages, communication and new technologies has become widespread in major companies. Aside from those already in jobs, training for labour market entry and employability are always a part of social assistance schemes now, and they often tend to replace them. Hence there is a constant tension in educational agencies between the social functions which they have been given and their educational purpose in the holistic or popular sense (in Eastern Europe, on the other hand, there is a close association between adult education and social service — E. Ambrozik).

Another aspect of this close link with the economic sector has been the privatization of the training market, a fast-growing sector that acts as a lodestar in the field of adult education, which is affected by government budget cuts. This has encouraged innovations, in training practices, the recruitment of trainers, planning and management styles (with an important place for partnership), technologies and learning environments, research and development, etc.

The world of the trade unions, and the public authorities, have changed in the light of this dynamic development of jointly managed training, and of some companies that have become "sensitive" to requests for partnership and to issues of social responsibility (S. Gowen). However, there are still strong tensions between the productivist goals of companies and those of promoting the rights of workers pursued by the world of education and trade unions. Partnership can be fragile, being at the mercy of changes of government, for example, and companies' "rationalization plans" (J. García Orgales).

Aside from classic paid employment and training tied to the primary labour market, new types of voluntary association enterprise and alternative networks of the "plural economy" have appeared, linking work, education and training and community organization together more organically. The old formula of getting a job in the economy, which was always temporary and unstable, has been transformed into more permanent workshops linking training activities, commercial production, and service to the community and participation in local development. Such experiences have radically changed the perceptions, practices and administration of basic education. They are reinforced by the fact that living conditions have generally deteriorated, public services have ossified in many countries, and traditional democratic regimes are in deep crisis. There is a constant tension between traditional modes of work, training and citizenship, and the alternative formulae of the social economy, and between the new actors in the "political ecology"[7] and the former elites.

Social environments

Closer to the world of basic education has been the shift in the way of viewing illiteracy (*illettrisme*): from individuals with shortcomings, who were thought responsible for their own exclusion, to social environments that take account of the phenomena of designation, stigmatization, loss of class status and exclusion. The school environment has long been questioned, and attempts are being made, against considerable odds, to improve it. The family and community environment has also long been the object of specific educational interventions (the Family Literacy movement is just one recent manifestation), through schools, cultural networks (libraries, museums, etc.) and community organizations. The new industrial environments and the reorganization of work have more recently led to studies of ergonomics that have changed perceptions of basic education in companies. Schemes for the social treatment of unemployment and exclusion have also been called into question in the large-scale phenomenon of social dialyzation, which is also known as social breakdown or "apartheid".

More generally, all the modes of communication between public authorities and citizens have been called into question. This includes the bureaucratic language that hinders communication, formal procedures, the complexity of exchanges between authorities, the computerization that is seen as responsible for a growing gap between the state and its citizens, and so on. In order to reduce the "illegibility" of the public environment, there has been an attempt (which is very difficult) to simplify language, to humanize exchanges, and to introduce mediation services in communications (J.-P. Hautecoeur). The latter have largely been rendered nugatory by the attrition of public services, particularly those for the most dependent populations. Local community development initiatives certainly have more chance of facilitating exchanges and breaking down communication barriers than attempts at administrative reform.

Cultural pluralism

Another significant shift in the ideological landscape of basic education is of a cultural nature: the change from a national monoculture (literacy) and a standardized set of competencies (basic skills) to variable multiple cultures and configurations of plural skills subject to varying degrees of recognition and cross-fertilization. National minorities in a number of regions have demanded the right and the means to reinvigorate their languages and cultural traditions, and even to achieve political autonomy. Racism and ethnic conflicts between "nationals" and migrants have invalidated former assimilation policies and have regenerated awareness of identity. The "new cultures" of sociological minorities are finding outward expression and claiming their rights, and are showing that they are different. The sometimes violent tensions and hostility which these attempts at pluralism provoke are well-known.

More generally, the dominant languages and cultures and elitist traditions have been subjected to "competition" from minority or minor cultures which had been forgotten or oppressed, delegitimized and despised. The mass media have played an important role in this intermingling and exchange, as have new epistemologies, the spread of information technologies, the anthropology of everyday life, the democratization of the arts, etc. Cultural research and proliferation has made more complex the old literacies, the hierarchical transmission of knowledge, and the traditional ways of legitimizing cultural skills.

Regional differences

In the post-communist countries, the picture is not always the same. In the field of culture, a number of trends run concurrently, sometimes exacerbating the tensions. The continuation or resurgence of authoritarianism leaves little room for individual initiative and the establishment of civil society. Subservience to the unfettered culture of the market, drastically reduces respect for education, the humanist ethic and any non-profit making activity. There is also a return to pre-socialist origins, to the restoration of the historical heritage and respect for traditions as well as to ethnic distinctions, which opens opens the way to both cultural pluralism and monolithic nationalism. The desire to have nothing more to do with backward-looking obscurantism and the ostracism of the West's new forms of colonialism also contribute to these concurrent trends. (A. Dede, E. Marushiakova, & V. Popov).

The former cultural and adult education institutions have to a large extent collapsed. Private organizations partially replace them where they are closely linked to the economic market, but they leave the new areas of local democracy empty and lacking in resources. There is a regrettable lack of experience on the part of professionals working in education, culture and social affairs in the new democratic landscapes, where reflexes and expectations are still suffering from authoritarian and hierarchical constraints. There is also an unfortunate rise in inequality in relation to primary services such as education.

Above all, basic education is seen as a missing social service in the face of the population's new poverty, social anomie, disarray and feelings of impotence. There is a serious need for innovation in individual and community self-organization, solidarity and collaboration (which is a controversial goal, given memories of the former regimes). There is also a need to provide alternatives to former dependence on the state and, in many cases, to the impossibility of taking advantage of the benefits of economic liberalism. But there is also the rediscovery of a tradition of basic education in popular cultures under the former regimes, in which make-do and mend, barter and a range of illicit activities were practised on a wide scale as community solidarity or in close family circles (S. Hubik).

DEFENDING WHAT HAS BEEN ACHIEVED

Catherine Stercq says, "our task is not to create an institutional environment that will encourage community initiatives and link basic education with citizenship rights [but] to defend what has been achieved and is under serious threat ... and to explore possible new perspectives." Although she is speaking of Belgium, a country under-developed socially, culturally and economically, I think that is true in all regions.

What are these achievements that are under serious threat?

- A number of basic human rights, among them "the right to full participation in democratic life, the right to accessible services, the right to information, the right to work and the right to learn";[8]
- the roles and responsibilities of the state in ensuring respect for these rights and the principles of equity and accessibility;
- essential services such as adult basic education and guaranteed quality;
- a democratic ethos applied to all relations between citizens, including those found in education and training; and

- the development of an active and autonomous cultural/intercultural life.

From what we have seen clearly over the last decade, development is not lasting, quality of life can regress, and progress is "chaotic". This also radically changes the view of adult education, and also the prospects for basic education. Not long ago, it was possible to believe that misery, particularly in the form of *illettrisme,* would gradually disappear. Much was expected of states that were going to legitimize and take over the voluntary work of literacy networks. What has happened is that mass semi-literacy (*illettrisme*) has spread, misery has become commonplace, the state is powerless in the face of the global market, and everything is directed towards economic competitiveness, which is now likened to a new worldwide cold war.

The goals of basic education have thus changed, as have the status, roles and responsibilities of the actors involved. For most people, the goals are no longer adaptation or re-entry into the labour market, given the experience that "the rich no longer need the poor",[9] that the harassment of the poor is becoming harsher, and that training courses are in many cases a dead-end as regards rehabilitation and participation. The goals have become those of resistance to any further erosion of living conditions and active resistance to exclusion, where possible in the form of *socio-economic initiatives*.[10] Those who do the resisting can only be the poor themselves, alongside voluntary, professional and public agencies working together. They no longer expect new policies and additional funds from services and public authorities, but rather a guarantee that their rights will be preserved and defended.

> Having defended the right to literacy, we now have to "defend" the rights of our illiterate public ... rights which include the right to literacy teaching of quality ... [and] also include the right to refuse literacy, which is nowadays offered systematically to anyone designated illiterate, whatever their aims in life. The rights of illiterate people also embrace their rights to culture, work and vocational education. And these rights are far from guaranteed today.[11]

The Right to a high-quality basic education

While in many countries, the rights to adult basic education are enshrined in legislation, the principles of accessibility and equity are not. This is because of the selectivity of programs, cuts in resources, neoliberalism on the part of those in government, etc. Teachers' conditions of work are deteriorating while the numbers enrolled are rising under the pressure of social policies. Services seldom match participants' expectations and requirements, and in consequence "losses are considerable" (S. Wagner).

This sector of adult basic education, which in principle aims to provide access to the higher strata of (second chance) formal education, has to be consolidated if it is to meet adults' learning demands and long-term goals adequately. While the principle of accessibility applies to adults in the same way as to young people, and teachers' conditions of work need to be modified, the sector cannot accommodate all the populations, all the requirements and all the objectives of informal basic education. It is not cut out to play a social assistance role.

There is a strong tendency to shift from public educational services to the private sector and NGOs. Excesses are particularly denounced in Eastern Europe (A. Dede, V. Popov, E. Marushiakova). There is a countervailing tendency towards standardizing basic education structures and services in a single public network. These excesses are also criticized (M.J. Estéves, N. Druine, D. Wildemeersch, S. Wagner) because of the centralization of programs, control of innovation, reduction in the number of approaches, etc. Taking national differences into account, there remains a need for a permanent adult basic education service which is free and is accessible in all regions, provided with adequate infrastructures and, above all, supported by competent staff whose conditions of work are comparable to those of schoolteachers.

The right to work

The upheavals in the economy have rendered the right to paid work for everyone more or less obsolete. A growing number of people are becoming outcasts (the entire active population in some regions, notably Albania), and at the same time they face a deterioration in social services and a chronic shortage of essential goods. These conditions obviously do not encourage any educational enterprise. The provision that is repeatedly made for the outcasts, even in the wealthiest societies, is a period of training, or an assisted period of alternating training and work. For most of these "trainees", training is seen as a substitute for paid work, which they cannot get (and that may also be the case for the trainers), and as a demeaning social stopgap.

Literacy and training designed for the numerous under-qualified "populations" are severely criticized because they do not take account of individuals' and groups' priority needs, forms of social organization, and economic and cultural practices in everyday life. The proposed literacy and training are based on external programs, the professional traditions of the educators, and the practices of the primary labour market. They prove counter-productive because they do not take into account the informal economic practices which many individuals and communities use in order to survive. They can in fact suppress such skills and destroy traditional and alternative networks of exchange (E. Pieck, F. Anghel).

> In the face of the economic crisis, young people and adults in marginalized areas have resorted to all sorts of economic survival strategies. What these populations want is opportunities to work, and educational support. In this unprecedented context of a scarcity of employment and social inequalities, adult education should take account of the wide range of activities in which people are engaged. Programs face the challenge of finding the skills and knowledge that can help people to solve their everyday problems more effectively: training linked to independent employment and alternative survival strategies.[12]

While training cannot solve all the problems associated with the crisis of work, it faces more challenges than keeping busy the cohorts who are unemployable, picking out the "unusable", and trying out new types of social services. Educators are called on to adapt to the aspirations of their fellow citizens by building on their skills and consolidating their projects, rather than setting out to match their "clientele" to the competitive labour market. That requires in turn a professional transformation. It also implies a different commitment on the part of training agencies, and investment in experimentation of a cooperative rather than a productivist nature. It implies a transformation in the training market, in which voluntary associations are in competition rather than in organized, coordinated networks (P. Freynet, M. Hamilton).

In order to bring about these transformations, public authorities have to intervene. They are expected to:

- recognize devalued forms of work (building maintenance, environmental work, restoration of the architectural heritage, personal services, craft work, waste recycling, etc.) and the social usefulness of these alternative enterprises;

- help create jobs in these sectors of activity;
- encourage the development of training suited to local initiatives;
- make public infrastructures available to civil society organizations;
- facilitate professional collaboration between actors who are often antagonistic to one another;
- establish normal conditions of work for training staff; and
- bring the legislative apparatus and administrative rules into line with the aims of development and of strengthening new civil society enterprises and organizations.

A stimulating cultural environment

Basic education also has a major role to play in the relationship of individuals and communities to culture. This has three complementary domains: information and means of communication (including writing) living culture or socioculture, and the arts. A living, creative and democratic cultural environment must also be maintained and regenerated at the risk of reinforcing the morbid phenomena of the degeneration and destruction of cultures and exile movements, which particularly affect rural areas, suburbs and urban ghettoes.[13] In these fields of culture, innovation and spectacular investment are often less urgent than safeguarding what has been achieved, and defending the most precious human rights: the ability to find information and to think freely, to imagine, to express oneself and to exchange ideas: "the treasure within".

Opportunities for access to free information are restricted for many categories of citizens who are subjected to mass programing, the rules of the market and political control. The funds to buy new information and communications technology equipment are not within the reach of poorer classes and impoverished groups. The closure of public libraries has become commonplace. In Central Europe, entire networks of cultural centres are often affected. While the state no longer has room to manoeuvre in this field — which is heavily subjected to privatization, concentration of the press and free market agreements — it has acquired a vital role in ensuring the quality of information, the redistribution of resources in accordance with the principle of equity, and the coordination of geographical arrangements. However, these functions of public authorities need to be buttressed by voluntary associations and businesses which have given themselves a "citizens" purpose.[14]

The sociocultural world, made up of the collective inheritance, of the cultural capital of a community, and above all of the liveliness of exchanges between generations and professional and interest groups, is the most powerful antidote to the universalization of the market. This is also the experimental field of new forms of horizontal democracy, an indispensable precondition for the reconstruction of fractured societies. Local initiatives, new contracts of employment based on usefulness, and participation in the sustainable economy, have above all to capitalize on citizens' basic education: the skills they have acquired, existing relationships and potential networks, projects, and the imagination and inventiveness of individuals who need to be stimulated and mobilized.

Defending what has been achieved in the living culture and everyday life of groups is a priority task for basic education which should be rooted in communities' memories, feelings and abilities (D. Findeisen, E. Pieck, F. Anghel, E. Ambrozik, S. Hubik). That means:

- recognizing and maintaining the value of what is used and exchanged in traditional and contractual networks in the face of the devaluing forces of the market;

- renewing existing energies and resources instead of leaving them to become prematurely valueless;

- encouraging the development of voluntary sociocultural dynamics and activating existing infrastructures and institutions, instead of making exorbitant investments and bringing in new resources; and

- appreciating people's ordinary language and methods of communication, the diversity of their customs, and the ingenuity of certain tools and techniques, etc.

The arts are far from being a luxury for poor people. They have long been their unknown authors. They deserve and have the right to take a full part in them. Particularly in Central Europe, popular arts and traditions have been taught, practised and maintained in every village, even under communist regimes. Music is still a popular art in some countries at all religious and secular festivities. The theatre and puppetry are familiar activities in some regions, with whole generations and classes taking part. Recently, writing workshops and other experiences of artistic expression have reintroduced aesthetic research and experimentation with the imagination into basic education for mixed populations instead of creating "illiterate ghettoes" or opening more classes for "functional communication".[15]

Perhaps this is the greatest challenge facing basic education: to reanimate creativity where it has been assumed that there was nothing but incompetence and mediocrity.

NEW PROSPECTS

Education "within society"

Gradually, an autonomous world of adult basic education has grown up, mirroring schools. Whether intermingled or separate, these two fields have a close relationship, having in common a strong tendency to standardization, intolerance of what is different, and the illusion that they are pursuing the only true path.

In the face of corporatist intentions, there is a manifest desire for openness, usefulness, solidarity and cooperation in all regions, and especially at the bottom of the social scale, where many teachers find their vocation. There is a desire to set education and training on "the right path", in and amongst other social interactions and in every aspect of everyday life. There is a wish to break away from the mechanics of separation and to rediscover the desirable organic links between people, projects and activities. There is an attempt to create the mental and ecological preconditions for participation in projects that can improve the quality of life.

The Delors Commission came to similar conclusions:

> The increasing focus on the role of local communities needs to be encouraged and supported. Education needs to be seen by the community as applicable to their real life situations.[16]

Basic education has to be part of the activities that people believe to be the most urgent, the most useful, the most up-to-date and the most inaccessible, making it possible for them to express themselves and to communicate, and helping them to get things done and to pool their resources. To do so, it does not require a corps of professionals and specialized institutions. Sustainable activities have to be mobilized which were not designed for other purposes.

Basic education can therefore not be cordoned off in separate authorities. Its functions cut across all organizations. It is characterized by mobility, adaptability, plurality and multiple use of resources which are not its own. It can, where necessary, be concentrated in special workshops and specific places at particular times. But it can, if necessary, also be diffuse and widespread (M. Hamilton, S. Gowen, F. Anghel, M.J. Estéves).

Relevance to local communities

Local neighbourhood services are either based on a geographical division, such as the district, village or municipality, or are co-operative, community networks. They can also be hybrid — involving both public, community and private organizations and can be managed locally, with an office in a voluntary association, a cultural or community centre or a municipal building such as a library. They must above all, provide communication between all citizens in a locality, professional organizations and institutions. They may be linked to a mass communications network, as in the Czech Republic, for example (S. Hubik).

Such services are part of a community economic model. They are not profit-making but presuppose combined *ad hoc* budgets drawn from public and voluntary sources, or private, non-monetary reciprocal exchange. They are jointly managed on a voluntary basis, in accordance with the normal practices of the organizations' participatory democracy. They may be part of local or regional development plans (e.g., the "Plans locaux d'insertion par l'économique" — PLIE — in France), which lay down priorities, ways of cooperating and criteria of quality, etc.[17]

The aim of these services to individuals and the community, which are called "neighbourhood services" because they encourage people to come together and share competencies through solidarity contracts, is to *learn together* following a model of voluntary, mutual exchange of information, services, knowledge and skills. They make sense in local development projects in which the principle of subsidiarily, which has been tried out widely in the European Union, is applied.

According to Hugues de Varine, "the principle of subsidiarily is complementary to the principle of solidarity."

> According to the principle of subsidiarily, the state, a geographical collective or a public service must never replace the initiative and responsibility of people and groups at the level at which they can act effectively, nor should their freedom be infringed.
>
> According to the principle of solidarity, any individual can contribute, with his or her fellows (in the community) to the common good of the society, at all levels...
>
> A particular, progressive pedagogy is needed, based on the idea that the community has expertise and is a reservoir of energy, imagination, skills and commitment.[19]

In several places in the draft versions of the agenda for the Fifth International Conference on Adult Education, it is said that there is a common preoccupation with rooting educational programs in communities and local development projects:

> The challenge of the new emerging vision of adult education is to develop national adult learning initiatives which deal effectively with global issues, while emphasizing the centrality of community participation and the necessity of integrating local-based perspectives... The objective is to encourage people to become more independent and active citizens within their communities.

As regards literacy, an initial recommendation is "to integrate literacy and basic skills into all development projects and encourage grassroots organizations to promote their own learning and development initiatives."[20]

Joint planning of provision and demand

The criticism most frequently made of traditional literacy and basic education programmes is that the planning of provision controls demand, or that provision is simply imposed on a "public" that has no voice in the matter. Demand is planned from on high, in the name of a higher interest called national economic competitiveness, socialization and labour market entry, mobility, etc. The justification for the abuse of power is technocratic: the professionals know best, and the illiterates will find out in due course.[21]

The idea of lifelong learning, appropriated by individuals in their own communities and projects, presupposes turning a programed approach into a process of dialogue. It must be possible to build up the demand for information, assistance and education services on the spot, within the context of people's lives and in accordance with existing resources: explicit and potential provision. Such meetings, dialogue and negotiations do not exist in the traditional methods of managing public affairs, or in the competitive market. They have to be created. This is a precondition of local democratic life, the emergence of autonomous initiatives, and the development of economic solidarity, which can also create what is useful and bring about participation and autonomy.[22]

The expression of demand and the joint planning of provision are a new test for traditional communities, and for societies that were long subjected to totalitarianism. This test becomes a vital object of learning and experimentation, a prime task for basic education. From an economic and organizational point of view, its main requirements are partnership, while from a political point of view, what is important is the application of the principle of "active subsidiarily" or collaboration between different institutional and geographical levels. From a cultural point of view, what is important is the creation of an active, creative environment that feeds on living culture and intercultural exchange (see above). And from an anthropological point of view, the main requirement is lively individuals and communities prepared to defend their rights and improve their fortunes.

Partnership

Partnerships have to be created on several levels:

- **Between public institutions involved in basic education activities**. This is difficult to achieve, as a number of reports have shown (P. Freynet, M. Hamilton, C. Stercq, S. Wagner). There is tenacious competition, watertight administrative divisions, professional cultures that take the concrete form of corporatism, societal traditions to be overcome (such as the slogan "struggle against illiteracy" in France), and budgets to be shared. But federal regimes have had to institutionalize bridges between states and geographical divisions. Some recent policies, such as urban and rural policies, have been the occasion for imagination and compromise. The responsibility for promoting educational and local development initiatives can no longer be left to one or two ministries.
- **Between economic actors and sectors**. We are operating in a mixed economy: partially subsidized by the state, sometimes obeying the laws of the market, and sometimes independent, using non-monetary exchange between co-operative agents. There may be

rivalry and incompatibility between the three types of actor, largely because of the experimental, even marginal nature of these activities. But partnership between these entities is helped by the recognition of the third actor (sometimes called "active citizenship") and ethical rules.

- **Between citizens, local organizations and municipal or elected elites.** Experiences of local democracy overturning traditional models of consultation and decision-making. But new models of jointly managing local development and the administration of public affairs are being applied quite widely.[23] Basic education is also for elected politicians and administrators (D. Findeisen).

- **Between levels of competence** (for the complex *top down-bottom up* model, see S.G. Stein), as the principle of "active subsidiarily" reminds us:

  It is at local level that truly integrated and appropriate public action can best be defined. But active subsidiarily stresses that no answer can be found to a single level, that it is the *articulation of competencies* between levels which is the keystone of tomorrow's governance.

  The second innovation is based on following what the exchange of experience teaches us: *general principles* of relevance to public action rather than universal recipes. Active subsidiarily therefore suggests that action should be based on the *obligation to be relevant* and not on the obligation to use what is available (applying recipes).[24]

These new modes of operating require coordination and should ideally be undertaken by public authorities or by independent agencies. Whether they are termed partnership or a national, regional and international coordination, there is a desire for globalization here too, from a world ecological perspective.

Exchange of experience, research and evaluation

Large-scale experimentation, the diversity of actors, and the need for effectiveness and visibility of results, call for widespread action-research on the ground. Also important is the regular dissemination of information in and between networks, and meetings for the purposes of exchange, analysis and evaluation. The European Union, for example, has encouraged the spread of these practices by making support for development projects conditional on the visibility, networking, evaluation and theorization of the activities, with the collaboration of research and resource centres. Such contractual conditions are part of the quality criteria that deserve to become universal.

The traditional split between university staff and local actors can be neutralized by joint participation in these cooperative projects. These research practices, which are already applied in many places, also deserve to be investigated, evaluated and shared (E. Pieck, M. Hamilton). The new cultures of education to be created in intercultural communities proceed from communication between disparate elements and networks, and the imaginative handling of information at minimum cost (do-it-yourself and recycling) (S. Hubik). The dichotomy between the literate and the unlettered can only be overcome by changing the perception of skills and radically altering hierarchical or "top-down" styles of communication.

LEARNING TO LIVE TOGETHER

We set ourselves the task of opening up the field of vision of adult basic education, taking as our inspiration the many experiences from Eastern and Western Europe reported in *Alpha*, and taking into account the critical evaluations of the major trends of the last decade. We are looking for "possible forms of political practices that will offer greater resistance to the order of things and will devise more useful, fairer and perhaps more effective plans of action."

We followed in the footsteps of the International Commission on Education for the 21st Century, adopting the same desire to incorporate a *new spirit* into adult basic education projects. We share the Commission's primary objective, which is to learn to live together. It has become imperative to create a web of links between individuals and communities in order to resist the world competitive order and to establish alternative models of life, in a perspective of sustainable human development.

At the same time, we wish to support the strong determination of many agencies to *defend what has been achieved* in human rights, which we believe to be irreversible, and the minimum conditions for education and training. Much has been achieved, including the right to citizenship, to work and to education for all. The state's responsibility to ensure the principles of equity and accessibility in all public services; the availability of suitable, high-quality adult basic education services; and the creation and maintenance of a cultural environment that will stimulate individual and collective creativity are also important achievements.

In accordance with the new perspectives that have to be applied to basic education, we have called attention to ways of *managing resources intelligently*, in accordance with the principles of subsidiarily and solidarity. We have stressed the need to support local requirements, projects and structures; the need for partnership and coordination at several levels; and the usefulness of action-research, evaluation and the dissemination of the results of experiences.

We have tried to avoid educational programs that are independent but cut off from the aims and life of the community. We bring educational activities back to *local initiatives* and *integrated development plans*, which must enable everyone to participate without discrimination. Basic education is globally addressed to individuals and communities that are engaged in projects within the social economy. The model is the joint planning of the provision of and demand for services in a plural economy that combines public, private and community resources. It rests on the practice of local democracy, which presupposes the creation of new methods and relationships of communication between citizens.

This *commonality of learning* is, in the context of their national traditions, a cooperative model of basic education which relies on the skills, imagination and desire of each person to live better. Communities should not put up with contempt at the end of the 20th century.

Notes

1. In the proceedings of the American National Education Goals Panel: *Building a Nation of Leaders* (993), the sixth goal of the *Educate America Act* reads as follows: "Every adult American will be literate and will possess the knowledge and skills necessary to compete in a global economy and exercise the rights and responsibilities of citizenship." quoted by G. Stein in "Getting clear about where we are going", above.
2. *Learning: the Treasure Within*, Report of the International Commission on Education for the 21st Century to UNESCO, Paris: UNESCO Publications. 1996, p. 22.
3. Hanna Fingeret, extract from "Literacy in the USA: the Present Issue" quoted in Jean-Paul Hautecoeur, "A Political Review of International Litercy Meetings in Industrialized Countries", above.
4. *Learning: the Treasure Within*, op. cit., p. 111.
5. Stanislav Hubik, "Television and Literacy Development in the Czech Republic", *Alpha 94*, Toronto: Culture Concepts Publishers and Hamburg: UNESCO Institute for Education, 1994, p. 197.
6. European Commission, *Local development and employment initiatives*, Brussels/Luxembourg: Office for Official Publications of the European Communities, 1995; *Social Europe*, Supplement 1/96 — New Activities, new jobs: what development strategies?. Brussels/Luxembourg: Office for Official Publications of the European Communities, 1996; *Territoirs*, l'économie solidaire sur le champ, No. 368, May 1996; *Insertion-formation*, a study conducted by the

ECOTROPE Society for the Délégation à la formation professionelle, 1993 (distributed by Groupe permanent de lutte contre l'illettrisme, 20 bis rue d'Estrées, 75700 Paris, France).

These references give examples of the Western European context. For North America and Central and Eastern Europe, see especially *Alpha 92, Alpha 94 and Alpha 96*, in the same series as *Alpha 97*.

7. *Transversales science/culture*, 42, November-December 1996.
8. *Une société sans barrières*, Montreal, Institut canadien d'éducation des adultes, 1991.
9. The expression was coined by Pierre Calame of the Fondation pour le progrès del'Homme.
10. "Learning means capacity-building and autonomization, but entails also resistance and the creation of alternative models. "Initial proposal to Start and Open Dialogue on the Draft of the Agenda for the Future, Hamburg, UNESCO Institute for Education, 19 December 1996. (Unpublished working document.)
11. Catherine Stercqy, "Thirty Years of Literacy Work in Belgium: Where has it got us", above.
12. Enrique Pieck, "Making up for Lost Time", above.
13. Ermitas Fernandez, "Prescolar na casa — Teaching parents to teach children", *Alpha 94*, op. cit. pp. 51-63; Adela Rogojinaru, "A Way out of the Crisis of Work: Community Self-Education", *Alpha 96*, op. cit., pp. 161-170; Mechtild Hart, "LIteracy and mothers' work", *Alpha 96*, op. cit. pp. 33-56.
14. Hilario Hernandez Sanchez, "New Cultural Development Options", *Alpha 94*, op. cit., pp. 79-86.
15. Daniel Seret & Christine Mahy, "Turkish Faces and Landscapes — An Experiment in Creative Workshop Leadership", *Alpha 94*, op. cit., pp. 133-145.
16. *Learning: the Treasure Within*, op. cit., pp. 122-123.
17. *La lettre de l'insetion par l'activité économique*, No. 19, October 1996.
18. Claire & Marc Hébert-Suffrin, *Echanger les savoirs*, Paris, Desclée de Brouwer, 1992; *Le cercle des savoirs reconnus*, Paris, Desclée de Brouwer, 1993.
19. Hugues de Varine, "Economie solidaire et développement local", *Territoires*, No. 368. May 1996, pp. 9-17.
20. Preparatory documents for the Agenda for the Future, Hamburg, UNESCO Institute for Education, 1996 (unpublished).
21. J.-P. Hautecoeur, "Generous Supply, Flagging Demand: the Current Paradox of Literacy", in *Alpha 90* — Current Research in Literacy (Edited by j.-P. Hautecoeur), Hamburg, UNESCO Institute for Education/Quebec, Ministry of Education, 1990, p. 113.
22. Jorge Orgles, "The Project of Economic Equity", *Alpha 96*, op. cit., pp. 171-190.
23. Jean-Louis Laville and Laurent Gardin (eds.), *Les initiatives locales en Europe*, Paris, Centre national de recherche scientifique (CRIDA), 1996.
24. FPH, *Carte d'identité et project 1996/2000, Paris, Fondation Charles Léopold Mayer pour le progrès del'Homme, November 1996, p. 48.*